INNOVATION AND E-LEARNING

Innovation and E-Learning

E-BUSINESS FOR AN EDUCATIONAL ENTERPRISE

By

IAN ROFFE

UNIVERSITY OF WALES PRESS
CARDIFF
2004

British Library Cataloguing-in-Publication Data.
A catalogue record for this book is available from the British Library.

ISBN 0–7083–1757–X

Printed in Great Britain by Cambridge Printing, Cambridge

I Siân, Huw ac Elin

Contents

Preface

Educational enterprise conveys all the actions to develop education in a creative and businesslike way. The reasons for doing so are now very familiar: a changing context for higher and further education; increased competition for students and resources; a shift of emphasis from faculty and teaching to students and learning; and raised expectations in applying technology to support learning. These trends are not new, but have emerged in recent times as relatively more important than others, since they are driven by both the demands of increasingly competitive markets and the supply of ideas and information at much faster speeds and lower costs. Decision-makers in every institutional context have concluded that, in order to continue to be successful, it is necessary to function in an entrepreneurial manner and compete for business and students. Consequently, learning methods and management approaches that offer promise and seem practicable are applied eagerly to improve the performance of a group, department or institution.

In this context, electronic learning has emerged as a novel means for firms and learning providers to gain competitive advantage in the Information Age. It appears as an opportunity to reconfigure delivery and support without, seemingly, sacrificing the quality of learning. Internet-supported learning, especially distance education, has had a major impact on the flexibility of teaching and learning processes. A whole set of services has opened up, such as networking between students and the facility to participate in online discussions.

For these reasons and others, e-learning looks set to be at the forefront of educational development in the future, bringing with it far-reaching changes for the educational enterprise and learner alike. It offers the global educational marketer a key method of reaching new clients; for the curriculum and training designer it presents a new platform for the delivery and support of students; while for the learner it offers personalization, convenience, information, savings and choice. For a company it can mean a key source of competitive advantage in human resource development, as well as in the support of customers.

As educational enterprises around the world seek to integrate technology into education and training to transform the way we learn and to understand how e-learning can best be used, a number of common issues and puzzling questions arise for decision-makers and practitioners faced with similar problems. What are the practical implications of e-learning for business? How do the roles of teachers and trainers change in the new learning paradigms? What are the implications for teaching and learning? How can we assure quality in e-learning? How should human resource policies change to support e-learning? What are the strategic choices open to us? How can we innovate with e-learning? How is it possible to maintain a dynamic in an e-learning innovation? What are the markets for e-learning? How do we attract clients, especially small firms? With e-learning available from everyone, why should a customer register with one educational enterprise, rather than with any one of a host of others? When clients are faced with many offers of e-learning from different providers, where does a particular supplier gain an advantage? These are crucial considerations in trying to establish a sustainable competitive position. The issues are many and varied, but often recurring. The aim of this book is to help formulate answers.

As all educational enterprises embrace Internet technology, the application of the technique as a means to distribute and support learning as a comparative source of advantage is quickly nullified. Consequently, there are decision-makers in every institutional context interested in solutions, as competition in educational markets intensifies. These include heads of institutions, departments, units, deans, administrators and educational managers. The book is written, then, for those who want an insight into the key business dynamics in implementing an e-learning programme. People are also joining groups to develop e-learning all the time, often with little direct prior experience of the processes. E-learning provides new opportunities for them and their organizations. It brings together teams of professionals for design and delivery – business managers, administrators, IT specialists, designers, teachers and tutors – who might enter this arena for the first time. There is then a need for people to capture the essence of the processes quickly, and this book is also aimed at them.

The book builds on the many valuable contributions already published on the development of e-learning. Selecting from just a few of them will illustrate this: the challenges and experiences of transformative change that affect a whole university institution engaged in flexible learning are reported by Betty Collis and Jef Moonen (Collis and Moonen, 2001); the practical factors involved in creating a technology-based learning organization, for a department of open and distance learning, are described by Tony Bates (Bates, 2000); Svava Bjarnason and a team studied the business of borderless global education, which laid the foundations of the E-university project in the UK (Bjarnason et al., 2000a). Each brings a different perspective on new academic developments, organizational transformation, structures for technology-supported learning and the characteristics of a borderless education market. Implicitly or explicitly, however, they address the case of students who are essentially a captured market, in the sense that once recruited on to a mainstream, long course, such as a degree programme, they will stay to graduate, or drop out, rather than choose to leave for another provider. Many questions are resolved, but still many that interest me, and that arise from the education and business environment in which I work, have not been.

In Lampeter, as elsewhere, new education curricula, educational processes and technologies have been designed for electronic learning (e-learning). It serves a range of different audiences: professionals, lifelong learners and technology-supported distance students, in local, regional, and international markets. The emphasis in this book, however, is on e-learning for small firms. Everywhere, this is a difficult market to service: the clients are not captive, customers can be very selective and the competition is high. To develop and deliver provision in this area means that we must confront not only conventional issues of overcoming resistance to change, motivating faculty and encouraging collaboration, but also a range of business and educational management issues, including competitive strategy and performance analysis.

Learning is a potent force, but to gain most benefit it needs to be combined with active management and technology. The potential of e-learning involves sustained enhancement in technology, learning and e-business processes. This is true for the captive markets of corporate employees of large firms or campus-based students, as well as for the open markets of distance lifelong learners or employees of small firms. A sustainable position does not come solely from competing on price, but rather from enhancing the perceived value of a range of intangibles in the educational service. Value assurance, enhancement and innovation are practical and systematic ways of enhancing a service. The theoretical foundations are present in teaching and learning theories, distance education and corporate strategy principles. The technical basis lies in a variety of techniques, but with support by the Internet as a common thread.

This train of thinking will help explain the choice of content and the order in which the chapters appear. The first chapter begins by exploring the forces that are driving the need for educational enterprises to become more competitive and addressing vital issues for an educational enterprise in developing e-learning, together with the relevance of learning, technology and business dimensions. After an initial overview of e-learning in chapter 1, the experiences of addressing a supply chain of small firms are presented in chapter 2 as the context for the following chapters. Analysing the performance needs of a small firm rather than a standard course offer leads to an examination of the options for bespoke learning and technology delivery options that might better meet client needs (chapters 3 to 6). The ways of sustaining a business advantage in a competitive educational environment are discussed in chapter 7. These point to enhancing the perceived value of the intangibles in a service through innovation, value assurance, value improvement, staff development and evaluation (chapters 7 to 12).

Of course, no one can speak authoritatively about *all* the new developments in e-learning and their implications. The new frontiers are simply too vast, too complicated and rapidly changing. This context makes innovation crucial, with the speed of past responses less effective; it changes the task and skill-base for staffing; it encourages staff into innovative problem-solving; and it makes the optimum process of innovative curriculum design similar to that for a commercial enterprise. The educational and training world has experienced technological change for as long as I can remember. What has changed in recent times is the widespread availability of technology and networks, making online learning a viable option for individuals, enterprises and organizations. E-learning is already a major source of learning innovation for both companies and educational enterprises. The choice for firms and educational enterprises is simple: join the new wave in education, or fall behind.

Acknowledgements

A kaleidoscope of ideas, experiences and encouragement have come together to help shape the content of this book, and these influences are difficult to separate out. I am grateful to many people for constructive comments and embellishments, although any blemishes are mine. Thanks are due to Carl James from IAGO (European Consultants Ltd) and to all my colleagues at the University of Wales, Lampeter, in particular Alan Rogers, Jenny Thomas and David Thorne.

1

The educational enterprise

E-learning, the way people learn and communicate electronically, is emerging as a key application of the Internet. It draws many providers, making it a competitive arena, where solutions are created by a fusion of technology, learning and business. An educational enterprise can compete in this milieu through innovation, and by developing a value proposition based on personalization and authenticity. There are challenges, though, from regional, national and international competitors. Consequently, a mosaic of niche provision seems to be emerging, in which digital technologies not only affect learning delivery, but also expand information and can change the environment where people live and work. It makes sense to use the power and flexibility of learning technologies to meet a wide range of development needs, including those of lifelong learners, corporate learners and employees in small firms.

CHANGE AND CONTINUITY

Today, education and training providers are in the middle of an e-revolution. A simple Web search for 'e-learning' turns up more than a million records, when none existed just a decade ago. More than ever before, education and training professionals are concerned with the impact of technological change, and some even more directly with techniques that can be applied to improve an educational service-provider. Learning itself is recognized as a critical component of national economic success (WAG, 2002: 5). New curricula, educational processes and technologies have been designed to support business. Indeed, business and innovation concepts themselves are applied in education, often to the discomfort of traditional educationalists. All serve to fuel the search for new ways to support learning, which are challenging traditional forms and signify a rapid evolution and innovation in learning.

Nevertheless, in the general fervour to apply technology in order to advance educational processes, it is easy to assume that the application of electronic learning changes everything; that old educational practices, gleaned from experience of delivery with an array of support services, may appear a quaint vestige of an old economy beside the new knowledge media. Yet, while the Internet and related technologies do provide immensely important tools for existing providers and opportunities for new entrants, the means for open, distance and flexible learning (ODFL) have existed in one form or another for generations and served the educational purposes of millions of people well. There are, then, twin effects of change and continuity at work with e-learning.

Continuity exists, because the teaching process is essentially unchanged. Technology can convey information, engage people in seminars and support collaborative learning, yet all these can be done in a conventional classroom. Where technology-supported learning (TSL) has had a major impact is on teaching and learning processes in distance education. A whole set of services are opened up that were once difficult, such as networking people together and their ability to participate in online discussions. Technology, therefore, seems to change the framework more than the purpose. An educational enterprise that applies electronic means to support learning programmes is not entering a new industry, but, rather, is using powerful new tools to enhance learning performance and amplify demand. This, in turn, has awakened the recognition that innovation is not a special field, but part of the general educational architecture. Innovation, in short, is in the mainstream of educational life, both intellectually and in the practice of e-learning.

THE 'E' IN E-LEARNING

E-learning has quickly gained a strong band of proponents in both education and the corporate world and the reasons for this are not at all hard to discover: it simply presents so many benefits for educationalists, employers and students, as well as new possibilities for innovation. When John Chambers, the Cisco Systems CEO, said 'education is the next killer application for the Internet' he encapsulated a prevalent view among e-learning professionals on the potential significance of the development (Chambers, 2001). However, what exactly do we mean by the term 'e-learning'?

Certainly, 'electronic learning' has a degree of elasticity in its meaning. Apparently simple terms, such as 'e-learning', 'technology-based learning' and 'Web-based learning', are defined and used in various ways by different organizations. What seems clear from all models, though, is a convergence on the use of the Internet as a means of communication. To equate e-learning solely with Internet use, however, just seems too narrow a concept. Electronic-learning programmes, for example, can be devised solely for CD-ROM, or for an Internet Website, or by a combination of these two methods or other means. A more comprehensive interpretation is needed.

E-learning is a shorthand term for the ways people communicate and learn electronically. That is the meaning taken here, an interpretation that springs from a lead given by Cedefop:

> learning that is supported by information and communication technologies. E-learning is not limited to 'digital literacy' (the acquisition of IT competence) but may encompass multiple formats and hybrid methodologies, in particular, the use of software, Internet, CD-ROM, online learning or any other electronic or interactive media. (Cedefop, 2001: 5)

It is certainly true that an educator or instructor can choose from a variety of electronic technologies to try to effect learning, but considering the 'e' term exclusively as 'electronic' misses the human purpose of learning. An e-learning course designer has to find the optimum match between educational content and the potential learner. This dimension has to do with other, more human, 'e's: the engagement of the learner, the enhancement of learning, the ease of use, the empowerment of the learner to control the learning schedule and the execution of the learning programme (Roffe, 2002: 40–50).

A FUSION OF THEMES

What characterizes the present situation is not only the range of electronic applications available, but also an increased interest in the nature of teaching and learning, together with the business processes that extend their scope. Technology allows the reach of even a small educational enterprise to be global, while traditional hegemony in a regional market can be challenged from near and far. As a result, professionals in enterprises of all sizes are reassessing the entire learning process to discover where, how and when learning occurs. They search for technology-supported learning methods that are well presented, clearly conveyed and effectively supported. It makes e-learning, in one sense, a fusion of learning, technology and e-business. All three are omnipresent, although their relative importance depends on the actual application. Certainly, each component is evident in the practice of supporting e-learning in firms and organizations.

There are good reasons for this effect. As technology evolves, so systems increase in their sophistication. There are complexities of design, in application and in the organization needed for their operation. Education, by its very nature, takes on a growing responsibility in furnishing the skills needed to manage and control an enterprise that is expanding and using technology. Consequently, it makes great sense to use technology, not simply as the means for increasing production but also as a method to raise skills and performance. Taking a very broad interpretation of e-business as any form of business or administrative transaction, or of information exchange that is executed using any technology, then contracting and supporting e-learning students involves a business transaction.

Technology also helps to shape new competition. Learning technologies allow new providers of education to undertake selected parts of what the traditional educational service provides, without the extensive capital investment needed to build a conventional campus. The design and service cost of new computer-mediated courseware then act to push enterprises that make these investments to seek larger markets, to compete with other providers at home and abroad.

EDUCATIONAL ENTERPRISE AND E-LEARNING

'Educational enterprise' is a term which conveys both the initiative that propels a new venture and all the actions taken to develop education in a creative and businesslike way. Over the past ten years or so, it has become apparent to every form of educational enterprise that, in order to continue to be successful, it is no longer sufficient to think solely in terms of the bricks-and-mortar classroom approach. There are powerful reasons to support this idea, since we live in an era when the number of students appears inevitably to increase in relation to the number of teachers. With e-learning, though, there appears an opportunity to reconfigure delivery and support, seemingly without a sacrifice in the quality of learning. Opportunities exist for an educational enterprise to innovate through e-learning and are a dominant reason for engagement with the practice.

E-learning presents a wide variety of possibilities for such innovation. This can extend directly to the curriculum to deepen the penetration of learning. It affects teaching and learning methods through improving flexibility for students, which can represent a relative shift from teacher-centred to learner-centred learning. Innovation can be applied to the methods of support, to provide novel or enhanced participation. Learning technologies present many possibilities for creating highly interactive, collaborative classes that make good use of simulations, case-method discussions, games and other means of provoking discussion between students and tutors. Learning systems can provide better management information, through more precise monitoring of the effectiveness and efficiency of learning. Innovation can also extend to methods of entry into new markets that can extend the range of influence of a provider.

The first wave of Internet applications led organizations of all types to explore the opportunities of electronic learning. Initially, the boundary between higher education and corporate learning led educational enterprises to focus development actions on to captive audiences. Corporate-learning providers fundamentally focused on creating business value by raising performance from the collective knowledge and skills of employees. Higher-learning institutions focused on existing groups to improve flexibility and access, such as MBA students. Some cross-over activity also occurred (Harris, 2002: 27–33). New providers, as well as old, tried to enter different market segments. The situation today is such that the field is much more fluid, with different types of provider trying to enter and service different market segments.

No single development dominates currently; rather, the growth of e-learning can be explained in terms of many parallel developments for particular groups of learners. E-learning for flexible delivery to campus students might be the primary application for one provider, for example, as it supports an existing client group and may offer an easier managerial option than continuously recruiting and supporting distant students. An educational enterprise may also choose to serve a small-firm market, a customer group that is likely to continue to be important for government policy-makers, but which makes special demands on the provider in terms of business support, themes developed in chapters 2 and 7. Higher education, with more complexity in goals and stakeholders than companies, addresses a wide range of student groups. Indeed, the governing themes of the general economic good that higher education brings are its contributions to economic competitiveness, life-long learning, social inclusion and regional development (NCIHE, 1997; DTI, 2000).

CHOICES

Whatever the target group of students or technology, in launching an e-learning programme a provider is informing people of the services on offer and transacting business by enrolling students. Building student numbers and online services through continuous improvement can then help develop this line of business. There are broad choices and compromises to be faced by decision-makers, though, in support of e-learning.

In conventional settings, strong revenues are created by lecture courses given by academic celebrities to large classes of students. Similarly, with Internet delivery one way is to attract large audiences with authentic content by well-known figures, but with a minimum of feedback and interactivity, in order to keep down marginal costs and take full advantage of economies of scale. The courses that result may prove attractive in terms of student recruitment, but may fall short of achieving the full potential of learning technology. There is a danger that, in order to enlarge the size of audience, providers will favour simple material over more demanding courseware (Bok, 2002: 7–29). Minimizing interactivity, of course, may cause students to learn less. There is an alternative to large-scale courses for the maximum number of students. This lies in a variety of courses with low numbers, where the course content is continuously updated (Peters, 1998). Such an approach is applicable to all types of courses, including conventional campus-based learning, distance learning and e-learning. There are certain advantages in doing this by e-learning, though, because it is more feasible economically to deal with a personalized track through a learning programme. Good online education, then, entails more than simply accessing course slides, or converting traditional campus lectures for distribution over the Internet.

PERSONALIZATION

In an open competitive environment it is inevitable that competitors try to match the value in an e-learning offer made by a provider. In order to compete, an educational enterprise needs to ensure that its e-learning service remains different from the products offered by rivals. Direct competition comes from other e-learning service-providers. Competition can also come from substitution by other modes of learning, such as conventional classes, part-time evening classes or traditional open-learning courses that existed before the arrival of e-learning. Establishing a competitive position means making a different form of offer to tempt a student to enrol. This places a responsibility on a provider to innovate, to create a value proposition that will fit different market requirements. Innovation then becomes a systematic competence of an enterprise, because it can create perceived value for clients, a theme elaborated in chapters 7 and 8.

The requirements for conventional campus provision are different (normally) from a programme of distance e-learning for independent lifelong learners or employees in small firms. For a conventional higher-learning organization that recruits young people directly from school or college for a full-time degree course, the offer to meet educational needs will be a value proposition, together with social, community or business networking. For employees in small firms or independent lifelong learners, in addition to meeting learning needs, personalization of the programme and distance-learning support can form a powerful core to an e-learning value proposition.

Personalization is a key e-learning value source. Its significance lies in the opportunities for individualizing the interaction between the provider and client. With individualized pathways through a course, the prospect of creating attractive individual value propositions by means of e-learning increases. There is the potential for personalized access to experts and for easier and flexible contact. E-learning techniques can create special tracks and assessment through a programme, with personal Web-pages for dialogue on a one-to-one basis with a tutor, or in small groups for tutorials.

Personalization can be achieved through a diagnosis of the needs of an individual, analysis of the learner's objectives, existing skill-sets, interests, career objectives, job profiles, attainment and style. All of this can help establish an individual profile for a particular learner to address specific learning needs. Personalized design means that the content can be tailored to specific areas of interest, without wasting time on areas with which the learner is familiar. It can be executed by human or technology mediation, or a combination of both. This represents a marked shift of emphasis from a 'just-in-case' model that requires individuals to acquire information in a class-bound environment, much of which will never be used. A personalization technique can be combined with a 'just-in-time' approach, as this allows individuals to learn at the precise time and place needed and adds even greater flexibility.

The learner focus that is facilitated by personalization is a shift of emphasis from the educator to the learner, which can make learning more relevant and dynamic for the learner. Every learner is different. The variety extends to prior knowledge, learning style, and so on. Consequently, some compromise is necessary to move a class as a group through the schedule of a curriculum. With e-learning, an individual can take part in a customized programme that presents the precise material needed in the best form for the learner, thereby moving from instructor-managed to learner-managed. This can result in more relevant and dynamic involvement by the learner.

AUTHENTICITY

Authenticity is another source of value. Issues of authenticity, in knowing who is providing the e-learning and the credibility of the content, arise because of concerns about the quality of material that is available over the Internet. An e-learning programme operated by a recognized educational body becomes a value proposition because the institution's status and quality processes guarantee that the content is accurate and the information provided is bona fide. These features of value assurance need to be presented to a prospective student, but for some markets there are more than just conventional quality-assurance concerns.

Independent learners face a bewildering range of options from learning portals, accredited or non-accredited courses, and in selecting from hundreds of thousands of options on the online learning market to run on their personal computer. Selection is made more complicated because there are few measures of quality with which to compare products. Not everyone is comfortable with the responsibility of making a selection on their own. Even for existing students who are adopting flexible learning methods, e-learning brings greater independence, but with the twin needs of more self-direction and motivation. Therefore, the authenticity of the e-learning product is crucial to avoid post-sale dissatisfaction for individual cases, and the danger of low standards in general.

Authenticity for students can extend beyond accuracy, comprehensiveness and normal institutional quality-assurance methods. The learner needs confidence in the programme and assurance that the content is relevant, additional dimensions that create value assurance in the offer. A programme on how a company can market on the Internet, for example, may be accurate in describing the necessary steps. It may be comprehensive in coverage, including all the current issues, and have relevance in matching content to the knowledge of the manager group for which it is targeted. The programme may have educational credit. Nevertheless, authenticity can still be missing if the learner does not believe the situations, steps, solutions and cases are real. Building a level of credibility in the programme involves adopting approaches that anchor the learning programme in an authentic context. This means content with cases to which a student-client can relate. The goals need to be personal and meaningful. The subject content needs to engage the learner with tutor support that is stimulating and timely. The approach needs to lead a student logically to work on his or her own real-life implementations. As the business environment is dynamic, then each of these components must be reviewed and revised to maintain authenticity.

Many new providers of e-learning as distance learning choose to provide non-accredited provision, but the dominant efforts of higher- and further-education institutions are in accredited provision. The public will continue to view these latter providers as responsible for the quality of the e-learning provision and expect similar standard to mainstream courses (Eaton, 2001: 15). Decision-makers in established providers, therefore, have a responsibility to provide guidance to the public and company clients on how to reach judgements about quality in electronic settings, which include what to examine, whom to contact and how to make comparisons. For an educational enterprise, the pursuit of authenticity means working to keep its fundamental values intact, assuring the quality of credits in a distance-learning environment and providing clear communications to students about quality issues. Authenticity is, therefore, just as much an educational issue as a business one.

An educational service-provider, building authenticity and value assurance for students, will sooner or later be confronted by other providers trying to serve the same market. Value assurance, the effectiveness of enhancing value and innovation, then become important operational competences for the enterprise. Value enhancement covers the processes in which a service is constantly reviewed with the aim of upgrading. Innovation can help improve the efficiency, or effectiveness, or the perceived value of an educational service, subjects developed in chapters 7, 8 and 10.

MOVING FROM REGIONAL TO INTERNATIONAL MARKETS

Change is already affecting course prospectuses. The typical external programmes serve a range of regional audiences: adult working professionals, recreational lifelong learners, more traditional part-time credit-based students and firms. The existing markets for these operations are regionally constrained. The region is a primary target market, because of brand recognition and local reputation that can drive students in their selection for these programmes. There are, in addition, national and international audiences for in-company learners, distance learners, franchised courses and graduate studies. E-learning makes access possible to local, regional, national and international markets.

E-learning is ideal for export by e-business. Weightless and with high value, learning is held in esteem in all countries and cultures. There are three core business assumptions, however, that face an educational enterprise in entering export markets. First, that the additional customers will provide additional value to the e-learning service. This is a state of affairs that will be beneficial if any additional costs of delivery, such as in developing new cultural contexts, or in providing tutorial or technical support to students working in different time-zones, are to be feasible. Secondly, that forecast revenue will exceed the predicted additional costs. Thirdly, that the technology infrastructure will provide reliable support. Around the world, many providers firmly believe that these conditions can be met.

Classic distance-learning already has a significant international dimension, with countries using distance technologies to enlarge their own programme and degree offerings, as well as to import and export education programmes and services. Countries such as South Africa and India are importers of distance-learning programmes, as they endeavour to expand the educational opportunities for their citizens quickly. China, Thailand, Turkey and Indonesia also employ distance-learning techniques to develop their own programmes and degrees, as a means of supporting their existing higher-education systems. Eastern European countries are determining the place of distance-learning providers alongside their traditional education providers.

On a global basis, the United States, Australia and the United Kingdom are major exporters of higher education by means of electronic technology. For these developed countries, a favourable balance of trade has existed from the export of education for many years, through distance-learning programmes, overseas studies centres, course franchising and the validation of courses. The federal University of Wales, for example, registered over 7,000 students on validated courses overseas in the academic year 2002/2003. Existing higher-education providers are alert to the threat that new electronic brands or new e-learning provision might lead to a destabilization of the existing structure of international education provision.

Applications of e-learning in corporate universities and software firms offering products and services for the e-learning industry mushroomed initially in the United States. Applications of e-learning are growing quickly and in parallel in the major international education markets of the developed world, in North America, western Europe and Australia, as well as in the east Asian region. Such applications of e-learning vary from country to country, as do educational developments, conditions and financial resources. Not only is the situation complex, but it is changing rapidly. The enormous impact and diversity of the Internet on global educational practice can be judged from reports on the practice of virtual education drawn from different regions, countries and continents, such as that compiled by an observatory at the Commonwealth of Learning (Farrell, 1999, 2001).

Despite all this activity, it still appears that the market in e-learning for distance education is not organized. Supply and demand are not aligned and the markets are still forming. One strong market demographic, relevant to all distance-education providers, is the number of geographically dispersed individual life-long learners, who have niche interests with the time, place and resources to pursue them wherever they arise. One challenge for decision-makers in an e-learning service-provider intent on gaining a wider audience is, therefore, to move from regional delivery to presenting a relevant value proposition to national and international learners.

GLOBALIZATION

The issues involved with globalization are not new and are certainly contentious. What is relatively new, however, is the movement to embrace education as part of the debate on globalization. At a national level, it is arguable whether education represents a genuine market, because of government intervention. Leaving aside the influences that pervade national policies, access to education markets is engendering much international debate.

At the international level, the General Agreement on Trade in Services (GATS) (*www.gats-info.eu.int*) is being negotiated currently under the World Trade Organization and includes education as a service-sector industry. GATS is designed to liberalize international trade, and educational services are believed to be a billion-dollar-a-year service-sector industry, with particular barriers to trade. These apparent barriers include accreditation arrangements that favour domestic institutions and qualifications, taxation that handicaps foreign institutions, and so on. Observers have mixed views on GATS. Some see benefits in the movement of providers into countries where domestic capacity is in under-supply, others that liberalization may compromise crucial facets of quality assurance and capture the best students along with revenue streams; but in any event the issues are contentious and open to interpretation (Knight, 2002: 21). The discussions are of real importance. If education is a market, then according to GATS there can be no 'national education market policy'.

In a wider context, the issue of globalization, that is, the process of worldwide economic integration, is affecting the environment for firms and economies. A debate has ensued as to whether homogeneous or heterogeneous products are called for. An early proponent of the global product was the marketing specialist Levitt, who argued that the globalization of industries was inevitable, producing global products because of the homogenization of the needs and desires of people around the world (Levitt, 1983: 90–102). He suggested this process was driven by technology, communication, transport and travel, and led to standardized but superior products, produced at lower prices and sold in standardized ways to customers the world over. A contrary view is that markets are not so homogeneous. Customers in different parts of the world have different needs, which cannot be met by a standardized product, so that a local or country-based approach to competition that aims to customize products for local needs is optimum (Douglas and Wind, 1987: 19–29).

Between these two contrasting viewpoints and their resulting strategies, either geocentric or locally responsive, lies a middle way that has been described as a transnational approach and popularized under the slogan 'think global, act local'. Originally adopted by the 'green' environmental movement, this idea is currently adopted as an advertising 'strap-line' in the UK by HSBC Bank as the 'local global bank'. Although customer needs around the world had become similar, the fixed costs of meeting those needs had escalated, creating the need for global products (Ohmae, 1987). Sufficient differences still occur, however, to make totally universal products unrealistic. A similar argument is that transnational firms should have structures that combine strong local managers, who supervise the local customization and marketing of their products, with strong global supervision of the production process (Ghoshal and Bartlett, 1998).

There are other globalization factors that impact on education. For example, the globalized economy, with a growing demand for standardized products and services in regional markets, together with technical and human resource infrastructures that can support these requirements. Another factor is the emergence of the knowledge-driven economy, driven by new ideas and knowledge, innovation in products and services, investment in skills development and the imaginative deployment of knowledge and creativity. There is also a growth in demand from the working adult population for access to higher education, propelled by the rapid changes in the economy and the need to gain, maintain, upgrade and accredit skills for employment. Moreover, there is an increase in student numbers and costs of higher education, combined with reluctance on the part of government to fund the growing demand for education fully.

Globalization can have positive as well as negative consequences. The ability to benefit from the new opportunities associated with the effects of globalization on society and the economy seems related to access to productive assets, including education and skills. As a result governments are increasingly looking at improving en bloc the education of every member of society, rather than just selected groups. Lifelong learning and distributing learning across communities are both encouraged as the means to prepare and support people. At the World Summit on Sustainable Development, in Mozambique, Tony Blair commented:

> Globalization is not just inevitable . . . it is a good thing provided that it is combined with good governance, proper developmental assistance and awareness of environmental issues as well as fair trade through open markets. It is the fairness of, and what comes with, globalization that will determine its character. Free trade is vital and neither the EU, the US, Japan or any other wealthy nation should be retreating from it. (Blair, 2002)

GLOBALIZING EDUCATION

Globalizing education implies a move towards standardized curricula and modes of delivery. There are clear public and policy interests in whether technology is actually transforming education and learning, as can be seen from the many investigations into e-learning by all kinds of interest groups: governmental, professional, commercial, as well as from education communities (Bjarnason et al., 2000a; Block and Dobell, 1999; Close et al., 2000; Cunningham et al., 2000; Farrell, 2001; Kerry et al., 2000; McCrea et al., 2000; Peterson et al., 1999; Ruttenbur et al., 2000; Urdan and Weggen, 2000). In essence, these reports found a great deal of descriptive information, but also a lack of coherent data and much hyperbole on available provision. Each study concludes that electronic learning is serving to stimulate greater competition, creating international markets for learning and offering the means of extending learning opportunities.

The primary concern of an Australian research team that examined the convergence between global media-networks and higher-education provision (Cunningham et al., 1998), was that such convergence could lead to mega-suppliers of e-learning. Their application of standardized, or internationally accepted, curricula and modes of delivery, would be to the competitive disadvantage of existing providers. Analysis of the impact of media companies on borderless education led this research group to suggest that globalization may not lead to a homogeneity in e-learning content. In fact, a more likely scenario involved the emergence of a complex 'mosaic' of area- and language-specific content, tuned to cultural preferences and political sensitivities in different countries, rather than universal standardized content from a few global providers. Educational enterprises that identified a niche and strategy to meet the needs of the relevant stakeholders were likely to be in the best position for global trading.

Standardization rather than heterogeneity may, of course, well suit a company. A firm may choose to develop a corporate university that allows the effective and efficient delivery of a common curriculum in different countries for workforce development. The process can be made simpler and easier by the standardization of a core product, with elements of local customizing introduced as necessary. Large corporations in the IT industry, notably Microsoft and Cisco, have rolled out standard technical certification for international enrolment as a separate, but credible, method to the offer by traditional providers of accredited learning.

NICHE PROVIDERS

Some commentators hold that large global providers of e-learning will hold sway, others that there will be a complex patchwork of niche providers. In practice, fragmentation rather than integration of the world markets appears to be happening, with the emergence of very many niche markets on an international, national and regional basis rather than on a global scale. An aggregation of niche providers currently seems most likely to continue and several patterns seem to be emerging.

First, a global standardized model will not serve to fit all countries, cultures and languages. Apart from special cases where a multinational company might wish to support workers on overseas assignments and local employees with a standard programme, customizing for local requirements is a necessity. Local customizing of IT products is already practised by suppliers, so that moving to electronic-learning products that are customized and supported by the same IT platform presents only a small incremental step.

Secondly, the resources needed to provide the ongoing support of an e-learning programme with a large enrolment would be sizeable. After the development of a course, there is often a requirement to provide online tutors, with, for example, a ratio of one instructor for every thirty students. In an online business course, such as an MBA programme, although the faculty of a provider may have top-quality expertise involved in the course content development, the delivery of a programme with a large student enrolment will inevitably rely for tutorial support on less distinguished and less expensive resources. Not only is this a substantial expense if these instructors are faculty members, but there is a responsibility and discrete workload in managing this faculty group. There are, therefore, substantive issues of scalability for an e-learning programme.

Thirdly, the position of a niche supplier in a global market appears viable. A niche is a group of customers who require very specialized products, which sets them apart as a market group. E-learners use all the resource-investigation facilities of the Internet to seek out unique provision, just as learners in developing countries seek the opportunity to access scarce, top-quality expertise from the developed world. There is then an element of threat. An e-learning enterprise as a first mover may service a market niche that can prove an alternative to existing conventional provision. This first-mover position can continue to create a dynamic that adds value to an offer, such as greater course flexibility, better opportunities for networking or enhanced online services. Such advantages can help sustain a stronger proposition for a first mover in e-learning over secondary launches.

Niches can also arise for educational enterprises in servicing economic clusters, where learning occurs for cooperative advantage among participants. Clusters are geographic locations where industry specialization occurs and firms develop economies of scope and scale that it was once thought only single, large firms could manage. Today geographical concentrations of scientific and creative knowledge are the key resources. These require a support system including major injections of research funding, financial investment, management, specialist incubators and learning support for human resource policies. Firms often find it vital to acquire, through learning, new knowledge that is a significant asset to their business performance. An industry cluster, with an economic development agency and a responsive educational provider, is therefore the basis for a profitable interdependence, with numerous examples in Europe and North America (Cooke, 2002).

Niche provision is not exclusive to corporate clients or business studies. It can occur across all areas of provision. Here are just a few cases:

- Malta is the setting for an online postgraduate programme in IT and Diplomacy, where the University of Malta, working in collaboration with Geneva's Graduate Institute, has students distributed in the Balkans, the West Indies, Middle East, Africa and the Far East (Caruana, 2002: 376–81) (*www.medac.diplomacy.edu.default.htm*). The programme addresses diplomacy, based on relevant case-material for the target group, which is not wholly derived from the context of the richer nations of the G8 Economic Club.

- Personalization of learning through an enhanced IT-based form for supporting learning, with students' learning qualities measured and reported online (Niemi, 2002: 370–5). In principle, learners can improve through an understanding of their own preferred learning qualities and so the potential market for this is enormous.

- Volunteering studies designed for online support of students working in volunteer situations (*www.lamp.ac.uk*). Volunteering is a practice for very many people, but without the matching number of educational support schemes. Provision aimed at individuals working in volunteer organizations can access this large market segment.

- A global e-moderating course as a means to teaching online, based on the five-stage model of Salmon (*www.centrinity.com/e-moderating*) and (*www.oubs.open.ac.uk/e-moderating*). E-learning is a growth field that requires a cadre of competent tutors to support the increasing body of e-learners. A systematic and structured approach to online teaching may capture a substantial number of these professionals.

INFORMATION AND NICHE SEGMENTS

An information expansion is affecting all niche segments of society. The volume of production of digital information worldwide is estimated at between one and two exabytes (one billion gigabytes) per year, which is increasing hyperexponentially (Brown, 2000: xiii). Brown suggests that a key task ahead is to stop the volume of information from overwhelming its value. The heart of the problem is not in embedding information into social life, but rather in the interpretation of information by members of society. Access to information runs along a continuum from good to poor, which in turn presents different challenges for the e-learning provider.

Teenagers are growing up in an information ecology, and so the challenge for e-learning designers and practitioners is how to influence a digital generation by integrating appropriate forms of media into each discipline. Søby suggests that an appropriate form of response is in creating Internet applications that adopt the practice and expertise of computer games (Søby, 2002). It leads the teacher into innovative, prototype learning environments that are adaptable to the learners' needs. There might, not unreasonably, be an accompanying expectation by young learners that their teachers do 'action research' on their needs and on relevant technology-based learning solutions.

Digital technology also equips potential students with a level of information that was previously unavailable. A starting point in choosing to enrol for many students is an institutional Website. Prospective students may get as much information from this as a printed prospectus, but the Website itself can be a dynamic source of information and a point of comparison of an institution's capacity to employ learning technology. Once enrolled, a student can compare the approach taken in one course with that in other courses at the same provider, and courses at other institutions. Such transparency can only help create a greater level of competition and increase the demand for skilled uses of technology. Each institution, no matter how great its prestige in the traditional mode, will therefore need to compete effectively through the skilled use of technology to enhance learning.

In contrast to this 'digital-rich' environment, people living in low-income neighbourhoods are assumed to be 'digital poor'. To benefit from technology, citizens will need a suite of e-skills, not just in digital literacy, but also in a range of associated key skills, such as in collaborative working and learning to learn (*www.europa.eu.int*). Citizens from digital-poor environments are less likely to be able to use the most common methods of training or points of access to learning technology. A 'digital divide', then, separates people who have access to digital and online media and those who have not. This divide can exist between the rural and urban areas of a country, and also between developed and developing countries (Venkat, 2002: 14–16; Young, 2001).

Among the many ways in which ODFL and e-learning are addressing aspects of the digital divide, UNED (*www.uned.es/cued*) (Universidad Nacional de Educación a Distancia, Spain) is converting its international courses into e-learning format with a focus on Latin America. Working with the World Bank Institute, the Interamerican Development Bank, UNESCO and the Organization of American States, it is providing a range of services as part of its international activity. This involves delivering training in Bolivia, Brazil, Costa Rica, Cuba and Colombia, where UNED is collaborating with Universidad del Valle, Cali, to get former guerrilla members to return to civil society.

Gaining technology skills can lead to better opportunities for people to participate fully in the local economy and greater social inclusion. This, in part, is the thinking behind the European movement on lifelong learning (EC, 2001). One approach to providing better access is to collectivize and centralize technology resources in order to make them available for social purposes. Access centres, for example, are equipped and staffed to support the needs of disadvantaged learners. E-learning offered through access centres may then serve to widen access and participation in learning. A range of barriers are found in practice, though, and constrain the involvement of individuals from poor neighbourhoods in the take-up of technology in the UK (DTI, 2000). These barriers include an uncoordinated approach to policy and strategy, poor promotion, unattractive content and relevant competencies of staff, as well as the actual and perceived costs. The recommendations for improvement are many, and include coherent policy presentations to the public on technology access, better technology awareness, familiarization training and so on.

E-LEARNING FOR COMPUTERIZED WORKPLACES

Firms are a major market segment for e-learning services. Economic forces on the corporate world act to influence businesses to improve quality, reduce costs and create an organizational capability to adapt to change as a route to success. Superior learning ability for an organization and individuals becomes a competitive advantage, since it can change behaviour faster and allow a quick response to new opportunities. Learning can attract and hold on to better people. By making an offer to staff, such as 'if you join our company we will do this for you', learning becomes a part of the value proposition of the internal ecology of the enterprise. Learning, in short, becomes the social glue that holds an extended enterprise together. For companies, e-learning is not just about putting courses online to address a specific training issue, but is a core element of any workforce optimization initiative that addresses business issues, such as reducing costs, greater accountability for learning and increasing competitive agility (Manville, 2002).

Learning is expensive. Investment in employee development therefore merits close managerial attention to the actual performance of programmes. The achievement of the delivery of learning on cost forecast, standardization in content for all employees, flexibility in its multiple dimensions and scalability in size for different groups, are all attractive benefits for an organization. For managers in general, and human resource managers in particular, e-learning methods offer the ability to track the progress, record and performance of each and every registered learner, thereby greatly improving the data collection and interpretation of the efficiency and effectiveness of learning programmes. Although e-learning is still emerging as a field of practice, the benefits are attractive because they are so radically different from a classroom-based learning environment, yet still hold the real prospect of performance improvement for employees.

A prescient analysis of the future of work, by Zuboff, predicted that learning within an information organization would become the new form of labour and that information would become the source of value and wealth (Zuboff, 1988). An 'informated' workplace was the term she adopted to describe an information-based organization, where ideas and information can move quickly and cheaply. This has certain consequences for the organization. First, it needs fewer levels of management than the traditional command-and-control organization. Next, it can unbundle activities that do not present opportunities for advancement into senior managerial and professional positions, and allow outsourcing of such work to external contractors. Such reorganization requires smart people to address complexity, and so intellectual skills are needed at every level. Wealth creation in an organization, therefore, depends on the ability of its employees to learn to manage information. E-learning can serve to match the learning needs of such an organization by providing learning at the point and time that it is needed, a process termed 'just-in-time open learning' (JITOL).

Much time and effort has been applied to workplace computerization in enterprises in recent years, through systems such as enterprise-resource planning (ERP), a common organization-wide network. This is a way to enhance the performance of a business through streamlining the information flow in a business by bringing important processes together. It is not a single system, rather, it is a network of systems that brings together all the business units together under a single software system. The biggest benefit of ERP is integration; all employees can use the same information and business processes to receive the same results from a system query. There are other reasons for its popularity, as it provides a firm base for the next generation of technologies and applications. It also consolidates key business functions for internal goals and can improve customer-order processing. Learning is therefore seen as a key activity for employees to assimilate technology, product, market and competitor information, at least in some large-sized enterprises (LSEs).

There are three other major systems that can help an informated firm. Supply-chain management (SCM) systems seek to automate the relationships between suppliers and a firm to optimize the planning, sourcing, manufacture and delivery of products and services. Customer-relationship management (CRM) systems are intended to provide integrated information on the relationships between a firm and its customers. Finally, knowledge-management (KM) systems seek to capture, store and disseminate the expertise and knowledge in a firm.

WEALTH CREATION FROM SMALL ENTERPRISES

Small and medium-sized enterprises (SME) are widely seen as a vital component for economic competitiveness. Addressing their development needs is, therefore, crucial for wealth creation in a region. The notion of a generic enterprise based on size might be beguiling, but it is still profoundly misleading. Although it is convenient to classify enterprises by the number of employees and size of turnover, companies that make up the group of SME firms are in reality very heterogeneous. Companies are drawn from every industrial sector and are at all stages of an enterprise life-cycle. Indeed, the only common denominator is size and the accompanying resource limitations.

The European Commission categorizes enterprises according to quantitative criteria (EC, 2003). Under this regimen, to qualify as an SME a company has to satisfy criteria for the number of employees and also one of two financial criteria: either below the maximum turnover, or below the maximum balance-sheet (Table 1.1). Management must be independent, with less than 25 per cent of the company owned by an enterprise that is not a SME. Consequently, an SME is a business based on the criteria of effective management independence and under 250 employees, with either a maximum annual turnover of 50 million euros or a balance-sheet total of 43 million euros (EC, 2003).

Table 1.1 Definition of an SME (EC, 2003)

Factor	Medium	Small	Micro
Max. number of employees	<250	<50	<10
Max. turnover	≤€ 50 million	≤€ 10 million	≤€ 2 million
Max. balance-sheet total	≤€ 43 million	≤€ 10 million	≤€ 2 million

The economic importance attached to SMEs seems justified, because they are the backbone of wealth creation in most regions of Europe. They are an important and large source of employment, while the taxes paid by them and their employees provide financial support for government policies. Even in regions of Europe where employment is dominated by large enterprises, SMEs still play a crucial role as suppliers, subcontractors or retail enterprises. Their limited internal resources and capacity to modernize mean that they often need external services to help with economic and technological change. Because of their size, though, they can be more adaptable.

The significance of SMEs can be judged from economic data. Across the EU, 99.8 per cent of all businesses are SMEs; this translates into more than nineteen million firms (Table 1.2). They provide seventy seven million jobs, which represents two-thirds of employment in the EU, or twice as many people as are employed by large firms (EC, 2000). Even though larger enterprises are more productive, they cannot replace the impact of SMEs in employment or business operations. Indeed, the real challenge for policy-makers and business-support services lies in raising the performance of SMEs.

Table 1.2 Classification of SMEs by size in the EU (EC, 2000)

Size	No. of enterprises in the EU	Average no. of employees	Value added per employee (€)
Very small	18,040,000	2	38,000
Small	1,130,000	20	44,000
Medium	160,000	90	62,000

Government policies in Wales, as elsewhere, recognize the contributions SMEs make to employment, turnover and job creation. Policies are complemented by financial support measures, under a plan to develop entrepreneurship that includes a businesses' information resource online and stimulating the supply of learning by making educational enterprises more responsive to the needs of small firms (WAG, 2002). These measures are needed, since Wales is amongst the least entrepreneurial of countries in terms of activity, opportunity and capacity (Brooksbank and Jones-Evans, 2002). More encouraging facts, though, come from the analysis of the fastest-growing indigenous Welsh businesses in the knowledge-based service sector businesses (Jones-Evans, 2001: 19). Six key areas appear to be particularly important: recruitment consultancy, training provision, marketing and PR consultancy, environmental consultancy, graphic design and technological consultancy.

Internet technologies have fundamentally changed the economic and technological landscapes in which SMEs operate. Businesses need to get information to help their employees perform better and faster than the competition. E-learning is a tool to help improve workforce learning in SMEs, but the right technology and delivering authentic learning programmes, though necessary, is insufficient. Studies on small-firm development in Wales, as elsewhere, show a range of internal factors for the SME that can influence success, factors elaborated in chapter 2.

Many variables affect a small firm, making this a market segment with its own complexities. Conventional approaches to improving skills commonly involve standardized training programmes and expect SME employees to enrol, but this approach appears overly simple. For acceptance by SME clients, content must be strongly linked with the firm's goals and operational needs, and must be work-based. Another layer of service support is necessary to identify performance improvement, create authenticity and support employee learning in various ways. For e-learning to realize its development potential for an educational service-provider, much more than technology, content and support are involved. Success depends on strategy and execution of business development by the educational enterprise.

DUAL THEMES

Change is inevitable with innovation, and e-learning is no exception. Managing change requires expertise in sensing both continuity and the opportunity for innovation (Bruner, 1966). It is appropriate, then, that the themes here are dual: what we know about how people learn in conventional settings, and how best they can be helped to learn with technology; what we understand about innovation from the commercial arena, and how it can assist an educational enterprise develop an e-learning prospectus; what place and meaning we give to strategy, and how this can be interpreted for new competition in technology-supported learning; and what we know about the business of supplying small firms, and how the experience can be transferred into e-learning.

E-learning can become a complex subject, even in the limited sense of building and delivering an online course for a group of employees in a small firm. The goal of e-learning, though, must be to optimize the way a learner transforms information into actionable knowledge, whereas the challenge for an educational enterprise is to develop effective ways that create a sustainable line of business, through value assurance and enhancement. To achieve this, there are three fundamental barriers for an educational enterprise to cross: the right supply, in the form of a learning programme with authentic content; meeting the right demand from a market niche; and the right responsive structure, in a technological and business sense, as the following chapters are intended to demonstrate.

2

E-learning in small and medium-sized enterprises

Small and medium-sized enterprises form a key part of the economy, and yet support for their growth through the development of their employees has proved a problematic area. An extensive literature base has catalogued the many difficulties. Performance analysis among small firms along supply chains in the media industry is a means to diagnose their business context, technology profile and development needs for their e-business environment. Case studies exist from different stages of their business life-cycle. Technology is the source of many operational difficulties that may need attention before the introduction of e-learning, and is a useful introductory theme for system-wide analysis. Small and medium-sized enterprises are a highly heterogeneous group, and to meet their e-learning development needs a variety of responses on the part of the education service-provider, but the potential applications for an SME are enterprise-wide. Finding the time and space for learning in the busy workplace of a small firm is a major issue for many people.

E-LEARNING IMPACT ON ENTERPRISES

E-learning has made an immediate impact on large businesses because it offers an obvious avenue for an enterprise to gain a competitive advantage. Right in the centre of the steel-and-glass headquarters building of Lloyds TSB in Bristol is just one example, a cyber-café. This is designed to give a relaxed environment, where employees can get support for their online learning, offered through Lloyds TSB Corporate University. As an electronic-learning centre, it is part of a network operated by the company to keep a professional sales and service force informed about changes in the business environment, customers and regulations that are distributed by its corporate Intranet. One would expect a company such as Lloyds TSB to have a sophisticated and well-deployed Intranet, both as a source of real-time business information and to support its workforce dispersed throughout the country. Building a learning platform to run over the internal Web of the company does not add a great deal to the cost of running the system. Cost savings result from the reduced need to travel to a training centre, while the savings made from not taking employees out of a branch or sales operation for training compensate for the learning development and administration costs.

There are other benefits that e-learning can bring. It is a highly efficient means of human resource development (HRD) for people, delivered precisely when it is required and accurately targeted at an individual's need. The prospect of self-selection of information makes it attractive. More learner control is possible, with access to learning whenever it is useful. Learners may access the relevant parts and navigate their way through a learning scheme by any desired route. In the process, they can bypass any unnecessary knowledge or skills, self-tailoring the information they need. There are good opportunities for experiential learning through real-life cases with rapid feedback, reflection and reinforcement. When implemented well, most technology-enabled learning can also double as a performance-support tool that is immediately available and embedded in the workplace.

Benefits like these make e-learning an attractive proposition for business, particularly for large organizations. For these large-sized enterprises, distributing costs over a large number of employees achieves a low unit-cost. Employees are a form of captive market, unable to move up or around a company without demonstrating capabilities set by the employer. This creates implicit and explicit requirements for vocational learning by the firm. These are explained in case studies, which, however, are almost wholly derived from large organizations with significant human capital to drive organizational change, either in the form of companies (Schank, 2002: Rosenberg, 2001), or of academic enterprises (Mason, 1998; Bates, 2001; Collis, 2001).

There are, of course, good reasons for this paucity of descriptions for small and medium-sized enterprises. One is that customizing an e-learning solution is often so costly that it may be beyond the budget of a small firm. Another reason is that supporting implementation in a small firm is very time-consuming, with relatively limited scope for scalable actions within the firm. Limited staffing in an enterprise can also inhibit the dissemination of good practice. Whatever the grounds, questions on e-learning practice in SMEs do exist, such as 'What are the practical implications of e-learning for a small business?' Such questions are relevant not only to SMEs themselves and their suppliers, but also, in terms of policy-making, because of the effect of SMEs on wealth creation. Much research effort has been expended on enhancing the business prospects of a SME, but comparatively less attention has been given to technology-supported learning for the improvement of small businesses.

SME GROWTH AND DEVELOPMENT

The economic importance of SMEs, the context of enterprise, the characteristics of high-growth small firms and the role of education and training in developing SMEs have stimulated many investigations over the past thirty years (Bolton, 1971: Stanworth and Gray, 1991; Storey, 1994; ENSR, 1997). The Bolton report identified the primary problems that challenge the management of an SME today, such as raising finance, costing, organization, delegation, information use, personnel management and technological change. Not all firms grow. Some small firms fail to stay in business, and the reasons are varied, such as financial difficulties, poor management, family problems, high labour turnover, difficulties in acquiring appropriate skills and technology (EC, 1993).

Technology is widely accepted as being central to the running of a business, and it facilitates the delivery of appropriate information to managers and employees. Size matters for company comparisons, however, because in large enterprises the cost of technology applications can be spread over a wider operational base, thereby reducing the unit cost. Much research into the use of technology in business is done on large firms, with comparatively less on small ones (Swartz and Boden, 1997: 53–65). Most models and methodologies taught in higher education are therefore based on the needs of large organizations (Doudikis et al., 1996: 189–201). SMEs may share many of the same technology concerns as larger enterprises, but differences appear in their direct application and in their constraints. Most SMEs use computers for operational purposes or for support tasks, such as accounting, stock control, payroll and word processing (Meldrum and de Berranger, 1999). All enterprises face resource constraints, such as on time and the cost of technology systems, but these are more significant in the smaller enterprise.

The business success of a firm is often critically dependent on its people. Employees can create a competitive advantage through their creativity, service quality or flexibility. An effective human resource management (HRM) strategy has an effect on operational performance, such as in lower costs of production, or improved product development. A firm needs to nurture and support employees, therefore, who can give it a distinctive edge. In a large enterprise, HRM is often viewed as a strategic function, needing specialist staffing to achieve organizational goals. In contrast, a small-business manager often needs to be a competent generalist, with HRM and concern for working relationships an integral part of the role.

Building a long-term sustainable business that is not dependent on the skills and effort of the founding entrepreneurs requires investment in employees. The outlay might entail building depth in the organization, or having trust in inexperienced employees to take key decisions. Upgrading the workforce, or recruiting new individuals for certain positions to replace or manage existing employees, are also areas of potential expenditure. Complex and sensitive issues are often at the heart of human resources management for any firm, regardless of size. In small enterprises and start-ups, it is common for everyone to do a little bit of everything. Then, as the business grows, as it tries to organize to achieve economies of scale and scope, employees have more clearly defined roles that are grouped into organizational units. The core of the human resources approach is that all managers recognize the importance of human resources, rather than leaving it as a specialist function of the personnel manager (Torrington and Hall, 1991). Everyone is a human resource manager in this culture, and developing employees to contribute to the success of the firm is the goal of human resource development.

HUMAN RESOURCE DEVELOPMENT

Human resource development (HRD) and workplace learning are terms that are gradually replacing training, development and workplace education as explanations of learning processes, because they are thought to be more comprehensive ideas. HRD comprises a wide range of activities and issues (Garavan et al., 2002: 60–71; Megginson et al., 1993; Weinberger, 1998: 75–93). One form of HRD is the training and development of people in work. Whatever terms are used, management literature strongly advocates that organizational effectiveness in the longer term requires expertise in learning, at both the individual and the organizational levels (Dixon, 1992: 29–49; Garrick, 1998).

A crucial question for both the policies and practices that support SMEs is whether or not investment in training affects the survival and growth of firms. The answer is not clear-cut in the literature. A DfEE study on training for SMEs is critical of previous research that explored training provision and small-firm performance (DfEE, 1997), as it found too many overly specialized, short-term, small studies that were difficult to compare. As well as failing to define training clearly, studies failed to take account of other management options open to owner-managers to improve performance. As Storey reports, 'there appears to be little evidence that small firms which invest in training perform better than those which do not' (Storey, 1994: 283). Although there is no positive correlation between management training of entrepreneurs and business growth, factors such as the nature of the firm, chosen business strategy and the nature of the entrepreneur seem crucial. In contrast, instances are reported where training and management development have shown positive links to business success (Lane, 1994). The results are mixed because it is simply too difficult to establish a cause-and-effect relationship between training and business performance, due to the problem of isolating training from all the other influences in a firm's environment.

A benefit of HRD is that the communication abilities of employees can improve, which enhances their adaptability. Better-educated workers can give the flexibility needed to switch production and better accommodate innovation, retraining and relocation (Godfrey, 1997). Adaptability is considered necessary for retaining employment and maintaining business competitiveness (Booth and Shower, 1996). A body of evidence suggests that SMEs do not have the expertise, infrastructure and general resources of large-sized enterprises. For instance, the manager of an employee is less likely to receive training, particularly job-related, formal training, if he or she works in a small rather than a large firm. When they are addressed, the management development needs for SMEs, even in the same size-bracket, may still be very different. The size of the firm ensures that it functions in different way from larger firms, with informality and the performance of multiple tasks often the management style in a SME.

A consistent picture of the conditions under which SME managers will undertake training includes the appropriate quality, timing and location (Temple, 1995). Training of appropriate quality is understood to apply to training that is directly relevant for the businesses and involves trainers who understand what it is like to operate an SME. Many managers are self-taught and hold no management qualifications; they may recognize the value of training but have difficulty in identifying their specific needs. Self-diagnosis skills can therefore be important for potential solutions. Owner-managers commonly rely on themselves and other members of the firm for training, supported by technical literature, equipment suppliers, private-sector companies and trade associations (Curran et al., 1997). They seem to prefer to acquire knowledge by external advice, networking and the exchange of experiences with other managers, rather than formal training.

For many SMEs, the problem is not so much with the long-term benefits of learning, but rather with the short-term problem of allowing employees who are stretched to capacity the time to take part in formal training. Owners or managers in micro-SMEs can view employee development as something that happens when necessary, and expect employees to be fully equipped for their work when appointed. This picture is not applicable to all SMEs, since the competitive forces in sectors such as IT mean that certain firms have to keep up to date with developments and also invest in their staff (Lange et al., 2000: 5–11).

A survey of management training by technology-supported training for heads of SMEs in Europe pointed to priority areas in business management skills (James, 2000). More specifically, these areas include marketing, international business procedures, quality control and application of business computer software. Tailor-made training, with programmes of high practical relevance that are sensitive to the different stages of development of a firm, was also highlighted, emphasizing the value of customizing and personalization in a technology-based learning solution.

FORMAL AND INFORMAL LEARNING

Formal and informal learning are both important methods of workforce development. The former is generally taken to be a structured investment. In contrast, informal learning takes place in the work context and relates to an individual's performance of their job, which is not formally organized into a programme by the employer (Dale and Bell, 1999). Employees engage in informal learning to meet organizational and individual goals in the course of participating in everyday work activities, which are not for the sole purpose of learning (Watkins and Marsick, 1992: 287–300).

Formal learning provides only a small part of work-based learning. Many SME managers are hesitant to engage in regular formal training. Although there might be adequate capacity for the supply of formal learning to business professions, these offers do not appear sufficiently attractive to meet the specific needs of SMEs in terms of content, methods and organization (Stahl, 1999: 51–60). Decision-makers in SMEs are more willing to agree to on-the-job training and informal learning where the direct link between cost and benefit is more evident (Lange et al., 2000: 5–11). For employee development to be supported as a discrete practice by SMEs, a link with business performance and relevant indicators, such as motivation and staff turnover, must be made. A rationale is also needed that connects directly to the aims and challenges of owners and managers (Hill and Stewart, 2000: 105–17).

Activities for developing the workforce in SMEs are often informal, in the sense that they may be in-company activities provided by personnel of the enterprise itself. Indeed, SMEs often resort to the training market only when they need to obtain specific skills that are not available in-company (EC, 2000). These firms are much more interested in custom-made courses, exactly tailored to the needs of their enterprise, than in open courses. Many studies on SMEs reveal a considerable degree of unplanned, unsystematic, reactive and informal training, where there is unlikely to be a personnel officer (Gibb, 1997: 13–29; Metcalf et al., 1994).

Informal learning appears to succeed because employees learn in the context in which their skills are applied and maintained. There are many sources of challenges at work that involve solving problems and coping with change. Learning then derives from thinking, trying out and communicating with co-workers. Organized support is sometimes in place to help this process of learning from others, which can come from teamwork, coaching or mentoring. Sometimes it comes from seeking information from customers, suppliers or professional networks. Practitioners draw from this the need to create a group climate for learning, characterized by ownership. Employees need to have a suitable degree of challenge in their jobs; they need suitable management with attention to the microclimate of the immediate work environment (Eraut, 1999). When implemented effectively, many benefits can accrue from informal learning; when learning is related to real events and put into practice more readily, it can increase employee confidence as well as improve relationships between employees and managers.

PERFORMANCE IMPROVEMENT ALONG A SUPPLY CHAIN

In Lampeter, development programmes for supporting growth in small firms started twenty years ago. Rurality, the relative remoteness and the small scale of operations are all critical local factors in delivery. Decision-makers in small firms in the area face a set of barriers to accessing conventional programmes, including inappropriate location, timing and form of opportunity, difficulties of finding information about what is available to meet individual needs and, superimposed upon these, geographical, economic and logistic barriers to access. Difficulties such as these, added to the learning transfer problem, led to a shift, some six years ago, in the process of delivery to small firms. This involved a move from the supply and sales of education and training courses into analysing and addressing performance improvement needs. Access to small firms was effected through performance analysis of the impact of technology on business strategy, operations, e-business and employee development.

Technological change is an opportunity for innovation everywhere. Trends in the knowledge media industry are relevant, as it exists to produce vast quantities of digital material and services for education, entertainment, information and training. Speake and Powell argued that 'knowledge media' was emerging as a new industry. This employed large numbers of people and created a new skill-set which embraced technology, learning and design and which they termed 'advanced convergent' skills (Speake and Powell, 1997). Worldwide demand they estimated as five to ten million developers. In the UK, however, the infrastructure to create these people had not yet developed.

In Wales the media industry is a high-profile sector of the economy, supported by the indigenous television broadcasting industry. It is a recognized source of entrepreneurial dynamism and a powerful magnet for attracting talented young people into high-growth small firms. A recent analysis of employment in the new economy for Wales concluded that some three and a half thousand people were employed in the digital media sector in Wales (Newidiem, 2002). Although 'digital media' was interpreted broadly, to include radio and television production, distribution and related audio-visual activities, it excluded software and IT services. Such a categorization makes it difficult to pick out the actual impact on employment of digital technologies in learning.

A study on SME firms in the media sector in west and south Wales set out to find the influences of change and the opportunities offered by technology and e-learning (Rogers et al., 2001). A performance-consulting approach was adopted as a holistic way to explore the problems faced in a small firm (Robinson and Robinson, 1989). The original concept was to work with a cluster of media companies affected by change due to technology. The value of such a cluster lies in the strength gained by the firms from competing together

(Porter, 1980). The rivalries between firms, though, made them unwilling to participate if information was shared among other firms from the same production sector. They would support an approach, however, to firms within their supply chains. Indeed, all companies along the supply chain agreed to participate, a feature attributed to positive referrals provided by the initial partners in the study.

The investigation involved a total of thirty firms. The initial focus was directed at firms in the media sector, but extended to include firms in their supply chains. All firms were small, with fewer than fifty employees, and each applied technology on a regular basis. The cases were based on interviews with the owners, managers and other key decision-makers. The following are a small number of the companies involved from the total casebook. The firms are dynamic, with a number of relevant changes under way and others planned, so that the picture is a snapshot of activity.

The findings represent different stages of the life-cycle of an SME: enterprise start-up, business development and maturity. They are summarized by six company case studies that represent three life-cycle phases (Table 2.1). These firms are sufficiently well known for a few features to be masked, and they are presented by pseudonyms: 'Melyn' and 'Coch' as business start-up firms, 'Gwyrdd' and 'Gwyn' in the development phase, 'Oren' and 'Porffor' as mature SMEs. A range of HRD needs arise during the phases of the life-cycle of an SME. The whole-systems approach to business analysis was adopted to understand the entire environment that contributes to the success of the learner in the firm and how to prepare for an e-learning environment. Access to the firms was gained by positive referral from clients along a supply chain, addressing technology performance needs in the firms studied rather than explicitly looking at learning practices.

Table 2.1 Company cases and SME business-cycle

Business phase	Company	Business operations
Start-up	'Melyn'	Specialist media suppliers.
	'Coch'	Television resource services.
Development	'Gwyrdd'	Media production.
	'Gwyn'	Office and computer supplies.
Mature	'Oren'	Publishing and printing.
	'Porffor'	Audio-visual and language services.

CASE STUDIES

Company: 'Melyn'

Two entrepreneurs with similar backgrounds in accountancy set up 'Melyn' three years ago, in a small town in Pembrokeshire. The company supplies a range of specialist media technical services to other television production companies. The founders knew each other well before starting the business. They registered as a partnership, with each having an equal share. The owner-ship structure operates successfully, with the business enjoying a steady growth in turnover every year. Even though they employ four people, they do not want the business to grow so large that they lose control over the business, and have no plans currently to employ more staff.

Technology profile. One partner is knowledgeable about technology and takes responsibility for all the computerization, while the other is less confident. The business has three computers: two desktop machines and an elderly portable to manage the business accounts. Both owners are competent in business applications because of their professional training. Word processing is also a key application used for letters, sales scripts and for promotional materials to market the company. Competitor companies are not currently threatening their business operations through the use of technology, in their view.

The company is contemplating several IT-related developments. The first comes from a growing line of existing business that would benefit from the creation of more professional packaging. They plan to purchase a colour laser-printer and have sought advice on PC-based software for graphic design work. The second opportunity involves the exploitation of the Internet. Although the company has a modem, it has no Internet service provider (ISP). Acquiring e-mail is a priority to catch up with competitors; its use will cut costs and increase efficiency, and the need for it is also driven by a significant rise in the adoption of e-mail by the company's suppliers. The partners also want a Website to promote the services of their company in the development of lines of e-business.

Learning and development. Both partners welcome professional development on IT in order to bring about more equality in their knowledge of IT. Workplace learning is favoured, but travel to university premises is also feasible. Accredited courses are not an essential requirement, although they are willing to attend certificated courses. The partners think that higher education could offer services to their firm at affordable costs. They value the knowledge base available in the university and want to harness it for their business. For the graphic-design venture, specific training on a PC-based software product would be needed. Advice on the business exploitation of the Internet would also be valuable for them.

Continuing learning is essential in the view of both partners. Heavy emphasis is placed on ensuring growth of business turnover and on professional updating programmes in accountancy. They have undertaken programmes in this area while in business. They both realize that there is a potential growth market in e-business, with future potential for increased sales and market penetration. For the company to capitalize on this market, technology and skills development are critical. As decision-makers, however, they need to decide on their priorities for entering the e-business market and devise an appropriate strategy to achieve a position. Once this is resolved, and with an effective Internet service in place, support for a learning strategy appeared feasible for each development direction. The kind of HRD consultancy they appreciated was a long-term relationship, with advisers understanding their particular business needs and developing relevant solutions for them. An initial intervention, with face-to-face development, could build capabilities and confidence for both partners and staff to progress to e-learning programmes, maintain their Website and exploit Internet marketing opportunities.

Company: 'Coch'

'Coch' operates from a rural location in Carmarthenshire. Founded by an entrepreneur, with high skill and energy levels, it has been trading for three years and has grown rapidly to employ five people. The business provides television resources and is setting up new premises to provide more space. Expansion of the business means that certain staff work excessive hours. Even so, the business is small compared with rivals. Recruitment by the company is not seen as a problem, but it does not expect to recruit in the near future. Instead, the solution perceived by the company is to increase the number of freelance staff, again a step not seen by the owner as an obstacle to further growth.

Technology profile. The business emphasis is on specialized electrical, audio-visual and camera techniques, not on business information technology applications. This means that only a very superficial knowledge of business IT exists in the company, which does not allow it to make informed decisions on business technology. The company currently makes limited use of computers. Manual systems prevail for sales, invoicing and inventory. The inadequacy of this situation revealed itself because the owner-manager complained of being distracted from running the company services by trying to remedy office difficulties, usually caused by computer problems. A single PC with modem is in use, for producing some of the business correspondence, running word-processing and spreadsheet packages, but it does not have an ISP.

The short-term business priority need is for effective business administration, since this part of the business is growing and the paperwork of the current administration takes a considerable amount of management time. A well-organized office, with e-mail to supplement fax and develop the Web as a business medium, to obtain contacts, as well as an advertising medium, are needed. These are not advanced requirements, but they are urgent. The current policy of do-it-yourself development is unable to deliver results in a realistic time period, because of the very limited starting competencies and the resources of time, energy and money needed for development.

Learning and development. Technology in support of business is changing faster than the owner-manager in this firm can respond. The owner-manager asserts that he is keen to train staff, but only in-company. A competent and sympathetic trainer might transform the business efficiency quickly by training in-company, establishing good office systems on spreadsheet, word processing, system security and backup. With a suite of e-skills, the company could receive ongoing support by e-learning.

Company: 'Gwyrdd'

'Gwyrdd' is an audio-visual business set up twelve years ago in Carmarthenshire by the current owner, who acts as managing director. The company is a high-growth business, currently growing at 20 per cent a year, a rate planned to continue for the foreseeable future. Management are keenly aware of the need for a strong profile in their industry in Wales, the UK and Europe and, to this end, balance promotion and business development with making themselves available to their own staff for consultation. Strong social responsibility is a recurrent theme expressed by the management. It is the biggest private-sector employer in their home town, with thirty staff. The business is rapidly developing and has successfully expanded to the point where the current accommodation is under growing strain. The managing director is faced with multiple decisions in business development for it to continue to perform. These concern not only direction, expansion, location and premises, but also human resource development, technology implementation and learning technology applications as a potential business line. A core competence of the company is a vibrant, dynamic company culture that can be the key factor in retaining and attracting valuable staff. Agility for new business development is another, as is the ability of the enterprise to change the way it works.

Technology profile. The existing premises are being networked. Even though the physical wiring is in place, not all the PCs are set up as networked workstations. A number of these have multimedia capability, and some experimentation with using technology-supported learning has occurred. There are plans to deliver Internet access to each workstation as well as to back-up every workstation to a single machine. The company has already contracted with an ISP and engaged an external consultant to create a Website to promote the business. Nevertheless, just a few staff regularly use e-mail, with only researchers employing the Web as an information and research tool.

The owner of 'Gwyrdd' is responsible for developments in IT, with support for existing systems provided by an independent service contractor. Contractors provide advice on future developments of hardware and software, with the quality of this current service viewed as satisfactory by the managing director. The company has multiple links with higher education and development agencies. The managing director is a leading figure in the industry and often gives presentations on development issues that affect the industry. Company confidentiality is a concern for them, because of the competitive nature of the industry and rivalry for contracts. The company is well integrated into the business support mechanisms available, but is critical of the tardiness of development agencies in relation to the real tempo of change affecting business. Aside from the fundamental problem of the inadequacy of business premises, the needs of the company are specific and relatively sophisticated. Work-based learning is considered desirable, although a problem for on-site tutoring might be the potential to disturb the work of other employees, because of the cramped accommodation. Certificate courses are regarded as too inflexible and are not a business requirement, even though they might prove a career help to certain employees. The need of the company is to be able to select support for the immediate and planned needs of the workplace.

Like firms of all types and sizes, 'Gwyrdd' is installing a variety of technologies for purposes of efficiency and to take advantage of the many benefits technology can bring to business. Even a small firm such as this has plans to install networks to enable their computers to communicate with each other, even though this is at present incomplete. The future technology requirement will depend partly upon its location, although it has an immediate IT requirement to complete networking all its workstations. The company will need to bring all staff up to a good core-level of IT knowledge and, in the process, embrace technology as a learning tool.

Almost all staff have a high level of familiarity with technology equipment. Some of this knowledge is highly specialized in its application, such as video-editing equipment. Employees are well qualified and experienced in their fields, and this proficiency has grown with the development life-cycle of the company. A company practice of multiskilling exists, to be able to compete with larger enterprises whilst still maintaining a small workforce. External pressures from the media industry put certain specialist expertise in high demand, which gives rise to a shortage of staff in certain technical areas and a practice within the industry of poaching staff. The company response is to recruit and train its own staff. Not only is it difficult in practice to recruit experienced replacements, but its human resource policy puts an emphasis on learning and development as a means of maintaining the culture and business dynamic of the firm.

The firm owns the copyrights for a large bank of photographs and videotapes, which is growing rapidly. Archiving, accessing and promoting the content is a potential new line of business and, at the very least, it will serve as an internal information resource. Sharing knowledge and information effectively is crucial to the future competitiveness of any organization. In this case, the positive features are the ownership of the initiative by top management, so that it can apply a disciplined process for capturing strategic knowledge; there is also a culture of continuous learning, with good communication and cooperation across the business. Negative factors are the current low availability of expertise and resources for managing electronic information systems. The nature of the business, the industry and competitors mean that this firm needs to follow technological developments in the media industry very carefully. The development of multimedia products for an expanding broadcast market might lead to the sale of these products on a high-volume basis, perhaps directly to end-users. This raises the possibility of e-business as the vehicle for such sales.

Learning and development. The managing director has imaginative ideas about future business lines and is keen to improve staff performance. A preferred route is by work-based learning, with support on the implementation of information technology. A case can be made for experimentation, with some staff trained in Web-page creation, maintenance and management, so that an employee could be assigned to the development of e-business. It is also feasible for this employee to be provided with support through e-learning and undertake an internal support role for other staff.

Company: 'Gwyn'

'Gwyn' was established eight years ago as a business providing office supplies, office furniture, computer media, computer equipment and software in an industrial town in Carmarthenshire. The founder of the company works as the owner-manager, and employs a total of twelve staff across its office and retail operations. The company has joined a purchasing consortium that enables small independent businesses to negotiate competitive deals with the major suppliers and then obtains an adequate trading margin for products. In this way the firm is able to compete with larger national and international chain suppliers.

A high-street shop serves as retail premises for the company. It also maintains a large catalogue of products that forms the basis of a mail-order business.

Another business offer is an installation service for computers, internal networking and software, presented as a 'total office solutions' service. The owner-manager faces certain choices in business development: a decision on redirecting resources away from revenue-earning work for clients towards business development for long-term growth, or optimizing all the short-term profits in the current business.

Technology profile. The organization has used IT since its start. For internal financial management it uses a turnkey system specifically designed for their business, which runs on an internal PC network. One member of the purchasing consortium has established an Internet server and now provides ISP facilities to other members, so that the company has a Web-page hosted by this service. The owner-manager has a plan to develop an e-business side to the mail-order business and has taken a great deal of advice on the process. An e-business application needs to be specifically tailored to the business practice since the company negotiates with clients, both private companies and public bodies, to produce a discount structure that matches the client's profile of ordered products. The higher volume of product sold to a customer usually attracts the greater discount, an arrangement that means that each customer has an individual account, with details of their personal discount structure. Any e-business implementation would need to incorporate this information as well as an electronic catalogue and ordering facilities. The sole responsibility for IT decisions lies with the owner-manager. He uses the Internet extensively, is satisfied with the bespoke software that the company operates and uses Microsoft support, as well as discussions with contractors.

Learning and development. The company does not lack expertise or training for the development of e-business; rather, there is a lack of management and staff time, with the need to divert this time from revenue-earning work. The company expressed interest in support for its e-business venture, particularly with on-site measures such as work-based learning and performance-improvement consultancy. The owner-manager was keen to introduce support for the e-business development that would engage other staff and spread the expertise in the company.

Company: 'Oren'

'Oren' is an established publishing business that has been trading for over forty years, with the son of the original founder now the managing director. It operates from premises in two towns. One site is run mainly as a sales office, the other as a production and management centre. Two purpose-built but ageing buildings comprise the company premises, which appear utilitarian and productive. The company employs some fifty people, ten located in the smaller sales office and the majority at the production and printing site. Staff turnover is negligible, with recruitment of new staff not a problem. There are a large number of long-serving employees in the company, and the management are conscious of the balance between progressive management approaches and their corporate responsibilities to the communities where they are located. The company has operated in a stable business environment for many years, but this has changed suddenly, due to the impact of technology and e-business. It faces challenges for the development of the business: to improve, in step with industry competitors, through applications of technology and also to compete in new markets through e-business.

Technology profile. Clear responsibilities exist for company IT, from the managing director down. Technology is applied throughout the firm, in design, scanning, page-assembly, image-setting and publishing. In administration, a client database is used to progress work through the company and deal with costing, personnel time-sheets and project planning. A Website, set up and maintained by an external contractor, has some fifty hits per week and has not generated many sales. 'Oren' is not prominent on Web search-engines for publishers, indicating that the site needs to be made more visible, by promotion and Internet marketing, to attract more e-business customers. The company is ideally suited to e-business, since the potential market is worldwide, but the customer base is very sparsely distributed. The customer base is well educated, has Internet access and is sympathetic to a business with the location, language and culture of the firm. Beyond the externally managed Website, with its small measure of e-business, there is little use of network technology.

'Oren' was trading successfully well before the technology and e-business boom of the past decade and has held a respectable position in a conservative industry. However, the advent of e-business has suddenly introduced new competitors into its own backyard. The response to these challenges is to work on improving the business performance by redefining job responsibilities to cover the new e-business dimensions, and to include in this role the monitoring and support of Internet information.

Learning and development. Staff experience of technology on the present scale extends back ten years, so a mature IT culture exists within the business. A substantial minority of staff, about 40 per cent, are regular IT users, although none have formal training or any certification in the subject. All were trained in-company, or are self-taught. Staff updating is still done largely informally, on the initiative of staff within their normal job function. The owner-manager, however, is keen to respond to challenges and believes that work-based learning, driven by the business needs of 'Oren', is the preferred solution. An on-site trainer, followed up by technology-supported learning, could achieve this. The company is interested in improving the performance of its e-business through Internet marketing development. Work-based learning with a tutor attached to the site is favoured, but certification is not essential.

Company: 'Porffor'

Porffor was founded fifteen years ago by the owner-manager in a small market town in Ceredigion to provide specialist audio-visual services for the media industry. It has been a market leader, an exploiter of technology and an innovator in services since it was formed. The company operates as a network organization, a relatively new form of work organization, in which a core staff is complemented by a network of freelance professionals to cope with any sudden surges in demand. The owner-manager has expanded its operations and 'Porffor' now operates from three sites, chosen for their convenience in meeting the requirements of its customers and also giving it optimum spatial coverage. These sites are a hundred miles or more apart, however, across slow country roads. Currently, the company employs about thirty people, together with, typically, twenty freelance and temporary staff. Staffing is stable and spread across all three sites, but there is an attraction for younger staff to move and work in the city, rather than in the rural offices.

Technology profile. A degree of autonomy has developed in decision-making at all sites, probably due to the large distances between them. Autonomy extends to the IT decision-making, with differences in the arrangements at the three sites. In the head office the internal networking is limited to a simple automatic printer-port switch, although there is interest in developing internal networking here. There is no internal networking at the second rural premises. At the third site, even though an external contractor had done some work, this appeared to be unsatisfactory, and the relationship between the company and this contractor was strained to the point of breakdown. External networking has been limited to e-mail, with the mail-server based in the city office and the other offices dialling in to collect e-mail. The three premises each have a different ISP, so that the external networking situation is somewhat confused, with three different e-mail addresses for the same business.

'Porffor' aspires to setting up a Website and developing an e-business line through an existing contract with an ISP. Despite a highly qualified workforce, the company recognizes the limited knowledge of this facet of business IT and of advanced applications. Consequently, it has depended on external advice for business support in this area, and that experience has been unsatisfactory. The firm identifies a business objective as better coordination of IT and is exploring options to resolve this problem, including the appointment of a new member of staff with specialist IT knowledge.

Learning and development. The company is faced with a difficult development problem in the pressing requirement for integration at three sites. A supporting need is for improvement in the use of technology in the business. It is a challenging project, and requires a substantial change effort that is beyond the resources of the existing staff. Since it is so closely aligned to the operations and performance of the company, it justifies adequate resources being applied for a resolution. Once this step is taken, then the information benefits to the staff will become available, with online learning enriching their independence and motivation for professional development. The owner-manager is committed to addressing this problem and to appointing a person to effect the integration of IT and improve communications, as well as aid the development of human resources across its networked organization. Existing staff have adequate IT skills for the current operations, but several future innovative developments are anticipated that will require a wide range of staff development, if they are to be successful. A major advantage for the company is that almost all the staff are graduates, well motivated and accustomed to professional development and adaptable to the changing environment.

'Porffor' is in large measure a distributed networked organization, dependent on technology, with a core staff of well-educated, creative and competent people. As well as transforming the relationships of a company with its customers, the Internet can also change the relationship with employees. Work can now be performed at a place and time that suits an individual employee. This means that a new psychological contract exists between an employer and employee that involves a high degree of trust, motivation, self-discipline and self-direction, and an appropriate learning and development strategy integrated into the working environment. The role of managers involves communicating a new business culture, managing and motivating a flexible workforce with specific expectations and demands. It means understanding the impact of flexible working on individuals and the organization and adapting management strategies, policies and practices for dealing with the e-workforce.

ANALYSIS OF CASES

These cases are observations on a series of small companies in a supply chain connected by the media industry in west Wales. No evidence was found of the development of 'advanced convergent skills' for the media industry. The conventional means of acquiring skills to complement the core business appeared to be through two strategies: subcontracting and multi-skilling, done primarily through self-tuition. Indeed, the major employment growth for e-learning production currently appeared to be among the public sector education and training providers that comprise a major employment segment in the area, rather than from the private sector.

Each firm operates in a turbulent business environment and is experiencing a series of challenges to improve efficiency through the development of technology. Change, brought on by technology, faces each business. The conditions for each company vary, as do their core competences, but there are some common elements in their strategies for coping with change. No overall strategy for adopting technology solutions is evident in the firms, instead it is more a case of following others, often in an ill-prepared and unstructured way. This leads to difficulties for management. These can range from displacement activity for management, in sorting out technology rather than in business development, as well as inefficiencies in the deployment of staff resources.

Few enterprises have the resources for dedicated IT staff; rather, their experience of technology is led by a member of the management team, who commonly relies on an informal network for information about technology developments. To help them in the change process, some firms are turning to external advice, but the quality of this support, as evidenced by the technical solutions and improvement gains, is not consistently good. Those SMEs that have taken this route recognize that an internal solution by means of a specialist member of staff offers a better medium-term solution than relying on external experts. They are all experiencing a series of challenges to their improvement in efficiency through the development of technology.

There is a pervasive interest among interviewees in e-business and the Internet, and a growing familiarity with e-mail and accessing information using the Web. These SMEs will register as e-businesses, according to some surveys, because they have PCs and modems. Despite the growth of the Internet and improved access by SMEs, though, e-business seems to have been slow in taking off. Each is some distance from having an operational marketing strategy to conduct an e-business. For those firms with a Website, set up and maintained by an outsourced contractor, there is an initial expectation that customers will be drawn to their site and conduct business. Practical experiences are different, with little custom unless continuous marketing effort is applied to the task. Past implementation of IT systems seem to indicate that the likely approach to e-business will be through informal information rather than on a sound business justification. A structured approach for improved communications and e-business may prove difficult, however, when the current IT solutions are only partially effective.

LEARNING AND DEVELOPMENT OPTIONS

Few companies have the time and resources to send employees to long classroom-based training courses, planned months in advance. What is also lacking is the call for academic business courses, such as MBAs, degrees, diplomas or certificates, online or off. Demand is centred on very specific skills, namely, competences and attributes that contribute directly to business performance improvement. Interviewees expressed a strong preference for in-company learning, in order to cut costs and increase efficiency by addressing real-life work problems. Interest in work-based learning fits with accepted good practice in the purchase of education and training so that learning is integrated into the job in the workplace. This eases the task of needs identification by comparing the knowledge and skills of staff with those required for their work, and it assists in the selection of appropriate learning materials to meet these needs. The companies interviewed either had no links with government support agencies, or found that they did not meet their needs.

Dedicated in-company training is a high-cost option, from both an SME client and provider point of view. Firms with more advanced technology applications seemed keen on e-learning approaches because of the potential in-company learning options. E-learning interventions, however, require a computer interface, connection to the Internet and an e-learning supplier. Management support in the firm is crucial in utilizing this approach, not only in encouraging employees to drive their own learning, but also, in a more basic way, of changing the management control methodology. Relaxing management control, specifically over access to a PC and the Internet, requires an underpinning shift of perception to view Internet use by employees as a source of information and learning, rather than a waste of time and resources.

The extent to which a firm is seeking to develop and sustain a Web-based platform for e-business is important in adopting e-learning. Keeping in-house control of a Website is a way of ensuring that the material is relevant and fresh for business-to-business transactions. It also helps introduce the perception that the Internet is a business tool and a suitable channel for employee development. Finding the time and space for learning in a busy multi-task environment is a substantive issue for many people, since reflective learning requires a protected time and space environment that is difficult to safeguard in a busy workplace, such as that observed in these small firms.

Most employees are self-taught in IT and this self-reliance will, no doubt, continue. Indeed, this motivation for independent learning is a positive attribute for developing skills in a dynamic business environment. Nevertheless, visits to help start employees with their local interface appeared to add value for them, prior to engagement with networked learning. Many employees also needed to develop e-skills and there are different ways to achieve this, such as through in-company support that can then lead to blended, or independent learning. When the e-learning links are in place, a range of learning and development options become available (Table 2.2).

Table 2.2 Potential e-learning development during the life-cycle of SME cases

Learning and development characteristics	E-learning dimensions
Life-cycle phase: start-up Enterprise development. Staff development to embrace technology as a learning tool, assisted by blended learning. Recruitment, induction. Business planning.	**'Melyn' and 'Coch'** Staff development to embrace technology as a learning tool. Internet technology developed for communications and transfer.
Life-cycle phase: development Forming a learning and development strategy. Aligning learning and development strategies with business goals. Developing the right management skills for business transformation. Innovation in product and market development for the e-economy. Communications and initial networking. Knowledge management applications. Practices for managing the e-workforce. Developing and integrating e-skills to support the e-business.	**'Gwyrdd' and 'Gwyn'** Integrating e-learning into a learning anddevelopment strategy. Linking e-learning to employee career delopment. Knowledge management, innovation and creativity for the e-environment. Developing a curriculum for e-business. JITOL learning.
Life-cycle phase: growth/maturity Performance management. Embracing technology as a learning tool. Restructuring training for company changes by e-learning. Re-engineering the business organization. Technology for e-business exploitation. Technology to aid transfer, aided by on-site HRD. Communications and networking.	**'Oren' and 'Porffor'** Communications and networking. Adopting and adapting new approaches to learning for the e-environment. Identifying and developing core competences for the e-environment.

SNAPSHOT OF A DYNAMIC SECTOR

The findings above are from work with small firms in a media supply chain. Typically, some fifty firms each year from all sectors take part in the whole systems approach programme. This performance analysis approach sets out to capture a wider set of information for business and learning development. There are clear deficiencies in large-size enterprise models for applications with SMEs, and there is low demand apparent from this customer base for the academic programmes of business schools.

The process demonstrates the difficulties in accurately determining e-business activity from Internet access data. In spite of greater access by SMEs to the Internet, it implies that e-business is used to meet very specific business needs. These typically might involve finding customers, matching products and services with Internet users, creating alternative products and producing competitive equality with competitors. Among the wider set of work on performance analysis, there are applications in small firms across all business sectors, such as a Web designer using e-business for better marketing; local newsagents are providing out-of-hours communications for customers; a small manufacturer is sourcing new components and suppliers; an engineering company is improving customer service; a sports club is using online sales and improved customer information by the Internet.

These practices do not compare with the sophisticated integrated e-business applications portrayed in the media, which bear little resemblance to e-business activities as experienced by most small firms. Not every firm with a modem and an ISP conducts e-business. The characteristics of SMEs themselves, their customers and their technology experience, or lack of awareness of good examples of e-business, may imply that selling products or services on the Internet does not apply to them. Doubts may also exist over the return on investment, while a lack of skilled personnel and the lack of consumer access to the e-market may inhibit them in the direction of e-business.

IMPLICATIONS FOR E-LEARNING DELIVERY

E-business applications open the window for adopting new approaches to learning in the business environment. More choices in fulfilling a development strategy become available with e-learning, but at the same time small firms find it hard to come up with the time for dedicated employee training in a hectic business environment. Implementation in a firm means there are classic issues for SME managers to address, such as aligning HRM development to business strategy. There are also contemporary ones, for example in defining new skill-sets and balancing 'just-in-time', or reactive e-learning, with traditional learning programmes.

For most companies today, the Internet is the method most likely to be used for computer communication with external contacts and information sources. It also provides access to business information and support, through a large number of Websites with market information, advertising, technical support and free software. There are prospects of easier access to worldwide markets, with e-mail giving fast communications with distant customers and distributors. Hence, SMEs have a business objective to connect to the Internet to promote the business, but with such a connection established, access e-learning becomes an option, with a range of potential benefits arising from flexible learning.

There are disadvantages in the delivery of e-learning to the workplace. It might be convenient for people to receive training by means of their desktop PC, though the small firm workplace is not always the best environment in which to learn. Interruptions can be difficult to control. Intentional learning needs some reflective time and space, which is difficult to construct in the SME workplace. This can displace learning for employees, from their workplace to their homes, in their own time and at their own costs. A number of other problems can arise for SME managers, not least in the initial cost and in concerns that it may not be effective. E-learning will often be an innovation for a small firm and there are pressures on the adviser, who is highly visible and expected to demonstrate quick results, even though the variety of human and technical factors are very wide. More variables affect e-learning success than affect face-to-face delivery. The factors, for instance, that affect outcomes can range from the initial e-skills, motivational and behavioural attributes of employees, to the speed of downloading programmes.

One solution for some SMEs is a form of mixed-mode delivery, blending face-to-face tutorial work with e-learning. A blended learning approach can involve a peripatetic support service that places a tutor in the SME for a series of short visits. Technology can complement a peripatetic training service, since it multiplies the time-span of student support at very low cost. Balancing the peripatetic and distance-support components for delivery will then depend on the overall approach to the costs and needs of the enterprise. The tutor delivers and supports learning in a way that is most beneficial and least disruptive to the SME. Businesses may have such limited staff numbers that the absence of staff, even for a few days, is seen as disruptive. Consequently external learning offers are likely to be rejected. Staff and owner-managers of these businesses also need to be given guidance in their working environment, in order that relevance of the learning to their enterprise is underpinned.

Conventional technology-supported learning applications are a high-cost way of developing a bespoke solution for an organization. The costs are such that they usually prohibit this as a solution for an SME, but sometimes an adviser can identify an off-the-shelf multimedia package that nearly meets the needs. More flexible learning solutions offered by Internet delivery can also give the distinct advantages of adaptability, lower development cost and thereby customized solutions.

With such a broad range of learning needs from a diverse client group of small firms, the need is to match this diversity by creating sufficient variety in the methods of meeting needs. Solutions at Lampeter include, therefore, offering support for business performance consultancy, diagnosis of IT and learning development issues. Content and support for Welsh-language communication skills, Internet marketing and a range of other topics has been developed. An integrated electronic learning environment has been created, together with content and a support infrastructure to support the learning and administration of participants. A learning centre offers a dedicated location with support for the development of managers and employees in SMEs. This provides access to a faster network than a dial-up connection, and gives learner support to participants with fewer disruptions than the workplace. These services complement the offer of blended learning with peripatetic workplace tutors, that combines e-learning with traditional tutor training. Eventually a compromise position is reached, between the level of support for the range of needs and an affordable cost for the service. As a provider, it then raises business development issues on how to optimize the content by scaling or extending delivery to other market segments, issues addressed in chapter 9.

Four basic rules seem to emerge for developing a blended e-learning programme for SMEs. First, that the technical specifications and limitations of the computers available to employees are identified early in the process. Second, that the capabilities of the SME-user's platform is the basis for design, rather than the high-end specification of the e-learning provider. Third, that the design is tested early in the project development process and any necessary adaptations made. Fourth, that assistance to SMEs across a range of enquiries on their specific platforms is necessary, as well as with learning subject content. Novice students who encounter problems online often want to speak to someone who understands the Website of the provider and the e-learning programme, not simply an automated (FAQ) response.

THE E-LEARNING VALUE PROPOSITION

The business and technology environments are very dynamic, and small firms work hard at achieving their business aims in such environments. Getting a new idea adopted by a business, even when the advantages are demonstrable, is often difficult. Technology changes quickly, but SMEs are spread out along a technology adoption cycle so that it is important to put e-learning on to platforms that are in widespread use. For e-learning to be considered as a means to delivering HRD by SMEs, therefore, its link with business performance needs to be articulated in terms of the business needs and goals of owners and managers. The major challenges for an SME are in competition, market specialization, product complexity, shorter product life-cycles and reducing skill gaps. Pressures for adaptation in working practices come from agile methods, speedy implementation, cost-effectiveness and a growing focus on performance. There are the pressures that drive the need for more efficient learning solutions. So for all SMEs, not only those sophisticated technologically, support through management advice is much needed.

Learning is only a means to an end in business. That end is workforce performance, which results in greater value, improved products, lower costs, greater innovation, improved market position, increased market share, business growth, bigger profits and so on. Delivering a value proposition based on e-learning to a small firm is the sum of its ability to save money and generate benefits. The perceived value of a service is based on the criteria of cost, service and authenticity that are provided by the e-learning offer. Underperformance on any of these parameters seriously degrades the value of the proposition.

3

The extension of learning

Open, distance and flexible learning (ODFL) has many attractions for managers in industrial and commercial organizations. Several models are possible, with transactional distance, autonomy and structure all influential in the design of learning systems. Internet-supported learning is a relatively new application and initiating development work can prompt a review of all aspects of delivery that can build on the foundations of knowledge about ODFL approaches. The terminology of e-learning, however, can be a problem.

EXTENDING THE REACH OF AN ENTERPRISE

Educational institutions are designed typically for face-to-face delivery. The rewards from extending educational opportunities by e-learning are so attractive, however, that it is challenging the way in which all organizations support learning. In the geographical area of west Wales, for example, all twelve higher- and further-learning institutions, built originally for conventional delivery, are now creating flexible learning by digital methods, whereas none existed just a decade ago. For many, this is their introduction to distance education. This does not diminish, of course, all the other efforts to extend education to new audiences by means of part-time study, evening classes, work-based learning and the like. It does emphasize, though, both the rapid and radical impact of e-learning.

In this changing environment, decision-makers in educational enterprises have the taxing job of looking for effective learning solutions wherever they arise and then guiding change. Some changes are more predictable than others and thrive on structured management controls. The less predictable ones require more decentralized and flexible implementation. For example, the Open University (OU) in the UK has applied ODFL techniques to distance learning for more than thirty years. Development was relatively predictable over the earlier decades, so that certain learning organizations chose to develop this form of delivery, but many others did not. The unpredictability with ODFL now springs from technology, particularly from the arrival of the Internet. It means that decision-makers have a straight choice to make: either join the wave of e-learning implementation, or lag behind.

Both experienced and new providers of ODFL face change as they adopt e-learning for their market environment. Experienced providers can analyse their current position for the change context and then choose the optimum development path, based on their particular organizational features. Meanwhile, newcomers without a legacy ODFL system can conceive of e-learning in ways that range from small feasibility pilots to major transformative efforts. Contextual judgement does not need to consider the delivery practices that should be preserved, but should focus on other factors, such as the capability, capacity, scope and readiness for change. Whichever route or whatever scale is chosen, previous efforts to deliver ODFL act to reshape teaching, learning resources and organizational structures. E-learning already looks set to follow a similar route.

ODFL TO SUPPORT BUSINESS, INDUSTRY AND COMMERCE

Making learning available for employee development has long been a major thrust of government policy and still is (WAG, 2002). The two fundamental aims are to develop the workforce and also to contribute to enhancing national economic competitiveness. Traditional classroom-based delivery for workforce development has limitations that seem all too obvious when listed. Constraints for firms are in delivery and travel costs, interruptions to work patterns, inflexibility of timing, content and the numbers of participants, as well as in the relevance of the content to the workplace (Scriven, 1991). As a result, many companies perceive traditional classroom learning as inefficient and consider technology-based solutions as an alternative means of developing employees. The limitations of conventional provision for employee development have spurred various UK government educational initiatives on ODFL over the years. The latest is 'learndirect', which has a broad strategic objective to lead vocational e-learning through the use of innovative technology solutions for learners (*www.ufiltd.co.uk*).

An educational enterprise that sets out to create learning opportunities for workplace learners in SMEs is, therefore, closely aligned with government policies. Such activities, when multiplied across a sector, can help grow the market base. Secondary effects may occur in raising an institutional profile by promoting areas of expertise. Moreover, successful delivery may well increase the utilization efficiency of the technological infrastructure in a provider.

The power and flexibility of open- and distance-learning technologies make them suitable for meeting a wide range of employee development needs (Calder et al., 1995: 10). Everyone unable to travel to a campus, for instance, can be offered access to a wide range of learning. Significant benefits like this are the experience of many learning providers implementing distance-learning programmes (Chute et al., 1998: 5), and there are others.

We found that ODFL delivery increases the impact of financial investment in learning programmes and facilitates the supply to more people, making the coordination of learning programmes easier. Programmes deliver consistent content, and support is scalable, to a certain degree. For the learner, it offers better access to learning provision and remote specialists and can reduce the travel costs and time.

A classic approach to the development of an ODFL programme involves a curriculum group devising content in a custom-designed format, often designing print-based content and audio-visual materials. The method becomes cost-effective when the course content is relatively stable, a long-term training need appears to exist and large numbers of people need to be educated in a relatively short period of time. Although authoritative, well presented and building on proven methods this can prove expensive and relatively difficult to adapt. Technology, however, has added greater flexibility in the design and publishing of text-based ODFL materials. Technology has also helped in hybridizing content by mixing content from print, Web and audio-video, with linkages with sources and between discussion groups.

Distinctions between initial and continuing education become blurred by technology. The practice of creating small chunks of e-learning means that these can either stand alone, or be aggregated into a programme aimed at different targets. This process also allows the meeting of individual or employee needs that require small elements of learning to address a micro-competence. Elements can be accredited and followed by employees undertaking initial or continuing education by ODFL. All ODFL avenues, therefore, become available by e-learning, so that an employee now has a wider choice of ways to learn than ever before. These choices include independent study, interdependent networked learning, attending a conventional class, taking a course through a learning centre or following an ODFL course.

A MIRROR ON DIVERSITY

There are pressures everywhere on higher-learning institutions to perform over a range of parameters, and the University of Wales, Lampeter, is no exception. Superimposed on these factors are geographical, economic and logistic barriers to access: contextual features, that make open, distance and flexible learning an attractive proposition for a student. Such features have shaped the long-term academic principles for the delivery of continuing education that are valid for the provision of e-learning. For example, the difficulties of finding information are addressed by making information about any course provision as simple as possible from the clients' point of view. The hindrances of travel leads to giving maximum benefit to the client from a minimum amount of provider contact. The suitability of the learning is determined by continuously seeking information on client needs and targeting those needs effectively, with solutions that make economic and financial sense.

At Lampeter, we started investigating ODFL provision some ten years ago as a way to provide educational access for people who needed to continue to learn, but who were unable to travel to our relatively remote campus. There was a pressing need to increase enrolments for economic and educational reasons, as local markets became mature. Distance learning appeared an attractive solution, but a wide range of course products already existed from large established providers. The quandaries facing us as a new entrant were to determine a new approach and secure investment resources to make the solution a success. A crucial step for determining a solution was a precise understanding of the dimensions of client needs that would be met by the system. Needs assessment provided the source of the data, while experimenting with curriculum design served to validate the needs and system design.

The work of the university over the past two decades has targeted various key groups of learners. These groups include heads of small firms and entrepreneurs involved with enterprise start-up. Certain members of these groups show a keen interest in the potential for e-business. For example, over the past two years fifteen graduates have launched businesses in areas as diverse as Web design and heritage consultancy, each one engaged in some form of e-business. Four of them fall into a smaller sub-set, involved in e-learning through providing customer-focused support for firms with the design and support of Web-rich content. These firms have Websites and develop collaborative alliances or networks with other small companies, in order to widen their expertise base. These are micro-sized firms with, at most, two or three employees, but they are competing with other firms for e-learning through business-to-business (B2B) transactions and also with the public sector. This group of entrepreneurs sees e-business as a way of overcoming some of the problems of rurality; the same understanding that we came to as an educational enterprise in proceeding with e-learning.

The first Lampeter initiative to develop e-learning in order to extend programmes to working professionals uses the brand-name *e-addysg.com* (e-education.com). The initial development was for specialist support for Welsh-medium small firms. Using a variety of e-learning methods, *e-addysg.com* now offers flexible, worldwide educational access to people who cannot travel easily to Lampeter.

HISTORICAL EMERGENCE OF TECHNOLOGY-SUPPORTED LEARNING

The speed of development and the sheer diversity of technology-supported learning (TSL) is remarkable. Yet TSL is not new. Long before the provision of learning by the Web, technology enriched the educational experience of learners: first through radio broadcasts and then by television. Other means of distance learning also proved viable. Thirty years ago, for instance, the UK armed forces complemented service training with forms of distance study applied to technical, language or educational programmes. Distance education was accomplished by print, often combined with audio-tape and film, and supported by local tutoring where possible. A variety of other learning tools were used, including closed-circuit television networks, films, recorded audio-tape programmes and print, as well as instruction for workplace learning. Cases like these do not transfer well into industrial or commercial practice, however, because the goals and contexts are so different; the dominant purpose of the armed services in peacetime is training to improve performance, for combat readiness. This does illustrate, though, that technology to support performance improvement by ODFL is not new.

In one form or another, computer-based training (CBT) has been in use for at least the past three decades. Efforts to use technologies in the learning process by bespoke computer-based training, laser disk and videotapes required large numbers of employees to receive the same instruction to ensure cost-effectiveness. These proved in certain circumstances to be expensive and time-consuming, without providing a breakthrough. For some technologies the speed of interaction between the learner and the process is too slow, for others the actual improvements in performance could not justify the cost of development. Commonly, they have been developed on closed technology systems, with the content inaccessible for transfer on to other systems that might give a wider circulation of the learning product.

Until recently, the high development costs limited TSL use to very specific high-cost areas of education and training. Then CD-ROMs, as a computer-disk technology with a large storage capacity, offered an impressive range of educational applications, particularly with the arrival of read–write disk drivers and DVDs. Simulations, involving PC-based stored programmes that provide a degree of interactivity for the learner, have become more realistic. However, it is the penetration of the PC as a standard tool linked to the Internet which has made TSL an attractive alternative for the delivery of ODFL.

INTERPRETATION OF OPEN, DISTANCE AND FLEXIBLE LEARNING

Open and flexible learning are terms sometimes used interchangeably with distance learning. There are distinctions between them, even though technology tends to blur these differences. Distance education is the provision of programmes of study to learners who rarely, if ever, attend face-to-face teaching or have on-campus access to educational facilities. The 'non-contiguous' nature of the supervision of learners by a tutor is a characteristic of distance education (Holmberg, 1989: 127). Courses might be delivered by written correspondence, text, graphics, audio- and videotape, floppy disks, CD-ROM, DVD, the Internet, Intranet, audio- and videoconferencing, TV and facsimile.

Open learning is a more elusive term than distance education, without a real consensus on a definition. It is distinguished from other forms of learning through the degree of autonomy given to the learner. Autonomy can stretch across decisions on place, time, duration and circumstances of study. It can also extend to learner choice of the curriculum through selection from a planned schema, or even developing curricula of their own (Peters, 1993: 10–18). Autonomy may also refer to an organizational approach that allows learners, to an extent irrespective of previous qualifications, to engage in programmes of study that widen access to education.

The range of practices in open learning can be conceptualized as a continuum of choices offered to a learner (Lewis, 1986: 14); a continuum that extends from pure contiguous to pure distance, but with most systems operating as mixed systems, somewhere between these two poles (Rumble, 1989: 37). Delivery methods can include face-to-face or electronically-mediated learning, provided off-campus and sometimes by delivery in the workplace. A similar continuum of openness exists between open learning and traditional learning. Many conventional classes can in principle include aspects of openness and flexibility, through assessment methods or by the pace of learning. Critiques of this continuum of openness point out that opening up the place or pace of learning does not necessarily equate with a shift of responsibility to a learner for full learner-centred provision (Carr, 1990). Nevertheless, open-learning applications are attractive to clients in business, as they can offer greater cost-effectiveness over conventional forms of learning (Lewis, 1987: 83–94). Lewis also comments that an ODFL approach permits the needs of employees to be addressed as they arise. Better targeting of needs is therefore possible, since it allows the selection of particular skills which are to be acquired rather than an entire course having to be studied.

Flexible learning aims to increase learner independence and implies learner choice over modes of delivery of instructional material. This can cover a wide range of parameters, including course content, medium of delivery and forms of learner support, as well as the assessment offered (McCollum and Calder, 1995). Since the learner chooses the key dimensions, flexibility represents a shift from learning decisions made in advance by a teacher and an institution. This degree of flexibility, however, can present considerable complexity to the developer. The key lies in balancing the options available to learners with a manageable range of tasks for the teacher and provider (Collis and Moonen, 2001: 11). Flexible learning can operate as a mixture of face-to-face teaching, often in block sessions, and independent learning that might use computer-based supplementary teaching materials. For the educational designer, complexity arises because flexible learning focuses on the learning process in the individual learner and also on the choice of methods employed in the process.

CO-PRESENCE AND TECHNOLOGY

E-learning has already proved a major influence in creating more flexible campus-based structures as well as distance-education provision for learners. When people cannot arrange to meet in person, however, they try to simulate this as closely as possible. This need for co-presence is endemic and is the basic mode of human socialization. Moreover, the degree of proximity people prefer for socialization leads to a hierarchy in the communication tools favoured to replicate co-presence (Boden and Molotch, 1994: 257–86). People prefer close simulation and, in general, trade down to less authentic methods only when necessary. Hence, the closer approximation of videoconference is preferred to audioconference. Similarly, the telephone is favoured over a memo, and prompt e-mail exchanges preferred to letters.

Co-presence is particularly relevant to business and learning interactions. In business it appears that a premium is placed on co-presence, especially higher up the organizational hierarchy; senior decision-makers frequently need to develop complex understandings, to arrange informal deals, or to address unanticipated tensions. The reason for this premium is that co-presence is dense with tacit information and reveals far more than any other form of human exchange. Consequently, co-presence is good for arriving at a business result, simply because it conveys so much implicit and explicit information to all parties.

The notion of co-presence extends to learning interactions, where technology can simulate co-presence between a tutor and a learner. Indeed, co-presence can be effected through many forms of communication: video- or audioconferencing, chatrooms, bulletin boards, voice-mail, interactive question and answer, structured text-based script or applying digital technology as an information source. As with traditional learning, co-presence is valuable only if it offers both teachers and learners benefits, such as stimulating interest or more interactivity.

The preference for co-presence does have implications for the support of learning. Programmes that do not allow significant co-presence between the key actors may run into significant problems, such as high drop-out rates. For practitioners of distance learning, support needs to be responsive to the demands for co-presence from learners. Clearly, risks can arise from the inequality of access to co-presence for certain student groups. Among these groups at risk of disadvantage are e-learners in small firms, who may have inadequate access to support, for a variety of business reasons.

DEGREES OF SEPARATION

Everyone who seeks to provide distance education is confronted by a common problem, namely, overcoming the separation between the tutor and the learner. This separation can be educational and psychological as well as geographic. A gap exists between a teacher and learner in all educational exchanges. For example, in a face-to-face classroom there can be a metaphorical distance between the understanding of the teacher and learner (Boyd et al., 1980). In distance education, a distinction between spatial and mental distance is made, with the term 'transactional distance' applied to the latter:

> separation leads to special patterns of learner and teacher behaviours: It is the separation of learners and teachers that profoundly affects both teaching and learning. With separation there is a psychological and mental space to be crossed, a space of potential misunderstanding between the inputs of the instructor and those of the learner. It is this psychological and communications space that is the transactional distance. (Moore, 1993: 22)

Transactional distance is greatest when the tutors and learners do not communicate at all, so individual learning requirements cannot be addressed. In contrast, distance is shortest when the teaching programme is open, with frequent interchange between tutor and learner in which the prior knowledge and interests of a particular learner can influence the teaching and learning process, such as with personalized tutorial care, e-mentoring and forms of blended learning (Table 3.1). Transactional distance depends on three variables: dialogue, structure and autonomy. These in turn are dependent on the people taking part, the content of the teaching, the aims and the methods of teaching.

Table 3.1 Variation of transactional distance with programme (adapted from Moore, 1977: 39)

Distance	Programme type	E-learning examples	Comment
Greatest	Teaching programme without dialogue or structure.	Independent learning by own reading or Web-search.	High autonomy Low dialogue Low structure
	Teaching programme without dialogue, with structure.	Teaching programme on broadcast TV, course-in-a-box.	High autonomy Low dialogue High structure
	Teaching programme with dialogue and structure.	Typical distance education course.	Low autonomy High dialogue High structure
Smallest	Teaching programme with dialogue, but without structure.	E-mentoring; tutorial care; blended learning.	Lower autonomy High dialogue Low structure

Dialogue gauges the extent to which learners can communicate with their tutors. Communications media have a direct influence on the scope and quality of dialogue between tutors and learners. A one-way educational programme between teacher and a learner, such as watching television, listening to an audiotape, reading a teach-yourself book, or studying a course-in-a-box, will have no dialogue, since no feedback path exists between teacher and learner. Even though an internal response can be generated in the learner, it is not available for feedback on an individual level to the tutor. In contrast, correspondence by conventional postal service or e-mail can carry two-way interaction and therefore dialogue. Dialogue from a postal exchange might even be more reflective than e-mail because it is slower-paced, but speed of delivery, feedback and spontaneity are detractions when compared with electronic communication. The interactive nature of the medium, therefore, is a major factor in determining the degree of dialogue that is present in a teaching and learning environment. The delay in providing feedback, or 'latency', can be modified by the choice of communications media. By selecting the appropriate media it becomes feasible to increase the dialogue between learner and tutor, thereby reducing the transactional distance. For an online course, dialogue can occur through many forms, such as e-mail, asynchronous chat, group discussion and so on. To be successful, though, it must be carefully structured into the course.

Transactional distance is affected by 'structure': these are elements in the course design that determine how well the distance-education programme can accommodate a learner's individual needs. Dialogue and structure determine the scope of distance in an educational programme. Reducing transactional distance is not always an objective, however, for example when independent learning is itself a key goal of the learning process. Autonomy is a third variable in assessing the capacity of a programme for independent learning. It is greatest when a participant can determine the learning aims and paths, which are not restricted by dialogue or structure. Conversely, autonomy is lowest when aims are prescribed, paths are determined by structures and control of learning is carried out by others.

Involvement, support and control are also alternative parameters to segment online learning (Coomey and Stephenson, 2001: 38). Involvement is created by various engagements with the learner, for instance in response to structured tasks or learner collaborations. Support is the most often cited feature of online learning and includes online tutorial supervision. In almost all cases, learners indicate that effective procedures for tutor–peer feedback are the most important features of a successful online course. Control is the extent to which learners have control of learning activities. This can extend to the management of a broad range of learning activities, overall direction and performance. Digital technologies vary in the control that they give to learners and can add to the complexity of the learning process, so care must be applied in giving control to learners with little prior experience (Oliver, 1998: 147).

MODELS TO BRIDGE TRANSACTIONAL DISTANCE

As technology has developed, so have delivery systems, institutional processes and the roles of teachers which all reduce transactional distance. Methods of bridging transactional distance have been classified into five models: correspondence, conversation, teacher, tutor and technology extension models (O. Peters, 1998: 18–25). Technology is also allowing another 'learner-centred technology model' to appear.

The correspondence model comes from an early approach to implementing distance learning, where a teacher writes letters and learners reply to them, giving rise to the term 'correspondence' for this type of learning method. Teaching and learning elements are: reciprocal answering by a written dialogue; personal address to a learner, implying that the teacher understands the learner's needs and interests; and that the tone of personalization adopted may compensate for the lack of proximity. The drawbacks are that personal address may become intrusive and irrelevant for certain types of learner, such as experienced professionals already familiar with individual study. Applications of the model in TSL are through asynchronous e-mail exchanges between tutor and learner. It is a relatively simple means of adding flexibility to complement face-to-face provision, or wholly distance provision.

In the conversation model, teaching content is presented in a spoken style as a form of instructional conversation between teacher and learner. A learner reading the text visualizes the teacher and carries out internal dialogues. The limitations of the model arise from its unsuitability for the presentation of certain subjects, such as scientific content. Another arises because the language of advanced learning in most disciplines is complex and demands long sentences that cannot always be reduced to short words and sentences. Furthermore, the change of medium creates different ways of thinking, expressing, studying and remembering; this requires a teacher to exploit various media, including writing, rather than to imitate oral teaching in written form.

In the teacher model, designers transfer their skill and expertise to the course content in order to transfer key teaching functions. These roles can include stimulating, directing and motivating learners, contextualizing lessons, unitizing the contents to help comprehension or providing feedback to ensure effective teaching and learning. The content often includes an organizer at the start with a summary of the main text, making the core problems explicit as well as the preconditions for comprehension. Learners are encouraged to develop their own activities, to pose questions and answer them, identify and solve problems. A self-instruction text with all the teaching functions integrated is the goal of many practitioners. Some professionals have a low regard for the model, however, as it is too similar to classic school instruction. Technology-supported learning can serve to reinforce this model, for example by online video-conferencing or many CD-ROM applications, because it makes careful planning and an empirical method an acceptable way of preparing for teaching. Not surprisingly, then, until recently technology served to extend this teacher-directed model.

In the tutor model the teaching content resembles a tutorial. The tutor providing help is not always responsible for the original content. A learner follows the programme independently and receives counselling when difficulties might be expected. The content ought to make the learner familiar with the objectives of the study units, the preconditions for successful learning, introduce the programme, indicate suitable study time for sections and help reflection and application of the content (Rowntree, 1992: 119). The approach is less obtrusive than in either the correspondence or conversational models, and has more independence than the teacher model, so being suited to the adult learner with a preference for independent learning. The tutor model is widely adopted by e-learning providers as a means of supporting and scaling delivery.

A description of online learning process for tutors and learners is provided by the 'five-step' model for computer-mediated communications (CMC), which attempts to structure the learning path in an online environment for learners that is likely to be unfamiliar ground for participants (Salmon, 2000). In the first stage the essentials for participation are established; those focus on the access and motivation to spend time and effort. The second stage involves participants forming their own online identities and finding others with whom to interact. In stage three, participants exchange information relevant to the course with their peers. In stage four, group discussions occur and the interactions become more collaborative. At stage five, participants look to integrate this form of learning into other methods and reflect on the learning process.

The technology-extension model arises when technology helps a learner attend teaching events, since access by technology can alleviate the expense to a provider of developing special distance-education programmes for learners. These all work by giving access to remote classes by electronic media and assume virtual attendance at a traditional class. Variations on the theme employ teleconferencing, virtual classrooms, virtual colleges and variations of teleconferencing. No pedagogical simulations of closeness are present, or any form of presentation specific to distance education. In principle, this is the reverse of the teacher model, because the course takes no account of any special needs of working adults and does not develop course material to enable self-teaching. The model is directly concerned with extending conventional education rather than with contributing to extending the range of traditional education (O. Peters, 1998: 27). Technologies, such as online videoconferencing, have been used predominantly to extend teacher-directed instruction. An example is the Welsh Video Network, where videoconference teaching from a campus, such as Lampeter, is accessed from further-education partner sites across mid-Wales. It is not suitable currently as a method for distribution to the premises of small firms because of bandwidth limitations and high infrastructure costs.

Technology development has progressed to make another model, a learner-centred technology model, feasible. The development of Internet-based education by asynchronous methods is firmly in the resource-based learning approach, but enables much more learner initiative and control than closed systems. Certain teachers take the view that learners should take more responsibility for their own learning; an approach furthered by the demand for competences in the knowledge economy, such as critical thinking, teamwork and collaborative learning. Self-direction in learning has previously been possible, but recent technology developments enable much more learner initiative and control of the learning process. Learner control means that an individual can access the source of learning whenever it is relevant, access just the pertinent portions and navigate whichever way is preferred through a learning scheme, even in a non-linear fashion, if necessary. Access can be almost immediate and the learner may even choose to bypass unnecessary or redundant knowledge, or skills. Difficult areas can be repeated to achieve competence, with support obtained when required from an online tutor. Networked learning with a well-structured design of learning paths and simple navigation is crucial. Such a programme, with suitable content, is also capable of acting as a work-based performance support tool. The model can fully support a learner or be taken by an independent lifelong learner. In this latter case, the role of the practitioner shifts in emphasis to that of a learning adviser.

DUAL AND MIXED MODE

Digital delivery has influenced the move of many providers from single-mode towards dual-mode, or mixed-mode operations. There is a fine distinction between them (Bang and Dondi, 2000: 2). Ordinarily, the term 'dual-mode' is applied to delivery through classroom-based education together with ODFL provision, in separate programmes. In contrast, an educational setting where a certain amount of face-to-face classroom work is integrated with ODFL, or viceversa, or other learning or organizational problems are addressed, is referred to as mixed-mode delivery. With dual-mode, a minority of teachers might be involved, whereas mixed-mode is likely to represent a more systematic process that affects the whole range of staff, including the majority of teachers.

A distinction can also be made between a section of a conventional provider engaged in distance delivery and an autonomous distance-education provider, such as the Open University (Keegan, 1993). Some of these latter institutions have grown to an immense size. For instance, eleven 'mega-universities' exist around the world as distance-learning institutions, with a learner body in excess of 100,000 active learners on degree-level courses (Daniel, 1996: 29). The success of these huge universities is due to a collection of factors, such as the cost-effectiveness created by mass production and delivery. They make efficient use of national communications networks to reach learners and have a capacity to address the lifelong learning needs of a wide variety of people. Even an autonomous distance-education enterprise like the OU, however, recognized from the very beginning the need to bring tutors and learners together as a group, through the provision of summer schools and tutorials, a practice that 'blends' distance with face-to-face education.

There are differences between the provision of distance education from an autonomous ODFL institution and from a section of a conventional provider. An autonomous distance-education institution often forms a course design team that is equipped with sufficient resources to produce audio/visual/text and technology-supported learning material, in its sundry forms, in glossy or permanently bound texts, which are mass-produced for large numbers of learners. In contrast, ODFL delivery by centres is often based on fewer resources, but with more flexibility and the potential for more frequent updating. Distance-learning programmes emerge as a response to perceived learner needs in specific subjects, so are not applied across all subjects. Very small teams prepare course content, which is not over-engineered, making it less costly to produce and easier to replace. This gives a flexibility to the materials that can be complemented by a personalized learner support service.

Electronic delivery eases the entry for new ODFL providers to supply distance learners, without the large upfront investment of an autonomous distance provider. In practice, it makes it simpler and cheaper for almost any section or group with the inclination to provide a form of online education; any individual teacher can adopt e-learning as a way to support students. This practice is very common, but the solo enthusiast can prove a discouragement to other staff if they perceive the work as too technology-oriented or overly time-consuming. For most decision-makers the appropriate response is not necessarily in encouraging solo developers, or in seeking to model the OU, but might be in forming a centre that helps groups sections, departments and individuals to collaborate and initiate provision at a degree, course, subject or interdisciplinary topic level. There are plenty of practical examples of this approach, although the scope of a group varies with the institution. Examples exist across Wales, such as a dedicated ODFL centre at the University of Wales, Aberystwyth, that emerged from a single department to serve all academic departments. In Coleg Sir Gâr, in Carmarthenshire, an e-learning section has developed from specific course delivery in IT. At the University of Glamorgan, entry into the e-learning form of ODFL has been from the subject-base of business and management (Cooper, 2002).

FLEXIBLE LEARNING IN TRADITIONAL SETTINGS

There are both benefits and problems with such integration of e-learning into conventional settings. Learners emerge as the main beneficiaries of the additional flexibility of e-learning, which can provide access to educational materials outside their institution (*www.sustain.odl.org*). The same study identified that transnational programmes also present learners with cross-cultural viewpoints from peers in other countries. It revealed that the ability of an educational enterprise to respond to integration depends on certain influences. The economics of delivery is important, as equipment and development support all need finance up front, which creates high initial costs before they are offset from increased enrolments and the benefits of more flexible delivery. Technology infrastructure is often inadequate for running large-scale ODFL operations, with insufficient support for teaching development in many educational providers. Learning and teaching are other factors, since teachers are not often sufficiently trained to organize and produce learning materials that support learner-centred learning. Educational organizations frequently do not have a specialist unit to support teachers in the production of interactive learning materials, or may have insufficient equipment. To make progress with integration, therefore, an educational enterprise has to address these issues and provide staff development to facilitate a learner-centred approach.

The degree of integration of the online activity into a programme produces three types of course (Mason, 1998a). A 'content plus support' model, as an online dimension, is simply an add-on to an existing course, with a strong separation between the content and tutorial support. A 'wrap around' model involves online materials designed to enclose existing materials. An 'integrated' model involves collaborative activities, learning resources, online discussion, accessing and processing information and carrying out tasks. The model implies a progressive move towards the fuller integration of online learning within a course and the formation of a learning community.

MODELS FOR THE ADOPTION OF TECHNOLOGY

The flexibility of learning technologies is blurring the boundaries between distance and traditional instruction. Providers now use e-learning in both settings. Distance is no longer the primary description of explaining the educational use of technology. Instead, technology allows learning to be distributed in time and space, regardless of where or when the learner and provider are located. The generally accepted conclusion from thousands of studies on teaching with technology is that it does at least equally as well as classroom teaching (Schramm, 1974; Bates, 2000: 199). This is known as the 'no significant difference' argument. Straight comparisons between TSL and classroom teaching are not very helpful, because different kinds of learning outcomes can best be achieved by the use of technology. For example, an Internet-supported course could be focused on finding, analysing and interpreting information, whereas a classroom lecture may be concerned with information acquisition and comprehension.

The adoption of technology in education can be described as a three-stage process, involving substitution, transition and transformation (Van de Westeringh, 2000). In the substitution stage, technology substitutes for another instructional aid without changing the actual process of education. Typical examples of the substitution stage are drill and practice routines, as well as simulation programmes. In the transition stage, the application of technology involves new teaching and learning techniques. Technology is used as a part of the teaching and learning process itself, with extensive use of the Internet allowing teachers and learners to get comprehensive access to information and to communicate with each other on curriculum matters. At this stage provision is made for online courses, teacher–learner contact by computer networks, cooperation with other learners internationally and the presentation of assignments electronically. In the transformation stage a fundamental change in teaching and learning occurs, in which the learner manages his or her own learning process and the teacher becomes a coach and adviser.

The adoption of TSL can have implications for the role of a teacher, therefore, which shifts from being a source of knowledge towards that of an educational manager. The development of more open systems places responsibilities on a practitioner for providing a suitable learning climate and, as a counsellor, for helping a learner to address content. Some closed applications of educational software, however, exclude the teacher. Such closed software tends to develop a pedagogic model that is rarely explicit. The designers have made decisions concerning the selection, presentation and progression of content, as well as the tasks, assessment and feedback to the learner, and this produces an internal pedagogy. The teacher is left to make decisions on how the software is integrated into a programme and for how long students use the software. Nevertheless, such decisions are important in determining the impact of the programme on the learner.

The development trend in the educational use of technology at all levels of education is to incorporate a more flexible approach. A spectrum of intervention by a practitioner exists, therefore, as software and networks move from closed to more open applications of technology, shifting control from the individual designer in the closed system to the teacher and learner in the open system. With more open software, all the decision-making can be with the teacher. The problem with this is that individual teachers will never have sufficient time, expertise or resources to do everything themselves on a large scale. It is more likely that they will utilize open applications for a shift of emphasis from information delivery to students, towards the support of learning.

RESEARCH AND INNOVATION IN ODFL

What does research on ODFL reveal? The most apparent feature is that research and innovation in ODFL is such a broad field. Efforts at developing ODFL have covered issues such as the changing needs of society and the effectiveness of the application for industry (Evans and Nation, 1993; Hoey, 1994; Thorpe and Gudgeon, 1987). There is scarcely an area of education and training where flexible learning methods are not relevant, although investigations into the ODFL approach have mirrored the relatively narrow interests of higher education (Tait, 1992: 4). Assessing the interrelationship between research and innovation with ODFL is complicated, however, because ODFL engages so many researchers, organizations, partnerships and projects that it is almost impossible to get a complete picture.

Table 3.2. Recent research contributions in ODFL (adapted from Wagner, 2000: 4)

Research area	Distance-learning aspects
Educational systems.	Regional case-studies development and networking.
Organization and design of teaching and learning process.	New studies or course programmes, target groups learning design and learning management.
Virtual education/ organization of ODFL.	Design of virtual-learning environments, transnational networking, new models for virtual education, designed and evaluated.
Technology, multimedia, Internet.	Applications and testing of technology for delivery and interactivity.
Knowledge sharing.	Distributed systems.
Teaching methodology and innovation.	Concepts on teaching approaches. Findings for innovative methods. Action research methods. Evaluation of innovation.
Student–teacher interaction. Sociocultural aspects.	Evaluation of learner-centred activities and issues. Psychological–sociological influences on distance learners. Promoting dialogue. Impact of virtual learning on learner users.
Evaluation and sustainability.	Effective models for mainstreaming.
Economic and policy.	Cost-effectiveness studies and policy implementation.

A review of ODFL research papers found ten different categories that reflect the range of different issues (Table 3.2). It concluded that research on innovation by ODFL is often a description, explanation or an evaluation. Little evidence existed, however, that research findings are the cause for driving political or practical innovation, with only some exceptions in the applications of new technologies. Changes in the organization, curriculum, technology or methodology that occur during ODFL development may serve to stimulate research on targets, concepts and practical improvement steps and, in the process, draw conclusions for innovative methods. In practice, though, research is often focused on small events or single projects, and it is not unusual to find no explicit foundation in existing knowledge for a new development effort.

Criticisms of ODFL research include a series of gaps in research, with many ODFL studies having only a very small empirical base, with questionable methods and inconclusive results (Phipps, 1999). Among key shortcomings, Phipps observed a lack of control of extraneous variables in experimental research, no randomly selected subjects or groups, insufficient proof of validity and reliability of instruments, and not enough awareness of reactive effects. The most serious challenges arise from the growing complexity of development in ODFL practice and the accelerating speed of change in systems and models. In the learner-support area, description and prescription outweigh empirical enquiry or research (Robinson, 1995: 221–31). The most relevant improvements could be gained by a careful theory-based clarification of concepts, terminology and categories. A reliable comparison of different models in ODFL is also important, rather than more applications of different technologies.

One difficulty from this categorization (Table 3.2) is that the interdisciplinary nature of ODFL is not obvious. The research community comprises a number of distinct but overlapping groups involved with basic concepts, funding frameworks, professional networks and organization. Many forms of interrelationships can arise, for instance, between culture and language, pedagogy and psychology, technology and management. Interest in the ODFL field, nevertheless, is still developing rapidly and shows four trends. The number of studies on evaluation is continuously increasing; this number is widening internationally; the emphasis on the application of digital technology is increasing; and there is a growing interest in methods to improve the quality of distance education (O. Peters, 1998: 3). There are many newcomers to the field who are investigating new course programmes and variations of technology for e-learning. There are so many diverse activities and sources, with much ODFL knowledge implicit in practitioners, that newcomers have to set out to explore the variety of existing knowledge that comes from different sources and then test out the linkage between target group and e-learning.

THE E-LEARNING UMBRELLA

Online learning has a certain degree of elasticity in meaning. Terms such as e-learning, technology-supported learning and Web-based learning are used differently by different groups, but there is a convergence on the use of the Internet as a means of communication. Various typologies exist to categorize approaches to technology-supported learning, based on the time and location where learning occurs. One form of categorizing Web-based learning creates three types: the desktop tutor, the online class, and the ultra-interactive model (Fryer, 1997: 10–15).

The desktop-tutor model includes computer-based training (CBT) on the Web and, for some interpreters, Web-based training (WBT). It is linked closely with applications in corporate learning for job-specific skills, because of the ease with which learning materials can be distributed. Flexibility and cost-savings can be gained from a course designed to be self-contained and followed without the aid of a tutor. The focus on job-related skills helps the design process, since it enables clear learning objectives and performance measures to be set. In this type of application, the potential learners are a targeted group, selected on the basis of the prerequisite skills for the course. The learning programme can then follow a structured path, with a sequence of self-assessed tests to provide feedback to the learner, while keeping the need for additional tutorial support to a minimum. This form of e-learning gives many people independence in learning without the constraints of compliance with corporate structures or academic accreditation processes. Fully independent learning offers the benefit of autonomous learning, but is not regarded universally as the best approach. Various forms of tutorial support add value to the learning process, by addressing points where a learner encounters difficulty. This can be achieved by combining Web-based training with tutorial support in various forms.

The online-class model occurs when tutors and learners participate in online discussions and other interactions. Learners are likely to be dispersed geographically and to communicate by means of computer-mediated communications (CMC). Participants are guided through a course programme, with other learners, by a tutor. Most Web-based learning courseware providers offer interactivity, in the form of electronic bulletin boards that are moderated and reviewed by an instructor. Learners may access a particular bulletin board to share information, ask questions of the instructor and receive updates.

The ultra-interactive model includes the virtual classroom, which incorporates video technology, and real-time audio- and videoconferencing with an instructor. This model entails distributing conventional demonstrations, tutorials, seminars and lectures by means of a telematic link to learners in distant locations. This typography is not universally accepted. In the opinion of some people, the term Web-based training might apply only to the first category, while the second category would also be known as online learning and the third as the virtual classroom.

Another typology characterizes ODFL systems by the nature of the mediation offered to the learner, and is described graphically by Blandin (Blandin,

2000). One discriminating characteristic is based on the presence or absence of a tutor, which identifies the human mediation aspects of the system. A second characteristic is the presence, or absence, of an electronic network, so recognizing the technical mediation dimension of the system.

BENEFITS OF E-LEARNING

E-learning has the potential to provide flexible and supportive learning that addresses the learning needs of adults, offering benefits that are radically different from a conventional classroom-based learning environment (Block and Dobell, 1999: 7; Close et al., 2000: 12). Frequently cited as advantages for learners are the following factors: accessibility, since learners can gain access from many locations and times; the blindness of the learning engagement, as learners may express a preference, perhaps because of a 'fear of failing' in a live group, or perhaps because a manager may not wish to expose a lack of understanding of a topic in front of a group of employees; and that it can be learner-focused, making learning more relevant for the participant.

There are many benefits, too, for the provider. Development of content is relatively low-cost, can be uniformly consistent, updated rapidly and delivered in real time. Changes can be done remotely and made available to every learner instantly, providing equity for everyone. Curriculum cycles can occur quickly, with unitized delivery, frequent delivery of courses and rapid feedback. The cost of technology is low, with a relatively low cost of entry for providers. Interoperability between different machines facilitates global reach through widely available browsers. In principle, the process of learning support can be scaled according to the size of the audience. This may take the form of individual support, or provide product or sales training and information to 100,000 employees in a range of countries. All this can be accompanied by real-time measurement of individual and group progress, generated to diagnose performance on course.

DIGITAL COLLABORATION IN WEST WALES

The potential for collaboration through technology is an interesting property of e-learning. Collaboration can involve learners cooperating together on a learning programme or bring practitioners together to target specific client groups. Partnership in providing e-learning material can help manage cost and complexity in the face of the competition that can arise from across the world. Collaboration can be time-consuming, and therefore the benefits need to outweigh the costs.

The main focus within a west Wales consortium is in addressing the needs of SMEs. Within the catchment area of the institutions, wages in places are the lowest in the European Union. In the rural areas, small businesses have a crucial role in the economy, with 98 per cent of employers employing fewer than twenty-five people, a higher level than for Wales or Great Britain as a whole. The push for economic development is encouraging providers to collaborate to support the strengthening of skills of the workforce through e-learning. It has led to the development of a range of services, including providing e-learning business and management, language services, computer training and wider accessibility to online opportunities (Table 3.3).

Table 3.3. Typical applications of e-learning for SMEs among west Wales partners

E-learning provider	Description
University of Wales, Lampeter	Welsh communications, business applications in SMEs.
University of Wales Swansea	E-learning environment, distribution of content, eMBA.
University of Wales, Aberystwyth	Online training information database, e-business for SMEs.
Swansea Institute of Higher Education	Digital design.
Trinity College, Carmarthen	Written Welsh.
Coleg Sir Gâr	Virtual college IT skills for business.
Coleg Ceredigion	Local geographical network for UfI e-learning access points.
Coleg Powys	UfI geographical network, focus on take-up by SMEs.
Gorseinon College	Website for tourism.
Neath–Port Talbot College	Computer-aided design.
Pembrokeshire College	Web design.
Swansea College	Health and safety at work.

E-learning applications in the west Wales consortium are directed at managers and employees in small firms. The content, predominantly in generic rather than job-specific skills, is intended to respond to increasing demand for employee abilities in these areas. Decision-makers and practitioners who guide the e-learning experiences, however, have responded with different interactions. The different degrees of interaction range from full-scale distance delivery to the application of technology in learning materials to support blended learning.

Providers are in different stages of preparedness for e-learning, ranging from very experienced to novice starters. Working together on e-learning, however, is helping to spread the continuum of core professionals involved in development and delivery. There is a heavy turnover of project staff, who engage with a scheme for a short period of time and then move on with enhanced skills and experience. This creates a continuous flow of people into development work, who often need particular skills and familiarity with current e-learning processes. These practitioners can access informal support networks that form around working groups on topics, such as training needs analysis, and then go on to practise digital collaboration.

DIVERSE TEACHING AND LEARNING METHODS

The debate on the processes of teaching and learning between those educationalists who consider that learning ought to be teacher-directed and those who think that students should take more responsibility for their own learning is not new. Until recently learning technologies have, however, helped the former much more than the latter. What is striking about the debate now is that it is occurring not only between educationalists but also among decision-makers and practitioners drawn to e-learning processes from all the other subject disciplines. Within the local consortium, the move to e-learning has caused a review of virtually everything that was previously taken for granted, including the fundamental views that guide decisions on teaching, learning, the curriculum and student support. There has been a focus on testing and comparing learning and teaching methodologies. This reflects a desire for more knowledge or understanding of these processes in e-learning. It may also reflect the different practices under the banner of distance education: 'In reality, distance education no longer has a distinct and common pedagogy. The pedagogy of synchronous remote-classroom teaching resembles the pedagogy of classroom teaching more than it resembles the pedagogy of asynchronous correspondence teaching' (Daniel, 1996: 56). Even so, the needs of SME clients are many and diverse, so that no standard application fits all their purposes. Variety is present in the choice of e-learning solutions. Self-directed learning using constructivist principles is well regarded, but other methods such as an instructivist approach can also produce an effective programme (Rogers, 2002). Problems can arise, however, when a fundamental pedagogy does not underpin an e-learning course, or if it is lost in the conversion from a conventional face-to-face course to an e-curriculum.

4

Learning and teaching with technology

Theories of learning and teaching remain as academic argument until they are applied to influence the actual conduct of education. Embedded in any decision on the application of technology, there are bound to be assumptions about the learning process. These surmises are often implicit, but are likely to be reflected in one or other of the major theories about learning. Such theories, in the form of behaviourism, constructivism, learning as cognitive growth and humanistic psychology, form sound bases for the exploration of e-learning. There is value, then, in considering how people learn by applying these theories, because the choice of method should be driven by a coherent and conscious view of how people learn. Applying e-learning to SMEs has other implications. The notion that teaching is the transmission of unchallenged information is confronted. In addressing adults, the application of adult learning theory becomes more prominent, for instance, with more learner control. Super-imposed on this are constraints imposed by the SME, so that learning is contingent on its requirement, resources and environment. Before we think about the technology of online education, therefore, we need to consider education itself and the aspects of the theory and practice of teaching methods that influence e-learning.

LEARNING AND TEACHING THEORIES

Educational design usually emerges from the deliberate application of a particular theory of learning. Arguably, it follows that effective design is possible only if the developer has a reflexive awareness of the theoretical basis underlying the design. For course designers there is a natural tendency to adopt the prevailing mode during their professional formation. Various views exist among practitioners, however, on the optimum approach to using learning technology. In certain academic circles, constructivism is the preferred paradigm for an approach to online learning. In workforce development programmes a more instructivist, teacher-directed learning model reflecting conventional instructor and trainee behaviour is a common model. The complication is that a blanket strategy does not fit all learners. Experienced learners do not always want collaborative learning approaches, while some learners may want a closed system such as a 'course-in-a-box'. This reflects the fact that adults are different and learn in diverse ways, so that a variety of methods can be adapted usefully for e-learning.

Concepts of how we learn have concerned educators for centuries. They still continue to generate controversy, as there are many complexities involved in defining 'learning'. Learning defies precise resolution because of the sheer variety of its applications. It can mean the acquisition of what is already known about something, or the extension and clarification of the meaning of one's experience, or an organized process of testing ideas relevant to problems (Smith, 1982). Nevertheless, a general distinction can be made between education and learning. Education is an activity designed by an agent of change, whereas learning emphasizes the person in whom the change occurs, or is expected to occur. 'Learning is the act or process by which behavioural change, knowledge, skills and attitudes are acquired' (Boyd et al., 1980: 100–1). We already know that learning is not the same thing as teaching, online or off. Theories about the nature of teaching address the methods employed to influence learning. 'While theories of learning deal with the ways in which an organism learns, theories of teaching deal with the ways in which a person influences an organism to learn' (Gage, 1972: 56). Simple as this appears, it masks different approaches by learning theorists. For some, learning is a process by which behaviour is changed, shaped or controlled. Others perceive learning in terms of progression, the development of competences and fulfilment of potential.

A learning theory adopted by a practitioner will influence the teaching theory applied in the design of a programme. In planning an e-learning course, the practitioner will need to choose certain techniques from those available. The full repertoire of teaching strategies has emerged from psychological, physiological and philosophical considerations. Although it desirable to select one on the basis of a clear assessment between the learning and teaching principles and objectives, it is more likely that the actual selection is made on the repertoire of principles known to the designer. This leads to different applications of learning and teaching theory in the development of e-learning courses.

BEHAVIOURISM AND INSTRUCTION

The basic ideas of behaviourism are that all complex forms of behaviour, including the attitude of an individual, can be traced back to a specific stimulus–response event. Once the stimulus that produces a certain response is identified, then an individual's behaviour can be predicted. It follows that if the stimulus is controlled, an individual's behaviour can be controlled. According to behaviourist thinking, most of human behaviour is learned through stimuli–response. Educators who accept the behavioural perspective assume that the behaviour of students is a response to their past and present environment, and that all behaviour is learned. Since learning is a form of behaviour modification, it is the responsibility of the educator to construct an environment in which the correct behaviour of the student is reinforced.

The basis of behaviourism lies in a series of systematic investigations into the phenomenon of learning, by exploring the effect of behaviour on subsequent behaviour (Thorndike, 1928). The findings, generalized as the *law of effect*, proposed that a response is strengthened if it is followed by pleasure, weakened if followed by displeasure or pain. This principle has become a cornerstone of behavioural theory, known as 'reinforcement'. Such concepts of control and shaping were at the centre of Skinner's treatment of learning: he maintained that an individual learns by having certain aspects of behaviour reinforced while other aspects are not (Skinner, 1968: 10). The conditioning-of-behaviour approach is reflected in many teaching strategies, ranging from the use of programmed instructional learning through to direct instruction. In programmed learning, the curriculum is organized along carefully sequenced lines. Subject content is formulated into small, understandable steps or frames, each step followed by a question that the student can almost always answer correctly. The object is to reinforce learning through an immediate response and reward of the right reply.

Behavioural objectives imply a rational model of learning, in which learning proceeds in a logical and orderly manner (Davies et al., 1974). Although appearing teacher-centred, the emphasis is on student needs and responses, with an awareness by the instructor of student understanding being a feature that can be incorporated into the method. Direct instruction as a cognitive strategy has acquired a number of different practices, but has a set of essential characteristics, which include: beginning a lesson with a short review of previous learning and a short statement of goals (Rosenshine and Meister, 1995: 143–9); presenting new material in small steps and providing for student practice after each step; giving clear instructions, detailed explanations, providing explicit instruction and a high level of practice for all students; asking a large number of questions, checking for student understanding and responses from all students; and guiding students during initial learning phases, monitoring and providing systematic feedback with corrections.

More recently, direct instruction has migrated from narrow definitions of tightly sequenced instruction with constant feedback, to definitions that emphasize the development of cognitive strategies. In this adapted approach, it is an explicit strategy for an instructor to explain the strategy, as well as when, where and how to use it and why it should be used. All learning outcomes are stated clearly in advance. There is a gradual transfer of the responsibility for learning from the instructor to the learner. The focus is on constructing meaning and problem-solving (Idol et al., 1991).

The principles of behaviourism have proved useful for managing both classroom behaviours and instructional delivery. Critics of the approach, though, consider that it oversimplifies human behaviour and views the individual as an automaton, rather than a person of independent will and purpose. Although the design of computer-based training has been strongly influenced by behaviourist theory, the essential feature of classical behaviourism is that it ignores the role of conscious strategies, or self-will, in learning. The role of the teacher in this scenario is to manage the learning environment so as to create the most appropriate learning outcomes. Learning occurs through the impact of the external environment on the learner, who seeks rewards or avoids punishment. Commentators argue that this approach is not compatible with the ethos of adult education, because no account is taken of the unpredictability of student-centred learning that involves a constant redefinition of goals in the exploration of learning (Robinson and Taylor, 1983: 355–70). Moreover, the specification of objectives may function as an authoritarian support for the teacher, in the sense that they are part of a controlled learning process where failure can only be the result of the learner's failings.

The behaviouristic approach has exerted a strong influence in the field of learning. The rapid growth of PCs fuelled an explosion of educational software packages involving computer-assisted instruction (CAI) procedures. Behaviour-modification principles are used to programme these CAI packages, and therefore underpin many existing e-learning applications. These principles include: having a statement of the purpose of the software; applying appropriate reinforcement by text, visual or audio, depending on the application; the use of shaping, chaining, modelling, punishment and reward principles; scoring, or monitoring, is often present; providing progress reports; and applying varied forms of CAI, such as drill and practice activities and simulations, as well as tutorials. An e-learning designer with a behaviourist understanding of learning might seek a systematic, step-by-step approach, with frequent testing that results in positive or negative reinforcement, in order to produce the prescribed learning outcome.

Instructivist principles are adapted and applied to underpin a set of courses on IT skills for business developed for a virtual college (Rogers, 2002). The student is presented with clear objectives and a step-by-step guide for each of the many IT tasks within a module, and with small-sized units of learning that build into an acceptable level of competence in the topic. Every learner is allocated a personal tutor at the start of the course, and the learner and tutor agree a personal training plan. The virtual learning environment (VLE) in support of the course provides efficient management of student progress and assessment, which can reduce stress on students and the workload on staff.

CONSTRUCTIVISM

The constructivist view of education emphasizes that all knowledge is context-bound and that learning cannot be separated from the context in which it is used, so that the goal of education is to help students construct their own understanding. Context refers to the real-world factors surrounding the learning environment, or the environment in which the task to be learned might be accomplished. Complementary to this perception is the idea that learning needs to occur in a rich context, so that the constructive process can happen and facilitate the transfer to other environments beyond the classroom, or learning platform. These factors may include the physical, organizational, social and political issues related to the learning and application of the new knowledge. Learning them needs to be 'situated' in problem-solving in such real-life contexts, where the environment is rich in information.

'Situated learning' emphasizes that it is important that learning should (usually) relate to an activity, a context and a particular culture. The method of 'situated learning' or 'situated cognition' is to ensure that students learn to understand concepts, anchored within the context of a particular area of study. Rather than abstracting unrelated pieces of information in areas of study, a student learns about a subject area by immersion in that culture. The goal is to produce a student who understands how a practitioner in a certain professional domain acquires knowledge in that field and integrates this knowledge to solve problems in that particular area. This is in contrast with a conventional classroom approach, where knowledge is presented in abstract form, outside a context. A rich context for problem-solving and social interaction becomes part of this component (Brown et al., 1988: 32–42).

The constructivist view of learning is that the active engagement of the learner is an essential element of learning. This implies a shift from what the teacher may do through explicit instructing, to what the learner does as an active agent in making sense of information (Poplin, 1988: 401–16). In constructivism, students are not assumed to absorb knowledge passively, from external sources such as experts, books, databases, but rather are active constructors of knowledge, by integrating and combining new information with their own experiences and prior knowledge. A premise is that, in order to learn, learning needs to be situated in a problem-solving situation, a real-life context where the environment is rich in information and where there are no right answers. Tasks must be authentic (Duffy and Jonassen, 1992). Moreover, two primary varieties exist: personal and social constructivism.

Personal constructivism focuses on transformations of understanding in the minds of individual learners, such as the individual's existing understanding, knowledge and interests and how these extend through personal interactions with events in their daily lives. Learning occurs as an inner process that affects the entire personality. It cannot be observed directly and does not necessarily result in outward reactions. An individual makes active selections and adaptations to stimuli. The intrapersonal dimensions of learning are emphasized, with the view that knowledge is not transmitted directly from one knowledgeable person to another, but actively built up through exploration and discovery, rather than direct teaching. Learning situations that reflect this perspective would design practical activities that challenge learners' prior concepts and encourage learners to reorganize personal theories. This leads into contributions from areas of cognitive psychology and information processing (Driver et al., 1994: 5–12).

Social constructivism focuses on the growth of subject matter for individuals in social domains (Rogoff, 1990; Davydov, 1995: 12–21). The emphasis is on the growth of an individual in a social context, on how an individual makes sense of experiences from socially-shared perceptions. This process of construction is distinguished from the position that an individual learns best from self-discovery, being a position that advocates collaborative inquiry. Meaning is negotiated through interactions with others, where multiple perspectives on reality exist. This is best achieved when learning takes place in well-structured contexts.

Constructivist assumptions are that learning is best facilitated by the design of constructivist tools and learning environments, rather than by instructional interventions that control the sequence and content of instruction. The role of the designer shifts from creating learning situations to developing environments that require the learner to construct knowledge that is most meaningful to them. Such an environment is constructivist only if it allows individuals, or groups of individuals, to determine their own meaning for what they experience. Constructivist instructional principles to achieve this end include: designing an authentic task and anchoring all learning activities in a larger task (Savery and Duffy, 1996); designing the task and the learning environment to reflect the complexity of the environment in which learners should be able to function at the end of learning; supporting the learner in developing ownership for the overall problem or task; encouraging the testing of ideas against alternative views and alternative contexts; and providing opportunity for reflection on both the content learned and the learning process.

Practical strategies for developing constructivist teaching for Internet-based learning include: learning objectives being prepared with student collaboration, based on the learner's needs; encouragement being given to student autonomy and initiative; problems presented to students and solved having personal relevance to learners; tasks being framed using cognitive terminology, with terms such as classify, analyse, create and predict; teachers enquiring about student understanding before sharing their own understandings; and students being encouraged to engage in dialogue with the teacher and peers, with learning measured through direct observation and dialogue (French, 1999: 9–24).

The computer can enhance learning in situated cognition by providing environments that simulate situations in the real world that are difficult to re-create in a conventional classroom. Software tools and applications, such as databases, multimedia and virtual reality, spreadsheets, word processors and graphics packages can all be applied to represent realistic simulations. The Internet can also provide rapid access to expert knowledge and the cognitive strategies that specialists use to solve problems. The potential for interactivity with the learner and the ability for a programme to be customized for an individual give computer applications the means for students to construct their own knowledge. The PC and network can be a conduit for distributing cognition between those involved in the social interaction with a constructivist philosophy in two ways (Salomon, 1993: 620–7): it can alleviate some of the mental processing of the learner and free processing space for higher-level mental activities; it can also act as a channel, through which communities of learners can interact to construct knowledge in a dynamic way.

A social constructivist approach to e-learning is adopted in an interpersonal skills programme for volunteers at the University of Wales, Lampeter (*www.lamp.ac.uk*). The design of the course and the supporting VLE reflects the need to bring individuals into a welcoming group whose members learn cooperatively. The success of the course, therefore, strongly depends on the group dynamic generated by a number of like-minded people working together to mutually enhance their skills and knowledge. The course attempts to make use of a participant's actual experience in voluntary work to inform learning. The VLE offers several support-resources, including links to relevant education and government Websites, open fora for feedback on course content and structure, private student fora to allow interchange between participants taking modules and a 'social club' as a completely open discussion group, with a student directory which allows students to display their curriculum vitae and photographs for viewing by fellow students.

COGNITIVE THEORIES

Cognitive theories examine what happens from the moment we sense stimuli to the point when a response occurs. With cognitive theory and development, the driving force is the urge to discover meaning, coherence and wholeness in everything. Relevant questions are: 'what happens when we learn?' and 'how do we solve problems?'

Two contrasting views of cognitive development are those of Piaget and Vygotsky (Piaget, 1970; Vygotsky, 1978). Each believes that learning is an internal process of constructing meaning from experience, but the means by which this knowledge formulation occurs is dealt with differently. In his theory of intellectual development, Piaget considers the idea that individuals construct their own meaning through the interacting processes of assimilation, adaptation, accommodation, equilibrium and the extension of ways of thinking, which is related to personal constructivism. His second concept is cognitive structuralism, which connects to the idea that cognitive growth in children occurs through a series of stages, with each distinguished by different cognitive structures. Piaget believes that, in each of these stages, there is a characteristic way in which children think about the world and solve problems (Cellerier, 1987).

The role played by social factors in the external environment in constructing meaning is an emphasis of Vygotskian theory (Vygotsky, 1978). His theory for social constructivism emphasizes the interaction between a supportive learning environment of teachers and peers and the individual's internal manipulation of information to facilitate meaningful learning. Vygotsky places emphasis on the elements of proximal development, holistic education and mediated learning through social interaction. He uses the term 'proximal development' to equate to an individual's range of potential for learning where it is shaped by the environment in which it takes place. 'Holistic' implies that the division of material for a unit of study should be the most meaningful unit, rather than the simplest or smallest. 'Mediated learning' is guiding instruction that develops an increasing mastery of the language of learning so as to acquire conscious awareness and voluntary control of learning (Moll, 1990).

Certain learning theorists, like Bruner, see learning as a process of growth, the development of competences and fulfilment of potential, from a perspective of cognitive psychology (Bruner, 1966). Bruner argues that learning is an active process in which a learner infers principles as well as rules and tests them out. Cognitive development argues that what is learnt are mental structures and that problem-solving involves insight as well as trial and error. Cognitive strategies are a priority for some educational theorists and are based on the idea that an ultimate goal of instruction is to ensure that the student becomes an efficient self-learner (Bruner, 1961, 1971).

For teachers who accept the cognitive theories, it is important to assess the limits to which a particular learning technology enables learners to develop and test their own inferences. It is also important for learners to explore for themselves the underlying structure and assumptions of a subject. The extent to which technology enables feedback and criticism to be provided for learner-generated inferences is significant, as is the degree to which learning technology can substitute for direct physical experience.

A cognitive-instructivist e-learning approach is taken on a Managing SME Business on the Internet course at Lampeter. Selection of students is by a technology and skills audit, which establishes that students have a basic understanding of issues related to the subject. Students provide problems from their personal work situation, on which they then work during the course.

Mediated and peer-to-peer learning is organized as participants progress through exercises, casework and problem-solving to test their interpretations. The tutor communicates motivation and encouragement, reminding students on the completion of assignments or in sending additional information that might prove useful.

TEACHING THROUGH INQUIRY

The discovery method, inquiry method, self-directed learning (SDL) or problem-based learning (PBL) have roots in cognitive theory and with the ideas of Dewey (Dewey, 1938). Experience is the central concept under this system, and the foundation of this system is the will of an individual to learn. The central problem for education based on experience is to choose the kind of current experiences that can inform subsequent experiences beneficially. A notable proponent of the discovery method, Bruner, considers that there are three roles for teachers in the inquiry form: as communicators of knowledge, models who inspire and symbols of 'education' (Bruner, 1966: 40–1). A theory of instruction for inquiry teaching must address certain areas: first, the experiences that implant in the individual a predisposition toward learning; second, the ways in which knowledge should be structured so that the learner can grasp it readily; third, the most effective sequences in which to present the materials; and fourth, the nature and pacing of rewards and punishments in the process of learning and teaching.

In terms of e-learning instructional materials, the kinds of questions that may decide whether they address the four areas of the theory of instruction are: do the e-learning materials increase an individual's desire to learn? How can the e-learning programme designer make an individual eager to learn? Are the e-learning materials appropriate for the level of the learner? How is the best sequence of learning presented to the learner? When will feedback be provided?

Problem-based learning (PBL) is rooted in experiential learning, since it is problem-centred rather than discipline-centred. The inclusion of problems as a stimulus for learning is used in higher education in areas as diverse as architecture, computing, engineering, social work and business. Teachers encourage student learning, by using case studies in tutorials, for example. A problem-based curriculum differs from the traditional subject-based curriculum in four primary ways: first, in cumulative learning, where a subject is not learned in depth at any one time, but introduced repeatedly at increasing levels of complexity over the course of study; second, by integrated learning, where subjects are presented as they relate to a problem rather than separately; third, through progression in learning, since the methods that students use to learn change as they acquire skills, knowledge and maturity; and fourth, by consistency in application, so that the goals of problem-based learning are present in all aspects of teaching and learning (Engel, 1991: 29).

A PBL approach can situate written-language learning in real-life applications. This supports the principle that learners should develop their understandings of the conventions of language by using it in real-life applications, rather than as a set of rules. A course on Welsh translation at Lampeter draws participants from a range of small enterprises. Learners bring problems based on their real-life work, which they explore with the tutor, so that the course is relevant to the learners' situation. E-learning support is complemented by a day workshop once a term. During the inquiry process to develop solutions, participants need to use language to document discussions, present findings and write effectively. They construct these solutions on work-based content, which then gives added cost-efficiency to the employer.

SELF-DIRECTED LEARNING

Self-directed learning (SDL) is a core principle of adult learning, which strengthens its identity as a distinct field of practice and inquiry. SDL is associated with several terms in adult education, such as learner-centredness, independent learning, self-teaching and autonomy. It allows seemingly limitless interpretations of how it should be applied (Tennant, 1997: 14–18). Two important dimensions of SDL are self-teaching and personal autonomy, but they are relatively independent. Self-teaching arises when an individual learner is capable of taking control of the processes of teaching in a particular subject; personal autonomy, when the learner takes control of the goals and purposes of learning (Brookfield, 1986; Candy, 1991).

An individual may have a substantial degree of personal autonomy, but still elect to learn in a teacher-directed process, for reasons of speed, convenience or learning style. This choice does not mean that the individual has relinquished control because of the choice of access to learning. Conversely, if an adult does engage in self-teaching it does not make that person autonomous; for example, an independent e-learning course may have all the requirements set by a tutor. For most teachers, the more important aspect of SDL is building personal autonomy. The premise that all adults have a full capacity for self-teaching and personal autonomy in all learning situations is not, however, commonly accepted. This issue is addressed by Grow, who argues that any learner in a particular learning situation is likely to show different capabilities and preferences; therefore, self-directed learning is situational and the role of the teacher is to match styles with student (Grow, 1991: 125–49). Grow proposes that a student moves through four stages: from dependent, through interested to involved, and to self-directed. The teacher at each of these stages functions as a coach or authority, guide or motivator, facilitator, consultant or designer.

A number of supposed 'myths' surround self-directed learning. One is the notion of self-directed learning in isolation, which is strongly refuted (Brockett and Hiemstra, 1991). Another is that facilitating self-direction implies an easy option for teachers. It is necessary for an effective tutor to establish a special relationship with learners, and it appears that conversation by synchronous communication is a better way than asynchronous methods to establish such a relationship between tutor and learner. Real live conversation includes non-verbal communication, so that conversation by telephone or even videoconference is impoverished in this respect. The roles that a tutor needs to undertake to promote self-direction in learning, according to Brockett and Hiemstra, include promoting discussion, the raising of questions and small-group activity to stimulate interest in the learning experience. There is a role in working with learners outside formal settings as a stimulator to develop a positive attitude towards self-directed enquiry.

An underdeveloped area for e-learning designers is in the difference between the genders in learning. There are difficulties in getting the right balance of approach in a single model. Autonomous, self-directed learning has been challenged by various authors, who emphasize the significance of interconnectedness and interdependence as qualities that reflect a woman's method of connecting with the world (Shrewsbury, 1987: 6–14; Cafarella and Olsen, 1993: 125–51; Hayes, 1989). Even so, much e-learning is designed and presented on closed systems for self-directed learning.

INFORMATION-PROCESSING THEORIES

Information processing in learning is concerned more with the inner mental processes during the learning experience than with external factors of influence. The theory of information processing involves students actively processing, storing and retrieving information. Teaching helps learners to develop information-processing skills and apply them systematically to their studies. Learning theory based on information processing concentrates on the processes that occur in the individual's thoughts during the learning experience in a purely cognitive means of learning. The concepts that support the model derive from efforts by learning psychologists to represent the variables in the learning process by mathematical equations. Another source is from computer scientists exploring the limits of information processing by computer. Information-processing theories also reflect work from linguistic scientists in interpreting how people learn and apply language.

Two information-processing theories applied in the design of e-learning are the computer as a model for human learning and the 'chunking' of information (Millar et al., 1960). The first considers the processing of information, which occurs in sequential steps and is a fundamental cognitive process of the human mind in which it performs like a computer. The mind takes in information, performs operations on it to change its form and content, stores and locates it and generates responses to it. In this way, information processing involves gathering and presenting information, or 'encoding', holding information, or 'retention' and getting at the information when required, or 'retrieval'. The second idea is 'chunking', the idea that the capacity of short-term memory can hold only five to nine chunks of information, where a 'chunk' is a meaningful unit (Millar, 1956: 81–97). Both aspects are widely applied in the design of 'unitized' e-learning content.

Information processing implies that there are limits to the amount of information that learners can process effectively. The predominant model of human memory divides the information-processing model into three parts: input or sensory registry, short-term and long-term memory (Huber, 1993: 35–46). Sensory registry has input primarily from sight and sound, with processing in three to five seconds, but with the input going to the short-term memory for processing. Information transferred to the short-term memory can remain active for about fifteen seconds without rehearsal, but has a capacity limit of between five and nine items. Three means of handling cognitive tasks in short-term memory have been defined: chunking, breaking into sub-parts in order to process one at a time, and the practice of skills until they are automatic. If the working memory is overloaded with processing, it becomes unable to cope with the demands and processing becomes inefficient. Long-term memory is where information for future reference is stored and is thought to have unlimited duration, with prior experience having a major effect on how information is retained and stored.

The learner needs to be actively engaged in the processing of the information for transfer from the working memory to the long-term memory. A variety of practical learning strategies and techniques, such as whole and part learning, repetition and drill, distributed practice, elaboration, review, rehearsal, summarizing and chunking, may all help retention once the material has been processed. Furthermore, content that is meaningful is learnt more easily and retained more effectively than non-meaningful material.

Information processing has a significant influence in the design of e-learning. Stimulating conditions for the learner are not simply stimuli to which they react; they can be viewed as supporting remembering and performing in the learning experience. Instruction can include: presenting the e-learning programme so as to capture the student's attention; emphasizing learning through helping students to focus on the most meaningful details; encouraging students to make connections between new information and what they are already familiar with; providing for repetition and practice of applying strategies in new situations; presenting content in a clear organized way; and focusing on meaning, not recollection of information.

SOCIAL COGNITIVE THEORY AND
OBSERVATIONAL LEARNING

Social cognitive theory was originally termed social-learning theory or observational-learning principles (Bandura, 1986). Learning is achieved, under this theory, through observing the behaviour of others. An individual learns to imitate through receiving reinforcement for performing certain behaviour and maintains the behaviour through continuous reinforcement. Positive or negative effects of a model's behaviour, called vicarious reinforcement or vicarious punishment, can then influence the behaviour of the observer. Observational learning can be explained in terms of behaviourist conditioning, if a person can imagine the reinforcement and the behaviour of models.

A system of teaching by modelling, where the teacher behaves in ways intended for the learner to imitate, was developed by Bandura. As a result of bringing a learner into contact with a model, a 'modelling' effect occurs as the learner acquires new forms of response patterns. An 'inhibitory' effect arises where behaviour acquired by observation is practised or not, depending on the perceived rewards and punishments that might apply. Moreover, an 'eliciting' effect occurs, where behaviour similar to the modelled behaviour is performed and the learner receives from the model a cue for releasing a response.

Under the social cognition model of learning, culture is the prime determinant of the development of an individual. A student acquires many ideas and knowledge by way of culture. The culture enveloping a student provides that person with the processes of thinking that are called the 'tools of intellectual adaptation'. Culture provides a student with what to think, therefore, as well as how to think. Cognitive development arises from a process where the student learns through problem-solving experiences that are shared with someone else, perhaps a teacher or peer.

Observational learning has an influence on certain aspects of teaching and the formulation of the curriculum. It implies that students need to observe and model behaviour that leads to positive reinforcement. Since much of what students learn is through interaction, then the curriculum should be designed in such a way as to emphasize the interaction between the learners and the learning tasks. Designers and tutors need to encourage collaborative learning, since with this approach much learning occurs within social and environmental contexts. A learned behaviour might only be performed when the environment is right, and tutors need to provide such a supportive environment. In terms of tutoring, an appropriate strategy might be for a tutor continually to adjust the level of help in response to the student's level of performance. Assessment methods need to take into account the actual level of development and the level of potential development, which might be attained with help from a tutor.

Observational learning can be applied to e-learning, although a low level of co-presence can diminish the amount of implicit information that a participant might receive. It is often not possible to immerse a student fully through the use of IT simulations that the student can learn to observe and model. Experiences, however, can be provided for the student that imitate good practice. In the field of health and safety at work, a collection of fifteen self-standing learning objects, each of about fifteen minutes' learning time, has been created using Macromedia Flash and XML at Swansea College (*www.swancoll.ac.uk*). The learning objects are distributed on CD-ROM, or downloaded from a Website. The learning objects can be selected by the learner in any preferred way, and are incorporated in the health-and-safety-at-work education of employees to represent model practice. The teaching is highly visual, with clear graphics that are free from distractions and text presentation kept to a minimum.

HUMANISTIC LEARNING THEORY

Humanistic psychology is concerned with the 'self' and a reaffirmation of the human qualities of an individual, such as personal freedom and the validity of personal experience. Learning is accomplished by the learner in conformity with his or her own interests, values and opportunities for study and practice. With a learner responsible for setting goals, the role of the trainer is as a facilitator, providing a supportive environment through which learning can take place largely through discovery. In practice, this means that taking account of the individual learner enhances the likelihood of successful learning. Writers as varied as Maslow, Freire and Rogers have all emphasized the importance of considering the specific characteristics of individuals and using them as the point of reference for learning (Maslow, 1968; Freire, 1972; Rogers, 1951).

Humanistic psychologists are in a sense at the opposite end of the spectrum from behaviourism. They argue that every person acts in accordance with their own perception of the world, placing an emphasis on the wholeness and uniqueness of an individual, a concern for improving the human condition as well as for understanding the individual. With this view, the most basic drive of the human organism is toward self-actualization – the constant striving to realize inherent potential. Once the various alternatives are clearly perceived, the individual chooses the path of development. This process has certain characteristic elements that include personal involvement in the learning event, with the whole person engaged. Self-initiation, in the sense of finding out and comprehending, always comes from within the individual, even when the stimulus comes from the outside. The locus of evaluation also resides with the learner, since the learner knows whether the learning meets personal need, whether it leads towards what the individual wants to know.

For distance educators, the interest in the humanistic approach arises from the potential of new technologies for developing an interpersonal relationship at a distance, as distinct from a human–machine relationship. Knowledge is constructed by each individual, testing the meaning of external events primarily through feedback from social contact with people. Learning, therefore, requires this interpersonal communication between a learner and a facilitator to whom the learner can personally relate.

STUDENT-CENTRED LEARNING

Learning is a completely internal process controlled by the learner, according to Rogers (Rogers, 1969). His model emerges from the concerns of humanistic psychology with developing human potential, not merely with its adequate functioning. The assumption that individuals, when given the proper encouragement, can decide for themselves the best course to follow is an approach formulated by Rogers, based on client therapy (Rogers, 1951). He distinguished between two types of learning: cognitive and experiential. Cognitive learning corresponds to academic knowledge and includes learning vocabulary and multiplication tables, while experiential refers to applied knowledge, such as learning about motors in order to repair a machine. The key difference between the two is that experiential learning addresses the needs and wants of the learner.

The concept of learning as a completely internal process controlled by the learner led him to conceptualize a student-centred approach to education, based on five 'basic hypotheses':

1. 'We cannot teach another person directly, we can only facilitate the individual's learning.' This focuses attention on the learner, rather than the activities of a teacher. It arises from suggestions in personality theory that everyone exists at the centre of a continually changing world of experience and reacts to the environment as it is perceived and encountered.
2. 'A person learns significantly only those things which he perceives as being involved in the maintenance of, or enhancement of the self.' This emphasizes the need to make learning relevant for the learner and highlights a contention with the academic tradition of devising courses for group conformance.
3. 'Experience which if assimilated would involve a change in the organization of self, tends to be resisted through denial or distortion of symbolization.' This implies a requirement to provide a supportive environment for the learner to accept change and responsibility. The third and fourth hypotheses are similar, because learning may often appear threatening to an individual.

4. 'The structure and organization of self appear to become more rigid under threat and to relax its boundaries when completely free of threat. Experience, which is perceived as inconsistent with the self, can only be assimilated if the current organization of self is relaxed and expanded to include it.' A threat-free environment is necessary for the acceptance and integration of learning. This depends on the perception of the learner and so it places responsibility for learning firmly on the student.

5. 'The educational situation which most effectively promotes learning is one in which (a), threat to the self of the learner is reduced to a minimum, and (b), differentiated perception of the field is facilitated.' Here the two parts are almost synonymous because differentiated perception is most likely when there is no threat. Undifferentiated perception arises when an individual sees experience in absolute and unconditional terms and confuses fact and evaluation, relying on ideas rather than reality-testing. In contrast, with differentiated perception, an individual sees things in limited differentiated terms, is dominated by facts and not concepts, evaluates in multiple ways and is aware of different levels of abstraction.

A prescription for the qualities of a good facilitator or tutor includes genuineness, prizing, acceptance, trust and empathetic understanding (Rogers, 1983), although these are such subtle qualities of human relationship that it seems self-evident that direct human contact is needed to establish them. The idea that, given the proper encouragement and advice, individuals can decide themselves the best course to follow is an implicit belief for free-agent e-learners. The practical complications for them start to arise in finding the right course from the myriad of courses on offer.

CONDITIONS OF LEARNING

In addition to the major categories of learning theory, theorists emerge with adaptations and variations to these models. For instance, behaviourism has gradually absorbed new elements with an interest in the mental processes of learning. One representative of this position is Gagné, who described himself as somewhere between behaviourism and cognitive science and summarized his position on learning theories neatly as: 'I do not think that learning is a phenomenon which can be explained by simple theories despite the intellectual appeal that such theories have' (Gagné, 1965: v). There are several levels of learning that require different types of instruction, according to Gagné. He identified five major categories of learning: verbal information, intellectual skills, cognitive strategies, motor skills and attitudes. Different internal and external conditions are necessary for each type; for instance, to learn attitudes, the learner must be exposed to a credible role-model or persuasive arguments.

Similarly, for cognitive strategies there needs to be an opportunity for learners to practise developing new solutions to problems. Gagné proposed that learning tasks for intellectual skills can be organized in a hierarchy, according to complexity (Gagné, 1985). The hierarchy identifies the prerequisites that should be completed to facilitate learning at each level, and these provide a basis for the sequencing of instruction.

Learning is a process involving both outer stimuli and inner conditions, in the view of Gagné. To be effective, a teaching programme should take into account nine elements, termed the 'conditions of learning'. Different types of knowledge and skill require different conditions for learning. If an instructional experience does not include the instructional strategies required for the acquisition of the desired knowledge or skill, then effective, efficient learning of the desired outcome will not occur (Gagné et al., 1992). Instructional strategies can be verified by empirical test and are natural principles, not arrived at by collaborative agreement among instructional designers or learners. Key instructional events in the order in which they arise, together with the internal processes within the learner and the design implications for e-learning, are shown in Table 4.1.

Table 4.1. Nine instructional actions for effective learning (after Gagné, 1987)

Instructional action (Gagné's event)	Internal processes and effect on e-learning
Gain and maintain attention	Stimulate perceptions within the learner through a range of varied and attractive presentations that engage and actively involve the learner. Leading questions can be posed, or scenarios, or demonstrations, or Web-pages that stimulate curiosity, and then explained.
Inform on outcomes	Create level of expectation for learning, either explicitly in words or by means of demonstration. This event gives meaning to the instruction from the start. Learning objectives can be listed, as well as what the learning assessment is intended to measure.
Stimulate recall	Retrieve and activate short-term memory by stimulating the recollection of relevant prior learning or experience, or 'scaffolding'. Review prior knowledge or experience, hypertext links and connections with new materials.
Present the task	Engage selective perception of content and ensure that this fits the objectives and the learners. This can be directly presented to students or by providing the means for them to discover the materials.
Provide learning guidance	Systematically encode for storage in long-term memory. Provide prompts to paths and further

Table 4.1 (*contd.*)

Instructional action (Gagné's event)	Internal processes and effect on e-learning
	information. Opportunities can be created for self-learning or group collaborative learning by means of discussion questions, listings of resources and progressive assignments. The autonomous nature of online learning makes the opportunities for student-led learning important.
Evaluate performance	Student responds to questions for verification. The event is intended to show comprehension through an understanding in tests and assignments.
Provide feedback	Reinforce and assess correct performance. Timely, exact and specific, based on a learner's progress and success or failure. Prompt and reliable feedback is essential for the online environment, and can be to an individual or a group.
Assess performance	Retrieve and reinforce content as final evaluation to determine that learning has occurred. Assessing performance can include multiple-assessment strategies to determine the reliability of performance. It can include the learner in online assessments, graded projects or threaded discussions.
Enhance transfer	Retrieval and generalization of learned skills by a student to a new situation. Practice can be provided to reinforce the application of a new skill. Students can construct course portfolios that show progress on the course or course-long projects that summarize overall learning on course.

The full set of actions provides a comprehensive range of conditions, from gaining and controlling the attention of a learner, through to ensuring post-course retention by the practice and application of a new skill. Actions within Gagné's framework are a helpful and practical guide to operational planning for an e-learning strategy. The principles of Gagné's framework are that different instruction is required for different learning outcomes, and that specific conditions of learning need to be present for learning to occur. In the context of e-learning, some of these actions assume greater importance, due to the nature of the learning and the learner. Moreover, the specific operations that comprise instructional events are different for each different type of learning outcome. However, the instructional design method proposed by Gagné is criticized by Laurillard because 'Gagné's approach is essentially a logical case of what must be the case, rather than an empirically grounded theory' (Laurillard, 1993: 72).

INSTRUCTIONAL SYSTEM DESIGN

The principles of behaviouristic and cognitive theories form the basis of the instructional system design (ISD) model. The assumption of the model is that an expert instructional designer can represent the external world in an objective way that is independent of an individual's mind, which means that everyone can, in principle, understand the world in an objective way. Learning depends strongly on external stimuli, with an instructor responsible for: programme control; the source of objective knowledge; the control of the material; and the pace of the learning process. One of the characteristic traits of this approach is that it separates the content of the teaching from the methods. Behavioural psychology makes a significant contribution to the formulation of the systematic process through programmed instruction, task analysis, behavioural objectives and criterion-based evaluation (Rosenberg et al., 1999: 22–45).

The key concept behind ISD is a generalized systematic model that provides a guide for instructional designers for the main stages of the process. In the first stage, the requirements of the learner and task are analysed in order to determine the precise instructional need. Then an instructional programme is designed on the basis of the analysis, with objectives and testing linked back to the need (Mager, 1975). Instructional materials are then produced and delivered. These delivery methods can be standardized on methods, such as case studies, role-play or instructional lectures. At each stage, evaluation is performed and revisions made, so that the outcomes of instruction match the identified needs as closely as possible. One type of systematic ISD model, accepted as the foundation of the practice, is known by its acronym, ADDIE (analysis, design, development, implement and evaluation). This model is applied widely as the basis of training design for industrial and commercial praxis and so is often familiar to managers and employees in SMEs.

TRANSFER OF LEARNING

As the evaluation of instructional programmes has developed and improved, it has become apparent that instructional programmes alone cannot meet a variety of needs. Regardless of how well certain programmes were designed, learning did not always result in improved performance. Indeed, as instructional designers became adept at identifying problems, it was discovered that the whole variety of instructional solutions could solve only a group of these problems. The core problem is that the transfer of knowledge from training to the job is much more complex than was anticipated in the original formulation of the ISD model, and this is a major theme of cognitive research.

Why is the transfer of learning in the workplace so low? The search for answers has prompted a critical assessment of the effectiveness of learning transfer. Few experienced managers, for instance, believe that they can easily convert underqualified and inexperienced employees into star performers by training alone. Transferability can be viewed as an individual competence, as well as being the most important outcome of the process of vocational education and training. Viewed in these terms, transfer is the process that effects transferability, and can be defined as a phenomenon involving change in the execution of a task as a result of the prior performance of a different task (Gick and Hollyoak, 1987: 9–47).

Transfer of training is the effective and continuing application by trainees to their work, of the knowledge and skills gained in training, both on and off the job. Whereas learning might be seen in part as knowledge acquisition, transfer is something that occurs later, when the knowledge has to be used in practice. In some types of training, such as in technical skills with clearly defined procedures, the workplace provides support for immediate transfer. An assembly-line worker, for example, can apply statistical process-control skills straight away and the performance shows immediately. Similarly, a secretary can use word-processing skills directly and the effect on performance is observable. In these cases, transfer problems can be identified promptly and corrective action taken speedily. In other technical situations, however, the transfer problems are not immediately recognized or effectively addressed. An assembly worker may make mistakes in calculations that are not found promptly and cannot be traced to an individual or particular site. Similarly, the supervisor of the secretary may discover repeated errors, but may not know what corrective action to take (Broad and Newstrom, 1992: 5–11).

A distinction arises between 'far-transfer', the creative use of knowledge, and 'near-transfer', the routine use of knowledge. Far-transfer arises when knowledge is successfully applied to a highly unusual problem. A manager who might learn the principles of economics and apply this knowledge in social and personal interactions is likely to participate in far-transfer. A manager facing a more predictable aspect of the job, which requires a more routine application of knowledge, is likely to engage in near-transfer. When people are trained for job-specific performance involving near-transfer it seems that they are less able to make adaptations to their performance to accommodate unanticipated changes or novel situations. The repetitive practice of a skill on similar types of problems apparently hinders creativity. Similarly, when creativity is encouraged through assigning people to constantly changing problems and environments, the performance for a specific problem is retarded. In curriculum design, the task of enhancing creative problem-solving and at the same time promoting practical skill lies in achieving a balance between the two; on the one hand, for near-transfer, providing opportunities to work on certain problems that enhance practical skill and on the other hand, for far-transfer, providing as wide a range of creative problems as possible.

Research finds that learning transfer is more likely to occur when certain strategies for enhancing it are present (Tennant, 1999). These strategies include that: learners are exposed to 'authentic' activities with the opportunity to access a full range of learning resources; learners are presented with multiple situations and multiple examples; there is a capacity to learn from experience, by practice, analysing experience and developing strategies for learning; learners have the capacity to be self-directed and control their own learning; and that a supportive climate for transfer also exists, such as supervisor support, opportunity to use learning, peer support, supervisor sanctions, positive personal outcomes, as well as the encouragement of further learning.

Transfer appears to be enhanced when training involves multiple examples and encourages learners to reflect on the potential for transfer (Anderson et al., 1996: 5–11). The amount of transfer depends on the attention directed at it during the learning event and the amount of practice with the target task. Combining abstract instruction with concrete examples is better than either one alone. Moreover, training for skills to be applied in complex social environments is best done with a combination of individual training and training in social settings.

Traditional training approaches in support of performance change are claimed not to work, mainly because they are not system-oriented in their approach to resolving performance problems (Rummler and Brache, 1995). Hence, an emphasis on the full diagnosis of performance problems led to a genre of performance-consulting approaches aimed at improving organizational performance (Brinkerhoff and Gill, 1994; Mager and Pipe, 1970; Robinson and Robinson, 1995). The aim is to achieve improvement by means of organizational analysis of a system, the identification of obstacles to performance and the indication of suitable solutions for operational impact.

HUMAN PERFORMANCE TECHNOLOGY

Efforts to improve performance in the workplace has given rise to a field of practice called human performance technology (HPT). The foundations of the practice derive from general systems theory applied to organizations, groups of people and technology (Checkland, 1981). Although HPT is concerned with systems, it applies to productivity-oriented systems, which make it especially relevant for commerce and industry, where organizational goals and objectives are generally well defined. The development of the ISD model is widely regarded as essential to the establishment of the field, with other major influences from learning psychology, analytical systems, information technology, cognitive engineering, human factors, feedback systems, organizational development and change (Stolovitch and Keeps, 1992: 3–13).

Human performance technologists adopt a systems view of performance gaps. They systematically analyse the gap and the system, and aim to design cost-effective and efficient methods to close that gap. Viewed in this way, HPT is a form of engineering approach to achieving certain attainments from human performances. The core of the approach is a performance audit to identify what the system is currently accomplishing and what the system needs to have done (Gilbert, 1978). A realistic level of exemplary performance is identified and measured, and the potential for improvement determined and translated into a measure of economic savings.

ADULT EDUCATION AND ANDRAGOGY

Adult learners require a particular set of processes and practices, which together constitute a characteristic form of education termed 'andragogy' (Knowles, 1980). Consequently, Knowles restricted the term 'pedagogy' to the teaching and learning of young people. This 'pedagogical' model was designed for teaching children, with the teacher having full responsibility for content, method, timing and the evaluation of learning and students having little or no input into the curriculum. Knowles theorized that adults need to self-direct their learning, know the purpose of what they are learning, apply their relevant experiences to their learning and require a problem-centred approach and he termed these processes 'andragogical'. The two models of learning lie on a continuum, where pedagogical methods are used with the less mature mind and andragogical methods reflect the adult's needs as a self-directed learner.

The humanistic approach and applications of experiential learning appear to influence the views of Knowles. The andragogical model is based on a set of assumptions, in which adult individuals are perceived as autonomous learners who desire self-improvement, are self-directed and not influenced by social structures. Each person is considered unique, and individual differences are respected and nurtured to self-fulfilment. The precepts of the theory are that adults need to know why they need to learn something, maintain the concept of responsibility for their own decisions and enter the educational activity with a greater number of and more varied experiences than children. Moreover, adults have a readiness to learn things that they need to know in order to cope effectively with real-life situations, are life-centred in their orientation to learning and are more responsive to internal rather than external motivators.

The facilitation of learning by andragogy involves a set of procedures for involving adult students in learning (Knowles, 1990). These techniques are climate setting, involving learners in mutual planning, in diagnosing their own needs for learning and formulating their objectives. It involves learners in designing learning plans, helping them carry out their learning plans and involving them in evaluating their learning. The process of facilitation emphasizes the relationship that exists between the learner and facilitator. This places the responsibility on the facilitator to provide an accepting, respecting, helping and social atmosphere. These themes are developed for e-learning in chapter 11.

The principles of andragogy laid out by Knowles form an integrated concept of the operational role of the andragogical teacher. They are intended to have general application in the education of adults and, as such, all may not be appropriate to every e-learning situation. The themes from adult learning theory that appear relevant to e-learning are its learner-centred approach, with self-directed learning and recognition of the prior experience of the learner. The case against the andragogy model, however, is based on its alleged limited applicability and its failure to provide a social rather than a personal objective for education (Tennant, 1997). There also seems to be a lack of quantitative evidence in the literature on the effectiveness, or otherwise, of SDL.

LEARNING STYLES

The learning-styles approach emphasizes that individuals perceive and process information in very different ways. It implies that what an individual learns in an educational experience is geared towards that individual's learning style. 'Learning styles' has its basis in the classification of psychological types, with a style being the preferred way an individual organizes experience. It is distinct from ability and appears to be a relatively stable trait that affects everything that the individual does. Style can be divided into two concepts: cognitive and learning styles, terms that are frequently, but incorrectly, used interchangeably (Messick, 1984: 59–74).

Cognitive style refers to consistent individual differences in the ways of organizing experiences into meanings, values, skills and strategies. Such cognitive styles are considered to be more stable traits and refer to an individual's typical method of acquiring and processing information. On the other hand, learning style refers to broader preferences for modes for learning. They do refer to consistent individual differences in the ways of changing meanings, values, skills and strategies.

Cognitive and learning styles are value-neutral, so that there is no best way to learn for everyone. Individual adults are able to learn effectively, whatever their preferred style. Each style, however, may be an advantage in certain circumstances and a disadvantage in others. A central premise of learning style is that individual learner preferences will lead individuals to being less effective in learning situations that require them to depart from their preferred learning strategies and style. Adults tend, moreover, to select learning situations that are congruent with their own preferred style. It is likely, however, that individuals will find themselves in circumstances outside their preferred learning style. In such cases, unless a broader array of learning skills is acquired, they may struggle if there is a mismatch with their natural style.

Adults, it is commonly accepted, have a tremendous variety of attitudes, abilities and approaches, and this diversity extends to learning styles. Indeed, most individuals adopt a mix of styles for learning (Honey and Mumford, 1982). There are 'activists', people who like to get involved immediately, with the attributes of enthusiasm, gregariousness, open-mindedness, short-term attention, barnstormers who may prefer novelty to quality. 'Reflectors' are people who observe others in action, collect data, think over it, are cautious and quiet and, when they act, do so with a broad perspective and with some awareness of the implications. 'Theorists' are individuals who are systematic and logical, serious and objective, and suspicious of subjectivity. They prefer to work from first principles and compare suggestions against these constantly, and become troubled if events do not match with their constructed and expected rational reality. 'Pragmatists' like to test ideas by experimentation and are less likely to engage in extensive prior discussion; a typical response to a problem is to perceive it as a challenging opportunity and to do something practical in response.

Extensive research into learning styles has established that people learn in different ways. Structured learning opportunities are said to benefit certain types of students, while others prefer self-organized processes. Modules are available for diagnosing learning-style inventories, designed to help people develop their learning, behavioural skills and capabilities (*www.peterhoney.com*). There is a well-known divide between holistic and sequential approaches to learning, and then there are the visual, auditory and tactile learning preferences. In terms of the perceptions by learners of the media, it is also clear that differences exist. These different perceptions affect the amount of mental effort the learner will make in engaging with material in any one form (Mason, 1994: 118).

The variety amongst adult learners is enormous, yet the greater the knowledge about students, the better it is for e-learning practitioners for planning and design purposes. With a wide variety of students and content, an e-learning delivery team needs sufficient variety to cope with the design and support of provision. Curriculum design should try to connect with all four learning styles by using various combinations of experience, reflection, conceptualization and experimentation with different media.

EXPERIENTIAL APPROACH

The premise that adults learn best when new information is presented in a real-life context has led to the experiential approach becoming practised widely in adult learning. Experiential learning involves learning as a cyclical process (Kolb, 1984). Learning, in this model, is concerned with the interaction of content and experience, in which the job of an educator is to transmit new ideas and modify old notions that may inhibit the new. To determine an individual's learning style, a student completes an instrument called Kolb's Learning Style Inventory (KLSI) (Kolb, 1976). This includes four learning styles. A 'converger' is someone who wants to solve a problem and who relies on hypothetical–deductive reasoning to focus on specific problems. A 'diverger' solves problems by viewing situations from many perspectives, and relies heavily on brainstorming and the generation of ideas. An 'assimilator' solves problems by inductive reasoning and an ability to create theoretical models. An 'accommodator' experiments and carries out plans adapted to specific circumstances to solve problems.

Kolb's experiential learning model provides a model for experiential learning research and for experiential learning practice (Kolb et al., 1979). Kolb also defined a four-phase learning cycle: 'concrete experience', where a perceiver absorbs information through direct experience by doing, acting, sensing and feeling, and possible e-learning content takes the form of simulation, case study or demonstration; 'reflective observation', making sense of an experience by reflecting on and thinking about it, and an e-learning approach might take the form of discussion in small groups, or as designated observers; 'formation of abstract concepts and generalization', where an abstract perceiver takes in information through analysis, observation and thinking, and an e-learning approach might take the form of sharing e-learning content; and 'active experimentation' by testing implications of new concepts in new situations by applying theories to make decisions and solve problems. An active processor makes sense of an experience by immediately using the new information in learning by doing or results driving the influence of learning, and e-learning may include practice sessions or on-the-job experience.

These four phases are tied into learning styles. A converger favours a learning cycle of active conceptualization and experimentation, for example, since these two cycles involve learning by doing and thinking. Students prefer one learning style to another, but can move between learning cycles in the process of growth. Critics of the KLSI indicate that there is low test–retest reliability (Ruble and Stout, 1993: 115–17) or that there is little correlation between factors that should correlate with learning styles. HRD practitioners, however, increasingly emphasize experiential learning as a means to improve the performance change after training. For e-learning course design, the model can be applied at a course level so that the learning experience is designed to include the four phases.

PRIOR EXPERIENCE

The prior experience of an adult can serve to shape or inhibit new learning. Each individual has a potential which, if fully realized, would bring benefits to the individual and also to the working group in the organization (Argyris, 1991). The personal development of an individual is affected by the kind of situation in which a person works. Argyris identifies the importance of overcoming an inherent tendency in an individual to resist new learning that challenges the existing mental schema that have resulted from prior experience. The terms 'single-loop' and 'double-loop' learning describe two relevant effects: 'single-loop learning' is narrow problem-solving in identifying and correcting errors in the external environment that fits in with prior experience and existing values; 'double-loop learning' involves the learner reflecting critically on his or her own behaviour, in order to identify how they might go about identifying and solving problems. Commonly, 'double-loop learning' will require learners to change their mental schema in a fundamental way (Argyris, 1982). Prior experience that shapes the bias of an adult towards new learning is, therefore, an increasingly important area in the field of professional development.

Related work concentrates on 'knowing in action', which is the type of automatic response that allows the performance of daily actions (Schön, 1987). In contrast, 'reflection in action' involves reflecting while performing to determine when existing schema are not appropriate and to change the schema as appropriate. He propounds that the most effective practitioners and learners are those who are successful at 'knowing-in-action' and 'double-loop learning'.

Mental models are one of the core characteristics of an individual's experiences and allow an employee to perform efficiently on a day-to-day basis (Senge, 1990). These may also be responsible for inhibiting change, since many people will resist this if it does not correspond to their mental model. To become more effective as a learner, an individual needs to identify his or her mental model, test it and then learn to change the model. E-learning can offer learner-management arrangements that allow the performance of an individual, group or whole organization to be assessed, monitored and adapted with appropriate content.

COLLABORATIVE AND COOPERATIVE LEARNING

'Collaborative learning' and 'cooperative learning' have become fudged in popular usage so that distinctions are not often made between them. Collaborative learning is an umbrella term for many forms of learning, ranging from small-group projects to a more specific form of group work, called cooperative learning, and is often mentioned as a characteristic of adult education (Brookfield, 1986). It has roots in a number of movements, such as student-centred learning and problem-centred learning, and assumes that knowledge is socially constructed by communities of individuals. The characteristics of collaborative learning are that tutors and learners become active participants in the educational process as the hierarchy between them is eliminated and a sense of community is created (Imel, 1991).

E-learning makes creating a community of learners much easier by facilitating learner-to-learner electronic interactions. Various forms of collaborative learning can provide students with the opportunity to think for themselves, compare their thinking with others, conduct small research projects and investigate subject matter with fellow students. It can provide activities that develop better judgement through confronting biases and the accuracy of their understanding about previous learning. There is, however, little empirical evidence on the effectiveness of collaborative learning on learning outcomes in adult education.

Cooperative learning exists when students work together to achieve joint learning in groups (Johnson and Johnson, 1983). Groups are given structured tasks to perform and members often receive designated roles, and the completion of the group task requires that group members work interdependently (Stahl, 1994). Both the group as a whole and individual members are held accountable for completing the activities and demonstrating a satisfactory level of learning. Groups are asked to complete written evaluations on how well the group worked as a team and on the contribution level of each group member. Consequently, cooperative learning is a specific type of small-group learning with the distinctive elements of positive interdependence, individual accountability, structured activity, teamwork skills and group processing.

CONTEXTUAL LEARNING

The most common theme from adult learning theory is that teaching ought to be much more self-directed and that participants probably learn better as a result of more learner control. When applied to SMEs, one of the challenges for designers of e-learning programmes is that teaching is no longer the transmission of unchallenged information. Practitioners have a responsibility to give their clients more effective involvement in education. SME clients, in general, have greater experience of training and ISD as a process to aid employee development than of other forms, but their overriding concern is on the effectiveness of the learning process on workplace performance. In practice they seek contextual learning, rather than educational theories.

For practitioners, a variety of learning technologies can be applied to support all manner of learning and teaching methodologies for adult learners. There are new opportunities and challenges. Internet-based delivery, for example, gives the opportunity for students to network together and explore the variety of knowledge that comes from very many different sources. Students need critical and analytical skills to do this. The challenge in this case is that there are so many sources on the Internet that students need to be able to make critical judgements on their value.

5

E-learning and computer technologies

Advances in technology over the past twenty years have aided the presentation and storage of information for learning. Indirect applications, in the form of improved overhead projectors, software presentation tools, calculators, personal computers and photocopiers, have assisted learning indirectly. Formal learning, however, appears less affected by technology than have been other dimensions of everyday life. There are exceptions in delivery methods for flexible and distance learning, especially by e-learning, where digital technologies are applied enthusiastically for the management, communication and transfer of learning. Learning technologies are based around communication components that use computer, telephone, video or Internet technologies, either singly or in combinations. Applications extend to many client groups; for small firms, they are an important design choice and certain cases are examined here.

COMMUNICATION SYSTEMS AND LEARNING

E-learning needs a communication process to convey information. Indeed, a form of communication system is essential for all teaching methods; only the components vary with the application. A system is needed for digital data exchange between two PCs, such as when a student might seek to download content, or e-mail a course assignment. Similarly, a system is needed when information is conveyed in face-to-face conversation between a teacher and student. The components used in these two systems are markedly different, as the information is carried in data and speech respectively. Nevertheless, everyday life depends on communication systems to carry information by means of the telephone, radio, television and computer for education and entertainment in both our personal and professional lives. In fact, there is a complete field of academic study, Information Theory, which deals with the transmission of messages through communication systems (Shannon, 1948: 379–423).

Communication systems consist of a number of generic components. The source of messages is the person, or machine, that produces information contained in the message. An encoder associates each message with an object that is suitable for transmission over a channel. This object can be a series of sounds, as in speech, or a sequence of binary digits in digital computer applications. The channel is the medium over which the coded message is transmitted. A decoder operates on the output of the channel and attempts to extract the original message for delivery to the destination. This whole communication process can be disrupted, however, because of the effect of noise, a term for anything that produces errors in the message. The system is the sum of the components and mechanisms that link the source of information to the destination.

Communication is not always an electronic issue. The same systemic model is applied in marketing communications. In educational marketing, the message can comprise a promotional campaign for a recruitment programme from a Website, or information to persuade people to participate in an e-learning videoconference link, and so on. Marketing messages are encoded and sent to target audiences, who decode them and then, it is hoped, respond. Marketing communications can also be applied across cultures, but these cases can generate more complex issues. There are clearly greater chances for misunderstanding the meaning of a message and so greater care is needed in scripting content. The practice raises profound questions for providers of e-learning who target international students over the efficient use of uniform content for delivery to all cultures, or the extent of local customization and support that can offer greater personalization and tailoring.

DIGITAL CONVERGENCE

Digital technology, with its capacity for countless replication, easy storage and retrieval, has pushed analogue communication techniques out of most application areas. The emergence of international video compression and decoding standards, such as the MPEG family of standards for the digital coding of moving images, makes it possible to transport digital video and multimedia as well as to standardize low-cost receiver devices, such as PC cards, or plug-in software components. When images are encoded in this format they can be manipulated, modified and transmitted in the same way as other digital information. Once encoded, the systems that store and convey the information are insensitive to the content of the source material. The practice of digital source encoding forms the basis of a convergence in the media. Media convergence, however, is an elusive term to define. The expression is often assumed to describe the 'ability of different network platforms to carry essentially similar services, or the coming together of consumer devices such as the telephone, television and personal computer' (EC, 1997: a). It is driven by the availability of cheaper, faster and smarter technology components throughout the media supply chain. Convergence brings direct benefits for consumers in the form of lower prices, more features and greater choice. There are also less costly cameras, PC-based recording and editing hardware, and a substantial drop in the costs of digital memory, that lower the entry threshold for new entrants wanting to be e-learning producers.

Convergence is also apparent in courseware authoring. Desktop publishing and word-processing applications, such as Adobe Pagemaker and Microsoft Word, give the option of converting text documents to HTML. Likewise, the multimedia authoring applications, Macromedia Director and Asymetrix Toolbox, can produce multimedia episodes that can be delivered by the Web. Books with CD-ROMs linked to a Website can provide additional learning resources. Other high-capacity storage media may be used for the distribution of courseware such as DVD-ROMs, ZIP disks or JAZ cartridges. The convergence of synchronous communication and video-on-demand is another nexus of importance for education. Teachers can record real-time delivery and then make it available for further use by students through an asynchronous Web environment. Consequently, an educational service-provider can create its own library of classroom presentations and interactive instruction.

DISPARITIES ACROSS THE MEDIUM

Technology in support of learning is leading to another point of convergence between on-campus and off-campus teaching. There are still important differences, however, in the requirements of campus and distance students. Applications that run over fibre-optic cable or fast Ethernet on-campus will probably perform poorly over a narrowband public telecommunications network. A learner on a campus-based local area network (LAN), or corporate Intranet, will be able to receive more content-rich learning material in a certain time than a learner at the end of a slow-speed modem. Hence, complications may arise when learners on the same programme, in different locations, have different network connections and capabilities. Care needs to be taken when targeting distance students.

The speed and time of transfer over a channel are directly related to content complexity. Consequently, designs that are effective for campus applications do not necessarily transfer to Internet-supported distance education. A simplified layout, designed with minimal graphics to facilitate downloading by a distance learner, may serve a dual purpose for on- and off-campus use. For distance learners, special attention to the front page of a Website is merited in order to prevent excessive waiting times. The initial page should display a very limited number of objects, such as icons, GIF files and JPEG images. A course designer can reduce the amount of data that needs to be downloaded and, with it, the time that a learner spends waiting, by using care in design and with graphics. These student-friendly factors are important for a designer to examine in the initial design of a course.

Practitioners of distance education face a big inequality in resources across a communications link. The provider has all the resources for digital delivery: the content, learner management, expert opinion, academic validation and technical support. In contrast, a distance learner operates with combinations of resource constraints that can arise from the infrastructure, interface and inexperience. This can be a frustrating experience for non-technical newcomers, because the learner needs to know enough about the infrastructure layer to be able to troubleshoot common problems. A novice e-learner may lack the expertise to resolve interface problems, and also be unable to set up the learning exchange, which means that new learners must know where to get help for problems they encounter.

DIFFERENT DIGITAL SIGNALLING RATES

Computer communication systems involve a two-way flow of data. Developments in communications have lagged behind those in computer technology because of the slower pace of the physical upgrading of telecommunications networks. In reality, it is bandwidth as a measure of the information-carrying capacity of a channel that is critical to the performance of the delivery of an e-learning service. Bandwidth determines the digital signalling speed and dictates the time needed to receive a certain message.

Compression techniques are extensively used to give greater apparent bandwidth than the communication channel actually supports, such as in the common V90 modem connection, which provides 56 kbps over a dial-up telephone circuit. Even though over 80 per cent of SMEs in the UK have access to the Internet, most are likely to be using a dial-up telephone line, with a modem and an Internet connection provided by an Internet Service Provider. The same is true currently for the majority of home Internet users. After a slow start, between the cable companies NTL and Telewest who offer cable modems and BT broadband services, in 2003 there were nearly 1.5 million homes and small businesses in Britain with broadband facilities (Durman, 2003: 9).

The problem with a narrowband connection is slow speed, most noticeable in the time spent in waiting for large files to download. This can be problematic; for example, an SME involved in the publishing business will frequently deal with large data files, containing a mixture of graphics and text to be transferred, and this may require the high cost of a leased line. On narrowband, the download of a single large file can take hours. This may require the recipient to make individual contact with an ISP to alert them. Therefore, speed is often a critical requirement for an e-learning system delivery because access times can be a problem in distribution to premises and homes. The only way to gain a substantial increase in data rate above current modem speeds is to move away from dial-up connections into broadband.

BROADBAND

Bandwidth can be improved dramatically with a broadband connection to a telecommunications network. Digital signalling rates can be more than ten times faster. As the connection is always on with broadband, there is no requirement to dial up to make a network connection. Faster rates bring a range of other advantages: quicker access to Web-pages, the transfer of large e-mail attachments, quicker responses to customers, or the use of IRC to chat with customers. Broadband allows a subscriber to create a virtual private network with other offices. There are other benefits, such as access to application service providers (ASPs) to rent online packages, or to have data backed up automatically to a remote location.

There are a variety of broadband communication services available at present in the UK; for example:

ADSL technology converts an existing telephone line into a higher bandwidth channel. The service is asymmetric, with more bandwidth from server-to-client than client-to-server. This means that download speeds are much faster than upload, typically 512 kbps download and 256 kbps upload. To obtain the service, however, the client must be within five kilometres of a service connection point.

A *cable modem* also offers asymmetric speeds of 512 kbps downstream and typically 128 kbps upstream, wherever cable is available.

Satellite is becoming available for broadband format through an asymmetric service, with data signalling at 256 kbps to 2 Mbps downstream and 64 kbps to 320 kbps upstream.

Wireless Ethernet, or Wi-Fi, is appearing across the UK to create Wi-Fi hot spots. These allow a small community of users to share one broadband connection by using inexpensive wireless cards to create local area networks. Amongst the different, wireless network standards, Wi-Fi Ethernet is the most widely adopted, using the IEEE 802.11b standard. In practice, indoor distances range from dozens to several hundred feet and outdoors up to several kilometres, with the distance covered depending on impediments and line of sight.

Lease lines offer a secure connection between two or more points for a high fee, based on agreed data rates, which are usually from 512 kbps upwards.

This list of approaches may create an impression that is overly favourable of the real options available from different services. A chronic problem for the rural areas that cover most of Wales is that these services are either simply not available, or are too expensive for the small firm, or home learner. Rural telecommunication services lag behind those for an urban conurbation, with the result that the media for distance learning continue to be constrained, both in bandwidth and application, long after urban improvements. Learning technologies offer many advantages to rural and isolated distance-learning students. They offer the possibility of sharing scarce resources in the form of subject specialists, digitized resources or student experiences, for example. However, they may simply serve to widen the equity gap between rural and urban life. For many small rural firms, therefore, the extant challenge is to try to prosper with narrowband in a broadband world.

INTERACTIVITY

The degree of interactivity in an e-learning offer is a primary decision for a provider. As interaction increases, so do the expense of systems and the cost of expert time to support the level of interaction. Just what constitutes inter-activity, though, is not always clear. For some people, interactivity is enabling learners and teachers to share ideas in a virtual chatroom. For others, it represents posting questions on a bulletin board. Interactivity exists between the student and the learning content in its various forms. There is also interaction between the teacher and the learner as well as between students, either in self-help groups, collaborative work projects or discussions.

Table 5.1. E-learning collaboration types (after Johansen et al., 1991)

Synchronous: higher co-presence, lower convenience

1.	Same time, same place.	Traditional face-to-face classroom teaching, tutor support for blended learning, or supervised simulations in a learning centre.
2.	Same time, different place.	Technology-enabled remote access by video- or audioconference, computer conference, video streaming, Web publishing.

Asynchronous: lower co-presence, higher convenience

3.	Different time, different place.	Distance-learning provision for non-campus-based learners. Chatrooms, e-mail, threaded discussion, whiteboard, video streaming, Web publishing.
4.	Different time, same place.	Flexible, open and distributed learning arrange-ments with e-mail, chatrooms, video streaming, Web publishing.

Interactivity is, therefore, influenced by a number of variables. The decision regarding which e-learning platform to use depends on these variables. The technology resources available to the decision-maker provide one set of parameters. The characteristics of the target audience, including the size of the target group of learners that need support and the intended impact on students, provide other criteria. The type of content to be delivered comprises yet another set. The compromise facing many decision-makers is one of collaboration, or convenience. Students want the flexibility of asynchronous learning, but often seek the co-presence added by the human component of a synchronous solution. Writing about teams and technology, Johansen et al. described four different collaboration arrangements of location and time (Johansen et al., 1991) (Table 5.1). These provide different examples of learning arrangements, student experience and degrees of co-presence.

SYNCHRONOUS LEARNING

Synchronous operations can involve substantial human interaction, but impose time constraints on the participants. The process is conducted in real time and requires students to log on to the Internet, or join a videoconference system or a conference call, at a specific time in order to participate in a class exchange. The format resembles a conventional classroom situation and the learner can behave in the same way as in a traditional classroom, only the tutor is not in the same room. Learners can engage with peers and with the tutor in real time in a virtual classroom, allowing students to ask questions and receive answers, or contribute to a discussion. While it can still be convenient compared to face-to-face instruction, it is more restrictive due to the need for timetabling and scheduling time of the log-on sessions. As a result, the solution often adopted is to programme synchronous sessions with a long advisory schedule in advance, on the time and topic of events.

Synchronous learning is suited to learners who need structure and immediate feedback in order to enhance the quality of their online learning. Synchronous techniques can help create the co-presence that technology-supported learning solutions often lack (Ruttenbur et al., 2000: 81). A basic approach is the use of collaboration features, such as chatrooms and e-mail exchanges conducted live online. A growing number of systems add synchronous audio, or live video, in broadband applications that link participants and the instructor in a real-time virtual classroom. Collaboration tools enable employees to communicate with others, sharing ideas and learning from each other in a way that creates an online community environment. Online tutors and mentors serve as a resource to answer questions and can give feedback to keep the learner involved and motivated sufficiently to complete the course.

Several companies provide synchronous and asynchronous delivery technologies. These firms aim essentially to bring the classroom online, providing live collaboration which includes functions such as voice over the Internet, software-application sharing, real-time data exchange and shared work-spaces. While not as flexible and convenient as asynchronous delivery, synchronous delivery is more interactive and personal, appropriate for one-to-one customer and sales interactions, seminar and presentation events, and learning and interactive teamwork sessions. Examples of companies that provide synchronous platforms are Centra Software (*www.centra.com*), NetMeeting (*www.microsoft.com/windows/netmeeting/default.asp*), Tegrity (*www.tegrity.com*) and WBT Systems (*www.wbtsystems.com*).

ASYNCHRONOUS LEARNING

Asynchronous learning is two-way communication, with a time delay between the transmission and reception of a message. Learners interact with the tutor, or other students, by means of a bulletin board or e-mail, but no real-time collaboration tool is necessary. This has benefits in terms of accessibility, but the drawback of less human interaction. Asynchronous learning is for people who seek flexibility in the time and place for learning, but still want access to instructors, colleagues and other learning resources that help their learning processes. Asynchronous is well suited for someone who travels extensively, or who has an erratic schedule that precludes commitment to a fixed learning schedule. A learner following an asynchronous distance-learning engagement needs to be a self-starter with self-discipline, however, since time structure will often be absent. Home-grown asynchronous solutions are very common. Some firms license pure asynchronous platforms that are independent of content, such as Eloquent (*www.eloquent.com*), Tegrity (*www.tegrity.com*) and Lotus LearningSpace (*www.lotus.com*).

MEDIA FOR TECHNOLOGY-SUPPORTED LEARNING

Learning technologies cover a wide variety of delivery media and tools to create content in electronic form. Each technology has different characteristics, which to a greater or lesser extent makes each appropriate for a particular learning need. These techniques are sometimes used singly and at other times together. Technology-supported learning (TSL) and face-to-face delivery methods have different attributes, for example, so that an approach that combines the two may lead to the creation of more imaginative educational or training events. In general, combining techniques can build on the strengths and reduce the limitations of a single method.

The presentational technologies and delivery methods for e-learning yield a range of options for course designers. The actual design choice emerges from various factors that include the degree of interaction, the value of the application and the likely number of learners in the target audience. In certain applications, the time-value of information determines the speed at which the information needs to be disseminated. This may then require subject specialists to create content directly, often by choosing the simpler media, like documentation. Each application affects teaching and learning, but they all require a view of teaching and learning as reaching out from the conventional classroom, as the following activities demonstrate.

E-mail

E-mail involves one-to-one or one-to-many communication between computer users, and is in extensive use in teaching and learning as a way of achieving dialogue between a teacher and learner, or between groups of learners. It can supplement conventional teaching and support communications for class announcements, for example, in distance learning. E-mail can also be used for administrative purposes in storing and archiving discussions, as well as sending out documents and other types of file. Tutors can set up a bulletin board that allows a tutor to post announcements to all members of a class.

E-mail is a relatively simple but powerful method for question-and-answer techniques. In learning applications, questions posed by a student can be left for a tutor to be answered at a later time. Indeed, these question-and-answer exchanges from individual students can be stored together for the whole course to see. The use of e-mail for creating dialogue in distance learning has other benefits. With international students across different time-zones, the students can determine the time of an interaction. There is more opportunity to reflect on a question and provide a well-considered answer. This feature seems particularly important in language learning. The experience of support- ing international students is that the time delay makes it possible for them to be reflective over the culture differences and to prepare their answers carefully in response to questions.

One learning-development technique that uses e-mail as a key technology is e-mentoring. This is relatively widespread in the USA, but less so in Europe and the UK. Elements that seem to make e-mentoring successful are the appropriate technology for sending periodic e-mails, and the commitment of both parties to the programme. The term e-moderating is applied by the Open University as a structured approach for developing a tutor–learner support relationship by computer-mediated communications (CMC) for distance learners (Salmon, 2000). Another application is Mentornet (*www.mentornet.- net*), which pairs women studying engineering with mentors in large compa- nies. The e-mentor follows a relatively simple model, in which one learner-client is matched with one mentor. The mentor and learner exchange weekly e-mail correspondence. Mentors provide prompts that direct some communications and arrange one or two face-to-face meetings to provide a personal connection. Finally, an evaluation is done, with recognition of success on completion of the programme.

Threaded discussion is an asynchronous tool that allows a tutor to post assignments to an entire class. Documents and other types of file can also be attached and sent to students. These can be located at a central site, where the class can view the assignments and respond at convenient times. All responses can be recorded and viewed by the tutor and class. It can be used for posting discussion questions for students and for students following collaborative projects. A chatroom is a synchronous tool that requires participants to be online at the same time. Communication is commonly by typed text, or by voice, or by a combination of the two. The tool allows small-group collaboration with a high level of interaction, in which experts at a distance can be invited to present to a class.

The Metä Institute Silva uses a collaborative document-sharing system to train employees during on-the-job apprenticeship periods (James, 2000). Coordinators set learners written tasks, and they send the answer back as an attachment for correction. After approval, the learner saves the answer into an online learning diary. A workplace-based mentor also has access to the diary, in order to check technical details in the answer.

Presentational software

Presentational software is one of a number of general tools, along with word processing and spreadsheets, that are increasingly important in education, but require some creative thinking from the teacher on their application. Their educational value lies in their use, because these tools do not have content. They do make it relatively easy for a practitioner to take text-based materials, add HTML code and post them on a Website.

One of the chief challenges for a practitioner is to consider the ways to break down subject matter into sub-tasks, in a way that makes the information effective. One approach, based on information processing theory, is for the designer to break the content down into manageable chunks that are based on what the student does with the information. Applying such task analysis follows three steps: defining what the student will do with the information; breaking the task down into a logical sequence; and working out how to chunk the information for delivery. Key words can also help form a structure, so that a hyperlink can be made from certain terms to take a student on to further exploration. Frequently asked questions (FAQs), where hyperlinks are attached to a number of questions that students often ask and which lead on to the answers, may also be used.

As a learning technology, presentational software is in ubiquitous use. Microsoft PowerPoint is a relatively easy way to convert course content into an electronic course form. Text alone gives very low user retention, although it can be improved with the use of graphics. Slides can be created and converted for publishing, with study notes, on the Web. However, to exploit the full potential of incorporating graphics, charts, video excerpts, audio clips and animation requires a greater measure of expertise. An instructor can create complex applications for face-to-face delivery, and this normally requires a laptop PC and a data-projector. A big difference between distance and face-to-face presentations, though, is that a simple approach is often better for transfer to distance learners and saves time for them on downloads.

Multimedia: CD-ROM

Computer technology provides opportunities to combine different media technologies and allows learners to interact with them. Multimedia is a collective name for a range of systems that allow the creation, integration and manipulation of text, graphics, video and still images, sound and feedback cues (Latchem et al., 1993: 19–38). In one sense, it is an upgraded form of computer-based technology (CBT), where the issues for practitioners are concerned with hardware. 'Multimedia' also means the media used to support learning, where the issues are based on instructional design. It becomes important, therefore, to distinguish between instructional design and hardware matters. Here the central concern is multimedia for the purpose of learning.

One common applications format is the CD-ROM. When CD-ROMs and, more recently, DVDs became available, they held the prospect of holding so much data that they would be free from the limitations of floppy disks. A CD-ROM as a storage device with 650 Mbyte capacity can incorporate content and multimedia. The trend, however, has been to add as much multimedia in the form of sound, graphics and video as possible, at the expense of instructional content. Such an approach can rapidly fill up a CD. Most networks are not yet able to transfer video to client computers because of access download speed, but video excerpts are distributed frequently by CD-ROM courseware or by DVD. Nevertheless, video in different forms has already proved to be a cost-effective means to provide self-paced instruction and information to students.

Once a non-recordable CD-ROM stand-alone disk or DVD is produced and distributed, the instructional designer cannot change the content easily. This is a potential drawback in learning applications, because the content may become outdated quickly. Moreover, it is difficult for an educational service-provider to track the performance of a learner following this form of training. Despite the static nature of the content, its large data-storage capacity means that this form of CBT can deliver multimedia presentations without the bandwidth problems that face Web-based learning. Coding of the CD-ROM can allow hotlinks into a Web-support site, with a password for access by students. This can overcome some of the stand-alone disadvantages by introducing additional features, such as content updates, downloads for the learner and hotlinks to related sites, as well as generating information for tracking the progress of an individual or groups.

One example is a complete learning and assessment course for Microsoft Office XP applications and Windows 2000, produced by McGraw-Hill (*www.mhhe.com*). A computer-based training program teaches skills using a variety of methods and media, including text, graphics, interactivity, narration and animation. Learners can practise and improve their efficiency in a simulated and non-threatening environment. By proceeding through a series of exercises, the learner is required to apply skills to solve problems. A progress review helps to track the skills a learner has completed. An assessment component then examines the proficiency of the learner directly, on an application. There are many other CD-ROM-based learning programmes that focus on IT skills, which is a very popular application area for multimedia. For example, several different CD-ROM suppliers (*www.electricpaper.co.uk*) support the European Computer Driving Licence (ECDL) programme.

Another example from Ireland (*coaching@iol.ie*) uses practice in four companies, SIFA Fine Chemicals, Aughinish Alumina, Golden Vale PLC and Guinness, on a CD-ROM aimed at SME managers and entrepreneurs. This uses multimedia to convey its message, combining video, audio, animation and text. The intention of the program, 'Professional Tools for the Entrepreneur', is to enable SME managers to learn about best practices applied by these four leading companies and to benchmark themselves against these best practices. Topics include organizational change, business, personal development and entrepreneurship.

Video streaming

Video streaming is an application of the Internet in which video and audio are transported from one Website to another. Ideally, video and audio are streamed across the Internet from a server to a client, in response to a client request for a Web-page containing embedded videos. The client plays the incoming multimedia stream in real time as the data is received. A client uses one of the de facto standards, RealVideo, Microsoft ASF or Apple Quicktime, to view the message. To achieve this, the video material must be captured, edited and converted to a video compression standard for transmission. Full file transfer, however, often means very long, unacceptable transfer times and delays for playback.

With media streaming, organizations can record live presentations for the purposes of distributed learning over the Web. There are powerful attractions in delivering multimedia by means of the Web, but most organizations do not have the bandwidth for reception. Streaming video is an effective way to engage a learner and can create an experience similar to watching television, but limiting the bandwidth serves to make a less satisfactory viewing experience, because of small viewing windows and choppy video. There is also the danger that a sudden load of data, in the form of video files, may create a bottleneck that could cause the whole of a local network dealing with its normal day-to-day business to come to a halt.

Videoconferencing

Videoconferencing can offer access to specialist subjects to learners separated across a wide geographical area. Tutoring by videoconference has been in use across the federal campuses of the University of Wales for the past decade, in an environment designed initially to share teaching resources and enable the transfer of face-to-face delivery between five videoconference suites located on the campuses of the federal institutions around Wales. It is an application aimed at creating a virtual classroom environment, with a subject specialist on one site using a range of presentational tools, such as slides and graphics, that are then accessible to learners at remote classroom-studios.

The results in terms of online learning are very effective, although the business model for sharing and charging for teaching support determines the inter-collegial take-up of courses. In terms of the impact on the employees of companies, the primary effect lies in the opportunity to attend a campus video-suite to link into national and international presentations, or to attend a campus class using the videoconference link. This network facility was recently upgraded to form the Welsh Video Network (*www.wvn.ac.uk*), with videoconferencing and other video facilities at all further and higher institutions in Wales. The network supports eighty sites and is capable of operating via ISDN and Internet Protocol (IP) networks. It claims to be the largest single IP videoconferencing network in Europe and one of the most advanced in the world.

A recent project funded under the EU SOCRATES is establishing videoconferencing as a mechanism for the training of SME managers (*www.-tempotc.com*). Videoconferencing is used to provide distant access to campus education and as a substitute for face-to-face meetings. It is also creating new services and potential uses, including meetings, interviews and consultations. International meetings and learner exchanges can be planned and prepared, so that visitors and meetings are more informed and productive. It can be used for mentoring, where someone requires point-of-need advice and support. Moreover, it can be applied for assessment and verification procedures in work-based assessment, where these processes can be managed remotely. Master classes can be arranged by accessing a specialist who can contribute to a seminar at a distance. Interpreter services in order to translate between point-to-point locations can be provided by using multi-point conferencing. Virtual visits and cultural exchanges can be organized. Learners wishing to practise a foreign language for business and also get some engagement with cultural issues may have a virtual visit to another country. Case studies covering the use of video-conferencing range from language teaching and research methods to the teaching of mathematics and entrepreneurship (Alexander et al., 1999). Applications are likely to grow further, through the use of video-streaming applications, along with the availability of low-cost PC desktop cameras that allow more one-to-one applications.

Multicasting

Multicast is a network technology, just emerging on the Internet, which offers the prospect of greater efficiency in the distribution of content, like video, from a single source to many receivers simultaneously. Multicasting combines the best aspects of broadcast and unicast, as one copy of the data is sent and directed only to the parts of the network where there are users interested in receiving it. It is achieved because routing processes keep track of the data streams in use and adjust the data-routing rules accordingly. All the users act as peers, with each sending and receiving network traffic. This situation is common during interactive videoconferences, but is made much more efficient by the multicasting technology.

Terrestrial, cable and satellite television

Television broadcast programmes are a proven means of distributing educational programmes to reach mass audiences and cover large areas. Terrestrial television requires simpler receiving equipment and is widely available in homes, giving it more potential viewers than cable or satellite. A major obstacle for providers is the cost involved, although this is decreasing, over time, for satellite users. These result from the expense of content generation and also the costs of technology to transmit or to lease access to a channel. Nevertheless, a small number of organizations seek to provide regular schedules of learning programmes, such as the OU, in partnership with the BBC. There are others.

One current initiative is the Wales Digital College (*Coleg Digidol*). Formed by S4C and BBC Wales, together with a partnership of private companies and education-service providers, it is examining the potential of digital television and associated technologies for attracting learners at home. Programmes are broadcast on S4C digital television, from Monday to Friday mornings, and the channel offers a satellite broadcast channel to reach large numbers of potential learners. One example of programme content is an ODFL programme on the environment, designed at the University of Wales, Lampeter, in partnership with the National Botanic Garden of Wales. This created broadcast-quality video content, transmitted on S4C digital to provide trailers for learners to enrol on an accredited e-learning distance programme. The television channel, therefore, provides a promotional avenue to help recruitment to this provision.

Satellite broadcasting can be employed to deliver live business information or professional-development practice classes, spread across a wide geographical area. The Ford Motor Company uses satellite broadcasts to broadcast hundreds of hours of training a month, to distribute content to salespeople and technicians in retail outlets across North America (Conley, 1999). Viewers have a degree of interactivity because they can respond to questions on the broadcasts by electronic keypads. Across south-west England, the University of Plymouth, in conjunction with the Royal College of Surgeons, provides satellite broadcasts of medical procedures and discussion fora for practitioners (*www.plymouth.ac.uk*). Interactivity with the discussion from the receiving sites is achieved by electronic-dial telephone connection.

An alternative approach to dedicated channels, with the continuing demand for large amounts of programme content, is to have a regular programme on an existing channel. This solution is adopted in Ireland by RTE, with the programme maker AV-Edge, a spin-off company from University College, Dublin. This company produces a weekly half-hour programme on learning and development. For example, it has produced a series of case studies on the management of change in Irish and Welsh small firms, with specific strategies for coping. Each case study was broadcast as a weekly feature and provided the basis for a studio panel discussion, supplemented by telephone and e-mail contact lines to subject matter experts.

Electronic performance-support systems

Electronic performance-support systems (EPSSs) are intended to embed necessary learning into software tools that an individual uses while doing a job. The aim of a performance-support system is to help an employee along a learning curve for improved job performance. They are applied to improve employees' performance and learning at the point of demand. An EPSS can help a novice employee to work at an acceptable level or give a more experienced employee access to specialist information. A common example is a pop-up menu in a word processor that tells a user that a word is misspelled. EPSS is implemented by a computer-based system that receives, stores and distributes organizational knowledge on demand.

The information in an EPSS is directly related to an individual's performance or job responsibilities. It can be applied as part of an Internet-based learning strategy to bring information to an employee at the point of need in the workplace. Consequently, every work-based EPSS is different, and they can range from simple stand-alone procedures to complex knowledge-based systems. The Benchmarking Forum of the American Society for Training and Development (ASTD) has been collecting best practice since 1994 (*www.astd.org*). These examples of EPSS applications show that they can improve customer service by using an online guide, holding information on products and services, that is accessible to relevant staff. An EPSS may dramatically reduce the time staff need to access necessary information. A US study on the use of EPSSs in companies revealed that they are most often used in customer service, operations and sales departments, with Visual Basic reported as the most common development tool (Benson, 1997: 48–9).

Virtual reality

Business simulations are emerging that combine virtual-reality settings with traditional case-method teaching. One example is the Business Navigator Method developed by CALT. Business Navigator develops a virtual interactive business environment (VIBE) in a realistically simulated business context, which the learner is invited to explore. The research and development department at the Center for Advanced Research in Technology for Education, University of Southern Carolina, has also developed two virtual instructors, Steve and Adele, for use in training (*www.isi.edu/isd/carte*).

Simulations

Simulation programs are at the high end of interactivity, requiring constant attention by the learner, and can be very expensive to produce. This means they are developed where processes are essential to protect public safety, limit liability or risk, such as with aerospace applications, or with engineering training for the management of a chemical plant. In such cases simulation is often used to complement formal training. There are situations where synchronous simulations can provide an unmatched dimension of learning, not otherwise achievable except in extreme and hazardous positions, such as in flight or battle simulators. The additional expense of simulation, which provides high levels of comprehension and retention of information, is deemed worthwhile in view of the critical safety requirements. Reality simulation in these circumstances is deemed to be worth the high cost, simply because failure can prove even more expensive. For most industrial and commercial situations, however, the task and potential scalability of the learning content will not justify the expense of a detailed simulation.

Exceptions can be found in business training, where software simulation and games can be achieved without great cost. The Conglomerate virtual-business game simulates a commercial environment in which managers run a small multinational company and make realistic team decisions. Teams compete against one another, over a period of up to two months, and decisions made impact upon one another. They are set certain decisions online, discuss the best response and key in their answer online (*www.mbgames.com*). Another business example is the marketing strategy simulation provided by Markops, which creates a competitive scenario for gaining market share for a product manufacturer (*www.markops.com*). Tools such as these are useful even within a conventional learning environment.

Integrated electronic learning environments

Integrated electronic learning environments are a recent development in supporting the delivery of learning. They combine a range of functions needed to provide students with a full range of learning experiences and administrative support for the course. Terminology is often a problem with learning environments. The term learner-management system (LMS) is applied to tracking the performance of learners through a series of assessments, but it can be overly restrictive. Another term widely applied in the UK and used by JISC (*www.jisc.ac.uk*) is managed learning environment (MLE). This indicates that there are not only technical issues involved, but also substantive issues that affect people. MLE describes a system that uses technology to make the network of relationships between learners, teachers and organizers of learning more effective, through the integrated support of communications and activities. The implication is that the technology is managed in order to free time for teaching and research. Another term taken as synonymous with MLE is the virtual learning environment (VLE). Other terms are used interchangeably, including course management systems, learning management tools, online learning environments and collaborative learning environments.

Integrated electronic learning environments aim to provide a complete framework for online course delivery. For corporate e-learning applications, the ability to track the performance of employees through a course programme is a key advantage of e-learning in the business environment. The progress and changes in performance of individuals and groups can then be monitored in real time to provide accurate and timely management information that can contribute to calculations on the effectiveness of a programme.

Mobility by wireless

Wireless networking is becoming available to cater for the demands for mobile connections to businesses and consumers. The benefit to individuals working from offices and homes is mobility, so that e-mail and Internet access is available where it is needed. Installations can be made without the need for cables or fixed fittings. Wireless capability on laptop PCs is becoming standard, so that in many cases campus-based learners are able to become more nomadic by using wireless technologies linked to laptops. Learners can access a teaching and learning environment by means of mobile telephony in their residences, from all academic buildings and dining halls. It also allows employees who have to travel as part of their job to improve their communication links.

Mobile, or m-learning, is a term applied to learning on wireless devices, such as mobile phones and personal digital assistants (PDAs), putting the emphasis on wireless operation. M-learning has been relatively slow to grow because most wireless devices that are non-PCs have small screens, low resolution, slow processing and limited storage capacities. It appears, though, that m-learning seems suited to specific content areas such as sales or language courses. With the successful development of Bluetooth, Wireless Application Protocol (WAP), General Packet Radio System (GPRS) and Universal Mobile Telecommunication System (UMTS), the structures for wireless telephony are in place. There are many m-learning initiatives under way covering different devices and approaches (*www.ericsson.net/leonardo/thebook/chapter4.html*). For example, Global Knowledge (*www.globalknowledge.com*) selected four of its most popular courses, including Telecommunication Fundamentals and Understanding, and made them available on hand-held PDA. The aim was to give reinforcement to a course while travelling or between meetings.

Stanford Learning Lab (*www.stanford.edu*) applied mobile phones in language teaching for Spanish at the university. Testing showed that access any time, anywhere, increased daily attention to learning and boosted motivation, but highly fragmented attention with leading-edge technology can result in a frustrating experience for learners. The team concluded that keeping the design simple, with content selected to be most suitable for audio, with small chunks of learning for very distractable adults, produced the best results.

Internet and the World Wide Web

The Internet is the generic name for the global interconnection of computers, a physical network that connects users in government, companies, research organizations, universities, schools and individual homes. This physical network supports the World Wide Web as a convenient way of sharing documents over the Internet. The Web has a client–server structure. A client program, the Web-browser, on one computer requests information from a server program running on another computer that is identified by its unique address, somewhere on the Internet. The server program replies by sending the requested information back over the Internet to the original browser program, which interprets it and displays the results on a PC screen. This transfer process means that access to the Web requires a PC with a connection to the Internet and a Web-browser, such as Netscape Navigator or Microsoft Internet Explorer, on the client computer. To deliver content, a server computer is needed that stores content, which is connected to the Internet and runs a Web-server program.

The emergence of the Web depended on the idea of hypertext, that is, text which when selected results in the retrieval of a document that may be located elsewhere. It also necessitated the formation of a hypertext-distributed database that operates on standard protocols. The transformation of the Internet into a transport medium for hyperlinked documents was realized by two computer protocols: Hypertext Transfer Protocol (HTTP) and Hypertext Mark-up Language (HTML). HTTP is the set of standards for initiating the request for sending a file when a link is activated, whereas HTML defines a set of formatting commands that permit the same materials to be displayed on different computers, running different operating systems using screens with different resolutions and sizes, through a Web-browser.

The formation of the Web therefore represented the convergence of five distinct technical developments: first, the concept and development of hypertext; second, the installation of physical transport media, the Internet; third, the adoption of a common standard for communication, HTTP; fourth, the specifying and applying of a standard for the formatting of Web pages, HTML; and fifth, developing Web-server and Web-browser software.

Extended mark-up language

The Internet provides the underlying connections by which e-learning can be distributed to students. Solutions that use Internet support must operate within this network-based, client–server environment, provided by the Internet or Intranets. Deploying e-learning will also normally lead to the use of a learner-management system that usually deploys a large, scalable repository to provide a means for sharing data between different processes, tools, applications and learning content.

An e-learning framework needs to support and manage learning content, as well as administrative and management data. One key to achieving an effective framework is metadata, which allows the online learning resources to be tagged with searchable properties, such as author, publisher name, keywords, version, language and learning objectives. Metadata can be written for course objects, like a wrapper around a book, and permits a level of automation and customization of content. The metadata is a code and the de facto language of metadata is Extended Mark-up Language (XML). This is a flexible programming language that allows the user to create new kinds of descriptors that can be detected by search engines and learning management systems, though they are invisible to users. The use of standardized metadata allows an organization to tag, store and retrieve online content resources in their own repositories. XML is a language with a set of rules for defining a syntax that you choose to develop. XML, however, provides several benefits over HTML in an e-learning framework, the most attractive being its simplicity. XML can enable business data and learning content to be served, received and processed on the Web as easily as HTML over such standard Internet protocols as HTTP, and also works easily across organizational boundaries.

The reason why Extended Mark-up Language is so popular is that it makes content management easier, allowing a document to be marked up with the tags generated in-house. XML is becoming a standard format for Internet and Intranet data-information exchange. It serves as a means for representing data to provide an open, Internet-based integration of cross-enterprise e-learning applications. For instance, metadata for an e-learning course defines tags for the start and close of a module, as well as all manner of tags for a title, place and date of publication. The same content can be taken and transformed into different outputs. Examples of information and data that may be exchanged in an XML format include learning-content catalogue records, learning resources, content documents, e-commerce transactions and electronic-content administrative records.

The World Wide Web

Online learning, Web-based training, interactive distance learning and Intranet-based training at one time were separate categories. Now the distinctions and capabilities between delivery methods are becoming fuzzier, as technologies cross-fertilize. The merging of capabilities from once distinct platforms is likely to continue, particularly in converging on the use of the Internet as a communications channel. Hence, there are an increasing number of Internet-based training programmes for SME managers and employees.

The ICM Business School MBA (*www.Internet-mba.com*) is based on action learning by Internet, with learners using e-mail and web-fora to communicate with their tutor and one another. Intranet-based training lends itself to academic provision. The human–computer interaction module at the University of Teesside makes extensive use of Intranet and Internet technologies. Course materials, including augmented online lectures and self-managed study assignments, are made available on the Intranet for learners to access at a time of their choice (Barker, 1999).

One example of an interactive environment is the Business Navigator method, which combines the case study and business simulation methods (Angehrn and Nabeth, 1997: 275–85). Business Navigator comprises a virtual interactive business environment, in a simulated business context of a company, which the learner explores. Whilst this can be used on a stand-alone basis, a better option involves a multi-user dimension, allowing interaction with other learners and experts. An example of this approach is INSEAD Executive Education World (*www.insead.fr/CALT/VirtualWorlds/*) that allows virtual meetings and lectures to be conducted.

Reference material or guides are a popular way of delivering large quantities of detailed information. Text and graphics can be designed using a word processor and published directly on the Web. Italian training-provider ISTUD (*www.sviluppoimresa.com*) distributes electronic text in management-training programmes in this way. Distance-learning courses by them are aimed at SME managers and cover traditional management areas of sales strategy and marketing, with course materials sent out by e-mail.

Table 5.2. Good-practice applications arising from EU ADAPT projects (ECOTEC, 2001a, 2001b)

Case provider	Description
Richmond upon Thames College BusinessClub.com.	Business support for home-based owner-managers. Website support with business information specifically for micro-businesses.
Calderdale Colleges Corporation Pre-On Line Learning Initiative	Targeted SMEs with fewer than fifty employees, in manufacturing, retail and services. Initially an introduction to online learning. Focus shifted to equipment loan and basic training.
London Borough of Islington Agora Project *www.agora-project.co.uk*	Mobile Internet Café, targeted hard-to-reach SMEs and micro-businesses.
University of Liverpool Virtual Training Centre Laser Engineering	Online learning materials developed to train SMEs. Website supports reference base on laser engineering.
University of Westminster *www.mmk.co.uk*	Web-based delivery and portal to assist SMEs in the media industry. Guides produced on e-law.
Thames Valley University IDEAL *www.ideal.tvu.ac.uk*	Targeting of SMEs in graphic design, photography and broadcasting. Several formats including online support and CD-ROM.

Another example is Directors' Briefing, which publishes a broad range of fact-sheets, covering key business issues, such as innovation and increasing profitability, with bullet points for managers and decision-makers (*www.bizhot.co.uk*). This has migrated over the past five years from a print-based system into a Web-based system, providing information for SMEs and support agencies.

Two distinct e-learning courses in tourism and customer care for SMEs have been created at Neath Port Talbot College (*www.nptc.ac.uk*). These are collections of learning objects, each one representing twenty-one hours of learning activity. The content was carefully chosen and supported with relevant case studies. Interactive e-learning is designed to be intuitive, requiring dexterity with the mouse and very basic typing skills. Assessment is by means of multiple-choice questions, with drag-and-drop text or graphics. The most challenging task for e-learning, however, is the 'people skills' of the customer care collection of learning objects. These learning objects may impart knowledge, but skills need to be practised and perfected by students in real interactions with customers. The application of Internet-supported learning is already providing a wide range of programmes (Table 5.2).

ADVANTAGES AND PROBLEMS FOR SMES

The advantage of e-learning is the flexibility of provision in supporting SMEs (ECOTEC, 2001a). Employers in various case-studies regarded e-learning as effective because it enabled them to train key staff who could not attend a conventional course; it was also cheaper. Direct costs were reduced because the trainee did not have to travel to a location away from the firm or home. The training was of a consistent quality, which could be checked before starting. It was also available when required, at a time and place convenient to both the trainee and the employer.

Technology-supported learning for SMEs does have its problems. The initial cost of buying computers and multimedia packages can be a difficulty if this is accompanied with the concern that it may not be effective. E-learning is often an innovation for an SME, which at times has difficulty in justifying face-to-face training, and managers will be sensitive to the costs and benefits. Employees find value in going away from work, in socializing on training courses and in the out-of-hours discussion. An e-learning approach might be perceived as devalued in the eyes of both the trainee and colleagues who have a traditional view of learning. Some people have a fear of technology and as a result are not attracted by e-learning. Others perceive face-to-face teaching as personal and social, but e-learning in comparison as cold and impersonal.

A recent survey, which polled 275 human resource executives, asked whether investment in e-learning had been a success in their companies, but

45 per cent of them replied 'no' (Eglin, 2003: 6). Implementing e-learning, it seems, can be difficult, but companies learn from the experience. Managers who adopt the e-learning approach make a number of mistakes, often concentrating on hardware rather than content. This leads them to spend money on new systems before studying the precise needs of their organization and the appropriate solutions.

APPLICATIONS OF TECHNOLOGY FOR LEARNING AND BUSINESS SUPPORT

Technology applications can be categorized by their educational application, and applications can be found in areas such as communication, collaboration and special teaching applications (Collis, 1999: 36–65), demonstrating the scope for e-business in an educational enterprise (Table 5.3). Applications in e-business include marketing communication and client support, that can lead to online course-promotion and registration and real-time financial transaction. The communication process can yield a value proposition to the learner in the form of customized or a personalized service. Collaboration and network applications involving groupware and Web-based environments can create an electronic space to organize and allow members of a group to work on the same design document. Electronic publishing offers the potential of hosting and promoting a Website to reach a wide range of users, or contributing to virtual-conference reports for the promotion of products and content-design tools.

Research applications can also add value to the business offer. Resource investigation covers a group of tools that provide a rich source of material to a desktop PC. This can include obtaining resources from online databases, sound clips and so on. The bundle of advantages can be formulated into a unique value proposition, such as 'learn faster with more authoritative content'. Management and development applications include identifying and recording workforce needs collected through interactive questionnaires or assessments, or the assessment of learners by means of computer or Web-delivered tests of knowledge. Tracking and recording of student learning can also provide information on the efficiency and effectiveness of learning for decision-makers.

TOOLS AND TECHNOLOGIES FOR FUTURE DEVELOPMENT

New hybrid media forms are emerging through the application of the Internet in learning. One example of such hybridization is the development of interactive multimedia forms on the BBC Website. Radio, cable, digital satellite and the Internet are all used as channels to distribute audio programmes. On the Internet, audio is accompanied by text and visual information. Another

Table 5.3. Applications for technology in learning and business support

Technology application	E-business proposition
Communication E-mail; computer-conferencing tools; Web-boards and Web-conferencing; software for text-based chat; Websites for voice e-mail; Websites for direct sending of e-mail; software for Internet telephony; software environments for audio-video desktop conferencing.	**Marketing and client support** Online course promotion; links from other sites, co-branding. Dynamic Web registration. Real-time financial transactions. Personalization of learning by one-to-one interaction.
Collaboration Groupware; Web-based shared workspaces; Websites for collaborative document-preparation.	**Collaboration and networking** Course design by virtual network. Student networking with peers and tutors. Group choice for students: local, regional, national, international.
Publishing Word processing and HTML editors; Websites and browsers; Websites with linked database environments; document attachments for e-mail; tools for cross-application document access.	**Promotion and design tools** Website content design. Personalization of Website. Hybridization of online learning linked to range of products. Personalization of Web-pages.
Research and resource investigation CD-ROMs with information resources free-standing or linked to a supporting Website; Web search-engines; Web portals and Web vortals; Web-based search-engines; Websites for information organization; tools to retrieve, access and display stored resources, including streamed audio and video.	**Resource value added** CD-ROM linked to Web URLs with restricted access to research libraries and data. Access to selected Web resources creates unique value proposition; learn easier and faster.
Special applications Web-based learner-management systems (LMS); software for tutorials and simulations, resource collections; interactive assessments; video-capture tools for lecture; videoconferencing for point-to-point and Web-casting; Web environments.	**Management and development** LMS for immediate student-performance tracking; customizable reporting. VLE eases flexible delivery. Relationship marketing. Measuring learning effectiveness. Website-visit monitoring.

area of hybrid development is in the evolution of the conventional textbook. The book is extended with an interactive CD-ROM and supporting up-to-date information on a linked Website. For example, Encyclopaedia Britannica (*www.britannica.com*) provides a CD-ROM, with links to a Website with internal content, and gives out recommended URLs to Websites in the same subject area.

Bespoke course materials are also available from major publishers. Pearson offers a showcase for technology solutions grouped as book-specific Websites, discipline-specific Websites, course-management systems and other technology solutions (*www.pearsoned.com*). Pearson will customize an existing text-specific Website for teachers who enrol 250 students, with a course syllabus, assignments, handouts and Web links. The online content can be combined with a number of course delivery platforms, including WebCT and Blackboard. Similarly, McGraw-Hill (*www.mhhe.com*) offers online learning centres, in thirty-eight subject areas, that include lecture materials, quizzes, interactive exercises, PowerPoint slides and other supplements.

Constant change in technology-supported learning looks set to continue, but what is less assured is the real impact that such change will have on an educational service-provider. Learning how to apply a new technology in an optimum way for an instructional setting always lags behind the introduction of the technology itself. One challenge for designers is to recognize and apply technology for a justified use. Instead of spending time trying to understand how a particular technology works, simpler technology systems can serve to shift the focus to direct application, to solving problems and improving learning and work performance. This is starting to happen, through the consolidation and integration of proprietary virtual learning environments and their increasing ease of use for practitioners.

However advanced the technology, it is always the case that it is its widespread adoption by people that really allows its application for distance learning. The PC is at the heart of technology usage in corporate, SME and consumer markets. For existing users, it appears unlikely to be replaced in the short term by the growing trend in laptops, PDAs and mobile phones. For new users, though, laptops with wireless connectivity are an attractive and nomadic alternative to desktop PCs. The actual adoption of a technology is the area on which providers of e-learning need to focus, otherwise extra time and effort is spent on introducing the technology, rather than in applying the system for learning.

Moving ahead of reliable technology holds dangers. The practical effects of technical shortcomings in delivery are well illustrated in a study of technology-supported learning for adult learners (Selwyn et al., 2002: 23–41). Technical problems in distributed learning centres, supported by an unreliable network and imperfect software, often led to dissatisfaction and disengagement of learners. The promises of leading-edge technology applications, such as streamed video with an Internet connection for interactive access to online tutors, had significant shortcomings in the quality of service. Such findings only serve to reinforce the argument for the design of e-learning delivery methods to be based on proven, reliable and widely applied technology.

6

Implementation

E-learning is an attractive solution for learning and development, but requires attention to be focused on content, infrastructure and support. The key to implementing an effective system that will really work for business lies in adapting these dimensions to produce an effective and efficient service by the provider. Often this is achieved by a project-management approach, leading to the creation of an electronic learning environment. Changes are required, not just in the environment, but in the organization to support effectively and promote these services on a continuing basis. Digital delivery shifts the costs of learning delivery. It also brings with it concerns over a range of issues such as intellectual property, privacy and security. Partnerships can add value in added distribution channels and brand enhancement, but can be time-consuming, and need screening for their utility.

CREATING A COMPLETE ENVIRONMENT

Creating a complete learning environment requires the construction of three distinct layers: content, infrastructure and support. The content layer comprises the subject information, exercises and other material created for a learning process. The content layer is the material the designer creates for a learning engagement and needs to be tailored to the infrastructure, which stores, presents and delivers the content to the participant. The infrastructure layer is the connection between the content and the learner, discussed in the previous chapter. The support layer determines the services available to a participant, the tutors, technical advisers, learning centre or business liaison staff. The service may include business improvement, technical assistance, guidance on academic matters for registration and progress, tutorial support, scheduling or learner-management information. A primary goal for the designer is to create a perception for the learner of one holistic environment. However, a problem with any of the layers may diminish the learning experience, with the risk that the learning objectives will then not be met.

There are different ways of implementing a complete learning environment. In a large corporate setting it can be started by a 'top-down' strategy (Rosenberg,

2001). In a university it can form part of the transformational efforts for adopting flexible learning across a whole institution (Collis and Moonen, 2001). Probably the most common approach for developing technology-supported content is by an individual academic member of staff, a 'bottom-up' model that has advantages in experimentation but also disadvantages in terms of poor dissemination (Bates, 2000). There are supporters for all these methods, as there are drawbacks. For example, strategic 'top-down' approaches may require large resources and massive cultural change, while 'bottom-up' approaches may lack resources, completeness or effectiveness when scaled up. Between these poles, there is a middle way to implement the processes of digital delivery, in the form of project teams or centres.

Implementing an e-learning environment is rooted frequently in the application of project management. Good practice from transnational, national and regional applications in e-learning certainly point towards the value of project management (ECOTEC, 2001a, 2001b; EC, 2002). Indeed, it is a standard practice for grant-awarding bodies to require applicants for research, development or innovation funding to provide details in the form of project work-plans. When policy implementers make the decision about how schemes operate, then project sponsors are required contractually to follow. The adoption of project-management practice is very common. In Wales, for example, at least eleven of the (twelve) higher-education institutions have adopted some form of project-management approach for development aspects of e-learning. Project groups can be quick and nimble when it comes to creating product to meet market demand, and this approach allows a public sector education-supplier to respond like a successful commercial enterprise. Such initiative-based funding creates a general problem of continuity on project work for technology-supported learning, with many completed but under-exploited projects and then the rediscovery of course design principles by newcomers. This is a problem, of course, that has more to do with policy implementation than with the efficacy of project management.

PROJECT MANAGEMENT

The factors in classical project-planning requiring consideration include organizational factors, the control and monitoring of projects, which has been studied in depth, and specific applications for software development (Kerzner, 1992). A simple categorization of project-management tasks for e-learning yields four overlapping actions: research analysis and forecasting, e-learning project development, administration and business development (Cory-Wright and Keith, 2000).

The overall operational management of the project is delegated typically to one person, the project manager. This person is often a team leader who engages with a group of individuals, who contribute different skills to the delivery of defined outcomes. These outcomes are derived from a set of deliverable objectives that make it clear at all times what a schedule of work over a certain time period is meant to achieve and when it is completed. A project-management approach is based on a plan that sets out the major components. These include the goals, project description, target group and supporting market research. There are then project-management processes, in design, risk assessment, staff selection, budget setting, monitoring, evaluation and closure.

Developers of e-learning need a conventional suite of project-management skills, as well as familiarity with the learning technologies and an understanding of the factors that shape the learner's experience in e-delivery. Resources to undertake the development work are defined normally at the beginning of a project. An effective resource-base is central to success in e-learning and in e-business. These resources include staff, technology, funding and time, since implementing an e-learning programme requires a realistic timescale. The core service needs a reliable technology infrastructure to connect the learner to the provider. The biggest challenge, however, is in the creation and building of an effective development team for the initiative.

THE VALUE CHAIN FOR AN E-L EARNING ENTERPRISE

One method of illustrating e-learning applications across an educational service-provider is to examine prominent applications of the Internet across the value chain. Value-chain analysis is a classic tool, separating activities that underpin the strategies of any organization and how they all link together (Porter, 1985). The underlying principle is that all the activities and departments of an enterprise must work together. Each department carries out value-creating activities to design, produce, market and deliver the products and services. There are applications of e-learning right across the value chain of an educational service-provider (Table 6.1).

This can highlight potential objectives of a project-management implementation, from registration to post-course follow-up. There are, of course, wide variations in the range of technologies in use, the focus of students, and the size and resources. Some providers make a sales proposition to decision-makers in companies, based on the ability to manage the learning of employees as well as deliver content. Management tools can be applied for class procedures such as student progress, needs and gap analysis, and so on. Another management application is in the presentation of results to decision-makers and stakeholders.

Table 6.1. Prominent applications on the value chain of an e-learning provider

Value-chain activity	E-learning applications
Primary activities	
Inputs	Online student registration. Enterprise-wide recruitment data. 'Roll-on, roll-off' enrolment and progression.
Operations	Integrated delivery. Online help-desk services. Maintenance of online directories and services. Comprehensive testing and reporting.
Outputs	Real-time order transaction. Student-client access to delivery status. Integrated channel-management.
Marketing and sales	Online sales-channels. Real-time client feedback. Online course sampler.
After-sales service	Alumni databases.
Support activities	
Infrastructure	Web-server, mirror site and mail server-storage. Web-based information. Web-based equal opportunities and environmental policies. E-skills and finance training. Online compliance standards.
Human resource management	Self-service personnel admin. Online staff-needs assessment. Online analyses, time and expense reports. Web-based training and development.
Technology development	R & D access to online recruitment and feedback. Online knowledge directories to enhance Website status and usability. Skills development for technical and marketing development. Collaborative product-design. Web-based analysis of competitor applications.
Procurement	Direct procurement via B2B links.

IMPLEMENTATION OF INTEGRATED ELECTRONIC LEARNING ENVIRONMENTS

Adopting e-learning as a relevant means of student-centred learning, rather than as another form of delivering text-based media, is time-consuming and challenging in many practical ways. It can involve preparing teaching staff for learners taking control, linking e-learning with strategic goals, quality assurance, ICT support and creating a partnership with the finance and budgeting process. There is no shortage of information on types of implementation, or vendors, or particular methods of solution (Whitlock, 2000; Epic Group, 2000).

The proliferation of technology offers a great deal of choice to a decision-maker for implementing e-learning. Nevertheless, decision-making about technology in either conventional or distance education is a complex process, requiring consideration of a great number of factors (Bates, 1995: 59). These various factors may differ according to geography, local technological infra-structure, company application or educational service. Decision-making in this area is ultimately about personal choice and driven by values and technical considerations, all based on a careful analysis of the situation. The appropriate selection and application of a learning environment depend strongly on the local circumstances. There are fundamentally three ways for migrating to an e-learning environment: home-grown custom design, full off-the-shelf learning environment, or selecting building blocks from pre-existing compon-ents (Inglis et al., 2002: 65–81). Whatever the route chosen, an e-learning practioner should not design an implementation process that the organization has difficulties in applying or is incapable of delivering. Complexity in design affects the level of sophistication with which any accompanying organiza-tional change must be tackled.

IMPLEMENTATION APPROACHES

The home-grown, custom-design approach involves building a complete e-learning system all the way up from an initial design specification. Home-grown solutions, which at one time were a major problem, are no longer difficult for a large educational service-provider. This is reflected in their widespread adoption. For providers with home-grown systems the option exists that, if the licence price increases, they are not tied to continuing with a proprietary platform. It gives greater cost control, because the cost variables are in-house rather than from an outside supplier.

The major advantage of a home-grown approach is that it can provide a system capable of being tailored to match the needs of an organization. It can be adapted, as the needs of the organization change, with enhanced services, new courses, or the implementation of new innovations. This option needs resources to develop a system, although in practice the cost can also be controlled and budgeted, so that it becomes a feasible option for seeking entry into the delivery field (McCormack and Jones, 1998; Hall, 1997; DfEE, 2000; Petre et al., 2000: 97–116).

Experience from corporate applications of e-learning offer a structured approach to implementation (ASTD, 2000). The core of a structured approach is to analyse the needs of the organization and target group, identify the internal resources, determine any special features and then set a budget. The key steps are: first, to determine goals and the business case for e-learning, then to apply this information to ensure support comes from top decision-makers; the project owners and members of the project team are identified; current practices are researched and organizational readiness assessed; a project team is formed and a strategic, marketing and communication plan created; technology applications needed to support the strategy are identified; and finally, the programme is designed, a pilot test conducted and, following evaluation, a plan for the future is prepared.

Choosing a custom-designed approach for an e-learning system at Lampeter resulted from a degree of inflexibility in proprietary systems. The environment was developed by a classic project-management route under the *e-addysg.com* initiative. This tailored the e-learning solution closely to the need for bilingual delivery and for a controlled measure of experimentation to be possible. Several factors influenced this decision. First, the system would have to match the needs for delivery and support of the Welsh language and Welsh-medium materials and be able to operate bilingual content. Secondly, an internal multi-disciplinary team of staff was available to implement and evaluate the systems. Thirdly, the commercial products available at the time were limited, and taking an out-sourcing option might, over the long term, reduce internal expertise in the area. Fourthly, an initial small-scale trial provided favourable feedback and showed that the costs could be regulated. The e-learning solution was developed, based on open standards and using a Linux operating system, with an Apache Web server and MySQL database. All the source code is available freely and there is a vast development community; this makes it relatively more secure, because the large development community addresses software problems.

Amongst North American university providers, the e-learning delivery platform is becoming a less important development issue (Edpath, 2002: 8). Large organizations have the resources to create an electronic community and want their learning environment to be integrated to provide e-mail, chat and whiteboard that are customized to the needs of distance delivery, integrated and adaptable with the library and with student registration. Since existing staff maintain all the other systems, however, it makes financial sense to use them rather than pay an outside supplier for a subset of their functionality, that does not integrate with other institutional systems.

The building-block approach is a version of the home-grown method, in which an e-learning system is assembled from a set of functional components that are available as commercial products. All sorts of permutations exist. There are thousands of asynchronous e-learning products available, dozens of synchronous learning products and hundreds of companies providing services. This method works because the different components can be brought together and tailored to the delivery model. It offers more customization than with the off-the-shelf approach, but involves dealing with a number of component suppliers. The main disadvantage is that it requires additional staff resources to manage, implement, maintain and update the system to ensure effective interfaces.

PROPRIETARY OFF-THE-SHELF SOLUTION

The development of a home-grown environment can present problems for small organizations, without the resources to develop their own system, and they may have to turn to a proprietary system. For organizations which have not invested in earlier learning-administration systems, or which are looking to migrate from a collection of independent software systems to an integrated system, this class of integrated systems may represent an appealing option. Purchasing an 'off-the shelf' system from one of the commercially available systems already on offer is a quick solution. For a decision-maker, there are issues here in the degree of customization that is possible and increasing licence fees.

Obtaining an all-in-one, off-the-shelf paradigm involves acquiring a licence to use an integrated electronic learning environment from a commercial source. These products are evolving through different versions that provide greater integration and functionality. There are dozens of proprietary management systems in the marketplace (Table 6.2).

Table 6.2. A selection of integrated electronic learning environments

Product	Company supplier	URL
Courseinfo	Blackboard Inc	*www.blackboard.com/courseinfo/index.html*
Docent Enterprise	Docent Inc	*www.docent.com/solutions/products/index.htm*
First Class Collaborative Classroom	MC2 Learning Systems Inc.	*www.mc2learning.com/products/FCCC/index.html*
LearningSpace	Lotus Development Corp.	*www.lotus.com/home/nfs.learnspace/*
TopClass	WBT Systems	*www.wbtsystems.com*
WebCT	Web CT Inc	*www.webct.com/global/webct*

Integrated learning systems combine a number of capabilities. They feature authoring tools that let organizations develop content, customize courseware and provide assessment and testing, along with comprehensive systems for learning management. The disadvantage with these environments lies in the opportunity for only modest customization. There are substantial ongoing licence fees and often the need to have a core staff for staff development and more sophisticated design capabilities. For certain multilingual applications, they are not effective in supporting the character set, and so have limited application.

Published comparisons and descriptions of e-learning systems can become out of date quickly due to the rapid development of products and features. Decision-makers could easily be overwhelmed investigating these online platforms. Fortunately, some observatories exist to offer a comparison of commercially available integrated learning environments. One source is the Center for Instructional Technology at Marshall University (*www.marshall.edu/it/webct/compare*). Another objective site, operated by Langdon, provides a comparison of online educational delivery applications (*www.ctt.bc.ca/langdononline*).

TECHNOLOGY UPGRADE

Technology is simply a means to deliver learning and not a goal on its own. The technology specification needs to be planned for realistic delivery expectations by the client, not necessarily to be at the cutting edge. In drawing up the technical baseline for support, there is a possibility that the technology solution can be over-specified. Over-investment in technology by the provider will not necessarily bring greater customer satisfaction. Even the latest technology will soon become superseded. Not only is it expensive to stay and support the cutting edge of technology, it is not relevant when clients have unsophisticated equipment. For a participant SME, the infrastructure technology determines primarily the quality of the link, rather than the technology of the provider. Many SMEs have unsophisticated technology, therefore the e-learning solution must meet their capabilities.

The rapid uptake of e-learning by distance learners can increase the load on networks and IT systems. The standards of support need to be addressed with the IT department, otherwise these may prove a major constraint to development. Preparing for e-delivery begins with a clear analysis of what the service is intended to achieve, the communications software and the resources. Videoconferencing for synchronous delivery, for example, will bring different demands from those of a low-key asynchronous e-mail response system. The operation of e-learning on a significant scale will involve a form of VLE, for managing the delivery of courses in an online environment.

The additional demand may require substantial investment in upgrading the IT infrastructure. The likely impact will be on servers, to hold and deliver material, and networks may need to be upgraded to cope with greater communications traffic carrying graphics, audio or video files. Licences for courseware-authoring tools may also be needed and software systems for managing the exchanges between the provider and students. The establishment of a 'mirror' server, to cope with emergencies due to unanticipated service failure, is also justified. Moreover, the whole technology position needs to be kept under constant review, since a rising volume of traffic from rapid growth in student numbers, or an increase in applications involving large file sizes will make greater demands on the system. Networks and major technology equipment purchases are often seen as one-off investments funded from capital budgets. The renewal, redesign and replacement of the IT infrastructure is an ongoing process, however, better treated as part of the operating budget, with technology replacement scheduled regularly.

Staff make the technology infrastructure work and maintain services. Technology support staff can operate in a central support unit, or in sections or departments to support localized needs, or in a mixture of both. Among e-learning implementation groups there is a growing trend for technology support staff to be attached to e-learning groups and to supplement central service support. Their roles are to ensure that the networks, servers, equipment and software are installed properly and functioning fully. Learning technology support staff may also support the creation of educational programmes using technology.

SECURITY AND VIRUS PROTECTION

Security is an issue that affects electronic communications. Technology and network staff work to ensure that Internet connections and corporate Intranets are secure, with adequate firewalls. It is important to know how a new learning system or application, delivered via the Internet, will interface with existing environments and whether the security of company information systems might be jeopardized.

The Web-server that connects a provider to the Internet and with distance learners is in danger of attack as a route into an organization's private network. Hacking attempts are common. Attacks on Web-servers are commonly made for two reasons. The attack can give the intruder information that can be used to gain access to a private network and change the information posted on the Internet. If an intruder gains access to a private network, a number of security problems will arise, such as stealing usernames and passwords, manipulating applications and a compromise in confidentiality. Another motive behind Web-server attacks is simply the challenge of hacking into a server, by an individual who wants to leave a mark. Web-server security is a complex security topic in itself. Whatever the cause of possible attack, it is important to protect the integrity of the Web-server through planning, organization and security.

Viruses are another risk factor for providers and clients. These can be spread by infected disks or over the Internet. Virus-protection tools, which can be purchased for installation on to individual PCs and servers, will scan for any programmed threats before they become a problem. Anti-virus software is an important part of preventing viruses and, because new threats are created daily, virus software needs to be kept up to date, with the best policy being to scan frequently for virus updates. The same issues of security and virus protection affect an SME, but it may not employ specialist IT or network staff. The adoption process for e-learning in the firm, therefore, needs to ensure security, and that all relevant staff in an SME address protection issues. This means that managers and participants should be aware of the need to maintain protection measures for their systems, but at the same time assured of the security protection operated by the provider.

INTELLECTUAL PROPERTY AND COPYRIGHT

Interest in intellectual property and copyright has grown in recent years, as people seek to generate more wealth from the material that they create. Observing the field as a non-lawyer, there appears to be a colloquial and a legal view of intellectual property (IP). The colloquial view is that it covers all things that emanate from human thinking, such as ideas, inventions, poems, designs, microcomputers and so on. From a legal perspective, however, IP represents the legal rights that exist in the things that we create. These rights exist to protect intellectual property, to allow investment in product development to take place more securely and innovations to be turned into product and financial benefits.

The primary issue of intellectual property rights in e-learning is the control of the copyright of academic courseware delivered over the Internet. The intellectual property of courseware is protected by copyright legislation. Legislation varies from country to country, and so it is difficult to generalize and important to be aware of the protection provided by copyright legislation for courseware in a particular country.

The common practice in the world of education is to publish research findings for the benefit of an academic community, which may lead to the author achieving a greater standing in his or her peer group. Publishing an invention, however, can diminish the chances of anyone investing in the IP. Patenting IP before publishing does not prevent publishing. There are ways to protect the various types of IP (*www.cranfield.ac.uk/sme/rdman*). For instance, know-how and trade secrets, which can cover any skill, or technical or commercial information, are protected simply by keeping them secret. Copyright deals with original literary and artistic works and gives automatic protection rights, but not in the USA. Design rights for the internal and external shape have an automatic protection right in Europe. A trade mark that covers a badge of origin is protected through registration at the Patent Office. In e-business, maintaining protection over domain names from predators is necessary.

Normally a person who creates IP owns it, in the absence of an employment relationship. If the person creates the work as part of the normal course of work, however, it belongs to the employer. It is generally accepted, therefore, that where there is no agreement to the contrary, copyright in work produced by members of staff in an educational institution belongs to that institution. For staff in UK institutions who create e-learning content in the field in which they are employed, the IP belongs to their employer. This means that the ownership of copyright issues is bound up in institutional agreements and employment relationships with staff (Bjarnason et al., 2000a: 95–104).

The issues become more complex if an institution hires a third party, such as a consultant or student, to produce material for a programme. The patents and copyright belong to them and the designs with the commissioner, unless there is a contract to specify otherwise. A potential area of difficulty arises from staff members who engage in personal consultancies. The ownership of the copyright in what is produced should be stated clearly in contract documentation. There are ramifications not only for royalties, but because controlling the distribution of content is a way of delaying access to competitors. Difficulties can arise when there are no explicit agreements in place to cover the legal position of work produced; for example, the mobility of staff means that someone with a key role in developing content may decide to leave, taking the content. Moreover, part-time staff may have several employment contracts and, with more mobility, may choose to move content between different providers. Contractors and consultants get work by applying their skills from one job to another, so that development expertise can be transferred to competitors when they are engaged.

There are many difficulties tied up with ownership, but the perception by staff of the ownership of content is often the most difficult. Even when the legal rights clearly rest with the employer, staff may still have difficulty in accepting the position on legal ownership. Ownership issues are addressed by established large providers of distance education. Newcomers, however, operating as mixed-mode providers, are beginning to encounter problems that have long been solved by others. This means that the topic of intellectual property rights remains at the forefront of unresolved agenda items for many decision-makers in e-learning in education.

PERSONALIZATION AND PRIVACY

An e-learning practitioner might optimize the match of a programme with the particular needs of an individual if personal information is available. Personalization of a learning programme, though, is loaded with questions regarding privacy. For the learner, the question arises as to how much intrusion into personal preferences is tolerable in order for technology to assist with the learning process. They need to be assured that the information that they produce in course assignments will be available only to those whom they choose. Once started, their progress, performance and preferences become tracked within a learner-management system. This raises issues for the decision-maker of privacy, protection, rights, trust and the safeguards that must exist to protect an individual. Managers in small firms, as well as line-managers and HR staff in larger companies, are concerned that their proprietary and confidential information remains secure.

In the UK, the Data Protection Act 1998 addresses the protection of individuals in the collection and processing of personal data and is relevant in virtual provision. A Council of Europe recommendation (R (99) 5, 23 February 1999) also deals with privacy issues on the Internet. It points to the fact that the laws of many European countries forbid the transfer of data to those countries that do not have an equivalent level of protection to that of the home country, except where the individual has indicated consent (Bjarnason et al., 2000a: 104–5).

BUILDING AGREEMENT

No universal rules exist for the acceptance of an innovation in e-learning within an educational enterprise; rather, it is about achieving the possible through people or politics. This means assessing how to build political support for an innovation. The process of achieving agreement with others to invest time and resources in a new and possibly risky venture can be both time-consuming and challenging.

The development of a political strategy requires the identification of who is needed for the success of the project and their level of agreement and trust, both internal and external to the organization. Building political support for an innovation requires constant effort. A methodical approach in building support for change will need to identify people to be influenced in support of the initiative. For external partner organizations and their staff, the situation is more uncertain, because relatively little is known about them as potential partners. An initial screening process ought to occur, of subject interest and relevant expertise, with a sound track-record and financial stability the important criteria. This allows an assessment of whether or not there is a viable alignment between the mutual interests of the partners. The search for international collaborators, in order to extend the international direction of the work, is even more difficult, because of the added complexity that different cultures bring to the search for, scrutiny of and agreement on an innovative measure.

Internal support for an e-learning strategy and change is seldom automatic. The reactions of various stakeholders need to be addressed, as do the practical interests of internal audiences as the focus shifts from planning to implementation. One way is to create an internal marketing plan, and like an external one, this can be structured into different stages. First, an audit is needed to identify the important stakeholder groups and determine their current views, concerns and attitudes. The second stage is to specify objectives for the actions needed. The third is to determine the strategy for how the audience ought to be segmented and the positioning of the proposition and plan as a necessity, as routine or an exciting challenge. The fourth stage is developing and coordinating the message, and the fifth is control by a project timetable and a method for monitoring response.

The University of Glamorgan provides an example of building support that illustrates the internal marketing for cultural change that accompanies e-learning (Cooper, 2002: 8). In this case, part of the challenge was to overcome internal segmentation and low cross-functional collaboration which inhibited innovation. A planning unit, aided by external consultants, set out to communicate a new framework and process to a key group of young staff. The objective was to gain commitment at all levels within two years. A strategy to segment staff most likely to encounter resistance was prepared, with exemplars to motivate rather than threaten younger staff. Four strands coordinated the message: a twenty-year vision; a new institutional approach to innovation through changing culture; enhancing partnerships; and a strategic forum to engage younger staff in change. The whole initiative operated within a tight project timetable with regular monitoring.

LEARNING CENTRES

An effective way to deliver and manage e-learning is through a learning centre (LC). This provides a dedicated training environment as a physical location in an organization, making it easier to market e-learning and provide a suitable image. Many individuals find support from a learning centre very helpful. Hardware and software can be standardized, with training courseware pre-loaded on to PCs. The LC can offer a secure place in which to keep valuable e-learning materials, where learners can study in peace. It can also act as a focal point, where support can be available from a tutor and where learners can socialize (BAOL and LLTD, 2000).

A learning centre is often a PC-based training facility with Internet connectivity and a range of learning materials, CD-ROMs, videos and so on, that are available for learners. Learners might arrange to attend the LC at a time to suit themselves and can learn at their own pace in a comfortable environment. Staff support normally depends on the size of the centre and range of materials. A facilitator, who ought to have at least good coaching skills, might be employed in a larger LC. Other responsibilities might include booking in and receiving learners, reacting to technical problems and monitoring usage. Learning centres might offer self-paced networked learning tools, coaching from tutors, a selection of learning resources such as CD-ROM courses, or audio- and videotapes and internal classroom training.

A learning centre might be used in a large organization to facilitate technology-supported learning. The size of such a centre, the range of learners, the variety of learning and the availability of learner support will ultimately depend on the available corporate budget. It is becoming standard for the learning centre to provide broadband access for clients. Sometimes the learning centre will form an access point to a corporate university. Facilities and support for employees and managers such as this are rarely available for on-site e-learning in small firms. Advice on an appropriate interface and infrastructure is frequently needed.

Learning centres that provide access to e-learning for the general public are now common across the UK. A learning centre in an educational enterprise with general access can also act as a central resource for SMEs and offer a learning infrastructure that the firm could not provide itself. This implies that SME employees are able to travel to such a facility, but in the process they will lose some of the main benefits of e-learning, such as flexibility of use, savings in travelling and so on. Since it is often too expensive to install the same level of LC-support in individual SME sites, this seems a pragmatic solution.

The operation of an in-company dedicated learning centre with tutor support is widely advocated to provide interaction between learners and tutors, but it is frequently outside the practical resources of many small firms. Such a service can provide SME clients with performance consulting, peripatetic tutor services, advice on forming e-learning spaces, e-learning courses with online tutorial support, and a fully functioning shared learning centre for employees from groups of different SMEs. To reach this stage, however, employees in the SME not skilled enough to install courseware and progress independently might need to receive help through a peripatetic tutor with technical and professional training expertise. Technical guidance might be required to resolve a range of pressing application issues. These include, for example, Website maintenance, ISP agreements, systems integration, connectivity and browser difficulties, as well as application problems for the support from e-learning.

BLENDED E-LEARNING

An e-learning course that combines Web-based training with a tutor-led element, or blended e-learning, can offer the learner a variation in delivery styles that might satisfy a wider span of learning styles. This can shorten the tutor-led event, saving costs relating to trainer time and travel costs. By applying e-learning to present preparatory work, it can provide learners with a better understanding of the subject before attending the tutor-led element, as well as making the overall course more varied and interesting. Another solution adopted to support SMEs without a technology infrastructure is to adapt the programme, as the firm develops, with different dimensions of tutorial support. The first dimension might be face-to-face support on the premises of the firm. Another setting might be in a formal learning centre to demonstrate applications more fully; a third situation might be back in the SME after the implementation of infrastructure and interfaces.

For a tutor working with blended learning, one of the first tasks is to work through the programme carefully to establish the necessary content, style and duration for the participant. The salient points for the tutor to consider are ways to develop the points to underpin knowledge from an assessment of contributions made by the e-learning dimension. The final blended learning course may consist of in-house e-learning products, or content bought in to widen the portfolio of technology-supported learning.

SHIFT OF COSTS

Digital delivery involves a significant shift of costs, compared with face-to-face delivery. A greater proportion of the costs of e-learning is required for the design, development and maintenance of the infrastructure required to deliver programmes, rather than for the salaries of staff involved in delivery. A larger proportion of the costs of resource-based learning are upfront, since all the resources and infrastructure need to be in place before delivery begins. Courseware development costs can be apportioned over the longer sales-cycle for the programme.

A course that requires extensive programming and multimedia applications is likely to be much more expensive. Sound, animation and video can lead to a more visually attractive and satisfying product for the design team. It also puts greater expectations on the remote learner: on technical skills, on the PC specification, the need for plug-ins, download times, all of which might create barriers to access. This may lead to greater activity on the help-desk to resolve running problems. There are also new maintenance costs associated with the technology for Internet-enabled delivery; these include the overhead costs of a Web-server, mail-server storage and mirror site, Website maintenance costs, staff costs attached to the administration and registration of students, and staff costs for the support of help-desks.

There are a number of other subtle changes that arise from the delivery of e-learning. There is a significant shift in the cost of delivery to the student. In place of printing and mailing learning content by the educational supplier, a learner will incur call charges in contacting the provider as well as in printing downloads. For an employer, employee development by e-learning can also mean a shift of costs. When an employee pursues a programme of learning at home, this is not normally paid time. The learner is likely to bear the call charges and operate from a domestic PC. These are all costs that might normally be borne by an employer for work-based learning, as well as the paid time for study and the costs of travel and subsistence.

Savings in employee-time away from the workplace as well as in travel are the major cost-savings for an SME from e-learning, as for large-sized enterprises. An illustration of the financial advantages in terms of the return-on-investment for a corporate provider is available (Schriver and Giles, 1999: 51–2); a report on experiences at Lockheed Martin corporate university, which operated as a charge-back organization, recovering all costs from services provided in generic training and development for a workforce of more than eighteen thousand people. The largest savings resulted from participants not having to travel to classes. Other savings came from less time being needed to complete certain training. Another contribution to cost savings arose because instructors were not needed to deliver the Web courses and tests. All records from Web courses were handled electronically, which eliminated all manual processing. Other intangible benefits were that space was freed up for other uses, employees no longer had to wait until a class was available and employees could complete training when it was less disruptive to production schedules.

In an assessment of the cost-effectiveness of technology-supported training, Hunt and Clarke pointed out that the identification of cost effectiveness has two key ingredients: the costs of technology-based training (TBT) versus the possible alternatives, and a means of measuring the outcomes and benefits of training (Hunt and Clarke, 1997). They provide an indication of the key benefits, such as making learning more interesting, improving the retention of learning, reducing the training time, reducing travel and subsistence costs and so on. Examples of the kind of cost savings cited range from 12 to 90 per cent, although they caution that many studies are based on the outcomes of pilot projects rather than on the results over an extended period of delivery.

E-LEARNING RESOURCE COSTS

Money can flow out of an enterprise through all manner of costs, but money flows in only through the prices an enterprise charges and receives for its services. For an educational institution, this is generally through the fees charged, directly and indirectly, for access to programmes. The major business reasons to move into e-learning are the expectations of reaching and recruiting more students who would not enrol ordinarily, and hence increasing fee income, and that it will lead to significant cost-savings. As business propositions, the former leads to more sales and greater turnover, while the latter reduces the costs of delivery.

Resources on a project can be cost-controlled by the application of some predictive techniques that can advise a project manager of the likely costs before they are committed. When equipped with information, the project manager can consider the implications on the project time, scope and quality. Without timely information, delays in effecting decisions and changes can increase the implementation costs. Effective cost-control can be achieved through the use of three useful reports, which have been applied in the development of in-house e-learning courses. A detailed plan, schedule and budget, prepared during the planning phase, is the first report. The next is a detailed comparison between resources expended to date and those planned. The third is a projection of resources to be expended through to project completion.

It is not technically difficult to cost ODFL systems. The actual costs for the development and support of an e-learning initiative will vary, depending on the degree of interactivity. There are wide differences in the constituents of e-learning, including the choice and mix of media and technologies, working practices, such as in the terms and conditions of employment of staff, production standards and the range of student support services offered. Substantial differences in the course length can also arise. At one end of the spectrum is a complete online degree course, at the other end a small contribution to a course unit, which may or may not be credit-bearing. There are particular difficulties in the analysis of overhead costs and technical choices over the treatment of capital costs and the treatment of costs to joint products.

Costs for e-learning can be categorized as different types, such as capital costs involved in the purchase of technology equipment, software licences and materials. There are programme-development costs, which are normally initially high. Programme-delivery costs are often similar from course to course, as are recurrent costs to operate a programme. Fixed costs continue the same, regardless of the throughput of students, but variable costs can change.

Such diversity makes it difficult to reach any hard-and-fast conclusions about the costs of different approaches. In costing ODFL budgets, recurrent expenditure, analysis of revenue costs, capital depreciation, overheads, course design, format selection, cost efficiency and effectiveness, and varying rates of return are all factors to be considered (Rumble, 1997). A number of additional cost-categories are needed for networked learning, which include infrastructure, maintenance, security and overheads. Specific cost calculations for the design and delivery of a Web-based course, based on experience at the University of British Columbia, are provided by Bates (Bates, 2000: 145).

ACTIVITY-BASED COSTING

Activity-based costing (ABC) seeks to derive the total cost of a course by aggregating all of the costs incurred in the provision of the service. The costs of delivery are subdivided, according to the major activities involved in providing distance learning. The ABC method assumes that certain cost objects create the demand for activities, which in turn cause costs. Cost objects are the products and services for customers, and are the reasons for performing activities. These activities are the processes that cause work, and are usually grouped together in activity centres.

An investigation into the costs of developing and supporting networked learning found broad agreement around the cost centres of human resources, development, production and delivery; equipment and consumables; facilities and administration (Bacsich et al., 2001). Furthermore, this group proposed a life-cycle approach, which would separate course costs into three phases: planning and development; production and delivery; maintenance and evaluation. The ABC method was found to be suitable for use in universities, without major adaptation. It uncovered the hidden costs that are normally absorbed by the institution, but not those that go unrecorded, such as staff overtime.

COLLABORATION AND PARTNERSHIPS

Partnerships for the development and delivery of e-learning are common, and a selection are illustrated in Table 6.3. The fundamental reasons for a partnership are to share development costs, or to distribute costs over a larger group of students, or to create more distribution channels, or to achieve a better market position for students in the face of competition from other providers. Learning technologies can assist the process of collaborative working, as they allow courses developed by one institution to be made available at others. The Internet, e-mail and videoconferencing can also help the administration and meetings of development teams. Collaboration by these means may exist at the local, regional and national as well as international level.

Table 6.3. A selection of partnerships with global e-learning delivery

Partnership/URL	Themes and partners
Universitas 21 *www.universitas.edu.au/members*	Intercollegiate course offers. Twenty-one long-established universities from North America, Europe, Asia and Australasia, including University of Nottingham, University of British Columbia, etc.
Cardean University *www.cardean.edu*	Business and vocational subjects. Programmes developed with Columbia Business School, Stanford University, University of Chicago Graduate School of Business, Carnegie Mellon University, London School of Economics.
Scottish Knowledge *www.scottish-knowledge.co.uk*	Intercollegiate course offers, marketing of Scottish HE and course development. All thirteen Scottish universities and commercial organizations such as Bank of Scotland, BP, etc.
EuroPace *www.europace.be*	Demonstrations of technology applications for learning. Information, project and training services. Approx. forty participating institutions across Europe, predominantly universities.

The emergence of partnerships designed to capitalize on international opportunities is really another visible manifestation of global competition in markets for learning. The effect of globalization is to encourage providers to compete through cooperation in consortia. The formation of partnerships is motivated less by altruism and more by self-interest, to strengthen international products that become more exclusive and selective, and inherently underpin a sophisticated value-proposition. For instance, the ultimate goal of Universitas 21 is to advance the interests of the members on a global front. A joint venture between Universitas 21, a consortium of eighteen universities from ten countries, and News International plc to offer distance-learning courses and degrees is now defunct (Universitas 21, 2000). News International presumably at one stage saw a business opportunity through this venture, but then reappraised its options. However, Thomson International has entered into an agreement with this consortium, in which it develops international education and training courses, while Universitas 21 awards certification to students. There have been failures. The conspicuous and high-profile alliance fathom.com for example, set out to offer intercollegiate courses from leading US and UK universities, libraries and museums, but encountered commercial difficulties and closed in 2002.

PARTNERSHIP DEVELOPMENT

Partnership development for e-learning is encouraged by regional, national and European government agencies for providers to share development costs and expertise, but has problems. Even small providers can be engaged with a range of partnerships at the local, regional and European level. At the national level in the UK, an e-university project, with the brand name UK eUniversities (UKeU) Worldwide, aimed to protect current international markets and to exploit a potentially large demand for higher education. Three pilot Master's degree courses formed the first offer from the University of Cambridge and the Open University, Sheffield Hallam University and the University of York. It failed to meet a target of 5,600 students and closed in March 2004 (*www.EducationGuardian.co.uk*).

In Wales, the Digital College (*Coleg Digidol*), as a partnership venture between broadcasters S4C and BBC, public-sector colleges and the communications company NTL, pursued a cable and satellite distribution method for television-based programmes. The goal of the initiative is to attract large numbers of new lifelong learners. Before its launch, however, it encountered problems with the supply of set-top decoder boxes, which served to delay its development; a case where learning delivery was on a technology platform ahead of its adoption by the majority of potential consumers.

Partnerships also exist at the local level. Members of the west Wales e-learning consortium partnership share development costs and gain access to a professional network of course-developers, as well as to the findings of market and evaluation studies. Partners see e-learning provision as an alternative mode of delivery that can draw additional domestic student enrolments. Members of the consortium cooperate on a range of multilateral partnerships, such as in franchising, developing lifelong learning and widening access. The e-learning arrangements exist to provide resources for members to create content for the support of a target group of SMEs, which can progress through accredited programmes at any of the partner institutions.

There are many drivers pushing an educational enterprise towards alliances for the provision of e-learning. The most common factors are strategic alignment, brand enhancement, risk mitigation and extra communication channels. A decision-maker will need to address the resource requirement of existing commitments in considering entry into a new alliance, with the prospects offered by a new partnership. The key parameters are likely to include questions on staffing. Is there sufficient staff capacity in relevant areas of expertise? To what extent is it possible to quantify costs and risks? How large is the market segment that the alliance will address? Will there be a significant contribution to the existing business? Will the alliance provide entry to new communication and new distribution channels? How will the resources of the alliance be managed? Who makes operational decisions? The proposed e-learning solution must, above all, make economic and financial sense to all the partners involved.

A COMPLETE IMPLEMENTATION

E-learning is not just a delivery mechanism; it involves all the processes associated with curriculum development, provision and support, as with traditional learning. To provide it well means engaging the learner across all the points of interaction and getting feedback from them on how well it is working. Students are familiar with the conventional signposts of learning, such as registration, personal contact with the tutor, meeting colleagues and graduation. Implementation of e-learning, therefore, has led to more attention on each of these areas, bringing the process of learning closer to conventional learning.

E-learning challenges existing operational processes. The administration needs to be prepared for new ways of registering students and the rapid adaptation of the programme. As learners become familiar with online learning, a growing number of them will want to make further progress with their education beyond a single course. Consequently, capacity building is needed to create course options for students to progress with their learning.

Every e-learning service-provider requires a technology platform. Once a platform is established, however, the technology no longer becomes a competitive advantage for the provider, because similar learning technology can be purchased or developed by rivals. The competitive differences shift to issues connected with the content and support layers. The effectiveness of learning still depends on issues such as authenticity, branding, performance, track record and perceived value by the participant. For decision-makers in small firms, the perceived value is related to the effect of learning on the operational performance of the business. The content and support layer secures these benefits. The combination of all three layers is needed, though, for a complete implementation.

7

Competitive strategy

E-learning gives an educational enterprise access to larger and more diverse pools of students as well as to new relationships with other providers and companies. By informing, distributing, supporting and charging participants for e-learning, an educational service-provider operates as an e-business. Initiating and sustaining this business involves developing and implementing a strategy. Once everyone offers e-learning and an authentic product, then competing on price alone is no longer feasible. The means of sustaining a competitive advantage over rivals then moves to a competitive strategy of addressing the perceived use-value to a client. Determining the dimensions of perceived value and focusing on ways to achieve it through value assurance, enhancement and innovation become important in sustaining competitive advantage.

E-LEARNING AS E-BUSINESS

An educational enterprise delivering e-learning operates an e-business. It is a knowledge-based business, where the needs of clients are constantly changing, the surrounding competitive circumstances are evolving and the technology relevant to teaching and learning are in transition. The scale of ambition, use of technology, application of learning methods and choice of target group might all vary. Nevertheless, creating an e-learning business by moving an idea to execution with an action plan involves a series of parallel and progressive moves, designed to help the educational provider in the face of considerable uncertainty. This needs a strategy that links e-learning with business goals, since the development of content, delivery and support will be a strategic step, requiring resources.

There are already several terms in circulation that cover electronic business activities: electronic trading, mobile (m-)business and e-commerce are prominent. Here, e-business is interpreted as any form of business, or administrative transaction, or information exchange that is executed using any information and communications technology (ICT). This is a broad definition of e-business, but, as with all businesses, the objectives are relatively simple: to increase revenue and to keep down costs. E-business can facilitate modes of transaction between a supplier and a customer as well as building value by removing, or reducing, intermediaries in these modes. The effects on the economic and strategic fundamentals of an enterprise are the same as for conventional business, but the boundaries of time and geography are diminished by electronic transactions and there are also effects on the distribution of value.

PERSPECTIVES ON STRATEGY

Success in the business of e-learning is the same as in any other business. An educational service-provider must address practical issues of strategy in the choice of markets and products, as well as providing an e-learning service rooted in authenticity, quality, price and service. A key challenge for an educational enterprise is to discover the core offer that makes customers content, and then to develop from this position unique selling propositions (USPs) for e-learning services that keep them satisfied. Turning even a sharply focused idea into an e-learning business, however, requires a strategy to become sustainable after the start-up phase. Consequently, a provider must also understand its position within the wider e-learning service industry.

All enterprises are involved in strategy, either explicit or implicit. There are different forms. Determining what business line to be in for the future and how best to operate is the purpose of corporate strategy. Deciding on and achieving advantage, in the competition between products and services in the marketplace, are the ends of competitive strategy. Implementing the competitive strategy in the role of a department or function, such as HRD, marketing, or teaching and learning, is the perspective for functional strategy.

Decision-makers and practitioners of e-learning come from many educational settings, such as in a conventional managerial position, at a project level, or even as an individual staff member. Certainly, as technology changes, individuals or small teams are able to respond first, followed later by institutions. Attracting and addressing the needs of e-learning students takes a provider into a different competitive arena than does the case for relatively captive campus students. Different kinds of strategies are needed, different student support, different marketing and even different products when serving people at a distance, as opposed to enhancing classrooms. The relatively decentralized structure of a university can also make it difficult to integrate all the systems and processes as well as manage the interactions with clients. This means that a full system-wide approach is not always possible. A development group nevertheless needs to be sufficiently agile, open and responsive to perceived needs and values in the client group, as e-learning applications diffuse through a market. A plan and method for dealing with competition, a competitive strategy, can help to sustain work for a group and institution.

LESSONS FROM DOT.COMS

The online market is changing the way that consumers buy goods and services. Despite the well-publicized problems of dot.coms, e-business in services is strong and even the most staid and traditional businesses, such as banks and insurance companies, would not be without their online service channels. E-learning is in many ways an e-business success. It is a weightless, high-value service that is held in esteem by most societies. However, at the start of the e-economy, some universities responded by spinning out their own e-learning companies. Many soon found, however, that this model did not work well. These new companies did not have enough product, or enough brand reputation, to gain market-share. Other universities hired marketing agencies, which again discovered that they lacked volume. Other attempts to acquire product volume have included the formation of university consortia, partnerships formed to market and deliver their services through new distribution channels. Some of these have also failed because of the conflict with university politics and attitudes.

Firms involved solely in Internet business have tended to move away from competing on quality, features and service and moved towards competition on price, with the net result that it has become harder for anybody in their industry to make a profit (Porter, 2001: 63). Up until the dot.com meltdown these effects were obscured. The proper strategic route for dot.coms, in Porter's view, is to break away from simply competing on price and to pursue their own distinctive strategies, rather than to emulate one another as established companies. A better position for dot.coms is to apply their distinctive strengths to yield an attractive proposition to their clients. There have been well-publicized failures from the dot.com Internet phenomenon and some successes, in industries such as online auctions and digital marketplaces. Its biggest impact, however, has been in the reconfiguration of existing industries, that have been constrained by high costs, for communicating, gathering information or accomplishing transactions. Leading dot.coms, such as eBay, E* Trade, Amazon.com, lastminute.com and ebookers.com, all have one thing in common – none produces a product. Instead, they create a saleable commodity by reaggregating, repackaging and customizing services over the online customer environment, thereby creating a flexible organization, with no physical assets.

Certain experiences of dot.com operations are relevant and transferable for e-learning enterprises (Matkin, 2001: 156–7). These include: knowing the target audience's view on quality and trying to sustain this level; a focus on the customer interfaces to create effective student support; defining the means to reach the niche and exploring the international market for opportunities; focusing the Website on information relevant to an e-learning programme and using sampler courses as sales tools; assessing the business impact of delivery online and its costs; and taking care in trying to be the first mover, since technology can be expensive and opportunities always exist for development. There are examples of e-learning enterprises that have applied new models through the Internet. ECollege (*www.ecollege.com*), for example, is a full application service-provider (ASP) that contracts with universities, for a fee, to put courses on the Internet and provide the required delivery network.

GROWTH STRATEGIES

Today's big problem for business is that most of the world's industries can produce far more goods than customers can buy. Overcapacity leads to hypercompetition and price wars. Currently, the overproduction of goods and services by corporations is causing a re-examination of the competitive dimensions of an enterprise and the techniques of valuing intangibles that enable enterprises to compete on something other than price. Education is intangible. E-learning, due in part to the fuzziness of interpretation, is even more intangible than traditional learning. It is also an area of delivery where a degree of crossover activity occurs, with for-profit and not-for-profit providers seeking to supply the same market segments. Many management tools originate in the corporate for-profit world, where they can give a business a temporary edge over competitors, at least until rivals catch up by replicating the practice.

Decision-makers in education have also witnessed an explosion of management tools, such as business process re-engineering, total quality improvement/continuous quality improvement and benchmarking (Birnbaum, 2000). Virtually every management idea contains a grain of value for some organizations. Keeping up with these ideas and tools and deciding which ones to use is becoming an essential part of every professional's responsibilities. These management tools are valuable, however, only if they help to improve performance. Applied with this end in mind, they can be an important part of the change process to improve decision-making. Better decisions lead to improved capabilities that can serve student needs better than the competition. These competitive advantages can then drive improved performance and superior results.

One management tool that shows the potential growth strategies is the product–market matrix (Ansoff and McDonell, 1987) presented in a simple four-quadrant form in Table 7.1. The Internet can allow adaptations and extensions of markets and products. The benefits to an educational enterprise in opting for additional growth are that it might prevent or inhibit competitors from gaining competitive advantage, exploit new opportunities and provide new revenue streams, which may help offset losses from declining activities and broaden the portfolio.

**Table 7.1. Options for applying e-learning to extend the product
and market potential of an educational enterprise**

	Existing product	New product
Existing market	1. Same product, same market. Market penetration.	2. New product, same market. Product development.
New market	3. Same product, new market. Market development.	4. New product, new market. Diversification.

Apart from the options to do nothing, withdraw from, or consolidate in some markets, four basic strategies exist. The primary strategies for an e-learning provider from the product–market categorization are:

Quadrant 1: increasing market share for present courses and students; a growth strategy by market penetration.

Quadrant 2: creating new courses to complement or replace existing ones; a product development strategy.

Quadrant 3: new markets are sought for the courses of an enterprise; a market development strategy.

Quadrant 4: both courses and student-clients are new for the enterprise; a diversification strategy.

Risk increases with movement away from current activities. A degree of innovation is required for strategies in quadrants 2, 3 and 4, accompanied by higher elements of risk than in 1. Investment resources increase between quadrants 1 (low risk), 2 and 3 (medium), and 4 (high risk). The low-risk choice is to continue to provide the same product and services into the same market, but this may not deliver the required growth in students. The next choices, of introducing a new product into the same market, or marketing an existing product into a new market, both entail greater risks. For classic vocational course development, market penetration is the lowest-risk option, since it can require fewer resources and builds on experience. A market-development strategy, in which the needs of different client segment groups are identified and then targeted, is a relatively low-cost way of generating extra students for the original course product and may offer a pre-emptive option against competitive rivals. Product development normally requires more time and greater resources. Without some form of proprietary barrier, this could involve the risk that competitors will replicate the product quickly. Finally, diversification with a new product for a new market represents the highest risk and greatest difficulty of all.

A Web presence reduces the risk in a market-development strategy. Trial offers can be made even before course development starts, to assess demand.

Even so, moving to serve different market segments merits a careful analysis to determine the specific needs of customers in this segment. What are the critical dimensions of perceived value? What criteria do they use to evaluate products and services? What is known about competitors? How is it possible to out-perform existing providers in this segment? These are all relevant questions for market development.

Curriculum (or product) development has a relatively long gestation period, moving from idea to design, validation and launch. With classic delivery methods, competitors can replicate the course rapidly before the originator can attain market leadership. Uniformity of curricula can be established quickly, with no individual programme allowed in the long term to operate a significantly different product. This process of normalization is assisted by the movement of staff among educational institutions, the circulation of information through quality audits and teaching assessment, as well as the inclination of staff to demonstrate and publicize an innovation to peers.

With an e-learning infrastructure in place, product development can also be made easier. New content can be formulated to fit within a defined learning environment, assisted by a core e-learning design team. E-learning serves to modify the curriculum development in some subtle ways. The notion of transforming a full-accredited degree course into e-delivery format not only represents a massive undertaking of time and resources, but also the time to generate and apply feedback is very long. Even on an annual cycle of delivery and evaluation, it can take a couple of years from piloting to evaluation and adaptation, by which time the students will have moved on, as might the original staff. Staff mobility can affect digital delivery. A team approach to e-delivery means that the departure of an individual can have less impact on the delivery of a programme, provided that effective systems are in place. One solution is to unitize the e-learning curriculum to speed up the cycle of delivery and testing with more rapid repetition. As soon as the e-learning product is launched on the Web, however, it signals to current and future competitors a new opportunity for them.

Efforts that take an existing enterprise out of its own field of experience and into diversification are, in general, rarely successful unless they build on common ground within an existing business (Drucker, 1994: 161). An educational enterprise should innovate, therefore, where it has expertise, through knowledge of the technology or market, as a new growth strategy is always sufficiently difficult not to attempt in an area that is not understood. Authenticity stems from the perceived relevance of content and expertise in the support of specific groups of learners. Diversification, though, can lead a provider into areas where the perceived value by a customer is diminished, which eventually may affect adversely the primary business.

OPENING AND CLOSING THE WINDOW OF OPPORTUNITY

The historical approach to sustaining commercial advantage was to maintain secrecy about processes. Nowadays, however, a commercial secret is a rare item, and competitors can always reach an equivalent quality or price. It is extremely difficult to prevent competitors from reproducing more quickly and enhancing new products, production methods and, especially, services. The Web aids the replication process. When the same technology is widely available to everyone, technology cannot provide a long-term advantage to anyone (Davenport and Prusak, 1998). Competitors can always reach the equivalent quality and price of the current product, or service, of a market leader. The mobility of people between organizations and the dissemination of ideas, practices and processes make it relatively easy for competitor organizations to acquire and develop competitive positions rapidly.

In e-business, it is a common and legitimate practice to create a new service offer that replicates competitors' products by reaggregating, repackaging, and customizing one's own. This method can help stimulate ideas for developing a portfolio for flexible or distance education. For an established provider, the defence is to use knowledge to supply a sustainable advantage and move up to a new level of quality, creativity, efficiency and perceived value. Once the core dimensions of perceived value are found, however, it becomes highly desirable to identify and construct a proprietary barrier, if possible, around the expertise (Roffe, 1999: 163–73). This can be through technical affiliation with manufacturers or suppliers, or from being recognized experts in the field, or in constructing a novel application that draws in learners.

This proprietary step is important because replication strategies by competitors mean that the window of opportunity on an innovation can open and close remarkably quickly. Taking advantage of the window is not just a matter of adopting the right process. Even when both a goal and a particular course of action are clear to an innovator, conflict can easily arise because of an internal struggle for investment resources. The proponent of an innovation will argue in terms of the strategic benefits that the outcomes might bring, while a financial decision-maker might take an opposing viewpoint on an estimate of the costs of the action. The result can be deadlock and a continuation of the status quo. Such an adversarial position is not uncommon in the process of negotiations involved in support of a business strategy, and this is relevant for the innovator because of the difficulties of analysing future benefits.

In situations involving investment decisions on innovation in technology-supported learning, the weight of investment is in people, rather than in direct capital investment. The Internet can act as a research, marketing and delivery tool that serves to quicken competition from all shared options. It makes uniqueness, distinctiveness and a niche segment important. The

Internet acts to stimulate the competitive environment, speed up the product life-cycles and thereby shorten the time-value of options.

In terms of e-learning, the same principles on growth options can still apply, but with more competitors and faster speeds of replication. The application of Internet-enabled learning serves to widen the competitor base from local and regional to global, while the presence of an existing virtual learning environment speeds replication. A proprietary option can arise in a surprisingly large range of technology-supported learning situations. They exist in aerospace simulations, military technology applications, computer-assisted learning, certain multimedia training environments and so on. Wherever an application can be accompanied by a patent, intellectual or other proprietary rights which effect an influence on the education and training development, it is reasonable to expect an organization with a proprietary advantage to maintain this protection and to exercise all legitimate means to keep it. It will try to continue to extract value, invest in further options and maintain the proprietary barrier, in order to develop fully the product–market opportunities as long as it remains feasible.

In contrast, for a shared option with no proprietal protection the competition is high. Such an area of high competitive activity is e-delivery of enterprise skills. There are very many accredited and non-accredited courses available as well as specialist sources of information. For instance, a useful source of bulleted information for owner-managers and decision-makers in SMEs and LSEs is Directors' Briefing (*www.biznews.co.uk*). Originally available in print only, this migrated three years ago to e-delivery and makes content on key business issues, such as innovation and product development, freely available to subscribers in the UK (Roffe et al., 2000).

KEY RISKS FOR E-LEARNING BUSINESS

Risks exist in developing e-learning for distance education. If resources are committed to the design, supply and support of a course, will sufficient students register? Will additional students overload the technology or support systems? The variety of e-learning applications makes it difficult to present a complete picture, but one risk is that many products, services and business models are generally unproven. There are also conventional risks in substitution from existing offline services with greater financial resources, as well as other online providers. Market factors can include long sales-cycles to convert interest into a firm contract. Expectations from e-learning can run ahead of the market demand. There are personnel and organizational risk factors, because the operation of a service-based business depends on attracting and retaining key employees and it is necessary to manage staff as well as the technology actively. For enterprises engaged in collaborative activity, there is a possible reliance on partners to complete the business model by contributing content, technology or support. There is always the risk that difficulties can arise in some, or all, of these areas.

Traditional financial measures have not always kept up with the pace of change set by new service models, such as partnership, outsourcing and other innovative ways of doing business. Service-oriented business providers are being designed around low capital investment and narrow profit margins. Applications of economic value added (EVA) management systems are increasingly popular in assessing the real options when seeking to maximize value from a business proposition. Economic value added is a measure that allows decision-makers to see whether they are getting an adequate return. EVA is a measure of profit less the cost of all capital employed. It is a measure that properly accounts for all the trade-offs involved in creating value, because of its simultaneous focus on profit and capital. With EVA, every business unit is explicitly charged for the use of capital through a 'line of credit' that bears interest at a rate equal to the cost of capital. A hurdle rate can then be set, below which performance is unacceptable.

Analytical methods are important in comparing plans with actual performance during project implementation. There are still risks of inaccurate predictions. Problems can arise from many sources: unclear objectives, overconfidence, inadequate funding, an ineffective team and so on. There is a risk even in trying to get full information if this overly inhibits development. In reality, most activities start by experimentation based on the best evidence available and develop from this position.

NEW PARADIGMS

Technology-supported learning is causing a reassessment of the best organizational structures for providers of ODFL (Bates, 2001: 36–58; Campion and Renner, 1992: 7–28; Rumble, 1995: 10–20). Making money from learning in conventional class-based settings often follows industrial, Fordist principles because high financial contributions can be made by polished lectures given by academic celebrities to very large classes of students. Similarly, the traditional approach to distance education is also based on the principles of the industrial economy, or Fordist organization, where the key to competitiveness is assured by mass production and sales volume. Examples in education are found in the large autonomous open universities and in massive higher-education institutions in the United States, Europe and the Far East.

The same economy-of-scale principles can be carried over into Internet delivery. One way is to attract large audiences with authentic content by well-known figures, but with a minimum of feedback and interactivity, in order to keep down marginal costs and take full advantage of economies of scale. The courses that result may prove attractive to student-clients, but fall far short of achieving the full potential of learning technology. The danger is that, in order to enlarge the size of the audience, providers will favour simple material over more demanding courseware. Minimizing interactivity, of course, may cause students to learn less.

Post-Fordist, or post-industrial, organizations are emerging because the basic paradigms of competition are changing the industrialization model. Increasing differentiation between products, various geographic markets and their personalization to suit different customer groups, serves to fragment production volume and reduces the applicability of the economies of scale doctrine. Examples of typical organizations that fit into this form are found in high added-value companies, such as software firms like Microsoft and Apple. Such organizations have certain characteristics. There is a dependency on information technology, customized products, empowered and creative workers. These in turn allow rapid product development, a swift response to change and a global view of operations. In e-learning terms, this explains the suggestion by Peters that large-scale courses for as many students as possible are no longer always needed, but rather a variety of courses with low numbers where the course content is constantly updated (O. Peters, 1998: 114).

The key to responding to this new scenario is to divide product development into two phases: platform design and personalization (Otala, 1995: 157–64). In platform design, a fundamental product-family design is achieved that can easily be modified to suit the demands of various customer groups and markets in which extreme standardization is the rule. The platform can then be rapidly differentiated and customized for a personalization phase, which will generate an array of seemingly different products, all based on the same standardized product platform, thus creating the benefits of volume production. In this way a whole range of personalized niche products can be presented from a single platform design, an approach directly relevant for breakthrough in technology-supported learning.

Three new paradigms can therefore replace the old Fordist 'economy of scale' model: economies of timing, scope and skill. With *economy of timing*, the timely concentration of actions towards a business breakthrough is important. The great benefit of this model comes from freeing management time to concentrate on planning a few large coordinated actions at any given period of time, which helps to reduce the problems of complexity. Actions should be orchestrated so as to succeed in one action at a time, by using all available resources in a coordinated and well-timed series of moves. The synchronization of all these actions into a consistent plan, based on the expected business impact, leads to economies of timing. When success on one objective has been achieved, the next one can be reviewed and the necessary series of moves organized. Applying this model needs a clear understanding of the strengths, weaknesses, opportunities and threats (SWOT) facing an enterprise, concentrated just-in-time processes and taskforces, together with the elimination of silo practices – the building of large quantities of information in organizational departments that are difficult to access.

The *economy of scope* model brings extra efficiency, gained through concentrating efforts, to selected areas of activity that comprise the business core in terms of markets, products and customers. Pursuing a goal of worldwide dominance in a market niche requires the application of this paradigm. This focus increases awareness on the critical success factors, a process that may restrict the scope to those areas where the enterprise excels, which can then serve to encourage organizational learning and boost the intensity of learning. Employing this paradigm requires a clear understanding of the SWOT of the enterprise, the benefits of empowered teams, the adaptability in the workforce and the elimination of rigid departments.

An *economy of skill* model exists in an enterprise when the primary operational requirement is the competence of employees. Staff are expected to have up-to-date knowledge of their profession or trade that leads to an increased call for up-to-date education and training. Fundamental imperatives for the paradigm are an accepted business strategy, open management, and clear and sensitive human resource policies. Economy of skill is attained through increased occupational and social competence for the individual and greater competitiveness for the enterprise. Applying the model requires a clear business SWOT, a solidly implemented lifelong learning culture, continuous improvement process, empowered teams and the elimination of any immunity reactions against lifelong learning.

CREATING AN E-LEARNING STRATEGY

These three production paradigms are ways in which an enterprise can create a new e-learning product and create a competitive edge through operations. Different institutions, however, adopt a range of planning approaches because of the variety of management challenges. Identifying subject strengths and service delivery strengths in a policy matrix is one way (Bjarnason et al., 2000a: 219–23; Sizer, 1982). Another approach is a more detailed top-down approach, which is advocated for corporate applications (Rosenberg, 2001). In general, the process involves marshalling facts on the current position, thoughts on forward goals for a desired position, anticipating and organizing ahead.

Most successful strategies for creating an e-learning business include the following actions. The current position is analysed as it relates to launching and sustaining e-learning. The influences causing change and the current internal state of learning and development, resources, technology and business strengths are assessed. A desired future situation for e-learning is described from the business position, competitors, rationale, funding and student groups. The mission for the educational enterprise is set in succinct terms. The gap between future and current position is analysed. The strategy to close the gap is defined. An action plan to execute the strategy is prepared, with adequate resources, timelines and milestones.

Successful strategies tend to emerge from patterns of small, individual decisions that can arise anywhere in an organization and are not totally planned in advance, according to Mintzberg (Mintzberg, 1994). For academic departments and sections engaged in e-learning, an emergent strategy based on planning and management is an iterative process, in which strategies that emerge are learned, applied and adapted in a deliberate and controlled way, suggets Bates (Bates, 2000: 210).

COMPETITIVE FORCES FOR E-LEARNING

Viewed as a business, higher education has been a very attractive proposition, with high entry-barriers for potential competitors, not very appealing substitutes, and a ready supply of well-qualified faculty and not very strong competition. There are substantial opportunities for higher and further education, represented by the increasing economic value of academic qualifications, the shift to lifelong learning, the acceleration of knowledge and the increase in leisure and early retirement. Technology makes it far easier for new entrants to come into the education sector, needing no campus, no library, lower capital costs, having ready access to course materials on the Web, and so on.

In an open business environment, it is inevitable that competitors try to match the value in an initial e-learning offer. The classic model of the competitive forces on a business in an industry describes how the economic value created by a service is divided between enterprises in an industry (Porter, 1980: 61). The central tenet of the model is that a business exists in an industry and to succeed, it must deal with the five competitive forces within that industry. The core of strategy formulation lies in addressing the competition and the intensity of that competition depends on how that industry is structured, its underlying economics and the competitive forces that go beyond the existing competitors. These five forces are in equilibrium, determined by a balance of power between: the threat of new entrants, the bargaining power of buyers, the bargaining power of suppliers, the threat of substitutes and the extent of the rivalry between competitors. The combination of the five forces determines how the economic value created by a service, product, technology or way of competing is divided between enterprises in an industry, or the collection of customers, suppliers, substitutes and new entrants (Porter, 2001: 63). The five-forces model has been applied to education provision to assist strategy formulation (Daniel, 1996; Collis, 2001: 7–24) and the analysis of competitive rivalry can be applied to the e-learning industry.

Barriers for new entrants can be reduced by the Internet, which dispenses with the need for a dedicated sales force, or access to physical assets. Internet applications are difficult to keep proprietary from new entrants and, as a result, a wave of new providers have come into many industries. Historically, entry costs into education have been very high, because of the substantial capital costs required to build a campus and make the associated investments in infrastructure and resources in areas like the library and IT. It takes time to receive institutional validation to gain accreditation. Even more resources are needed to appoint staff and develop a reputation that will attract students and researchers. The Internet represents a particular threat because it makes it relatively easy to start an enterprise with limited capital, since no campus is required. The convergence of technology also means that firms that have operated in different sectors, such as in television media and publishing, can more easily gain access to other markets because of their access to technology. Proprietal issues may exist around who owns the intellectual property rights of the content of a course, but new entrants can contract to commission content or negotiate a licence for existing material. Barriers for entry into corporate e-learning can be expected to rise as providers build customer loyalty, raise perceived value and increase product differentiation.

The threat of substitute products or services can come from the Internet as it influences the industry structure by making the overall industry more efficient and, in the case of e-learning, expanding the size of the market. The proliferation of Web approaches can create new threats. Substitute products and services for e-learning include conventional text from publishing companies, conventional distance-learning programmes, and classroom-based instruction from a corporate university, a new provider or a conventional university or college. In most cases a substitute product exists as an alternative to e-learning, although it might not be as accessible, but some alternatives have limited credibility. The motivations for study are strong, because accredited learning provides a way to realise vocational ambitions or work-related needs. It offers the benefits of personalization, access, social inclusion and self-fulfilment. The cachet of an accredited programme is high, particularly from a distinguished institution. The benefits of high-level qualifications in the value added to salary and earning power across a lifetime of earning is lodged in public awareness and serves to create demand for education programmes.

Sourcing by the Web tends to raise bargaining power over suppliers, but can give suppliers access to more customers. The supply of education has historically been a relatively minor factor in determining the market equilibrium. Academic staff are a crucial factor in the delivery of conventional higher education. The move towards e-delivery of ODFL is changing the roles of staff, making it easier to engage staff for different facets of delivery and content development. With this redefinition of responsibilities, lower-cost staff and graduate students as tutors can take over an increasing share of student support.

The bargaining power of buyers is affected because the Internet serves to bypass powerful distribution channels or helps improve the bargaining power over conventional channels. The Internet helps to strengthen the bargaining power of end-user consumers; it also assists them in reducing the costs of switching from one supplier to another. In education, until recently, the bargaining power of buyers has been weak. The bargaining power of customers is greatly increased when they use the Internet to compare prices and performance. Historically, the consumers of education are individuals with no leverage over the provider from whom they are buying education. They are invited to purchase a service whose ultimate value is discernible only after the event. Buying decisions are difficult because information is based on reputations and word-of-mouth referral that give rise to real or imagined differences between providers.

Rivalry exists among existing competitors. The Internet acts to reduce differences among competitors as regards products and services and makes it difficult to retain a proprietary control. The geographic market is broadened, which serves to increase the number of competitors. Competition moves to price and the effect here is to lower the variable cost relative to the fixed cost, thereby increasing the pressures towards discounting. Among providers in the education sector, competitive rivalry has been relatively low, with the limited capacity of an educational enterprise a big constraint on competition.

Strategic analysis such as this gives an insight into the generic forces at an industry level, but reveals less about the practical responses for small e-learning providers. The source of competition also varies from country to country; whereas in the US it arises from a mix of commercial and public providers, in west Wales it comes predominantly from public-sector colleges and universities. Direct competition comes from other e-learning service-providers and also from substitutes by other modes of learning, such as conventional classes, part-time evening classes or traditional open-learning courses that existed before the arrival of e-learning. In order to compete with them, an educational enterprise needs to ensure that its e-learning service remains different from the products offered by rivals.

VALUE PROPOSITION FOR E-BUSINESS

Value is a crucial concept in e-business. It can help a student distinguish between competitive offers. Customer value is the difference between the values that the customer gains from owning and using a product service and the costs of obtaining it. Consider, for example, Open University customers, who gain a number of benefits from registration, such as authoritative learning-programmes, some status and image values, flexible study-routes and recognized awards. Money, time and psychological effort are the costs. Students assess these values against the various costs of using the service. During the process of purchasing they will compare the value of using the Open University against the value of using other learning providers and select the one that gives them the greatest delivered value that they perceive.

Clients often do not judge product/service values and costs either accurately or objectively, but act on perceived value (Faulkner and Bowman, 1995: 5). Does the Open University really provide a better-prepared and more reliable service than other providers of distance learning? If so, is the Open University brand worth the relative price-difference that it charges to students? The Open University is a large provider of ODFL learning programmes, one of eleven large mega-universities across the world, with over 100,000 client-students each year (Daniel, 1996). Many consumers do, therefore, perceive value in the OU offer. The challenge for new entry educational enterprises is to change these customer value-perceptions, to find a new set of consumers, or to try to do both.

E-learning appears to make this challenge more feasible for a new entrant. As Christiensen argued in his study of 'disruptive innovation' (Christiensen, 1997), an organization can continue to service customers and sustain high standards of service and good product quality, designed by careful research and course teams. However, new disruptive technology arrives which cannot be integrated into its existing current operations in a rapid and straightforward way. These disruptive technologies require a different organizational structure in which to flourish. If they do flourish, they can transform the whole enterprise.

The challenge for the Open University is that the Internet is a sustaining technology in some areas, while disruptive in others. It is sustaining in that it extends the opportunities for students to communicate with each other, but disruptive because it allows a distance-learning system to be reconstructed and implemented by competitor providers. One such case is the rapid application of the e-learning technology mode by the University of Glamorgan in business and enterprise studies. Originally a collaborator with the Open University in the delivery of OU-sourced programmes to business, it attracted sufficient EU funds to create products and become a competitor. It operates as a dual-mode university in business studies, targeting similar customers to the OU Business School (*www.enterprisecollege.glam.ac.uk*).

Another point of disruption for the Open University arises from recruitment. A topical and popular short course may completely fill, with the overflow of potential students advised to register for a following course that may start months later. Deferring enrolments from students clearly risks losing them, but can also signal a system with an emphasis on sustaining processes, rather than addressing disruption.

VALUE FROM INTANGIBLES

Why should a customer register with one educational enterprise rather than with any one of the host of others on offer? In trying to establish a competitive edge, the Internet and its related tools for delivering learning will not in itself provide a competitive advantage. The Internet as a business tool is not necessarily a business advantage in every respect, since it tends to lower overall profitability for an industry and has a levelling effect on business practices, reducing the ability of any company to establish an operational advantage that can be sustained (Porter, 2001: 73). For many enterprises, though, the question is how best to deploy the Internet to retain competitive equity. Internet technology does offer better opportunities for enterprises to form distinctive strategic positioning than earlier generations of technology did.

There are six principles for establishing and maintaining a distinctive strategic positioning (Porter, 1996). First, start with the right goal. Secondly, strategy must enable an enterprise to deliver a value proposition different from those that competitors offer. Thirdly, strategy needs to be reflected in a distinctive value chain. To establish a sustainable competitive advantage, an enterprise must perform different activities in different ways. Fourthly, robust strategies involve trade-offs, abandoning some features, services or activities in order to be unique in others. Fifthly, the strategy defines how all the elements of an enterprise fit together throughout the value chain. Sixthly, strategy involves continuity of direction in maintaining a distinctive value-proposition.

Attaining a competitive position involves building on proven ways in which the Web complements traditional means of competing, but not setting these apart from established processes. An educational enterprise is distinguished by being better than competitors, for instance by being 10 per cent better on one or two key attributes. These attributes might be the ability to facilitate faster progress, greater cost-effectiveness, better learning support or even the perception of being more student-friendly.

Achieving a competitive edge will depend largely on how an organization manages both its intangibles and its financial assets, according to Low and Kalafut (2002), who attempt to quantify the influence of ideas and relationships on decision-making, using a value-creation index. They estimate that one-third of an organization's value is derived from intangibles – elements that cannot be seen, such as brand, reputation, strategy execution, know-how, relationships, work processes, innovation and culture. Low and Kalafut could not establish any statistical connection to market value for two value-drivers: technology and customer satisfaction. Technology, they concluded, is so essential to any company that its value is neutralized. A customer satisfaction measurement helps to determine customer requirements and identify better ways to anticipate and fulfil them, but this did not register with them as a value driver. It might be the case that customer satisfaction is embedded into other factors such as quality or innovation, or could mean that a particular level of customer satisfaction is necessary to remain competitive. However, maximizing satisfaction levels does not offer competitive advantage compared with other value-drivers.

Measuring intangibles has attracted attention recently as a means of competing on value. Stewart (1997) identified interesting ways to measure the contributions to human capital. One way is through innovation, by measuring the gross margins on new products compared to old ones. Another way is by employee attitudes – employees who feel they are learning and valued tend to be more productive. Other measures include tenure, turnover, experience and learning, which can give an indication of a firm's ability to retain and grow its talent base.

The University of Chicago is a pioneer in devising a value-creation index that can be applied to educational service-providers (Shannon et al., 2003). In their view, the key steps are determining the critical intangibles for delivery and formulating suitable metrics for each. Work at the Graham School of General Studies resulted in identifying the key intangibles for general education as leadership, reputation, strategy execution, human capital, technology, communication and brand. These are measured to create a baseline and then initiatives are undertaken to improve performance. This set of intangibles aligns well with the conclusions of Nohria et al. regarding essential management practices that result in superior business performance (Nohria et al., 2003: 43).

COSTS AND PERCEIVED VALUE

The notions of perceived usefulness and perceived ease of use for the adoption of technology emerged from empirical studies by Davis (Davis, 1989: 475–87). This leads to a way to judge the value perceived by a client, and consequently its influence on sustaining a competitive strategy, by a customer matrix (Faulkner and Bowman, 1995). The aim is to show the effects of changing price or value, and thereby clarify the significant actions necessary to maintain a competitive edge. Two parameters, perceived user-value (PUV) and perceived price, create the matrix. PUV refers to the perception of a client in purchasing and using a service; perceived price comprises the elements of price that concern the customer. For example, in purchasing an e-learning programme, the client may be concerned less with the initial cost of enrolment than with the recurrent costs to completion or the loss of employee-time for study. The aim is to show the effects of changing price, or value, and thereby help clarify the significant actions for maintaining a competitive edge.

Figure 7.1: Competitive moves on customer matrix

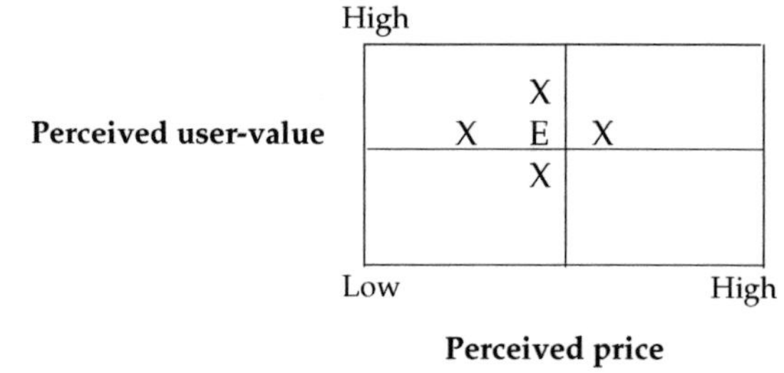

High

```
          X
     X    E    X
          X
```

Perceived user-value

Low   High

Perceived price

The competitive moves available to an e-learning enterprise (E) surrounded by other providers (X) as alternative suppliers are shown in Figure 7.1. The competitors cluster around E, as they all appear to a client to offer similar products and prices. All suppliers, in principle, have a similar share of the market. An educational enterprise can try to improve its competitive position by changes in perceived user-value and price. Most of the possible moves have disadvantages that can lead an enterprise into a different segment, a reduction in market share, or trade-offs between being cheaper or better. Nevertheless, two basic strategic choices are viable: cut prices, or raise the PUV of the e-learning services.

An enterprise can try to improve its competitive position by changes on the customer matrix in perceived user-value and price. The moves are:

North-east: raising PUV and price. Success with this move depends on groups of students prepared to pay higher prices. Another factor is the ease with which the additional PUV can be replicated.
East: increasing price without adding any more PUV. This can increase profitability if demand is strong enough and only if competitors follow the move rather than compete on lower price.
South-east: increasing price and decreasing value. A move which is feasible only if the supply is restricted but may lead to customer dissatisfaction. It can occur when scaling-up an e-learning programme in response to rising demand, if senior staff are not available and the only available staff are junior. It can also occur if the quality of the support service changes through introducing queuing in some form.
South: reducing value but keeping the price constant. This may occur through reducing tutorial support but retaining the same fees and will ultimately lead to a loss of market share.
South-west: cutting price and PUV. This may move into a new downmarket segment. This is viable only if it can supply against lower-cost competitors and it does not affect the brand image. It can occur by offering non-advanced provision from a higher-education institution, bringing competition from colleges and other providers.

West: cutting price but maintaining the PUV. To retain profitability, this move is feasible only if the educational enterprise is the lowest-cost producer and can sustain low prices in the face of cost-cutting by competitors.

North-west: increasing PUV coupled with reduced price. A feasible route to gain market share, which appears to be a winning strategy because the service appears better and cheaper.

North: increasing PUV and keeping the price constant. Adding more value for the same price should allow an enterprise to gain market share by attracting more students.

Costs are generally similar for the same kind of e-learning provider and similar types of activity, often constrained by staffing. Some cost-cutting tactics are available, such as making support levels adaptable to demand, offering programmes with a reduced service level, or limiting tutorial interaction (queuing at the point of demand or automated client-help systems). The scope for relative cost-cutting, though, is really very limited for similar levels of service. A provider who cuts prices will move to the west on the customer matrix, offering the same PUV as the competition, but at a lower price. As a competitive move this should increase market share. Some customers, however, perceive price to be a proxy for PUV; reducing price may lead to a move south-west and to falling profits. Ultimately, such a path can lead to marked reductions in PUV, which may raise questions of quality and the integrity of provision. Even without a link between price and PUV, the effect of a price-cut is likely to cause other providers to respond quickly to the move by cutting prices, thereby reducing the average price and profitability of the whole sector. Consequently, a provider can gain an enduring advantage only by continually driving down prices, and can maintain its position only by being the lowest-cost producer, sustaining lower prices for a longer period than its competitors, or finding sponsorships or subsidies.

Moving north on the customer matrix gives competitive advantage to the enterprise by offering more PUV for the same price as competitors. With this move, the provider tries to gain advantage through a clearer understanding of customer needs and what is valued in the e-learning service. These factors are translated into a set of PUV dimensions that can be compared with rival service offers, with the intention of continuously enhancing the relative value. Pursuing and sustaining a northward trip involves moving faster than competitors, while stripping out all PUV dimensions except those that maintain the movement northward. As an enterprise moves north ahead of competitor providers, it should attract an increased share of the market. Competitors will try to match the raised PUV and, given time, are likely to match the move. This leads to an overall raise in the minimum acceptable standards of the sector over time.

What can an educational service-provider do in such circumstances? Two feasible options exist. One is to keep moving north by staying ahead of the competition, through continuous improvement and innovation. Another is a move north-west, through combining PUV improvement with a reduction in price. Heading north-west can be a winning strategy, as the service is perceived by the client to be both better and cheaper than those of competitors, but it is a position that is not easy to achieve or to sustain. It requires a deep and continuing understanding of the criteria that a client applies to assess each dimension of value. The existing products or services must be reviewed constantly with the aim of upgrading them and enhancing their level of PUV, so that value enhancement of the e-learning processes becomes a systemic competence of an enterprise. The north-west move might be achieved through moving north to add value initially, to add scale and experience. As competitors begin to replicate the value, the enterprise cuts the price.

DIMENSIONS OF PUV

Collecting input from customers on a regular basis helps to understand their needs and satisfaction levels. This information can be used to improve customer loyalty by identifying and eliminating the barriers to customer satisfaction. It can also be used to identify the real dimensions of perceived value and to compare one service-provider with another. One approach to data-gathering and interpretation on PUV is to analyse a single segment of demand, such as the provision for small firms, in a structured manner:

1. Identify the PUV dimensions that are changing in meaningful ways by asking clients what characteristics of the service they value.
2. Weight the PUV dimensions according to their importance.
3. Query representative clients to determine a rating for each perceived dimension and then a score.
4. Sum the scores for each dimension to achieve a total score. This performance can then be compared and used as the basis of value enhancement.
5. Extend the analysis to other cases of demand.

In the following example, 'authenticity', 'personalization', 'flexibility', 'support' and 'accreditation' are identified as the dimensions that are important to our clients. We then gave a weight to each dimension, ranging from 30 for 'authenticity' to 10, 'accreditation'. Table 7.2 gives the tabulated result of the method, applied to a case of three competitors. With three providers, the values of 1, 2 and 3 – 3 being the highest – are assigned to the ratings within each dimension. So, for example, in comparing your own service relative to the two others, if your service is the leader, give it a score of 3 and assign 2 and 1 to the other services, depending on the clients' assessments.

When the weighting is multiplied by the rating, a score for each dimension is obtained. For example, taking the dimension of 'authenticity', which has the highest assigned weighting of 30, service A is rated the best, giving it a rating of 3; multiplying weighting by rating produces a score of 90. For this dimension, service C is second with a rating of 2, and a score of 60; service B is last with a rating of 1 and a score of 30. The process is then repeated for each of the five dimensions of PUV to determine an overall score for each service.

The maximum or ideal total for a provider is 300, meaning that it is the leader in each dimension. In the example, service A has a score of 220, currently offering the greatest perceived value, although not the lowest price as provider B, who has the lowest PUV score. These scores can then be charted on the PUV versus perceived price diagram (Figure 7.1).

Table 7.2. Calculating PUV ratings for competitors' products

Dimension of PUV	Weighting	Service A (own service)		Service B		Service C	
		Rating	Rating × weight	Rating*	Rating × weight	Rating*	Rating ×weight
Authenticity	30	3	90	1	30	2	60
Personalization	25	1	25	3	75	2	50
Flexibility	20	2	40	1	20	3	60
Support	15	3	45	2	30	1	15
Accreditation	10	2	20	2	20	1	10
Total (max. 300)	100		220		175		195
Price		£870		£840		£960	

* Compared with own service.

There are certain risks involved in this approach; among them are possible mistakes in the attribution of the weightings to the various dimensions, that can lead to the wrong score. Competitors are also working continuously to improve their service offer and so the relevance, importance, weighting and ratings of the dimensions will change with time. Moreover, the focus on a service cannot predict a 'disruptive technology' from making the service of all three providers obsolete. Another difficulty is that both PUV and perceived price are dynamic parameters and that perceived price can be distorted by price subsidy. For example, the figures in Table 7.2 represent an illustration of the initial price range, but if service-provider B secures a grant to subsidize a programme for SMEs at nominal or nil price then this will affect its market appeal. This will be attractive to SME clients and will distort the market unless, or until, providers A and C can make a similar offer. Market equilibrium will then be regained for as long as the subsidy remains in place, but the competitive emphasis increases on the dimensions of PUV. It seems logical that when all providers offer a programme at little or no cost, a customer chooses the product with the greatest value.

The advantages are that this approach strips away all the non-essential features and allows a focus on the fundamentals that drive an improvement in perceived value. It is both desirable and achievable for most providers to undertake an analysis of competitors, insofar as the amount of time and resources taken will not distract from the educational development process. The effort to determine PUV can be made proportionate to the value of the course or contract, and can also be extended across a whole portfolio of courses.

USE OF THE PUV TOOL

Devising a Welsh-language e-learning service will illustrate the application of the PUV tool. Initial development work determined that competition from three major sources was imminent: a media production company with links to broadcasters and a network of community colleges (service-provider B), as well as two other universities (service-providers C and D). In practice, the launch of a service at Lampeter in March 1999 preceded that of the competitors by between six and twelve months. Value analysis was applied at the end of the first cycle of delivery after nine months and before a major course revision.

Service-provider B appeared initially to be the leading competitor. It brought expertise from television educational programme-making and had access to advanced technology resources. It chose a diversified delivery approach: broadcast educational programmes, a CD-ROM incorporating video, and the possibility of video streaming. Substantial financial investment was made into broadcast-quality recorded programmes that targeted a wide range of subjects and levels. Studio-produced content was good, but offered little opportunity for flexibility or adaptation. Personalization was attempted through assigning an individual tutor from a community college. Support was judged to be poor, because most clients used dial-up modem connections from learning centres and homes, technical service breaks occurred, and problems arose with video-streaming for individual users. Despite the access to public-service broadcast television, service-provider B's experience underscored a key lesson for technology-supported learning: the technology must be in widespread use among the target population before it is applied as a platform for the delivery of learning. The lesson for us was to pitch and maintain our technology design by featuring easily accessible, simple asynchronous delivery, and to focus support on reducing technical problems for users. The wide range of subjects and levels made it difficult for service-provider B to focus on a specific area and claim authenticity. Mass communications also made it difficult to personalize an approach. And, because it came from a non-university provider, the content was perceived to have a lower level of accreditation and authenticity.

Service-provider C developed a full online degree programme, with the Welsh-medium elements a subset of a larger course offering. The main attraction was the opportunity to study for a degree without loss of earnings. This provider had attracted substantial government sponsorship and emphasized recruitment in full degree programmes, thereby meeting the requirements of its sponsor and bringing relatively high financial rewards. Personalization and support for this programme were strong, but little flexibility existed in accreditation and the source of content was relatively less authentic. We applied the PUV tool to test the demand for a degree programme among our client-base and found that it strongly preferred short, credit-based work. This influenced us to concentrate on shorter, credit-based specialist courses and to try to achieve economies of scale by attracting large enrolments.

Service-provider D, the last market entrant, competed on the basis of the experience of its staff in face-to-face instruction in the field. The launch product was based on text files designed for face-to-face teaching, but downloaded from a Website. Support was designed for part-time campus attendance, which reduced the flexibility for learners and offered no personalization. As a late entrant, the client-base it attracted was very small and so it had few financial resources for continuously improving the programme, leading to a continuing low level of support with low investment in recruitment and technical improvements. Internet support can complement conventional part-time study, but it seemed that providing e-learning in a full distance-education mode requires appropriate content design and effective learner support to help reduce the 'distance' for the learner.

Through PUV analysis, greater insights into competitor issues were possible in these cases than normal because of a contract to evaluate provision for firms. Distortions were observed in the perceived price due to intervention by EU subsidies. This evaluation work, however, revealed that we erred, by making overly generous assumptions about our competitors' capabilities, based on their promotional material. This, of course, is a relatively better position to take than to underestimate one's competitors. One way to check the reliability of the ratings, however, is to check with an analysis of recent market share, if this is available.

ANALYSIS AND EXECUTION

Analysis is incomplete unless it leads to execution. The real-life value of the PUV tool is its impact on the curriculum delivery process and its discovery of unique value. The evaluation stage is the rational point to test the methodology and processes, but evaluation often only extends to the immediate participants in a class. Results at this level may report high levels of student satisfaction, but extrapolating these results and concluding, without further testing, that the course continues to meet the perceived values of a specific market group can lead to mistakes. There is a danger that, while continuing to provide courses with high standards of service and good design, 'disruptive innovation' may occur that cannot be integrated into current operations in a rapid and straightforward way. This is the most dramatic situation, but more often this leads to a failure to adapt a course to changing work-practices and ends with the course reaching the end of its life-cycle due to low enrolments.

All this means that the proper strategic route for an e-learning provider is not simply competing on price, but in pursuing its own distinctive strategy to raise perceived value. Even so, achieving and sustaining competitive advantage is difficult. Adapting the PUV to improve the offer of an enterprise can involve a development shift to meet the perceptions of customers. The change requires a deep and continuing understanding of the criteria that a customer applies to assess each dimension of value. The existing products or services are constantly reviewed, with the aim of upgrading them and enhancing their level of PUV, so that enhancement of the value of the e-learning processes becomes a systemic competence of an enterprise. This implies that quality is a core systemic competence of the enterprise. Quality, or value assurance, is the effectiveness of the process that ensures constant cost-reduction without leading to value loss, with an accompanying decline in PUV.

Discovering client views of perceived value can be done in different ways, such as interviews and questionnaires, with a consultancy approach – placing clients in the role of adviser – often giving good results. Interaction with the learner is a valuable source of information that can be applied to improve the e-learning provision. Questions and answers to participants on their experiences of their learning environment and course support can improve the content and infrastructure. Monitoring the Website for user hits and traffic can also provide an important insight into activity levels on an e-learning programme. Detail can be revealed on the origins of information requests and the effect of marketing promotion. Continuing customer dialogue can then lead into innovation from such customer information.

The analysis can then be extended to other areas of demand. Each student base will have particular dimensions to its PUV, so that SME employees and recreational lifelong learners will have differences in the dimensions or their relative weighting. An educational enterprise can then construct a PUV for each student group. Improving perceived user-value, though, does need facts, from which to decide and develop the options for other demand areas. To establish these, an enterprise should conduct market research, to find out how the marketplace perceives its offer and identify any customer buying trends.

VALUE AND PROPRIETARY CONTROL

E-learning can create value, reduce costs or achieve a combination of both. Perceived value can be delivered to clients in different ways. Value can be built by more accessible modes to educational content, or creating personalized learning tracks, or by assembling and sharing knowledge among employees, networks or peer-learners. Establishing a competitive position means making a different form of offer to tempt clients to enrol, and therefore places a responsibility on the provider to create a value proposition that will fit different market requirements. The range of relevant competitive dimensions varies from one area of demand to another, but it becomes desirable to construct a proprietary barrier, if possible. This step is important in retaining control of the movement of the PUV.

One example of an aid to authenticity and proprietal control in e-learning at our university is an online dictionary. This dictionary is the only fully operational online Welsh–English dictionary, with more than 100,000 lexical items. A modest translation facility and grammatical detail are also included, offering value to learners who have to work in a bilingual environment. The contributors are leading lexicographers and the dictionary is continuously improved by client feedback. One respondent suggested that the addition of sound-files might add value to service, and so certain frequently used words have a sound recording to aid recognition and pronunciation (*www.geiriadur.net*). This source is not only authoritative, but adds perceived value to the learning offer; in effect, it tells clients that if they enrol on our courses, we can give them the means to help them with their daily work. The dictionary is available to anyone, including people enrolled on competitors' programmes, but we keep proprietary control because we maintain the dictionary database and can introduce a fee for access, if we choose, especially for selected areas such as medical terminology.

COMPETENCES TO ENHANCE VALUE

An educational service-provider building authenticity, personalization and other perceived dimensions of value for clients will eventually be confronted by other providers trying to serve the same market. Movements on the customer matrix to improve the competitive position of a provider can be achieved only by addressing the key internal value-creating competences. Changing all the system variables of an educational enterprise, however, may not be an option for an e-learning group. They can address only certain parameters within their control.

An educational enterprise can divide its competences into two categories: operational and system competences. In the former are specific technical competences that are relevant to operating in a particular market. These can comprise the creation of content, such as for a course on Internet marketing for small firms. They can also exist in the kind of learner support offered to specific participants, for example, by forms of technical mentoring of learners.

System competences span the range of activities undertaken by an educational service-provider and can be a major source of competitive advantage. These generic system competences include value assurance, value enhancement and innovation. These three generic system competences are important parameters for improving the efficiency, effectiveness and the perceived value of e-learning delivery to clients, and are elaborated in chapters 8 and 10.

Value assurance is the process that retains value in the course offer. It is related directly to maintaining authenticity for the client in the content. For an educational service-provider it is an important point of differentiation from the many other Internet-based providers from non-recognized educational bodies. Value enhancement covers the processes in which an educational service is reviewed constantly with the aim of upgrading and improvement. Both these processes are well established for different learning delivery modes by colleges and universities.

Innovation as a system competence is different. Even though the management processes of innovation are well understood, much effort is still underway across the world to discover new teaching, learning and support processes for e-delivery. This means that innovation as a competence to enhance value ought to be based on a systemic approach to develop and implement approaches that offer a large degree of proprietary control, and should use technology that is in widespread use by the client group.

FINDING THE CORE OFFER

Skill and technology gaps exist and, indeed, will always exist. The changes associated with the 'new economy' place a premium on knowledge, skills and training that, together with technology development, mean that there is likely to be a continuing source of innovative opportunity. The challenge for an educational service-provider is then to define and market a product that addresses gaps and to make the transition across them manageable for as many clients as possible. Converting a market opportunity into a continuing contract for learning, though, requires a sustained effort to maintain a competitive offer.

The general effect of market competition is to drive down prices or course fees. When this occurs, some education-providers determine that it is no longer cost-effective, cease to supply and withdraw from the market. This allows a new competitive equilibrium to form, with profit margins that are acceptable to the remaining competitors. The remaining providers are those which operate most efficiently, not simply on the parameter of price but also on authenticity and perceived value.

Formulating a strategy is one thing, but executing it is key to sustaining an e-learning business. The truly important act, though, is to determine the perceptions of the customer and detect the core offer that educational content designers, IT support and business recruitment staff are comfortable with, and then develop from this position. Gaining an understanding of perceived value through dialogue with customers seems more important than overlong strategic analysis of options. A practical approach through experimentation has benefits, therefore, in order to develop a fuller understanding of the customer, the dimensions of perceived value and the optimum supply methods.

8

Innovation

Innovation is a systematic competence of a provider that can sustain a competitive advantage and enhance perceived value. In education, innovation can affect curriculum design, teaching and learning methods, delivery systems, student groups and so on. Certain attributes of innovation have direct implications on the ease of acceptability of a novel e-learning service. E-learning is a source of opportunity for innovation by converting an idea into an e-learning service. There is unanimity in the literature on the general principles for the systematic process of innovation and how this is best done. Many of the studies are of large companies. The principles include monitoring sources of innovative opportunity and effective management to bring it to fruition. A classic response to gain a position that is timely in a new technology market is to set up a new and autonomous business unit to build new business around the innovation. Since the same technology is available to everyone, it cannot provide a long-term advantage to any particular provider. The emphasis then shifts to maintaining a competitive advantage by a dynamic and systematic approach to innovation through initiatives and projectization – converting work activities into discrete tasks and packages with defined resources and measurable outcomes.

DIFFERENT PERCEPTIONS OF INNOVATION

Education itself is in a constant process of innovation. Changes in knowledge and in the context and processes of teaching and learning provide both opportunities and constraints for people to adapt and practise their profession. Any shift in teaching and learning, purpose or priority, by an individual or group, can be construed as innovation. The term can also be reserved solely for major transformation efforts or breakthrough activities. The arrival of Internet-based teaching, using the Web as a delivery and support medium, is one such change. Whichever interpretation is preferred, for the people involved, the change efforts seem unique to the individual, the department, or the enterprise, even though, in practice, someone else has probably solved the problem, so that the real complication lies less in invention and more in finding and then gaining access to pre-existing solutions. E-learning is no different.

Innovation is a complex, rather subtle concept, interpreted in different ways in the literature. Some analysts regard an idea itself as an innovation, while others regard it as acceptance of change by an organization. Other commentators might regard it as something new for an organization. For certain observers, the term means an original invention. There is a degree of unanimity on the relevance of innovation for nearly every setting, but less agreement on the meaning of innovation, a point illustrated by the following definitions, by influential commentators in Europe, the United States and the United Kingdom:

Innovation is a synonym for the successful production, assimilation and exploitation of novelty in the economic and social spheres. (EC, 1996: 9)

Innovation consists of the social and managerial processes through which solutions are first translated into social use in a given culture. (Quinn et al., 1997: 3)

Creativity is the thinking process that helps us to generate ideas. Innovation is the practical application of such ideas. (Majaro, 1988: 6)

Systematic innovation consists in the purposeful and organised search for changes, and in the systematic analysis of the opportunities such changes might offer for economic and social innovation. (Drucker, 1994: 31)

An innovation is an idea, or object perceived as new by an individual. It matters little, so far as human behaviour is concerned, whether or not an idea is 'objectively' new as measured by the lapse of time since its discovery. The perceived newness of the idea for the individual determines his or her reaction to it. If the idea seems new to an individual, it is an innovation. (Rogers and Shoemaker, 1971: 11)

Each definition is descriptive, concerned with what happens when innovation occurs, and most make it quite explicit that the practical application of an idea is central to the purpose of an innovation. The variety of meaning includes the discovery of new ideas, the screening of ideas and methods of applying them to particular problems that bring them into widespread use. An innovation is often incremental, involving small-scale improvements; occasionally it can be larger in scope and, very rarely, it may be a breakthrough involving global commercial change. What it is not concerned with is trivial change, insignificant modifications or minor differences that may add slight variety or choice to the product, which for the customer is still essentially the same offer. These are not commonly construed as innovation, although products offering trivial diversity are often labelled wrongly as innovation, to distinguish between competitor products and to cope with over-capacity in an industry.

The difficulties with innovation are in discovering methods and applying efforts that focus on the dynamics of human behaviour: for instance, how people can coordinate their efforts in processes such as creativity and innovation, and how these can be applied to enhance how people learn, cooperate, identify expertise, capture knowledge, make decisions and work together. These are complicated areas. As soon as you start thinking about innovation you are confronted with certain difficulties, created because the subject base is vast, rapidly increasing, multidisciplinary and sometimes accessible only through high costs and difficulties (Nayak and Ketteringham, 1987). Much has been discovered about the processes of innovation, but often the bases for study have been large companies.

INNOVATION AND HRD IN ORGANIZATIONS

Innovation in e-learning, although used as a single concept, can have different implications for a provider. An innovation in teaching and learning for campus-based students may not result in major change for the organization. For example, it can occur at the level of an individual member of staff. Innovation can in such cases be a private attempt to improve the teaching and learning dialogue, for instance, mediated by technology. At the institutional, faculty or school level, innovation is most often driven by policy. In this situation, innovation might be a short-term strategy for maximizing profits or addressing an organizational difficulty, or might be a long-term competitive strategy and core competence. In the latter case, competitive strategy brings the nature of the innovation closer to the entrepreneurial features of industry and commerce. When competing for e-learning students in large companies or SMEs, it can draw an educational organization into direct competition with commercial providers as well as with other public-sector organizations. Innovation is, then, a tool for an educational enterprise.

There are other parallels. Recent research suggests that certain academics are not that dissimilar to entrepreneurs in business in terms of their behavioural attributes (Hay et al., 2002: 132–41). The major difference, however, lies in the readiness to take risks. Indeed, many aspects of 'intrapreneurship', or enterprise in large organizations, are found in both commercial and educational practice. In both settings innovation is a lever for an entrepreneur.

If successful creativity and innovation can lead to multiple benefits for an organization, in either the public or private sectors, what then are the implications for the decision-makers in creating a systemic competence in innovation in an educational enterprise? There is no shortage of material to answer this question, since the subject base is immense; the practical difficulties are in condensing it for a sensible overview. One approach is to consider the implications of innovation in an enterprise on human resource development (Roffe, 1999: 224–37). Table 8.1 gives a synopsis of the research, where the main elements are grouped under corporate strategy, competitive response, creativity culture, organizational structure and product development. These studies have been drawn largely from large companies, often involving product development rather than services. Such an aggregation does risk oversimplifying the interlinkages between innovation, creativity and all the other organizational activities.

Table 8.1. Synopsis of implications of innovation for human resource development (after Roffe, 1999)

Dimension	Innovative organization-development implications
Corporate strategy	Corporate strategy: clear direction, integration and systematic innovation (Kanter, 1983; Peters and Waterman, 1982; Drucker, 1994; Schumpeter, 1975 [1942].) Vision: experimental and leading an innovative organization (Quinn, 1985; Senge, 1990; Christiensen, 1997). HRM: emphasis on personal development and teamwork (Drucker, 1992; Kanter, 1983; Majaro, 1988; Peters, 1997; Tushman and O'Reilly 1997; Shrivastava and Souder, 1987: 25–41; Clark and Wheelwright, 1992). General management: function of management is the release of energy and potential of personnel (Drucker, 1994; Garvin, 1993: 78–91; Kay, 1993; Morgan, 1993; Quinn, 1985).
General environmental and competitive response	Learning to learn: as a core skill for performance improvement and managing information (Drucker, 1988; Garvin, 1993; Morgan, 1991; Senge, 1990). Improved leadership skills: to operate in a more informal and collaborative environment (Adair, 1990; Kanter, 1983; Majaro, 1988; Morgan, 1991; Nayak and Ketteringham, 1987; Peters and Waterman, 1982; Senge, 1990; Leonard-Barton, 1995). IT-understanding: as a core employee-skill (Drucker, 1988; Morgan, 1991; Nonaka and Tekeuchi, 1995). Marketing (Hamel and Prahalad, 1989; Kanter, 1983; Morgan, 1991; Peters, 1997; Roberts, 1988; Utterback, 1994; von Hippel, 1992: 117–22; Wiersema, 1997; Moore, 1991, 1995).
Corporate culture and creativity climate	Team training fostering interdependency, cooperation and interdisciplinary working (Amabile, 1996; Kanter, 1983; Morgan, 1991; Nonaka and Tekeuchi, 1995; Quinn, 1985; Robinson and Stern, 1997; Senge, 1990). Coaching as a means of performance improvement (Peters, 1997; Roberts, 1988). Employee participation: as collaborators in policy-making and execution (Kanter, 1983; Stacey, 1992). Innovation audit: systematic and regular innovation scan and evaluation (Drucker, 1994; Kao, 1996; Majaro, 1988).
Organization	Improved communications: open and multidirectional flow of information (Drucker, 1992; Kanter, 1983; Kotter, 1995: 59–67; Nonaka and Tekeuchi 1995; Majaro, 1988; Quinn, 1985; Robinson and Stem, 1997). IT for knowledge

Table 8.1 (*contd.*)

	management (Kao, 1996; Leonard-Barton, 1995; Nonaka and Tekeuchi, 1995; Ohmae, 1987; Stewart, 1997; Davenport and Prusak, 1998). Management of change: interdependency and open system, with multiple linkages based on functional collaboration (Beckhard and Pritchard, 1991; Burns and Stalker, 1994; Kanter, 1983; Kotter, 1995). Project management (Hamel and Prahalad, 1989; Peters, 1997; Quinn, 1985).
New product development	Development process factors and characteristics (Cooper and Kleinschmidt, 1987: 169–84; Cooper, 1992: 113–27). Product-development skills (Song et al., 1997: 88–101; Leonard-Barton et al., 1994: 121–30).

CORPORATE STRATEGY

Innovation is implicitly associated with change and is always a challenge for decision-makers. The research base shows that innovation has implications for them that extend from corporate strategy down to the operational level. Strategic and HRD plans and actions cannot be outsourced, or left entirely to someone outside the organization, since they are linked crucially to the future success of an organization. There is unanimous agreement that an integrated-type organization is best suited to develop innovation, rather than a rigid departmental type, and that innovation can be systematized, but that problems can often arise through the management of the change process.

The decision systematically to search for, identify and then develop an innovation inevitably leads to managerial choices in support of the policy, not only in terms of finance but also in terms of organization and personnel. The extent of the change effort depends on the starting position of the organization, and the emphasis will vary because of the diversity in values, norms, attitudes and responsiveness to change in organizations. On the one hand there are organizations that are intrinsically non-entrepreneurial and bureaucratic. The change effort is likely to be enormous and the organization will present a stifling environment for an individual with creativity and an innovative spirit. On the other hand, there are organizations that function as open and adaptive learning organizations and who have managed change successfully. For most organizations, that fall between these two poles, innovation will involve change to a greater or lesser degree.

Even though the process of change associated with innovation is well documented, it can fail for a wide variety of reasons, such as poor communication, fear of failure, employee resistance, lack of planning and preparation, a misunderstanding of what change is and ill-prepared employees (Kotter, 1995:

59–67). With so many pitfalls in the way, it is understandable that many organizations confine their innovation activities to special units where the effects can be observed, controlled and analysed. These special units can take many forms and names in firms and educational institutions: innovation centres and enterprise units are just some.

Continuous innovation occurs largely because top managers appreciate innovation and manage their companies' value system and climate to support it (Quinn, 1985: 73–84). Quinn concludes that, in successful innovatory firms, the culture and corporate strategy are mobilized to support innovation and creativity and managers take active roles in leading the innovation process. The key for decision-makers is to eliminate risk-averse climates and replace them with organizational cultures in which innovation is expected and failure accepted. Decision-makers in an innovative enterprise project clear and long-term visions for their organizations that extend beyond economic parameters. Such vision has a practical impact in attracting quality people and provides focus for their creative drives. These visions can channel growth by focusing on the actions that lead to profitability and recognizing realistic time-frames for innovation.

In contrast to the positive forces which encourage innovation, other characteristics can sometimes limit innovation in organizations (Quinn, 1985). These include the isolation of top decision-makers, which fosters misunderstandings and contributes to a risk-averse climate. Vested interests can focus on the parts rather than the whole and emphasize the defence of some areas against the encroachment of others. There can be short time-horizons, which emphasize short-term results over the potential for new ideas to generate long-term gains. Overly rational thinking, that tries to place creative and chaotic processes into systematic and rational sequences, may emphasize schedules over development needs.

Then there is disruptive change. The key contribution of Schumpeter to the question of knowledge transfer was to introduce the notion of disruptive change or creative development as the energizing process explaining capitalist development (Schumpeter, 1975 [1942]). An entrepreneur makes a discovery and transforms it into a commercial innovation sold on the market. This is quickly followed by a swarm of imitators producing the same thing at less cost, so that time and innovation erode monopoly.

GENERAL COMPETITIVE RESPONSE

An enterprise that wants to be innovative has to build enterprising management and be managed as an enterprising business. The desire to innovate and the habits of enterprise are needed throughout the organization. Large companies, in general, are successful as entrepreneurs when they use their own people to build the venture, because they use employees who they understand, who understand them and who know how to get things done to gain a competitive edge. This implies the ability of the existing workforce to learn how to learn in order to get better, applying technology to enhance skills and providing effective leadership to achieve the objectives implicit in a new venture (Drucker, 1994).

CORPORATE CULTURE AND CREATIVE CLIMATE

Every enterprise aspires to become more creative and innovative, because of the benefits for its business. Relative unanimity exists on the requisites to maintain creativity: the climate for creative thinking must be right; an effective system of communicating ideas must exist at all levels; and procedures for managing innovation must be present. All three factors are interconnected and should exist in harmony. The absence of any one would be sufficient to constrain the effective development of innovation in the organization. The climate of an enterprise is one of the most difficult development areas to change and always needs total commitment and involvement from top management. A climate open to creativity has certain features; for example, it will be open-minded to encourage flexibility and group involvement, perceptive in seeing things from the employee's point of view, respect everyone for the diversity each brings, stimulate the expression of ideas and give clear objectives and specific feedback.

Consistent corporate creativity can be promoted by addressing certain elements (Robinson and Stern, 1997). These include alignment, when the actions of all employees are directed toward the goals of the enterprise; also that individuals and teams own the problems and their solutions, so that intrinsic motivation is raised by self-initiated activity. Internal communications need to provide clear lines of communication, and diverse stimuli provide fresh insight into existing activity or identifying new development.

ORGANIZATION

Identifying talent and providing reward systems are crucial factors in developing the organization (Quinn, 1985). Most commentators stress the importance of communications in the innovation process as a primary driver of knowledge management, to capture and make accessible the formal and informal knowledge within an organization. Intranet network applications can serve to improve internal knowledge-sharing and understanding in real time. The aim of establishing an effective system of communication is to ensure that a systematic channel catches and examines as many ideas as possible and that wasted effort is reduced. Communication and collaboration are factors in stimulating ideas, since individuals, groups and organizations can learn from each other only if they communicate (Nonaka and Tekeuchi, 1995).

Large organizations try to capture the flexibility of smaller ones, especially the strong emphasis on lateral communications and cross-functional teams and taskforces. Research and development, in particular, traditionally a separate and independent function, is increasingly integrated into a team setting. Cross-functional teams comprise people from marketing, production and finance who participate in development work from the start of a project. Innovative organizations reorganize to create smaller divisions that can allow such creative teams to operate and encourage new ventures. These new ventures can then be taken forward as a series of projects, with project management a core competence of the organization (Peters, 1997).

NEW PRODUCT DEVELOPMENT

New product development has been studied in great depth in large organizations. Companies have organized product innovation in much the same way as other functional departments, although current best practice involves the use of multifunctional teams (Shrivastava and Souder, 1987: 25–41; Clark and Wheelwright, 1992). Organizations have been found to have more success when their skills are aligned with the needs of the new product (Song et al., 1997: 88–101). It has also been suggested that new product projects should be used to develop and deepen existing capabilities (Leonard-Barton et al., 1994: 121–30).

The problem for small organizations is that the research, from which the above results are derived, has been conducted almost exclusively on larger firms. For instance, locating a design team together has been found to be critical for large firms, but this is rarely an issue for smaller ones. Many authors (Hoffman et al., 1998: 39–55; Macpherson, 1997: 127–44) have identified the fact that small firms face a different set of issues in developing new products.

Small organizations developing new products for rapidly changing markets cannot assume the relevance of success factors that have been found to apply to large firms. There are many reasons for this and several are intuitive. Small firms produce in smaller volumes than large ones and so will not gain the same return for improving production technology. They tend to have lower market share and less market credibility than large firms; they also rely more on a small number of key customers. Finally, most small firms are severely constrained by the limited resources, both human and financial, at their disposal. An e-learning group operating in a mixed-mode provider might equate to such small organizations and face similar difficulties with resources and market share. Nevertheless, small size can provide agility, which can be combined with entrepreneurial management to develop rapid responses in e-learning services to opportunities.

THE INNOVATION CYCLE IN SERVICES AND EDUCATION

The Internet is facilitating economic, technical and social trends in services, which education as a service is likely to follow. Other services went through a five-step sequence, when confronted with major new technologies (Quinn, 2001: 28–36). Quinn argues that practically all service industries, including large banks, retail stores, large accounting firms and airlines, follow this sequence (Table 8.2).

Table 8.2. Development of five-step innovation sequence
for services (after Quinn, 1992)

Development step	Implications for education and e-learning
1. New economies of scale.	Consolidation of key activities into larger institutions.
2. New economies of scope.	Flexibility and common capabilities allow the service of multiple market niches.
3. Increased complexity.	Handled with new technologies at significantly lower costs.
4. New service concepts.	New alliances and customer-sets emerge and stimulate new sets of innovator-entrepreneurs.
5. Disintermediation and redecentralization.	As technologies become powerful they can support sophisticated local interaction with more personal contact.

The path of a bank, as another service-provider, illustrates the potential sequence. As it automates service operations, new economies of scale are created that can drive out or consolidate smaller companies (step 1). With properly designed system applications, the operations become more flexible and this can provide a capability to serve multiple market niches when previously these were discrete groups (step 2). As the cycle develops, the new technologies can process greater complexity with substantially lower costs (step 3). The technology systems then present the opportunity for new service concepts, by rearranging and matching elements in their knowledge base to target and service customers more precisely (step 4). Finally, as the technologies become powerful enough, they can support complex local interaction, in which the bank can reach out to customers to provide more powerful and accessible local services through ATMs, telephone banking or e-banking and to provide more personalized benefits to customers (step 5).

Presuming that e-learning services follow a similar trend, there are certain implications. The Internet allows the delivery of online courses to wider audiences, providing *economies of scale.* As more educational content in the form of text, video, audio or assessment is captured electronically, the material becomes more flexible and capable of rearrangement into customized programmes. These can be formulated into specially timed and sequenced packages for individual audiences, yielding in the process further *economies of scope. Increased complexity* in terms of topic content can be addressed and explained through greater interactivity, graphic and multimedia approaches. The scope for *totally new service concepts* arises from growing experience with the techniques and sophistication of customers, leading to individualized tracking of performance and enhanced customizing of programmes as well as new alliances. The distribution of Internet-enabled education programmes through learning centres, satellite campuses, corporate cyber-cafés, at the workstation or at home leads to greater accessibility for local interaction, which has been termed 'redecentralization' for more local access to more services. The personalization of an e-learning programme by a provider that is tailored specifically for an individual are features of 'disintermediation', or the removal of intermediaries.

The most critical impact for senior decision-makers seems to lie in the disaggregation and internationalization of educational activities. The 'totally new concept' is of great value. A new concept offered on the Web is picked up by another site and the potential variations explored in a 'kaleidoscope' fashion to uncover interesting modifications, or new combinations of product applications. An innovator might then add features or insights to launch a distinctively new set of ideas, products or services. This practice is well established among US e-learning software companies. For example, we have experience at Lampeter of registration on to e-learning provision for language learning from corporate employees of software firms in Washington and Massachusetts. The probable explanation is the trawl for ideas and knowledge growth, rather than the acquisition of the Welsh language.

Each twist on the original concept can open up a new set of opportunities, either singly or in combinations. Practitioners explore all these combinations for the potential benefit of themselves and their customers. With full product and market development, it is likely that the total value of an original application can be multiplied many times beyond the initial concept. For the originator, it means that a close look at all the anticipated uses and markets is merited before market disclosure, in order to assess fully all the potential concepts, markets and the potential for another round of innovation and growth.

EDUCATION AND DIFFUSION

Education is a social invention. Changes in the economy and society in which we live and work cause us to reconsider how we educate people for these times. All educational enterprises need to innovate, therefore, to respond to such changes and accompanying competition. Innovation can take many different forms, whether it is creating new programmes, organizing people to work in different ways, or introducing new technology-supported learning for students.

Transforming an innovation into widespread adoption by people is a major challenge in any professional discipline. The process by which an innovation is communicated by certain channels over time to members of a social system is known as 'diffusion'. Investigations into how innovations permeate a particular society began over a century ago, in a series of scientific enclaves. From the 1950s, diffusion emerged as a single integrated body of concepts, although researchers from different disciplines such as technology, management, marketing and education have studied the effect primarily on their own fields. The diffusion-research tradition in education is important in terms of the number of studies completed, but is less significant in its contribution to the theoretical understanding of diffusion (Rogers, 1995: 63). However, there is a strong potential for a rich contribution from the discipline of education, because organizations from all sectors are involved in the adoption of educational innovations.

A classic case of educational-diffusion research explained by Rogers is of the spread of programmed instruction among school administrators. What emerged from this analysis of thirty-eight administrators was that educational diffusion requires an effective interpersonal network. The initial adoption by a single, highly innovative, individual was not successful because his network with peers was not very effective and he was seen as too innovative to serve as a role model for others. Indeed, uptake occurred only when a group of six opinion-leaders favoured the innovation.

Diffusion is a challenge in itself, therefore, but it is inevitably preceded by innovation. Innovation in e-learning presents issues far broader than those usually encountered in curriculum development for education. Technology is only one part of this bigger picture. There are issues over devising new products, entering new markets and discovering methods of supporting people. Many questions emerge, such as how people coordinate their efforts in processes such as creativity and innovation, and how they are applied to enhance how people learn, cooperate, identify expertise, capture knowledge, make decisions and work together. These are complicated areas that are inextricably linked with the development of e-learning as a business. Nevertheless, a significant body of knowledge exists on the principles and practice of innovation.

For e-learning, the broad question is how culture and knowledge in all its various forms, skills, values and wisdom, are transferred and optimized electronically to produce more effective and knowledgeable people. In practice, the task of getting it adopted by a specific target market influences the work of transforming an idea into an innovation. The more refined question is how specific elements of knowledge, in its sundry forms, are transformed electronically to help particular individuals or target groups. There are always opportunities for innovation, whether incremental or in developing radically new products and services. Indeed, a recent study of innovative developments in e-learning among providers in west Wales observed that, whereas opportunities existed for everyone, the real outcomes reflected the actual efforts applied (Rogers, 2002). Providers did not need lots of different ideas; all they needed was a viable one that they were prepared to follow through in an entrepreneurial way.

ATTRIBUTES FOR E-LEARNING

Five attributes act as strong predictors of the acceptance of an innovation and explain why certain innovations are adopted more quickly than others (Rogers, 1995). They are: relative advantage, compatibility, complexity, trialability and observability. Each attribute may not be equally important, but each needs to be assessed in an e-learning innovation. This is a role that rests with the provider, rather than with learner preferences for one mode of learning over another. The process of e-learning is relatively new at present, so that most potential learners are not likely to have formed a view based on experience (Lewis and Orton, 2000: 47–51).

Relative advantage is the extent to which a proposed innovation is perceived as being better than existing alternatives. These benefits can be profitability, speed, social prestige, effectiveness or any other outcomes. The greater the perceived relative advantage of an innovation, the more rapid its rate of adoption. One perceived advantage for e-learning may lie in just-in-time access, getting information as soon as the need arises. Another might be its accurate focus on the precise skills required for a task, or its efficiency, compared with sitting through a conventional class covering a broader set of skills, or a 'roll-on, roll-off' enrolment process, or added services, such as a bespoke database. The perceived-value propositions for a user can be refined from the relative advantage of a particular e-learning offer over rival services.

Compatibility is the degree to which an innovation is consistent with the existing values, beliefs, past experiences or needs of potential adopters. It appears that if a new value-system is required, the rate of adoption will be lower. In contrast, compatible processes that fit more closely with a learner's life situation will require less adaptation. Attitude towards technology adoption becomes significant, in a marketing sense, whenever products are introduced that require a change in the current mode of behaviour, or the modification of other products and services we rely on. Such change-sensitive products are called discontinuous innovations. The contrasting term, continuous innovation, refers to the normal upgrading of products, which does not require change behaviour (Moore, 1991: 10).

When there is compatibility with previously encountered processes, the learner is likely to regard the innovation as familiar. E-learners are, therefore, likely to feel more comfortable with new learning technology if the online experience has familiar navigation and consistent interfaces. It follows that the design of a course programme that follows a sequence of progression to higher skill-levels should aim to maintain familiarity in the look and feel of the interface in a consistent house-style. Practitioners should aim, therefore, to retain consistency in the design of online work and download activity expected from the student. The expectations of a student with a highly mobile job are likely to be different from someone with continuous access to a PC workstation. A radical change in the proportion of online to offline work, or the nature of the service, or tutor support, can serve to disturb the working methods of a mobile learner, to make contact less familiar and perturb a newly established learning style. This might eventually lead to discouragement, or even disengagement. For these reasons, as a minimum the design of an e-learning service ought to make online navigation and interfaces familiar to the student, with consistency across different progression routes.

Complexity is whether an innovation is perceived as easy or difficult to understand or use. Innovations requiring new skills and understanding that involve steep learning-curves, of course, are slower to be adopted. The implication is that the apparent complexity of e-learning needs to be minimized for easy adoption. Installing a software plug-in adds complexity to the process for some learners and can act as a perceived limitation to the adoption of online learning. Applications can be rolled out with appropriate support, such as online help, or a frequently asked questions (FAQ) system, to reduce impediments to study.

Trialability is the degree to which an innovation can be experimented with, on a limited basis. Innovations introduced in instalments will, generally, be adopted more quickly than those that are not divisible, since incremental implementation tends to allow uncertainty to be reduced through learning-by-doing. The opportunity to try an innovation, without any requirement for continued or subsequent use, gives learners an opportunity to see how the product works under their own particular circumstances. It may help alleviate their uncertainty over the adoption of a new practice. In terms of e-learning, an offer of a short 'sampler' e-learning programme without obligation allows an introduction to the new learning technologies. Trialability is especially critical for early adopters with no precedent to compare, or no preferred learning style, with respect to the technologies and the balance of online learning. In contrast, later adopters may draw on the experience of peers. The 'chunking' of learning that often occurs in an e-learning design, enabling the body of knowledge to be more easily grasped, should allow a small trial-field to be sampled in detail by a prospective learner. The merit of sampling such a field of knowledge does depend on the ability to introduce the appropriate timing and placing of corrective action. The design, therefore, should aim to give opportunities without imposing any obligation to try the technique.

Observability is the extent to which results are visible to others and the benefits demonstrable. Easy, quickly demonstrable skills ought to be available first, so that the short-term and visible impacts can support the continued adoption of the longer-term goals of the innovation. The implications for e-learning are that the instructional sequence, which guides the learner through a flow of statements on a body of knowledge intended to transfer learning, will determine the degree of difficulty encountered by the learner in achieving an understanding. No single sequence is applicable for all learners. The optimum sequence, in any particular case, depends on a range of factors, such as past learning, the nature of the material and individual differences. Since the sequence affects the ease or difficulty, with some effects more immediate than others, greater observability is gained by a sequence that gives an early demonstration of impact. It is preferable, then, to position a specific item of instruction, which gives a quick demonstration of impact, early in the sequence; it will then be likely to be more visible and the results more quickly observable than with soft skills, which may take a long time to demonstrate effect.

WHEN E-LEARNING IS AVAILABLE FROM EVERYONE

What happens when e-learning is available from everyone? It seems that e-learning processes are likely to become a staple ingredient of delivery methods in every educational enterprise. As the method grows in its application of subject content, e-learning itself no longer becomes a source of differentiation between suppliers (as discussed in chapter 7). Are there, then, any parallels that might yield an insight into the ways of dealing with the predicament?

The movement for quality improvement has parallels. The quality movement started about twenty years ago across the EU, initially affecting manufacturing and production, then spreading to services and then into educational provision. When quality became available from everyone, though, it no longer became a source of competitive advantage. In a challenging assessment of such an environment, the need for building product-appeal and the importance of forging an identifiable brand are stressed by Peters (Peters, 1997). He reinforces the importance of constant innovation as the only strategy for survival for both the individual and the enterprise, and advocates gaining value within organizations by assembling professional services from staff units. These units need thoroughly to address five operational factors, which he called the '5 Ps': (a) projectization, by cementing activities into projects with definable tasks, durations and outcomes, (b) professionalism, by improving this dimension, (c) provocation, by challenging standards, (d) partnership, by operating as a professional practice, and (e) performance, by setting and attaining standards.

A consortium of disciplines is emerging that constitutes some understanding of the current processes of flux in business, and may afford a degree of control, albeit limited in span and duration (Peters, 1998). In his view, enterprises need to emphasize a new set of basic aims to enhance responsiveness through greatly increased flexibility and continuous short-cycle innovation, aimed at creating new markets for both new and mature products of world-class quality and services.

INNOVATION IN EDUCATION AND ENTERPRISE

Communications-technology development has been driven by the motivation to get a message as far and as fast as possible around the world and at as low a cost as is practicable. Now that it is possible to communicate a written message to any place on earth within seconds, the development goal is mutating to conveying richer message-content, such as audio, graphics or video presentation. Communications technology has itself become a commodity, acquired by anyone with sufficient resources and the desire to increase their scope of influence. This means that the technology to communicate at any time and to anywhere through asynchronous means is not in itself a factor in differentiating between education providers. It is simply the platform from which an innovation might spring.

Conventional teaching in further and higher education takes place in a course context, with an individual teacher responsible for a whole course. Many variations on this simple model can arise, such as shared course-teaching responsibilities for delivery of laboratory or workshop sessions, but this simple model dominates. The normal way to arrange the delivery of a course is over an extended period of time, such as a term, a semester or a session, the traditional academic periods of time. The large majority of work in e-learning developments still follows this same pattern, with a single enthusiast providing electronic support for students on a course. The model succeeds, probably because the member of staff focuses primarily on the teaching and learning needs of a class, rather than recruiting external students.

A major goal for innovation is that the entire process must be related to the needs of the organization and the marketplace. The commercializing process can be categorized into four basic elements (Roberts, 1988: 1–19). First, idea creation, where new knowledge forms around basic discoveries, extensions of existing understandings, or spontaneous creativity, made possible by individual ingenuity and communication with others. Secondly, initial application, where ideas are first tested in concept by discussions with others, or referrals to customers, clients or technical experts in the form of prototypes or samples. Thirdly, determination of feasibility, where the practicality and financial value are examined in formal feasibility studies that identify potential costs and benefits alongside potential market or applications. Fourthly, the final application, when a new product is commercialized or offered for sale in the open market, or a new process is implemented as part of normal operating routines.

Enterprise-driven activity in a company is concerned primarily with a reliable and predictable way of converting an idea into a new product. This requirement shapes a preferred single, linear and systematic model for innovation. All the evidence gathered over many years seems to indicate that innovation is a 'disciplined, systematic, organised and purposeful activity with its own fairly simple rules that offer a rational and repeatable way to convert an idea into an innovation' (Drucker, 1992: 1).

In education, two broad models of innovation can be found in the literature on education: the linear and the convergent (Robinson, 2001: 15–37). The linear model is similar to that for a business enterprise; it reflects rational planning and a top-down process of communication. It can be criticized for disregarding the social and political dimensions of project implementation in an educational institution. The second, convergent model views planning more as a participatory activity, with shared decision-making amongst staff. In comparison with the linear model, this opportunity for expression can make the process appear less orchestrated, more muddled and ad hoc, with the prospect of losing direction by trying to accomplish a wider ownership of the change.

These two educational models are comparable to a distinction made between approaches to change in education (Fullan, 1993). There is a rational planning model, with mandated change, a mission, objectives, a plan that involves linear and sequential activities that are controllable and predictable, a model that is to a large extent determined from above. From an educational setting this approach can be criticized because it does not reflect the complexities of change or match what actually happens. Alternatively, Fullan identifies a model that comprises an overlapping series of dynamic complex phenomena that engages both top-down and bottom-up strategies, focuses on process and is evolutionary in nature. This is more like an unpredictable journey than a route-plan, with its mission emerging over time, and is an approach that seems adaptable to a rapidly changing milieu.

During the past decade a major national project in the UK, the Teaching and Learning Technology Programme (TLTP), set out to create educational software for higher education with the objective of achieving wide circulation and adoption of applications in the sector (TLTP, 2001). As a government-supported programme, investment was on a substantial scale, with £32 million in grants directly from the state between 1992 and 1996, for seventy-six designated projects. Even with this scale of investment, most of the products had relatively little uptake or impact. An evaluation of this programme revealed that the few projects that did achieve success found a niche in a local setting, usually associated with the developer of the software product. The advice from the findings for future courseware-developers was to concentrate on developing materials and systems that can be used by large numbers of people (Draper, 1998: 5–8).

A number of other conclusions, germane to the development of e-learning initiatives, emerged from the TLTP programme. Ownership by senior academics and management was seen as a vital and critical component of the legitimization of the innovation, in view of the decision-making process of higher-education institutions. Support from senior management was a requirement of the TLTP, but in practice it was judged very weak, with awareness restricted to enthusiastic individuals (Stern, 1997). Institutional contractors tried to balance bottom-up enthusiasm and top-down planning tactics, such as by intervening when central support might be relevant for staff development, promotion systems and infrastructure development. Lastly, the practical implementation of network technology was often related directly to the need to pursue a fundamental and systematic change in the institutional culture. Whereas the majority of TLTP products were stand-alone schemes, formulated as discrete projects by groups of subject enthusiasts, the current development of e-learning is on a far greater scale, with most educational enterprises planning some form of provision. Even though individual enthusiasts are still very active, there is a greater breadth of involvement from more institutions that compels making this a higher priority for senior managers.

An educational enterprise can undertake top-down, bottom-up or enterprise-driven innovation, or any combination of these approaches, most often by a project-based approach. The effect of project-centred development is to form an approach to innovation based on a project-view, which is specific and insulated from the tremendous take-up of technologies in higher education (Goodyear, 1998). Several decades of category-specific funding have forged a project-view, with an emphasis on research output or delivered product, which is disseminated, often with disappointing acceptance. As Goodyear argues, an environment-centred framework is necessary to gain a comprehensive understanding of change affecting learners as well as to coordinate the complex tasks involved in the design and management of learning environments. A core challenge, therfore, is to discover what students as knowledge workers really do, and then to design supportive technology around them.

The rapid development of e-learning has stimulated innovation and led to a diversity of systems that are ahead of regulation as well as empirical research (Bjarnason and Edwards, 2002). In higher education, e-learning development practice indicates greater collaboration from corporate providers, more competition than cooperation and the requirement for more investment in human resources by releasing staff time for innovation, as well as for explicit strategies for e-learning. The process of innovation by e-learning affects many dimensions of the organization of teaching and learning, such as support for students during work-based learning, the development of transferable skills and more self-direction in student learning (Mason, 1998a: 139–40).

For applications of ODFL in industry by higher education, a review of fourteen case-studies highlights the quality of planning issues and the organizational factors for introducing ODFL (Brown, 1997: 193). Cultures, roles and values significantly affect the outcome of innovations and, when implementers of ODFL innovation are unsure of these factors, they are not likely to address them well.

CAPACITY FOR INNOVATION

The educational-development landscape is littered with completed but under-developed projects. Difficulties often arise because of the nature of project funding, which requires a budget to be set and spent over a fixed period. When the project comes to an end, a project team can split up and continuity in exploiting the outcomes can be lost. Another problem with projects and a project-management approach is that they are not widely accepted by academic staff, since they are associated with performance indicators, scheduling, objectivized criteria and managerialism, which are not congruent with the prevailing academic culture. Projects, though, are a major source of development funding for research, education and innovation from the government, EU and international bodies. They inevitably involve some facet of innovation and are operated on the basis of doing something new in return for receiving additional resources.

Maintaining a development dynamic requires the capacity to observe new opportunities, experiment and network. This capacity requires resources to cover the costs. Although larger organizations operate an industrial liaison office, or a similar support bureau, the specific tracking of opportunities is often so specific that it cannot be assigned effectively out of an e-learning project-development team. It means that, for continuing development, a core requirement is a role for innovation development among a project team.

SCANNING SOURCES OF OPPORTUNITY

An enterprise needs an effective means of monitoring sources of development opportunity, within and outside the organization. Decision-makers need to be receptive to these options, in order to transform the opportunity into a viable educational, training or support service which students and customers need. The process can take place at various levels: right across an educational enterprise, or in a school, department, centre or unit, or even at the individual level. An internal consultancy centre might also operate in one form or another – as an enterprise unit, business or innovation centre – and effect a similar service.

Seven potential sources of ideas for innovation exist, with four of these sources being within the enterprise and intrinsically symptoms of change (Drucker, 1994). The other three sources involve changes outside the enterprise or industry. The distinctions between these sources of innovative opportunity are often blurred, with considerable overlap between them, but each requires separate analysis, for each has its own characteristics.

Major internal sources for ideas include the unexpected, the incongruity, process needs and changes in industry or markets. The unexpected success, failure or outside event is the richest source of opportunities, least risky and easiest to pursue. Incongruity arises from differences between reality as it is and what it is assumed to be, symptoms of change that are clear to people close to the industry, in economics, products and expectations of customers, in the speed or logic of the process. Process needs yield ideas for innovation based on a need that exists in the operations of a business, industry or service. Industry or market structure may experience surprising changes that innovation can exploit.

External sources include demographic changes, changes in perception and new knowledge. Demographic sources include changes in the composition of the total population, its size, structure, employment, educational status, income and the likely demand for learning. Changes in per-ception include tastes, fashions, understandings and viewpoints that create innovation opportunities. New knowledge opportunities arise from scientific and non-scientific sources. This is a major source of breakthrough innovations, with the longest lead time-span, a high casualty rate and more unpredictability.

Structuring information is crucial. Information that is well structured, timely, relevant, accurate and easy to find can be applied more easily. Relevant information requires organizing, labelling and managing content. A careful review and monitoring of internal sources of opportunity is also needed to reveal further ideas for innovation. The key to accessing these sources lies not in building large silos of information that are difficult to access, but in providing immediate, real-time information to everyone who affects the business of innovation, rapidly. The mainstream adoption of the Internet provides an advantage, since it means that Web-based reporting to produce real-time information can be effective.

Table 8.3. Observation areas for timely information delivery.

Factors	Observatory source	Web address
Demographics		
Labour market	Labour trends	*statistics.gov.uk*
Skill trends	Skills	*skillsbase.dfes.gov.uk*
European initiatives	EU programmes	*europa.eu.int.*
E-learning		
E-learning	Observatory for Borderless Higher Education	*obhe.ac.uk*
E-learning and SMEs	Marchmont Observatory	*marchmont.ac.uk*
E-learning: US	ASTD learning circuit	*learningcircuits.org*
Learning environments		
	Educational delivery	*ct.bc.ca/langdonline*
	Integrated VLEs	*marshall.edu/it/webct*
		jisc.ac.uk
ODFL	Commonwealth of Learning	*col.org/virtualed*
	US Distance Learning	*usdla.org*
Business operations		
Business intelligence	BI	*business-intelligence.co.uk*
Customer relationship	CRM	*ittoolbox.com*
E-business	E-commerce	*ibm.com/e-business*
Enterprise	Enterprise information	*enterprisenetwork.co.uk*
	Business media	*vnulearning.com*
Technology		
E-learning	Technologies for Training	*tft.co.uk*
LMS observatories	Brandon Hall	*brandon-hall.com*
	E-learning magazine	*elearningmag.com*
	Masie Center	*masie.com*
Research	EU R & D programmes	*cordis.lu*

Monitoring sources of opportunity involves setting up the means to observe key areas and feeding the findings to a development team. Each situation will be different, but one useful starting point is to set out to cover the conventional political, economic, socio-economic and technological (PEST) factors as a basis for analysis of future structure and trends. These are very similar to the external sources cited by Drucker. The PEST factors serve to influence the shape of future markets. For example, political factors include GATS, environmental protection laws, employment law, education and training policy, economic development plans and European integration, initiatives and programmes. Economic factors that can play a part are business cycles, GNP trends, inflation, unemployment, disposable income and trade cycles. Sociocultural factors that are influential include population demographics, income distribution, social mobility, lifestyle changes, attitudes to work and leisure, consumerism and levels of education. Technological factors might embrace new research initiatives, new technology developments, technology transfer and rates of obsolescence.

An approach based on PEST factors can give an overview on future trends, but is unlikely to be sufficiently focused, or timely enough to provide detail for innovation in e-learning. Additional observational areas depend on the fields of application, but might include monitoring and gathering information on improving processes and technology. Specific technical developments, information on ODFL and e-learning are all relevant observation areas (see Table 8.3). Tracking information on e-learning is the business of several observatories, such the Observatory for Borderless Higher Education that provides an information service on international developments. The span of parameters scanned is a balance between comprehensiveness and the available time to find information quickly. Prioritizing the sites monitored is necessary to provide timely information and make the exercise manageable.

THE INNOVATION PROCESS

The innovation decision process is essentially an information-seeking, funnelling and processing activity. The basic steps for the process are monitoring sources of opportunity, screening, assessment, feasibility decision, development, testing and evaluating (Figure 8.1) as described by a number of investigators (Majaro, 1988: 10; Adair, 1990). First, there is a monitoring of the potential sources of ideas, then a funnelling of these ideas down to a position where a development decision is made. There then follows a development process that leads to a testing procedure. The operation of such a trial involves the comparison of the results of the test with some specified criteria.

**Figure 8.1. A model of the innovation process for education
and training (developed from Roffe, 1997: 90–6)**

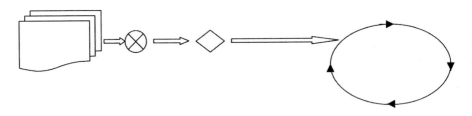

| Sources of opportunity | Screening criteria | Feasibility decision | Development project-based activity | Innovation testing as cycle |

Screening of ideas is often accompanied by criteria for compatibility with the organizational objectives. The remaining ideas are then assessed for their feasibility against sound educational, technical and financial criteria. A development decision made on the basis of feasibility will then lead into an implementation phase, when the idea is developed into an innovation.

All discussions of innovation agree that it is essential that the process is properly systematized. There is a strong emphasis on auditing the organization's effectiveness in the area of creativity and innovation, an audit that extends across the range of functional specializations and which is repeated on a regular basis (Majaro, 1988: 8–10). The process of examining, screening and evaluating ideas can be approached methodically to determine the attractiveness of an idea together with its compatibility for the enterprise's special needs. These two parameters, attractiveness and compatibility, can be used to form a matrix in which the merit of an idea is scored, or an algorithm method applied, to scrutinize the potential value of the idea to the organization.

CURRICULUM CYCLE

Does the production of an innovation follow a predictable pattern? A fairly simple model emerges from curriculum development, problem diagnosis and opportunity searching that gives guidance to decision-makers and practitioners involved in the development of e-learning. A learning path is often called a curriculum and progresses through a cycle. Learning and problem-solving are divisible into phases, described in various ways by different writers.

All descriptions appear to agree that this cycle involves the formulation of a trial, followed by the operation of a testing procedure, and the comparison of the results of the test with some criterion. It has variously been called trial-and-error, means-end testing, trial and check, discrepancy reduction, test-operate-test-exit, hypothesis testing and so on (Bruner, 1966: 51). The stages of a cyclic curriculum-development model involving the identification of needs, course design, implementation and evaluation, are regarded widely as stages in a cyclic approach. Similarly, experiential learning is described as proceeding through experience, reflection, generalization and testing by means of a learning cycle (Kolb, 1984). A cyclic approach to problem-solving also arises in the PDCA (plan, do, check, action) process recommended as a fundamental tool for quality improvement (Deming, 1982).

Operating a curriculum-development cycle is a means of continuously improving a course offer or value enhancing. The needs analysis and evaluation stages check on requirements and performance, a cycle which is normally repeated for academic courses on an annual basis. Continuing-education short courses can run more frequently, so the cycle operates more speedily and makes short courses an important test-bed for piloting and validating longer-course provision.

E-learning can lead to fast-cycle innovation, since a course launch can be monitored easily and efforts made to replicate it quickly. Student recruitment can be configured in a 'roll-on, roll-off' enrolment system. Demand can be tested before delivery, or even before the development of the course. Testing can occur with very small numbers of students, in order to validate the programme. The recruitment process is not tied to an annual or quarterly cycle of recruitment or necessarily dependent on classic classroom student numbers for a cohort to operate. An e-learning programme can also be designed in a unitized way so that the content and support processes are rapidly tested as a prototype for value assurance and then continuously improved.

PROBLEM-SOLVING AND NEEDS ANALYSIS

The start of a curriculum-development process is preceded normally by a detailed and comprehensive analysis of the needs and problems for a course to address, during a period sometimes called curriculum research, needs analysis or consultancy. This process is intended to verify, help define the scope and refine the requirements of a potential programme. This leads to an adapted curriculum development model (Figure 8.1), that informs the cyclic process at the needs analysis stage, with a project 'leadership' or impetus for problem-solving (Roffe, 1997: 90–6).

Problem-solving provides decision-makers with a relatively predictable way of transforming an idea, by conventional managerial practice, into a new course product, delivery system or student or administrative support service. Structures in conventional educational institutions, though, with segmentation into academic centres, departments, schools or faculties, can make multidisciplinary work difficult to orchestrate. There are other difficulties, such as staff contracts that may not address the need for work on e-learning, or in supporting project contracts, which can lead to a degree of inflexibility in working arrangements. The lack of staff time with sufficient capacity for innovation can also be a restraining issue. Ultimate success in developing authentic e-learning content, however, requires the best available inputs from a range of practitioners: researchers, designers, Web and e-business support.

Problem-solving activity can be viewed as a form of consultancy process, either undertaken internally by a project leader or sometimes by an external agent. By problem-solving and consultancy are meant a set of activities by an individual or group that helps an individual, group or enterprise to identify, understand, stimulate and maintain the change necessary for converting an idea into a development. The process is a series of linked and interdependent stages, dependent on the observer (Block, 1981; Robinson and Robinson, 1995).

The stages start with problem formulation, which identifies all process difficulties. Problem diagnosis is where an initial working definition of the boundaries of the problem is made. It involves screening the idea against technical, process and structural criteria, as well as data-collection by direct observation, individual and group interviews and surveys, using instruments such as questionnaires. This is followed by analysis, collation and interpretation of the collected data, and feedback with suggestions for actions designed to achieve implementation. Implementation involves assessing the proposed course of action against the possible benefits and costs. With e-learning, this is often likely to involve a complex process with the construction of content together with learner support and management infrastructure. It involves planning, team meetings and the training of people affected by the development. The various phases of the implementation need monitoring to observe and track what is happening. Evaluation of the success of the process is the final stage, carried out against a set of negotiated criteria.

LIMITS ON THE DEVELOPMENT OF INNOVATION

Searching for new e-learning courses, methods, materials and markets is essentially a quest for a uniqueness that is recognizable in every sphere of economic activity. Innovation, though, is not a universal panacea for all educational and training situations, or every aspect of organizational activity. Boundaries to its application can arise at the initiative or the enterprise level. For example, the scale and full potential might be unrecognized by the originators. An unexpected success might lead to a failure by the initiator to recognize the full potential of the innovation, or a failure to capitalize fully on the early development process. Even where the potential is recognized there might be a reluctance to undertake large-scale development, because of concern over loss of control, or lack of management experience.

Limits can arise for other reasons. Displacement activity may occur: the leader of the initiative, who may hold the key competencies for innovation, can be progressively drawn into other activities that displace and diffuse the focus of activity. This might happen through career self-interest, or top-down pressure, or as the result of the need to secure resources to sustain development; this may entail justifying time for political advocacy, either internal or external, on behalf of the enterprise. Another boundary arises when innovation becomes a goal in itself, and the pursuit of novelty in new products and markets becomes a dominant goal. The search for the next new application may provide the motivation, rather than seeking the full extraction of value from the initial development investment.

The politics of innovation may present another boundary. No universal rules exist for the acceptance of an innovation within an organization; rather, there are particular areas where it is welcomed and other areas of application where it would be discouraged. An innovator, looking at his or her own role, needs to assess what it is possible to achieve and how to build political support for the innovation.

An innovator must exploit the windows of opportunity. Education is dependent on people for design and delivery, but when content and methods enter the public domain they are rapidly disseminated and shared, so that the window of opportunity for exploitation can open and close with extraordinary speed. Exceptions can occur where this is delayed. The principal one is where a new course or process is dependent on technology that is proprietarily linked, such as e-learning tied with a software product. In such cases it is feasible to delay the onset of competition. The market launch of an e-learning product, however, will immediately signal the start of competitive rivalries.

Long-term alignment is needed with the aims of the enterprise. With competition inevitable, it is sensible to decide on the basis of sustainable competitive advantage, rather than trying to be all things to all clients. The aim should be to optimize the benefits of the innovation. Once the breakthrough is achieved, a reassessment of the best strategy for sustaining the development is needed, since sustaining situations do not always yield benefits for an enterprise. The concept should also be the right size for the enterprise; not so large as to overly stretch resources, or so small that the rewards for success would be unimportant.

EXPLOITING AVAILABLE TECHNOLOGY

E-learning is a rare case, when unfulfilled student groups combine currently with technology and educational drivers to sustain continuing educational innovation. For an existing educational service-provider trying to sustain existing programmes and students, new e-learning services will lead to competitive challenges from rivals. A classic way to gain an early position in a disruptive market is to set up a new autonomous business unit, in order to build a new business around the disruptive innovation. With the same technology available to everyone, though, technology cannot provide a long-term advantage to any particular provider. For new providers, there are significant advantages in becoming a first mover into a market. Maintaining this dynamic by aggregating knowledge and adding value to the service appears crucial, because of the difficulties in preventing competitors from copying quickly and improving on new products and systemic methods once they are launched. Although the purpose is educational, the fundamental competitive processes are those of e-business.

Technologies that will support teaching and learning in five years' time are available now, for example, wireless technology, but this is not in widespread use, and this is a problem for a provider. For an educational service-provider, a technology has to be in widespread application by a target population before it becomes usable. An individual can adopt a technology application more quickly than an educational institution can, but technology itself changes faster than the population as a whole can apply it. The direct challenge for e-learning decision-makers and practitioners, therefore, is to exploit the technology that is immediately available and in use through effective learning applications, rather than what might be available at some time in the future, or to put effort into trying to persuade people to adopt a new technology.

9

Markets and marketing

Markets for e-learning are very fragmented, but can be categorized broadly into three segments: corporate, consumer and academic. An innovation like e-learning diffuses through a market segment. Markets have different drivers and characteristics with different e-learning products and services on offer. The application of the value chain to an educational service-provider is a means of identifying potential applications for services. The Web is an extraordinary medium for marketing. It brings benefits to consumers in the form of convenience, savings, selection, information and personalization. There are advantages for the provider, with relatively low start-up costs, ease of market entry, time-independence and global reach. The Web presents an opportunity for practitioners to present integrated text and other media, through which advertisers and marketers can communicate with new and existing markets. With its panoply of novel advantages, Internet-enabled learning is creating new products, services and markets that form an e-learning industry. Taking an e-learning programme that has gained a market foothold with small firms into other markets or segments involves market development, in which the Internet influences the marketing mix and the branding of services.

DIFFUSION AND THE TECHNOLOGY-ADOPTION LIFE-CYCLE

Small firms are notoriously difficult to service. Our experience is that they are not a homogeneous group, and that diffusion of e-learning is relatively slow among them. According to the technology-adoption cycle on how technology is adopted by the masses, innovation is diffused in distinct phases (Moore, 1991). This adoption model predicts that when a marketplace is confronted with the opportunity to switch to a new paradigm, such as from stand-alone CD-ROMs to Internet-supported learning, customers are distributed along an axis of risk aversion. The risk-immune innovators are in the forefront, the risk-averse laggards at the rear. In between, the model identifies three additional communities: early adopters, early majority and later majority. Although many markets for e-learning are maturing, this is not the case as yet for our client-base of small firms in Wales, where firms are still working through early adoption stages.

Each community of adopters in the technology life-cycle model represents fundamentally different customers that require unique approaches: early innovators are offered a sales proposition in one way, the late majority in another. A key idea of the model is that the behaviour of early adopters may reveal how the mass market will respond. Successful providers are not necessarily those able to innovate with a new product, however, but rather those enterprises able to move successfully from consumers in one phase to consumers in another. Focusing marketing on a segment of the population that will adopt technology a little ahead of the rest seems a crucial activity in getting mainstream acceptance of a product. This knowledge can help plan a communications strategy for future launches (Rogers, 1995). Innovators and early adopters are critical to the successful launch of a new product, but they are estimated as representing typically only 20 per cent of the total market. Each phase of the adoption cycle has such fundamentally different customers that the goal is to create enough momentum to cross from one phase to the next.

The model proposes that product and market evolution move through consecutive phases of development, with the population present in each phase having distinctive behavioural characteristics. This life-cycle is in the form of a normal distribution, with each of the segments a standard deviation away from the norm. The early and late majority are one standard deviation away from the norm, each comprising about a third of the total population, while the early adopters and laggards are two and the innovators three standard deviations away. It appears likely that innovators in e-learning will follow this adoption process. This knowledge will help plan an e-communication strategy for future launches (Rogers, 1995: 263–5).

Innovators (2.5 per cent to 4 per cent of the total market). Members of this segment behave as nonconformist deciders who are adventurous, prepared to take risks and make quick decisions. The implication for e-learning marketing is that this segment requires informative rather than persuasive messages, creating targeted offerings with clear benefits that emphasize 'new' aspects of e-learning.

Early adopters (up to 16 per cent of the market). Flexibility and a willingness to take risks characterize members here. Influencers are very important in this group's decision-making. The implication is that providing information to advisers and influencers is vital, including cases from innovators.

Early majority (up to 34 per cent). Members of this segment like examples to follow. Despite being aspirers, they tend towards the status quo and in business sectors tend to favour incremental strategies. Influencers and consultants still can be key to decision-making, because competitors are likely to be established. Persuasive communication with a view to establishing differential advantages is important.

Late majority (34 per cent of the market). This is a much more conservative segment, slow to change and normally more price-sensitive. In the business sectors, these firms are usually adopting follower strategies with 'replicated' products. An awareness of the product and brands will be well established and communication will often be in the nature of a reminder, with sale promotions used to enhance the perceived value-for-money proposition.

Laggards (16 per cent of the market). These are the most traditional users in the market, conservative, cautious, cynical, even resistant to change, and they may fear the new experience. It can be expensive to win these final customers over. Communication messages should take the risk out of the decision.

From innovators to laggards, the profile and motivations of these user-groups can change significantly and therefore the messages of an educational enterprise and its media selection will need to be adapted accordingly. Developing a communication strategy to target specific students means that e-learning marketers must identify and profile segments of users against the phases of the diffusion process and then set objectives and devise strategies that will ensure adoption within each target group. The communication tools then need to be integrated and used in coordination to achieve objectives within each category of users.

NICHES AND COMPETITION

The classic approach to gaining mainstream acceptance of a technological product is to focus marketing on a segment of the population that will adopt a product a little ahead of the majority. This niche marketing can sometimes be geographic, such as a focus on Wales; sometimes demographic, for instance, small businesses in these areas, followed by home offices; sometimes a single vertical industry, for example, people providing customer-support services in the telephone industry. A key mistake is not selling into a niche, since efforts to sell in an undifferentiated way will not gain the momentum needed to get majority acceptance in the segment (Moore, 1991). A niche, according to Moore, is a group of customers who have a common application for the technology and who reference each other during the purchase process. Good niches are big enough to make a profit, but small enough so that an enterprise can dominate them. Domination is important, since it makes it easier to move into adjoining niches and command them. The high labour intensity and interpersonal nature of learning in conventional situations, though, inhibits domination.

The mechanics of the technology-adoption life-cycle were derived from observations of large fast-growth technology companies (Moore, 1995: 8). Moore asserts, though, that the patterns can be translated into industries outside the high-tech sector, such as insurance, health care, publishing and so on. Nevertheless, for each phase of market development, there are specific business strategies, sales and marketing activities that play out differently in each stage of the market-development model. In making a sales offer, therefore, it ought to be appropriate to the stage of market development. Propositions adapt to the stage of the market, in terms of competitors, pricing, support or the technology on offer. As different segments have different rates of adoption, it follows that a value proposition for an owner-manager of a SME may need to be different from that for a corporate decision-maker in a large organization, or an independent lifelong learner.

A marketing approach can apply to e-learning as to any other service. The customer does not buy goods or services, but rather solutions. Successful marketing relies on providing goods and services that people want to purchase, at a price that is attractive to them and yet it still being worthwhile to create economic value for the provider. Economic value, for an educational enterprise, is the gap between the price and cost of services. These can be, for example, enhanced skills, improved careers, better performance, identity or profits. The adoption of a customer-focused orientation means that colleagues and customers are treated as individuals, with an emphasis on managing relationships with customers. Once the culture is right, then educational marketing techniques have a firm foundation to work on. Even so, the multiple benefits and rewards are leading most educational enterprises around the world to develop e-learning as quickly as possible and to seek customers for these programmes.

An educational enterprise that occupies a particular market segment of e-learning is faced with twin competitive forces: the migration of other e-learning providers, as well as new entrants from traditional learning-providers seeking new customers for their particular solutions. Competition for providing services to employees of companies is high; it comes from commercial providers and conventional education centres. There are no dominant providers of conventional corporate training, probably because of the labour intensity of training. Two of the larger international providers are IBM and Oracle; like other large technology organizations, they have focused historically on providing customers and employees with training on their respective product lines. IBM has taken aggressive steps to establish itself as an e-learning solutions provider, and other technology firms can be expected to take similar steps. Providers like IBM and other leading technology firms are credible e-learning providers and should contribute to increased competition for corporate e-learning. Nevertheless, few incumbents appear currently to possess the content, technology, instructional know-how, brand and relationships to dominate.

INTERNATIONAL COMPETITION

E-learning is perfect for export. It has high value and esteem, and can be moved easily. With so many advantages, there is already buoyant international competition, as explained in Chapter 1.

New brands might lead to a destabilization of the existing structure of international education provision. E-learning applications, however, are growing quickly and in parallel in the major international education markets of the developed world. Applications vary from country to country. Not only is the situation complex, but it is rapidly changing and shows the enormous impact and diversity of the Internet on educational practice (Farrell, 2001).

THE INTERNET AS A COMMUNICATIONS MEDIUM

The Internet is a route where a client makes the first contact with a supplier, for instance, when a client seeks information from an e-learning provider (Deighton, 1996: 151–62). There are other characteristics. Viewing a Website, for example, engages the total attention of an individual. All the responses of an enquirer can be collected, stored and analysed for individual profiling, or group targeting, making it possible, therefore, for the needs of an individual customer to be monitored and addressed in all future communications with that client.

As a marketing medium, the Internet is like a large international exhibition hall, where potential buyers can enter at will and visit exhibitors and prospective sellers (Berthon et al., 1998: 43–54). A crucial problem for an educational marketer at a conventional exhibition is how to convert visitors who are touring a site into customers, at best, or into sales leads, at the very least. An Internet educational marketer has a similar challenge, turning individuals who simply browse the Web into registered students. This analogy places a Website in between personal selling and advertising. A personalized response is possible, through stored information, as well as presenting advertising messages to enquiries, with Internet-based e-learning services supporting a potential student with general and personalized information all along a purchasing decision-path.

Stopping casual Web-surfers at a Website is not the primary requirement; rather, the aim is to draw in searchers who are potential customers trawling the Web for specific business transactions. Attracting people to the Website, therefore, is just the first step in achieving registration. Certain techniques can help online sales. For instance, it helps to start by exploring the existing marketing promotion by drawing the site to the attention of all existing customers. If existing customers do not know about the opportunities to study online, they may go elsewhere, and so the Web address should be prominent on everything produced.

The ranking of a Website by a Web search-engine is crucial in the presentation to such an enquirer. Further prominence can be gained by registering with major search-engines, as free automatic registration is possible, and by demonstrating the e-learning services to potential visitors, rather than marketing information to potential customers. This is because the likelihood of interaction with an enquirer is far higher if a Website is presented on the first page of a listing from a search-engine rather than later pages. As the process of refreshing information on a search-engine is done periodically and automatically, it is worth utilizing their features with attention to the content, and choosing two or three key phrases for the site that customers will use to search for a product or service.

A customer normally follows a buying process in which certain questions are resolved, such as specifications, price, availability and delivery. It is not easy to ask questions of a person Web-browsing, however, so all the information they require for a decision must be provided for them. There are some straightforward techniques for turning browsers into customers, including making the buying steps as easy and as fast as possible. Complex forms and long delays can cause clients to change their minds. It is also best to avoid asking browsers to log on or supply any details before they look at the prospectus, as it risks most callers leaving the Website rather than completing a form. Names and addresses, in any event, can be provided once a visitor is interested in registering on a course. Simple presentation is best, with full contact details, including telephone number, e-mail addresses and the methods of registration. Flashing images and text can be distracting and visitors may quickly leave without exploring the site or the service offers. The Website ought to be kept up to date, with contemporary cases and a recent review date.

The analogy of a Website as an electronic exhibition case presents a Web address as the shop window in an electronic arcade, where a number of factors act to guide and retain visitors. As with all marketing communication techniques, specific communications objectives for a Website can help identify measurable ways of determining its success. Reviewing material is important so as to present contemporary content, and removing dated material can help, since an automated scan by a search-engine can locate and signpost current content. Web-pages to maintain the interest of visitors ought to be informative, attractive and sensitive to the potential user, therefore, without unnecessary downloading delays due to unwarranted graphics.

An Internet marketing approach can be integrated with all the other conventional marketing processes, such as the design of a prospectus, community relations activities and professional development activities with potential customers. Promotion of a Web URL can be done online through discussion lists, services, newsletters and bulletin boards, as well as by conventional media. Internet activity can be linked, for public relations purposes, to other stories in local, regional or national media. An event to launch a new e-learning programme can gain media coverage that may raise the profile of the Website on search-engines. A small-scale press launch in Lampeter of an e-learning programme attracted three local reporters who filed the story, making local, regional and national newspapers and three news bulletins broadcast on BBC World Service later that day. Another promotional initiative caused the Website to be featured as the Yahoo 'Website of the Week', with free banner advertising on the front page of this Web search-engine. A student from Slovenia who liked the music of the Welsh-language pop group, Catatonia, became interested in Welsh, was attracted by the Website and enrolled on a course. This was carried as a press release, attracting further enquiries and registrations. In each of these cases, conventional materials which include the Web address are linked with Internet promotional materials to attract additional browsers and to try to convert them into enrolled students. All these activities need to be measured, to discover where clients come from.

COMMUNICATION RELATIONSHIPS

Effective communications using the Internet involve the same fundamental steps as offline, namely: identifying a target audience, setting objectives, creating a message, choosing channels, setting a budget, deciding on a communications mix, measuring results and then managing the communication process. All major modes of the communication mix are open to the e-learning marketer, for example, advertising online or by conventional media that highlights a Website, personal selling and public relations. The Internet, as a marketing communications medium, however, can present integrated text, video, graphics and sound, through which educational marketers may communicate with potential and existing customers with a 24-hours-a-day presence (Berthon et al., 1998: 691–704). Moreover, the Internet supports two-way communication, in which three possible control relationships can be distinguished:

One-to-one communication. Here a unique dialogue between an educational enterprise and an individual student, or groups of students with similar needs, is possible. An example in e-learning arises in a two-way transfer of information between a tutor and a student. Personal interaction is also possible between a Website and an individual visitor, to track visitor interests and provide individual responses.

One-to-many. This represents conventional mass marketing, with limited tailoring of the message to the audience. It exists when e-learning content is transferred from a tutor to a group, or when a tutor leads and directs a discussion group of students, fielding questions and developing concepts, such as in an e-tutorial. Applications in educational marketing include visitor groups that can be selected from personal data and presented with a news update, or an invitation to join an online discussion or seminar group.

Many-to-many. This is a new marketing scenario in which interaction is with the medium itself, not between sender and receiver. Hoffman and Novak describe this paradigm as one where an enterprise provides content to the medium and consumers can interact and provide commercially-oriented content as well (Hoffman and Novak, 1997: 50–68). The model operates when companies provide personalized Internet services to certain accounts. Examples are Dell (*www.dell.com*), in providing bespoke services to clients, as well as eBay (*www.eBay.com*), in offering products for sale, whereby different parties make offers. One scenario in an e-learning context occurs when a group discusses a topic as equals, such as in seminars.

The Internet can function both as a communications channel, for messages to get from one individual to another, and as a mass-media channel. For the diffusion of innovation, a mass-media channel is effective in creating knowledge of innovations, whereas interpersonal channels are more effective in forming and changing attitudes towards a new idea.

MARKETS FOR E-LEARNING

E-learning is still a relatively dynamic industry, in which the shape of the market is evolving. In this environment, determining an attractive target market for an educational enterprise involves a process of selection and choice. A common way is to focus on a specific market with common characteristics that are aligned with the skill and competencies of staff. Once a target is chosen it requires a concentration of resources and attention to attain the marketing objectives. With the market exhibiting a degree of complexity, however, there are many ways in which the market might be analysed. There is currently no unanimity amongst analysts on the characteristics and variables for categorization and segmentation.

A broad approach puts the markets that e-learning providers set out to serve into three distinct categories. First is the corporate market, which includes corporate buyers for employee training, customer-focused e-learning for suppliers, customers or employees in large, medium or small enterprises. Second is the consumer market, with learners pursuing vocational continuing education as well as non-vocational lifelong learning. Third is an academic market, with a number of distinctive sub-sectors: pre-school, primary and secondary school, further and higher education, parents, lifelong learners and government.

THE CORPORATE MARKET

The corporate market is large and growing. The primary benefits for the corporate market are in skill acquisition and learning management. Advantages arise from the ability to manage the learning development of employees, to track the progress of individuals and groups as well as the extent to which skill gaps are being met. In a company with international operations, the organization's workforce may be spread all over the world, creating additional difficulties in keeping all employees up to date and making the economics of Web-based delivery highly compelling for executives and HR professionals.

Among other factors that drive the corporate market (Urdan and Weggen, 2000) are rapid obsolescence, since information and expertise can quickly become out of date, so managers need the capability to deliver skills to employees speedily and effectively. Considerable cost-savings for companies can be gained, due to the elimination of travel costs for the trainees and instructors, as well as the inconvenience of bringing them to the same place for learning. Courses can also be customized into a non-standard duration that can be distributed in time, to minimise the disruption to a business, or modified and made available across an entire network instantly. Cost-effectiveness of learning is offered, therefore, in the face of cost pressures on corporate budgets. There are also benefits in addressing the 'free-agent learner' mentality, in which mature individuals take responsibility for their career development and seek opportunities to enhance their career prospects.

Four groups of employees are evident in firms. One group comprises employees looking for statutory training for compliance with professional standards or legislation, such as in finance or health and safety. There are also groups of employees seeking essential specific product or company knowledge; examples here might include members of a salesforce team that need product development. A third group comprises employees with professional development interests, such as in management or technical development. Finally, there are employees with a general interest in development as part of their career projection. Challenges exist, therefore, in the formulation of an e-learning portfolio for employees, not least in their motivation and encouragement to become lifelong learners. Moreover, employees must be skilled enough in e-skills to participate in e-learning, which means that the professional, skilled, semi-skilled and unskilled may require different approaches.

CUSTOMER-FOCUSED E-LEARNING

One way for a company to provide e-learning is through customer-focused e-learning (CFEL). CFEL aims to educate customers and retain them as loyal buyers by providing ongoing customer support. The intangibles that add value to most products and services are knowledge-based. They include technical know-how, product design, marketing presentation, understanding the customer, personal creativity and innovation (Quinn et al., 1997). Customer-focused e-learning may help a customer optimize the use of a product and can add value to the product offer. Companies are turning to CFEL for a variety of reasons (Aldrich, 2000: 34–68): as a marketing tool to promote products and services, to fulfil a needed support-role for sales people and internal employees, to add a novel service not offered by competitors, as an inducement for potential buyers and to add a new revenue stream.

CFEL is following a similar development path to the adoption of e-learning. Hardware and software IT companies were the first to develop and apply CFEL models, other industries with intricate offers, such as pharmaceuticals and financial service firms, followed close behind, with Web retailers the latest and most visible practitioners. IT companies, such as Sun, Microsoft and Cisco, have all developed sophisticated CFEL programmes that offer combinations of e-learning, instructor-led training and certification programmes to individuals and business customers. Many conventional businesses are creating learning pages attached to their Websites to provide information for customers and site interest, such as Kodak (*www.kodak.com*) and financial sites, such as the company TD Waterhouse (*www.tdwaterhouse.com*). For consumers it offers an e-learning opportunity with little, or no cost.

CORPORATE UNIVERSITIES

A corporate university (CU) is another way of enhancing employee skills and can cover a variety of different types of organization, whether centre-based, centre plus electronic network, decentralized network or virtual. A CU has certain general characteristics; for instance, it occupies a strategic position, is proactive, extends beyond a training department and presents customized curricula for key jobs (Fulmer and Gibbs, 1998). For some large firms this has led to the change of corporate training departments into corporate universities, while in others the application of e-learning is used directly to support business performance. Corporate universities in the UK and the US show considerable variations in their application of e-learning (Beamish and Armistead, 2000; Bjarnason et al., 2000b), as the examples at BAE Systems and Lloyds TSB show:

BAE Systems CU. A corporate Intranet is the central technology platform for the delivery of employee education focusing on technologies, strategic research, leadership and development, worldwide engineering and business best practice. The CU has four faculties: best practice, learning, engineering and manufacturing technology, as well as a business school. The virtual university is advised by partner institutions about the content and context of the courses. Learning resources are provided for immediate employee reference and work application.

University for Lloyds TSB. The strategic goals of this CU are for development to match closely the strategic needs of the business, make learning more accessible, form collaborative partnerships and motivate people to learn. The CU intends to focus on distance learning and flexibility, providing a large proportion of provision of learning for externally recognized qualifications.

HIGH-TECH CORPORATE SEGMENTATION

One new approach to high-tech corporate-market segmentation is relevant
to certain clients in the corporate market (Dunn et al., 1999: 186–91). Dunn
et al. reported on a study of over a thousand mobile professionals in the
United States, defined by them as managers who conduct business away from
the office for at least 20 per cent of the day, using notebook computers, pagers,
cellular and smart mobile phones. Traditionally, technology providers use
vertical and horizontal segmentation to formulate marketing programmes
(Dunn and Thomas, 1990: 44–9). A vertical market occurs when a company
sells product into one or several specific industries, which can then be identified to develop lists of sales prospects. A horizontal market exists when a
firm markets product into a broad range of industries. From an analysis of
sales consultants' data, Dunn et al. concluded, however, that an alternative
four 'solution-based' market segments exist for emerging, unsaturated markets.

The first segment they describe as the specialized solution. It comprises a
'be-first' buyer, in which the user makes a significant investment in a specialized solution in order to get a sustainable advantage. The solution in this
segment is then aimed at a single buyer. The next segment is the 'customized
solution'. Here the solution addresses a business problem, rather than a technology problem, and is aimed not at a single buyer, but at a targeted group of
users who seek increased productivity amd cannot afford a specialized solution.
This segment then responds to aggressive selling. The 'value solution' is
another, but broader, market segment, where the customers respond to market-
pull. Buyers want quick affordable solutions in order to reach parity with
competitors who have already implemented solutions. The 'packaged solution'
completes the segmentation. Customers are retail-oriented with appeals to the
mass-market segment. They require ease of application for the user with
minimal hardware requirements beyond everyday equipment needs. The technology is sold on the basis of success with more sophisticated segments. Small
firms, home offices, the self-employed and professional consumers are the
likely customers. These buyer segments may be useful for decision-makers in
e-learning providers when tailoring a strategy to fit the different segments,
with marketing approaches and value propositions.

THE VALUE CHAIN AND THE INTERNET

Internet applications impact on the value chain through the cost and quality of
activities of enterprises from all sectors (Porter, 2001: 63–78). But they are not
the only influence. Conventional factors also play conspicuous roles through
the skills of employees, the physical assets, the product and process technology.

The technical options available to a company come from a range of advances, including relational databases and object-orientated programming as well as Internet tools. Current developments involve integration by linking together cross-activity processes, through tools such as customer-relationship management (CRM), supply-chain management (SCM) and enterprise resource planning (ERP) systems.

The value chain provides a template for business analysis and potential applications. It can be split into primary and secondary activities, with examples of Internet applications and e-learning across this range (Table 9.1). Five primary groups of activities exist: input logistics, which involves the acquisition, storage and distribution of materials; operations, where the various inputs are transformed into the final product/service; output logistics, which involves storing and distributing the product/service to the customer; marketing and sales, which includes sales administration, advertising, selling and communications networks that help users access a particular service; and after-sales service, which embraces all activities that enhance or maintain the value of a product/service.

Table 9.1. Prominent applications of the Internet and e-learning in the value chain

Value-chain activity	Internet/Intranet technology	E-learning HRD
Primary activities		
Input logistics	Real-time integrated scheduling.	Performance support tools.
	Firm-wide inventory data.	Skill development.
Operations	Integrated info. for firm and suppliers.	Performance support tools.
	Real-time info. for salesforce.	Health and safety.
	Links to component suppliers.	Quality management.
Outbound logistics	Real-time order transactions.	Performance support tools.
	Customer access to delivery status.	Logistics management.
	Integrated channel management.	Career development.
Marketing and sales	Online sales channels.	Salesforce product knowledge.
	Real-time customer feedback.	Customer-focused e-learning.
	Online product specification.	Essential product knowledge.
After-sales service	Online customer service.	Customer-focused e-learning.
	Service parts management.	Essential product knowledge.
	Real-time field access.	Customer installation support.
		Customer feedback support.
		Intro. to product upgrades.
Support activities		
Infrastructure	Intranet financial and ERP.	Performance support for quality.
	Online investor information.	E-skills and finance training.
	Online compliance standards.	Online information on standards.
Human resource	Self-service personnel admin.	Management development.
management	Web-based sharing of reports.	Employment-law updating.
	Web-based training and development.	Mandatory training.
		Health and safety.

Table 9.1. (*contd.*)

Value-chain activity	Internet/Intranet technology	E-learning HRD
		Developing lifelong learners.
		E-skills development.
		Learner management info.
Technology development	R & D access to online sales info.	Technical skills development.
	Online knowledge directories.	E-skills development and CPD.
	Collaborative product design.	Product development.
		Research and technology transfer.
Procurement	Internet-enabled demand plans.	Procurement compliance policy.
	Direct procurement via B2B links.	Customer-focused e-learning.
	Real-time availability information.	

Each of these primary activities is linked to support activities in the enterprise. The infrastructure involves systems for planning, organizing, information mangement, quality assurance and so on. Human resource management transcends all the primary areas and is concerned with recruiting, training, developing and rewarding people within the organization. Technology development is concerned with key technologies for the product/service, such as research and development and product design. Procurement acquires resources for the primary activities, which can occur through orders from many parts of the organization.

E-learning and performance support can be applied throughout the value chain, where the relevance to business requirement can be judged more clearly. Major applications of e-learning in an enterprise focus on compliance-oriented content, such as employment law and health and safety, and sales dimensions, such as insurance. Compliance-oriented content can be unpopular among employees and a multimedia approach can be a tool for ensuring that all required employees complete any compulsory training. Other applications for it are with employees in sales and marketing, who seek essential product or company knowledge, and individuals with professional, management, technical or general development interests. It might also embrace employees with a general interest in the conversion of users to lifelong learning and the support for long-term career projections.

Customized design can be a time-consuming and expensive implementation. The high cost of developing a customized e-learning programme for the company may prohibit this as a bespoke solution, but an off-the-shelf e-learning package that nearly meets these needs might offer advantages. In view of these costs, a business-needs analysis is a clear precursor for decision-makers, to support customized design. E-learning applications extend across the value-chain activities of an enterprise, as the set of applications, derived largely from large enterprises, demonstrates (Table 9.2).

**Table 9.2. Typical company applications of e-learning methods
(Click2learn.com, 2000)**

Activities	Company and applications of e-learning methods
Processes	*Bi Lo.* Cashier training for product identification and pricing.
Marketing	*Oxford Medical.* Information for better customer dialogue.
Sales training	*Buckman Laboratories.* Negotiation techniques. Customer financial measures. Career-planning tools.
Business	*First Union Bank.* Business process software instruction.
Operations	*Lloyds TSB.* Compliance training for financial products.
Manufacturing	*Boeing Company.* Customized video-intensive, text and graphics, computer-based job aids for factory workers and support personnel, covering topics such as aircraft hazard safety and shopfloor tasks. *Nabisco Company.* Enterprise-wide applications, supply-chain management and its custom computer applications. Performance support and instruction for factory operatives.
IT training	*PriceWaterhouseCoopers.* Training applications with SAP enterprise-system implementation.

SMES: THE 'FOUR-INFLUENCES LEARNING MODEL'

Drivers of e-learning for SMEs and large corporates are similar: skills development and learning management. Learning in the SME workplace holds many advantages for a firm, with the ability to customize training to meet work priorities high among them, according to interviews with firms in Dorset and the Isle of Wight (Kiley et al., 2001: 14). This study also noted the need to align learning to business strategy, which reiterates the theme emerging from performance-consulting studies on SMEs (see chapter 2). Taken all together, a complex set of perceptions in SMEs and influences on them seems to exist. These are relatively stronger than in larger-sized enterprises, arguably because of the greater importance of interpersonal communication channels.

Interpersonal channels are also important because they are effective in forming and changing attitudes towards a new idea. Most individuals evaluate an innovation, not on the basis of scientific research, but through the subjective experience of near-peers who adopt the innovation. These near-peers serve as role models, whose innovation behaviour tends to be imitated by others in the system. Observational learning of the behaviours of such near-peers may then serve as a powerful means for the diffusion of an educational innovation. One way of visualizing and grouping the influences on an SME is the 'four-influences learning model' (Beevers, 2000) shown in Figure 9.1. The model can help clarify marketing objectives and the optimum communications channel, according to the characteristics of the target audience.

The model is predicated on the notion that the environment of an SME exerts influencing pressures that can be grouped in four categories:

Top-down by an owner-manager, decision-maker, or the supply chain putting demands on the business for performance improvement.

Bottom-up from groups of employees or individuals concerned with getting the appropriate knowledge to apply to a job, or for career development. This can also exert leverage on e-learning for academic purposes.

Side-on from peer pressure, by a similar trade or occupational practice. Professional development can lead employees into becoming free-agent learners and stimulate demand from the consumer market for e-learning.

Side-on from community organizations that surround an SME, where there are interrelationships between the firm and its employees in the exercise of corporate responsibility. Managers and employees are members of the wider community and are likely to have family members who have relationships with these organizations as stakeholders or consumers.

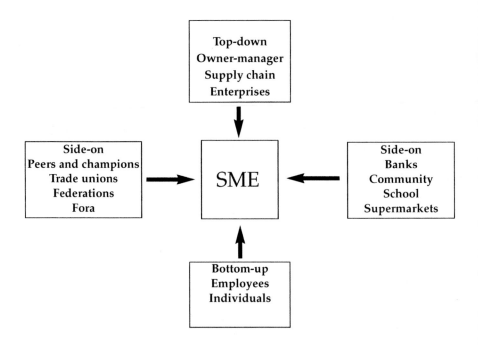

Figure 9.1. The 'four influences learning model' for SMEs

Promotional objectives, benefits and influencing arguments can be devised for decision-makers in SMEs for each of the directions of influence. Internal marketing can be applied for persuading employees. The model, although illustrated for a SME, can also be applied to a different target market-segment, such as lifelong learners, corporate employees, subject specialists or SMEs.

ADDRESSING SME BARRIERS TO SKILLS DEVELOPMENT

Research studies on SME and learning have focused predominantly on the top-down and bottom-up influences on learning, and this seems to carry forward into e-learning. The drivers for consumer and academic e-learning are addressed later in this chapter. But what do we know about SME employees and their managers?

The first characteristic of SME students is that they are not young. The average age of students on certain courses for SMEs at Lampeter is forty years old. This implies that they may have been out of full-time education for a long time and may be nervous about returning to study. Consequently, without good support services it can be difficult for them to complete a programme and feel successful. As well as an infrastructure to support students, effective communication methods and objectives are needed to attract and retain them on courses. This puts an onus on tutors to maintain contact with students to provide encouragement and to do this, telephone support can be a vital tool.

There is evidence that employees consider e-learning as being different from conventional training (Kiley et al., 2001: 14). For the majority of employees, their prior experience of learning was that of face-to-face contact in a classroom with other participants. Many had enjoyed being removed from day-to-day pressures and being able to interact with other learners. Employees needed help with their online learning and with developing confidence in using e-learning materials, especially during the initial sessions.

Simple internal promotional techniques can contribute substantially to increasing and maintaining employee participation. These can take several forms, such as holding an informal lunch while conducting a short seminar to demonstrate how e-learning is relevant to practical problems. Setting up a source of help is a useful way to advise employees on how they can get answers to their questions in person, by phone or via e-mail. The telephone and e-mail can be used to promote e-learning, provide useful tips, outline benefits and share suggestions. For SMEs with more structured employee-development plans, e-learning can be incorporated into a structured process in which suggestions for personal development activities can be offered at performance reviews. A tutor can tailor the interrelationship with employees to the level that seems appropriate and can be used for personal follow-up with less confident learners, to encourage them to work online.

The barriers to skill development perceived by managers in SMEs have been studied in depth and four categories of barrier identified: cultural, financial, access and awareness (Lange et al., 2000: 5–11). Cultural barriers can exist in the form of the right attitude to skills development and are one of the greatest impediments to training. Concerns may exist that training employees makes them more attractive for the labour market. Employees in large firms are more likely to have fixed job-descriptions, whereas those in small firms need to be multiskilled. Small firms that are developed by their owners appear to operate with informal and flexible personal relationships (Scase & Goffee, 1987). The experience and personality of the owner-manager influences the management of the firm. One possible way to gain SME support lies in enhancing management development in SMEs.

Financial barriers can be present, even in SMEs that appreciate the benefits of training their employees. The cost of training appears prohibitive for many small firms, even though many companies do not have an accurate method of assessing the costs or benefits of their training activities. Economies of scale are again influential in preventing small firms from benefiting from training, whereas larger firms may have structures and significant training budgets (Vickerstaffe, 1992: 1–16). The perceived cost of training may be linked to the culture and the type of skills required. The lack of financial resources in an SME often means that it does not have the resources to hire skilled people or adequate resources for training. Exploiting competitive advantages associated with the knowledge-based economy can prove an entry method to help a firm. Moreover, managers considering e-learning for their places of work need assistance in finding out what is available and how it can be applied, since access barriers can stop interested employees from accessing learning opportunities. SMEs also find it difficult to assess the quality of learning on offer by providers, have poor access to training information, or insufficient time for learning. Unless provision is credible in adding value in the eyes of employers, therefore, little positive action will be taken (Lange et al., 2000: 10).

Providers of learning addressing these barriers face a number of difficulties, but a range of indicators to the likely take-up of training may assist the targeting of small firms (Marchmont, 1999). These pointers include the size of firm, since larger firms tend to give more formal training than smaller ones; short-term economic benefits, with learning to improve productivity, reduce costs or increase sales an important driver; job-market conditions, as growing businesses located in areas of skills shortages are more likely to train; and main industrial activities, since firms using advanced technologies and attaching importance to R & D for the firm, the use of new technology and innovation strategies are most likely to train. There are many others.

Good practice in addressing the barriers in SMEs has been distilled into success factors that include providing business benefits by meeting commercial needs with immediate application (ECOTEC, 2001b). Other recommended features include offering flexible provision that meets client needs of place, pace, time and method so as to provide ease of entry and overcome barriers. Authenticity is important in using genuine experts, including businesspeople who relate to working in SMEs, with SME involvement in the development of services desirable to ensure that these are demand-led. Continuous improvement by ongoing service evaluation is necessary to ensure the provision continues to meet needs. Moreover, support systems ought to have staff able to respond quickly to enquiries and reliability to ensure that delivery and services occur on schedule.

TECHNOLOGY-SUPPORTED LEARNING FOR SMES

The application of technology-supported learning for the development of management skills in SMEs has been subject to an EU survey (James, 2000). Management skills are a sub-set of the general business development of SMEs, but James reported that the use of TSL delivery was not always the most appropriate method, because of a lack of knowledge of the method and a lack of human interaction. It concluded that educational enterprises which target SMEs ought to deliver customized learning, sensitive to the different development stages of a firm and, moreover, with high practical relevance. Priority areas for management development are business management skills, including marketing, international business procedures, and the quality, control and application of business computer software. Best practice in delivering TSL to management ought to incorporate human interaction. This might take the form of regular face-to-face tutor support, or through greater networking online through the use of chatroom-style discussion groups, or through teaching groups in which learners collaborate on assignments. A number of areas require attention in the TSL systems design for delivery to SME users, according to James. These include using a variety of media to arouse interest. The TSL design requires ease of use, with the provision of help features, learning objectives and progress checks. Virtual environments ought to assist in problem-solving and testing solutions, with technical support having easy access for learners. Customizing is also desirable, with the ability to enter company-specific data into the TSL.

Technology opens up significant prospects in the SME for lifelong learning, to develop skills in applying technology and the necessary skills for the future (Gray and Lawless, 2000). The limited empirical evidence, however, suggests that SMEs currently make very limited use of technology for learning. The barriers include deficiencies in SMEs in the use of technology, the low communication speeds, the high costs of ICT, the difficulties in differentiating between the myriad providers, the frequent changes in technology and, finally, the lack of skills for using technology effectively.

THE CONSUMER MARKET

The drivers for the consumer market comprise people who seek to learn for personal interests. The penetration of the Internet into domestic households offers a considerable market opportunity with advantages over a conventional retail channel (Peterson et al., 1999: 18). Consumer drivers include technology-aware schoolchildren, alert to technological developments that assist their studies. The Internet acts as a combined platform for such learners, enabling learning, play and social communications from the same PC. E-learning has the potential to make learning engaging and enjoyable from home; it can help present a value proposition around parents' aspirations for the best education for their children. For many people with busy lifestyles, learning has to be accommodated in irregular intervals, or episodes, or at unusual times, so that eliminating unproductive travel time and costs is a help. Lifelong learning is also a necessity for many consumers in a competitive job-market, for getting and then retaining employment.

The consumer market comprises both vocational and non-vocational learners. Vocational learners include those involved in continuing professional development (CPD), although those doing work-related learning are also included because the student is likely to bear the cost of paying for an e-learning programme. Even though an employer may reimburse the costs, the direct consumer will be making the buying decision. CPD is increasingly being made mandatory by professional associations, such as the Law Society, the Engineering Council and the various medical professions. The flexibility of e-learning gives people who seek professional development voluntarily an opportunity to improve their marketability. The techniques provide learning support for professionals remote from a learning site, or dispersed in small numbers over a wide geographic area.

'Free-agent learner' is a term that straddles both the vocational and non-vocational arena and refers to the growing numbers of independent and highly motivated adults who take responsibility for their own ongoing learning (Caudron, 1999: 26–32). Sometimes the term is restricted to people engaged in career-development learning that is self-directed and intended to develop competencies that can help career progression. At other times, it is applied more broadly to embrace learning for any purpose, including opportunities that relate to personal hobbies or interests. Many working professional adults are not able to accept the traditional portfolio offered in colleges and universities of daytime classes, aggregated credits, theory-based content, academically-oriented faculty and lecture-based format (Phipps and Merisotis, 2000: 6). The Internet is also used by individuals for research on non-vocational information. Purchasers of recreational e-learning are likely to be more sensitive to price than those buying work-related e-learning, who may be reimbursed for their course by an employer, or may ultimately receive added value in higher earnings.

THE ACADEMIC MARKET FOR E-LEARNING

This academic market consists of people directly or indirectly involved in providing, or receiving, formal education. It includes flexible approaches to providing learning on-campus, as well as supporting students at a distance. The academic market extends in age-range and level from pre-school children up to older adults returning to college after retirement, such as the University of the Third Age. This giant academic market can be categorized into a number of sub-divisions, such as pre-primary, primary, secondary and higher education.

Many factors drive growth in the academic market, including the need to attract new students continuously and provide more learning opportunities. Students who graduate need to be replaced by others enrolling, simply to maintain equilibrium. For growth, more students are required to enrol on existing courses, new student groups to be identified, or new courses to be designed. E-learning in this context has the potential to provide more learning opportunities rapidly, by creating among other things an additional distribution channel for distance learners. Flexible access can also widen participation in lifelong learning, which drives up public demand for learning opportunities. Lifelong learning is growing in importance, because of shifts in the economy and social structures, and because developments in science and technology demand more continuous learning to equip people with the knowledge to cope with increasingly complex demands. Time constraints on faculty staff can also be eased in developing content for presentation to student groups through reuse in multiple formats. For the student it offers flexible participation, at work or at home, whichever is best for study.

Technology has altered the ways in which people work and how society operates. The digerati, the accomplished communicators, of this society are young people who communicate with one another and organize easily in a multi-processing ecology. The tools for their way of life are e-mail, chatroom, cellphone, multi-player online games, MP3 music-players and instant messaging. They already live partially in cyberspace, with a range of online games and message boards. This mobile 'Net' generation have created their own language through instant messaging, which is quick, efficient, group-oriented and informal, and creates a sense of being connected to other people. They are comfortable in dealing with information and have honed information-skimming skills that are different from those of earlier generations, but little research has yet appeared on them (Søby, 2002).

National policies aimed at widening participation are developing the market for learning. The emphasis in the UK on lifelong learning is on social inclusion with a view to responsible citizenship. Education is seen as empowering individuals to develop a voice and combat marginalization or exclusion. The market structure for lifelong learning provision stretches from pre-school, through school and FE/HE, to adult education and continuing professional development.

The pre-primary education market is the smallest in this sector, but is growing, with the recognition by parents of the advantages conferred by education at a young age. Parents seek pre-primary education materials, both traditional and technology-based, that can help their child before reaching school age. They face a choice of materials, but are unlikely to be receiving guidance from a child's school on appropriate materials.

In the primary and secondary sectors, technology continues to gain acceptance as a teaching tool and as a means of accessing information. In the UK, the government is enhancing the ICT infrastructure for schools, for instance through the New Opportunities Fund (*www.nof.gov.uk*) and the National Grid for Learning (*www.ngfl.gov.uk*). In certain subjects, such as mathematics, science and technology, secondary schools are finding it difficult to recruit specialist teachers, because of a growing shortage of teachers in these subjects. Technology-supported learning may become a valuable tool to help students, if specialist teachers become fewer. Such resources can be accessed by technologically-inclined children and helped by increased involvement from parents (DTI, 2000). Teachers are stretched across a range of tasks, such as record-keeping, pastoral care of students, complying with new assessments and standards, integrating and undertaking new learning technologies, as well as teaching. E-learning can make a significant contribution for teachers, particularly since limited resources and time often inhibit travel. It can provide online continuing professional development (CPD) and administrative tools that help record-keeping and tracking, as well as being a resource for developing lessons and a medium for digital collaboration.

Post-secondary and higher education are subject to a number of influences from the knowledge economy, which offers better rewards for highly educated employees, a feature that serves to draw adults back into education in order to update their knowledge. Students from non-traditional populations may have more complex work and family obligations, so that flexibility can enhance the accessibility to learning for them.

MARKETING MIX AND THE INTERNET

The marketing mix was formulated originally around the four variables of product, price, promotion and place, used to define the marketing tools needed to realize a set of marketing objectives (McCarthy, 1960). Later adaptation of the model has extended the initial model to include the additional elements of people and processes, although some practitioners assume these to be already covered within the basic 4 Ps (Booms and Bitner, 1981). The Internet, however, provides opportunities to vary the constituents of the marketing mix in order to influence demand (Chaffey et al., 2000: 40).

Examples exist for each of the variables, for instance, new information-based products or services can be provided and product features can be adapted quickly. Customer service and brand values can be enhanced, with variants produced for certain markets. The price can be varied to influence demand. Internet distribution reduces the cost of conventional retail. Flexibility in price maintenance for profitability is possible, or price reduction to stimulate demand. The Internet offers a new sales channel for distributing products and so offers variants on place. Opportunities also exist for small enterprises through exporting, due to the ease of distribution of e-learning. The cost of distribution can be reduced compared with conventional channels, which means that a price point can be retained and the lower-cost route applied to raise profitability.

The Internet may serve to reduce the role of direct customer-contact and stimulate customer-relationship management. It can affect processes through the integration of the Internet with other marketing processes, such as telemarketing, PR and direct marketing. In terms of promotion, the Internet offers an additional marketing communications channel that can supplement advertising, sales promotions, PR and direct marketing.

PROMOTION AND SALES

Simple promotional techniques can contribute substantially to the success of an e-learning initiative in a firm by increasing and maintaining employee participation. There are several courses of action that can prove beneficial. E-learning incorporated into a structured employee-development process can be helpful for decision-makers, who can offer suggestions for personal-development activities at performance reviews. An informal lunch can be held while conducting a short seminar for decision-makers on how to demonstrate the ways in which e-learning is relevant to practical problems. E-mail can promote specific e-learning courses and its benefits, provide useful tips, outline benefits and share suggestions, with advice for employees on how they can get answers to their questions. The interaction between individual learners and a tutor will vary. The tutor can tailor the interrelationship with participants to the level that seems appropriate. The telephone is still a very important marketing tool and can be used for personal follow-up with less confident learners, to encourage them to work online.

A crucial element of any learning engagement involves securing a contract. One classic approach taken by educational institutions to SMEs is to offer to conduct a training-needs analysis, or to provide training directly. This is synonymous with direct personal selling as part of the promotional mix for a learning provider, but presupposes that training is the answer for each enterprise. Performance improvement is an alternative, described in chapter 2. This business improvement looks holistically at the technology environment and activities of the firm. Such a personalized approach adds costs to delivery, in the form of staff and travel to the firm for the business analyst. In this scenario, the potential for obtaining greater economies of scale is reduced, compared with free-agent e-learning, because of the increase in fixed and variable costs of business support. It does offer, though, a more customized service.

SERVICE CHARACTERISTICS

E-learning as a service is an act or benefit that one party can offer another that does not result, in general, in the ownership of anything. All services have four distinctive characteristics that greatly influence the design of marketing programmes: intangibility, perishability, inseparability and variability. There are, however, differences in these characteristics between conventional learning and e-learning services.

Intangibility. Conventional face-to-face education can only be experienced and cannot be evaluated before purchase, in a similar way to physical products. Customers look for tangible clues in appearance, location, customer handling, literature and personal presentation. In e-learning provision, a client can often try out part of a course before purchase. A portion of a course can be presented as trial product to help the customer appreciate the appearance and user-approach. The tangible clues that a customer then has to consider include: does the content link with personal or business goals? Is the content engaging with the appropriate use of media? Is the navigation friendly to the user? Does it assess where the student is, in terms of real-life assessment?

Perishability. Conventional delivery cannot be stored, so that an unoccupied place on a course has an opportunity cost. In contrast, e-learning can be stored and accessed again on multiple occasions at later times. This applies both to real-time events and to content prepared for distribution by storage and then downloaded at the convenience of the learner. The perishable elements in e-learning become synchronous forms, such as videoconferencing or live chat, but even these can also be stored although at the expense of interaction and spontaneity.

Inseparability. In conventional education the service is consumed as it is produced. The quality of the experience is, in general, inseparable from the quality of the teacher. In e-learning, a degree of separation can be introduced, so that the development of content is likely to be constructed through a team approach rather than the solo methods in face-to-face presentation. It is also probable that the support tutor will be different from the content originator. The quality of the content can be more easily maintained at a uniform standard. In a similar way, the quality of online tutorial support can be closely monitored to maintain standards.

Variability. Each experience is dependent on the quality of the teacher in conventional delivery, so that a significant challenge is to produce and maintain a consistent quality. With e-learning, the teacher variation can be removed through the application of standardized product content. Although online tutor support might still be a variable, certain measures, such as appropriate monitoring and scheduling, can be taken to counter or mitigate effects.

BRANDING

People need brands. They can instil confidence in the purchaser, save time in decision-making and, by choosing one, the customer will not be embarrassed. They project a message to other people. In educational terms, a brand can provide an identity and offer a way for an individual to relate to others. Branding of an educational service gives it a distinctive image to publicly differentiate it from competitors. The brand, however, means more than just the labelling of products and services to distinguish one from another. It includes intangible facets, such as quality assurance and symbolism.

Intangibles exist in the minds of people who form the market. The market is based on elements, some that a provider can control and others that it cannot. A successful brand is a certain service, augmented so that a client perceives relevant unique added values which match their needs most closely (de Chernatony and McDonald, 1992). Building such a brand requires a focus on two or three key attributes differentiating it from competitors. These can be defined objectively from research on the perceived value of the service from all angles, the students, staff and stakeholders.

Brands are crucial to Internet enterprises. The business challenges for Internet-supported learning are to build strong brand names, known for unique state-of-the art learning experiences where individuals, in a convenient way, can access first-rate content in an engaging, interactive virtual environment (Moe and Blodget, 2000). To determine a formal, precise definition, an educational service-provider needs to find the characteristics of its own mission that make it unique and analyse the competitors. Brand-name corporate-learning providers are operating in the e-learning arena. Writers and speakers, such as Blanchard on corporate leadership and development, and Peters on evolving competitive business-practices, have partnered with Ninth House (*www.ninthhouse.com*) to offer content that is interactive and personalized. At the same time, online companies such as DigitalThink (*www.digitalthink.com*), Skillsoft (*www.skillsoft.com*) and eMind (*www.emind.com*) are also trying to build their brand names on quality content, inclusiveness and accessibility.

Products and services are differentiated not only by how they operate, but also by what they symbolize and imply about the purchasers. Some companies mostly address corporate clients, such as Saba (*www.saba.com*). A number of firms target specific industry segments such as IT, one example being NETg (*www.netg.com*). Other e-learning firms help build learning infrastructures, such as Eduprise (*www.eduprise.com*). Brand-name content that is beginning to penetrate the corporate market is coming from traditional universities and colleges. By using the capabilities of the Internet, brand-name international business schools, such as Stanford (*www.stanford.edu*), Columbia University (*www.columbia.edu*) and the University of Chicago (*www.uchicago.edu*), are able to reach corporate employees as well as current students.

The general wisdom is that the online brand identity should be similar to, and support, the offline brand (Chaffey et al., 2000: 232). An established university, college or educational supplier probably has a stronger brand than a new e-learning service-provider. There are also more benefits than disadvantages to being aligned to the core of an institution through budgets and curriculum. Politically, a provider is probably better off as an integrated operation. Some companies, however, decide to differentiate their Web offering by using a different brand from their online brand, such as Cisco (*www.cisco.com*) through its Learrning Partners. The brand, of course, can be damaged if the site is difficult to use in any way, or if the graphics are of poor quality. Consequently, prestigious mainstream universities may undertake e-learning work under a new brand name. The possible failure of operations in the e-learning realm will not then taint the prestige of a mainstream identity. Separate branding protects the mainstream offer and repute, in which much time and effort has been invested, and distances the online offer, with potentially large enrolments and possible business difficulties.

There are strengths inherent in the current brand and image of an established educational service-provider. A potential student, drawn by the existing reputation, will expect a standard of service from e-learning that at least matches the expectations of conventional provision. This means that an e-learning service needs to be thoroughly scrutinized before full launch, with frequent feedback during trialling to monitor progress and rectify any operational difficulties. E-learning is not an activity where knowledge can be monopolized, so a new programme launch is quite likely to attract other practitioners to discover how it operates.

MARKETING E-LEARNING PRODUCTS AND SERVICES

There are a number of species of business model for how online companies can make money on the Internet. These groupings are not mutually exclusive and a number of companies derive revenue from more than one segment. Analysts categorize company activities into five models: access, content, commerce, software and services (Moe and Blodget, 2000). Access relates to firms that sell dedicated network services, such as Campus Pipeline (*www.campuspipeline.com*). Content involves companies providing what you see when you go online, such as UNext (*www.unext.com*), SmartForce (*www.smartforce.com*) and

Ninth House (*www.ninthhouse.com*). Commerce is the selling of merchandise, such as Textbooks.com (*www.textbooks.com*) for the higher-education market and Saba (*www.saba.com*) in the corporate-learning arena. Software companies sell software product that facilitates inter- or intra-enterprise communication and commerce. Service companies provide a wide variety of services necessary for the online environment.

A simpler grouping comprises three broad segments: content, technology and services (Urdan and Weggen, 2000: 30), although the distinctions between these three segments are not clear-cut. Content describes organizations that develop and distribute their own content, which can be text-based or some variety of multimedia content, and which includes any type of instruction, such as IT, business skills, lifestyle, academic or custom design. In the technology category are enterprises that offer technology platforms, or tools, as their core offering, even though they may provide content or another service. Service is a broad category that offers a range of assistance for implementing e-learning, such as a portal.

A learning portal acts as a front-door website for enquiries on learning. There are now well over a hundred, and each claims to offer individual enquirers or organizations consolidated access to learning resources from multiple sources. Typical examples of learning portals that operate as a gateway to learning resources are: *www.click2learn.com*; *www.ehow.com*; *www.learn.com*; *www.learnitonline.com*; *www.learn2.com*; *www.smartforce.com*; and *www.thinq.com*. This proliferation of portals is due to the need for content providers to expand their distribution outlets as well as to demand from consumers eager to find e-learning opportunities. Business entry is relatively easy since the cost of building an online portal is relatively small. Hence, consolidation seems inevitable as new businesses enter the market and they try to differentiate themselves from existing portals.

MOVING FROM REGIONAL MARKETS

The primary interest of conventional educational service-providers moving into e-learning is in the flexible delivery of content to new or existing student groups. Some newcomers seek to serve markets beyond their traditional regional catchment, but most seek initially to serve students from an existing market. Change is already affecting course prospectuses, however, on and off the Web. The typical external programmes serve a range of other audiences: adult working professionals, recreational lifelong learners, more traditional part-time credit-based students, as well as SMEs and in-company learners. Apart from the latter, the existing non-electronic markets for these operations are often regionally or nationally constrained. In terms of e-learning markets, however, these are regional, national and international. The region is a primary target-market because of brand recognition and the local reputation that typically drive students in their choices. A market demographic that is very attractive to all distance-education providers is that of individuals who are geographically dispersed, but who have niche interests, with the time, place and resources to pursue them wherever they arise. To reach them and sustain provision to them will mean continuing differentiation from rivals, which in turn means focusing on the effectiveness of value assurance, value enhancement and innovation.

10

Quality, value assurance and value enhancement

Digital delivery has direct effects on the academic work of educational providers; among these, it increases the sources of competition and influences the operating procedures for how quality is interpreted. Educational providers are now better informed than ever on the multifaceted aspects of quality assurance, through many cases of well-designed provision and codes of practice. Conventional criteria for assessing and assuring quality need adaptation, though, for the e-learning environment. Technical standards are important. Devising and delivering authentic e-learning solutions for firms presents another perspective of quality on value assurance for decision-makers in companies. Value propositions for firms are often defined by increased customer satisfaction, the improved readiness of an organization or an agile workforce. Devising sustainable e-learning for small firms seems to involve addressing perceived value, through conventional quality approaches, and applying continuous quality-improvement processes to ensure value enhancement. Customer-relationship management and supply-chain management may assist authenticity and the perceptions of value.

DUAL SYSTEMS

E-learning can alter the normal definition of an educational institution. An institution no longer needs to be fixed in location and time. The Web replaces campuses, borderless networks replace communities of learning and chatrooms replace lecture halls. The roles of staff are different, shared governance may be non-existent and the library and other resources may be accessible only electronically. Electronic communication provides remote access to virtual faculty–student interactions as well as student–student relationships. These factors have direct effects on further and higher education. Their impact includes new models of teaching and learning, revised and new job descriptions for staff and new types of organization to provide education. As the nature of provision develops, there is great diversity in the actual and potential delivery arrangements. E-learning poses questions, therefore, about the quality-assurance academic work of educational institutions.

Educational institutions are no longer the only source of accredited learning. The emergence of the knowledge economy has brought with it a dual system of accrediting courses. This new dual system recognizes two types of certifying authorities: the traditional national authorities and the major global industries, such as Oracle, Microsoft and Cisco. Whereas it has proved difficult to find an accommodation at a European level for mutual academic accreditation and recognition between countries, now global companies are emerging as forceful new players in accreditation. These companies are able to transcend state boundaries, policies and practices, with their own accreditation for proprietary products that prove attractive to students. Meanwhile, conventional authorities seem unsure as to how to deal with these newcomers.

Investigations of e-learning have highlighted worldwide concerns about accreditation, expressed by the traditional sector of education and government organizations. These bodies are seeking possible solutions to the problems of identifying, assessing and ranking of accredited courses and awards in a borderless market. The present quality-assurance regimes are based essentially on the providers' views of what should be delivered, rather than taking a customer-focused approach. Arguably, it follows that there is not enough incentive for educational institutions to change their approaches to teaching, as quality is not judged on market criteria (Bjarnason et al., 2000a: 32). Where market conditions do apply, such as in short e-learning events for formal and non-formal learning, or provision targeted on competitive sectors, such as in supplying firms, then more client-focused approaches appear necessary.

DIVERSE UNIVERSE OF PROVIDERS

Higher and further education in the UK are dominated increasingly by the influences of competition. Such a competitive scenario is not new in international terms and has existed for generations in the United States. In the American system of higher education, institutional autonomy is a primary characteristic, reflecting the early predominance of private colleges and universities and the traditional independence of these institutions from government control. Autonomy is perceived as critical for colleges and universities that serve complex public interests. The independent stewardship provided by governing boards of institutions is seen as a protection against both political influence and the impact of market considerations, when these contend with the public interest.

Under this system, institutional quality assurance is accomplished by establishing minimum thresholds through regional, national, specialist or professional accreditation. Resources are directed at maintaining this basic threshold and preserving the autonomy of institutions, with little effort made to assess the common quality of all provision and few people being concerned at quality differences between institutions. The market is left to sort out the differences between institutions. It is generally understood that the University of California, Berkeley, is different from Stanford University, and that they are both different from a local state university, or a Baptist college or a community college. Students choose the institution that is most appropriate for them and then apply to gain entry.

Within this market model for education, a great deal is already known about the impact of distance learning on higher education. Distance learning unintentionally challenges the core values of institutional autonomy, collegiality, shared governance, academic authority of faculty, the dominance of the degree, general education and a community of learning (Eaton, 2001). These core values are challenged in turn by consortia arrangements, the dispersion of staff and students, commercial software, the disaggregation of faculty responsibilities, competition for credits, the pervasiveness of training and the diminishing importance of the campus as a location for learning.

New providers of education by e-learning create two influences on the academic community. First, the growth of credit-bearing distance-education courses at degree-awarding universities and colleges creates greater competition. Secondly, the appearance of a range of new providers of higher education adds to this rivalry. These new providers of higher education represent a varied assortment of educational enterprises, which include free-standing, degree-awarding online institutions, consortia of degree-awarding institutions that offer courses online and corporate universities, as well as online programmes that are not associated with institutions and may or may not offer forms of credit.

These new providers of distance education, such as the University of Phoenix (*www.phoenix.edu*) and Cardean University (*www.cardean.edu*), take a customer perspective on learning. They believe that what matters most for many students is the relevance of learning to their particular job and, in this respect, conventional universities are not viewed as a source of practical knowledge. For this student clientele, brand names and job readiness matter more than collegiality and general education. This means that educational decision-makers must take the initiative in defining the difference that distance learning makes in maintaining the quality of the educational experience. They must also address the political challenges of assurance about quality and respond to the interest among industry, commerce and the public in providing reliable information on the quality of the learning experience in this new setting.

QA CHALLENGES FOR ELECTRONICALLY-BASED EDUCATION

Educational enterprises have wrestled with the issues and operational applications of quality for more than a decade (Barnett, 1997; Sallis, 1993). The primary difficulties arise because of the variety of stakeholders that make many varied and contradictory demands. Approaches to quality assurance that appear straightforward in a business application are often contested when applied in an educational context. Indeed, there is a view that in the educational domain, ideological conflict in quality assurance is right and that it ought to be acknowledged and studied (Lentell, 1992: 147–60). Learning technologies, however, appear to be creating a new flexible learning-environment by facilitating a three-way convergence of distance, face-to-face and electronic methods that is presenting challenges for educational institutions, ranging from autonomy to information resources (Eaton, 2001).

Consortia arrangements for electronically-based education challenge institutional autonomy by encouraging groupings that emphasize their similarity rather than their uniqueness. The growing mobility of students and educational transfer also challenges autonomy, placing more emphasis on the educational experience of a mobile student in all institutions that form a learning path. For some observers, e-learning questions the need for an institution, since delivery transcends national and state boundaries. For institutional decision-makers, the challenge is to define an appropriate balance between preserving identity and undertaking collaborative work, and to determine at what point cooperative engagement begins to weaken institutional identity.

Collegiality is a style of governance and decision-making that emphasizes optimum participation and consultation. The dispersion of faculty and students away from a single campus and system may challenge this value, with diminished participation in shared processes. Electronic participation strategies might be used by a decision-maker as a transition strategy to effect meetings and virtual debates and to disseminate information. The campus is a location of a community of learning, but e-learning and distance learning challenge and diminish the importance of place. The Internet for delivery of learning replaces lecture rooms and libraries. A transition strategy for this value consists of determining the added value of a site in the way that it supports learning and whether this can be accomplished in an electronic environment.

Staff determine course content as well as the requirements for student performance and directly work to support this in a classroom. A challenge to the conventional teacher–student interaction arises through commercial courseware, standard courses and online assessment, which can serve to decouple the curriculum and academic expectations and disaggregate the conventional responsibilities of an individual teacher. The dispersal of teachers and the use of part-time staff also contribute to this decoupling. A transition strategy for decision-makers is to develop the stewardship role of faculty. This might be achieved through encouraging teaching staff to make electronic tools work for them by creating courseware for online delivery. Other factors that involve staff include the use of part-time contract as opposed to full-time academic staff, which may affect student support. Moreover, teaching staff undertaking little or no research may result in a decoupling of research from teaching and course development.

There are other challenges. The verification of student identity in a virtual environment can be problematic. A prospectus may offer a limited range of programmes, reflecting actual or potential best-sellers. The standard of online information and library resources may also vary. This has led to the development of guidelines to evaluate the quality of Internet information sources which commonly relate to the scope, content, accuracy, authority, currency and quality of the quoted reference (*www.info.lib.uh.edu/pr/v8/n3/smit8n3.html*).

BEST PRACTICE IN QUALITY ASSURANCE

Quality assurance refers to the planned and systematic process of reviewing a course, programme or institution in order to determine that acceptable standards of education, scholarship and infrastructure are being maintained and enhanced (CHEA, 2001). There are variations in approach to quality assurance in higher education internationally, as well as in terminology. Differences appear, for instance, in the balance between institutional autonomy and external review. Quality assurance normally, however, includes an expectation that mechanisms of control are in place and are effective (QAA, 2000). The term in the UK also extends to ways by which an institution sustains and endorses that the correct conditions are in place to achieve the standards of an award. The objectives of quality assurance of teaching and learning in higher education articulated by the Quality Assurance Agency (QAA) in the UK (*www.qaa.ac.uk*) are:

(a) To contribute, in conjunction with other mechanisms, to the promotion of high quality and standards in teaching and learning.
(b) To provide students, employers and others with reliable and consistent information about quality and standards at each higher education institution (HEI).
(c) To ensure that HE programmes are identified where quality or standards are unsatisfactory, as a basis for ensuring that rapid action is taken to improve them.
(d) To provide one means of ensuring accountability for the use of public funds received by HEIs. (QAA, 2001: 3)

The approach to quality assurance in higher education in the UK is undergoing consultation at the time of writing, with reform a likely outcome. The basis of quality assurance for an institution is primarily vested in an internal set of quality-assurance procedures for its operations. External review validates the reliability and effectiveness of these procedures. Over the past decade, a comprehensive external review at the subject level has operated to examine the internal processes for quality and standards in teaching and learning. Consequently, the QAA no longer considers it necessary to maintain total external review at the subject level. The proposed new approach for future quality-assurance arrangements is intended to meet three principles. First, to provide consistent information for the public and stakeholders on teaching and learning in different subjects in different institutions. Second, vesting the primary responsibility in the institution for operating robust internal mechanisms for quality and for publishing key parts of that information. Third, the burden for quality-assurance arrangements is reduced to the minimum consistent with meeting the information needs and ensuring that the greatest value is gained from the resources applied.

The revised method resembles an external financial audit of an institution with a well-developed internal audit-system. The assumption is that an institution will approve, monitor and review its quality and standards through internal procedures. External scrutiny will then assess the effectiveness of the internal framework on a highly selective basis. The framework will be established by the QAA with standard benchmarks in each subject area, the qualifications framework, the code of practice and the programme specifications. A characteristic of the proposed method is that the intensity of the external review will operate in inverse proportion to success, thereby focusing review on programmes and institutions where there might be grounds for concern. Another feature is an assessment of the direct outcomes, through the quality and standards actually experienced and achieved by students.

QUALITY ASSURANCE OF DISTANCE EDUCATION

Dual-mode institutions, who provide face-to-face and distance delivery, have been required to develop quality-assurance protocols that demonstrate that the ODFL programmes on offer are of equal quality to those delivered by the traditional classroom method. The elements of quality control and assurance systems have been applied to modern open and distance learning for some time, such as in producing learning materials (Lewis, 1986: 9–13) as well as in monitoring correspondence courses and activities in study centres in an effort to eliminate bad practice (Tait, 1993: 303–14). The industrialized arrangements for ODFL educational delivery systems assisted the development of quality-assurance systems (Tait, 1997: 12–19), but these systems are similar to quality control, in the old industrial sense of the term, considering performance after it has been completed.

Guidance on assuring the quality and standards of higher-education programmes of study by means of distance-education programmes is provided by the Quality Assurance Agency in the UK (QAA, 1999). This advice is presented under six categories: system design, programme design, approval and review, the management of programme delivery, student development and support, student communication and student assessment.

Guideline 1. System design – the development of an integrated approach. A distance-learning programme at higher-education level should be underpinned by principles relevant to higher education, and designed and managed to ensure that these principles are applied. The purpose of these programmes should form part of an explicit strategy for achieving an institution's aims, and the learning system or systems designed to effect to that strategy. An institution should test its systems for administering and teaching and make contingencies to meet its commitments in terms of its aims and the quality and standards of its provision. A distance-learning programme should be financially under-written for the full period during which students will be studying on it, to an extent that protects the quality and standards that the institution has assigned.

Guideline 2. The establishment of academic standards and quality in programme design, approval and review procedures. The provider is responsible for demon-strating that the academic standard of an award is comparable to those of awards delivered by the institution in other ways. The programme should ensure coherence between the aims and the intended learning outcomes, the strategies for teaching at a distance, the scope of learning materials and the modes and criteria of assessment. External scrutiny should form a part of the course-approval process. Programmes of study and components, once designed, are monitored, reviewed and subject to reapproval. All learning materials remain current and teaching strategies and forms of assessment are enhanced in the light of findings from feedback, thereby providing learning enhancement.

Guideline 3. The assurance of quality and standards in the management of pro-gramme delivery. The provider should manage the distance-education pro-gramme in a way that safeguards the academic standards of an award. Feedback from the programme is applied regularly in order to enhance all aspects of the teaching, the learning and the delivery system.

Guideline 4. Student development and support. Explicit attention is given to the provider's responsibilities for promoting autonomous learning and enabling students taught at a distance to take personal control of their own develop-ment. The institution should set aims that are realistic and create practical ways for achieving them and monitoring attainment.

Guideline 5. Student communication as well as representation. Full information should be available on the expectations of a distance-education programme, achievement, assessment, academic progress, credit accumulation and how students interact with the programme. The institution should monitor and review the effectiveness of the information provided to students and deter-mine what methods of representation are realistic and appropriate for distance-education students. Student representation should be appropriate for students on distance-learning programmes.

Guideline 6. Student assessment. The provider should be able to demonstrate that summative assessment procedures for its programmes are appropriate and that these are conducted and marked and the results promulgated in a reliable and proper manner. The institution should have direct control of the summative assessment process and be able to demonstrate that it adequately assesses the student's achievement of the learning outcomes for the module and programme of study. Formative assessment should be applied during the design of the distance-learning programme. The assessment procedures should be monitored systematically and the practice adapted in response to feedback.

E-LEARNING BENCHMARKS

The growth of technology-supported learning has prompted many organizations to develop principles, guidelines or benchmarks to ensure the quality of the distance-education experience. Virtually all these strategies include topics such as course development, faculty training, student services, learning resources, infrastructure and outcomes assessment. Benchmarks such as these were developed initially for all types of distance learning and, as such, have existed in various forms for a number of years. The question that arises is whether they are applicable to Internet-based distance education. In short, are the current benchmarks appropriate and necessary to ensure quality Internet-based distance education?

A set of quality benchmarks for Internet-based distance learning has been drawn up, based on a study in US colleges that tested and identified practical strategies to achieve quality learning (Phipps and Merisotis, 2000). Benchmarks for quality Internet-based distance education were considered important by the sample and, in general, the institutions endeavoured to incorporate them into their policies, practices and procedures. The key areas affecting the quality of technology-supported learning common to all of the published benchmarks relate to the following factors:

Institutional support. A documented technology plan covering electronic security measures (password protection, encryption, back-up systems) in place with reliable operational systems for the integrity and validity of information. The technology applied is as reliable and as fail-safe as possible. A centralized system is available to support the delivery, development and maintenance of the infrastructure.

Course development. Guidelines regarding minimum technology standards are used for course development, design and delivery. Courses are designed to require students to engage in analysis, synthesis and evaluation as part of their course and programme requirements. Courseware content is reviewed periodically to ensure it continues to meet programme standards.

Teaching and learning. Student interaction with staff and peers is an essential characteristic, with feedback to student questions and coursework being constructive and timely.

Course structure. Before registering, students are advised about need for self-motivation and the minimum technology required by course design. Students are provided with clear course objectives and learning outcomes. Clear expectations are agreed by students and staff regarding student assignments and timelines. Students have access to sufficient library resources.

Student support. Full information on the programme requirements, such as admission, technical requirements and support services, are provided to students. Access to technical assistance is provided. The advisory and complaints structure is transparent, with a structured system in place.

Faculty support. Technical assistance in course development is available to faculty. Staff are provided with the resources for the transition to e-learning and to deal with issues arising from student use of electronically-accessed data.

The educational effectiveness is evaluated with the intended learning outcomes reviewed regularly to ensure utility and appropriateness.

The emergence and growth of e-learning means that the QAA guidelines for conventional open and distance education need to be reassessed. Institutions that apply technology to facilitate the interaction of students with content sources, information resources or other students, need to revise their quality-assurance protocols to ensure that they are focusing on the appropriate inputs, processes and outcomes. In an Internet-enabled environment, for example, the traditional measures of the size of the institutional library holdings and access to databases need to be replaced by measures relating to the mechanisms for information provision and support for the students' research work. An e-learning programme can be categorized under the same guidelines as the QAA ones for the quality assurance of distance education, but certain factors have more emphasis, due to the e-delivery and support (Table 10.1).

Each guideline has a precept for application in an e-learning environment. Compared with conventional support of distance learning, an individual can have a personalized route through an e-learning programme. Personalized branches can be repeated, with many different variations of casework, until proficiency is gained. The notion of a class cohort is unnecessary. The idea of class control is different. Feedback is more difficult to secure online, for a range of causes, including absence from the workplace. Other indicators, though, such as student progression and the immediate responses from synchronous contact, can be used as measures.

Table 10.1. Precepts for e-learning QA strategy

QAA guideline	Precepts for e-learning QA strategy
System design.	Clear governance and control throughout an organization, especially with a disaggregated design environment.
Academic quality and standards.	Attention to academic tasks to support the e-learning curriculum.
Management.	Appropriate choice and management of technology qualifications of staff.
Student development.	Electronic support for pre-entry counselling, motivation and autonomous learning needs.
Student communication.	Electronic participation to meet student needs, strategies for feedback, meetings and to disseminate information.
Student assessment.	Capabilities for e-learning for assessment and achievement.

System design. As with any provision, an e-learning programme should be in keeping with the mission of the institution. The curriculum design process and the provision of technical support and tutorial services may have been contracted out by the institution to consortia partners, or to commercial providers. In such circumstances, it is no longer appropriate to rely solely upon the procedures applicable to a campus-based setting to provide reliable indicators of overall academic quality. It needs to be explicitly covered through the partnership, franchise or validation agreement. Although the e-learning environment is new and for some an unfamiliar form of education, the resources, capacities and processes involved need to be scrutinized and assessed as appropriate for the expectations in terms of student outcomes, at every stage. Even more attention may be required when consortia or commercial models are engaged, in order to meet the conditions appropriate to electronic communities of learning.

With Internet-enabled delivery, a documented technology plan covering electronic security measures with reliable operational systems for the integrity and validity of information is essential. The technology should be as reliable and as fail-safe as possible. A centralized system should be available to support the delivery, with contingency plans to provide effective learner support in the event of operational disruptions of service. Before offering distance-education courses, an institution should test its systems and make contingencies to meet its commitments in terms of its aims, the quality and standards of its provision.

Academic quality and standards. There are different roles for faculty, different support environments and designs for the curricula between an online and a conventional classroom. The input, resources and components of an e-learning programme that need to be checked for quality include clearly-defined and achievable learning objectives, up-to-date curriculum content, well-designed teaching and learning materials, appropriate use of learning technologies, appropriate and necessary personnel support for learning and technical needs, planned resource provision and an outline review and evaluation cycle.

Management. The key management aspects for QA systems concern the appropriate choice and effective management of technology to meet all the expectations of the stakeholders, the emphasis on faculty training to enable them to operate effectively, as well as specifying and monitoring the experience of staff along the design and delivery continuum. The support of the technology environment is a crucial role for management, with a number of facets, including continuous access for the delivery of content any time and anywhere, and the provision of designated student support as well as support for the learning-management system. Staff skills need to be developed for designing and delivering a programme that is likely to include team building. Clear and explicit responsibilities for the operation of e-learning programme should be planned and managed to ensure that all relevant staff apply the principles of governance in administration, support and delivery to e-learning students. In e-learning environments, staff may have a different set of tasks. They may design curricula but not deliver it, or they may have shared rather than individual responsibilities for curriculum design and they may deliver as part of a team rather than as an individual.

Student development. To achieve the appropriate student learning, a provider must have systematic quality processes and practices for student management systems in the areas of pre-entry counselling, admissions, registration and orientation of students, assessment and recognition of prior learning and the accurate and secure management of student records. Potential students should be advised about the need for self-motivation, commitment and any other requirements in order to successfully complete the programme by e-learning, including the minimal technology required by the course design. Students should be provided with clear information on course objectives and learning outcomes, with clear expectations regarding student assessments. The provider should offer appropriate services to support the academic programme, through assistance for students with the technologies in use, and allow for learner involvement in decision-making, comparable to that for face-to-face students.

Student communication. The learning provider should advise the student on the characteristics of the e-learning and support environment and the best ways to interact with it. Advice should be given on the required skills in dealing with the technologies, on the requirements for using Web-based resources, the likely costs and the availability of learner support methods. Information on the arrangements for access to learning resources should also be presented. Arrangements for student representation should be explicit and include electronic participation methods to gain feedback and effect contributions at meetings and to disseminate information.

Student assessment. The e-learning provider should provide an educational rationale for the assessment strategy for the programme of study. Certain features of e-learning provision, such as potential for a fast cycle of curriculum review, rapid and universal content updating and the promptness of feedback to students, can affect the balance between formative and summative processes in the assessment strategy. Provider institutions should establish expected levels of student performance and record how well students perform against the expectations.

QUALITY FROM EVERYONE

When quality is available from every provider of e-learning, it is expected by a student and ceases to be an important differentiating factor between providers. Consequently, the competitive edge shifts from quality primarily to those who can not only provide quality and service, but also compete on costs and anticipate changing conditions, cycle times and discontinuous change, and respond with flexibility, innovation and continuous improvement (Bennis and Mische, 1995).

The dilemma for decision-makers in an educational enterprise is that improving is no longer the only important issue. Not only does an organization have to improve, but, crucially, it has to get better at improving. This means that processes are improved and the means by which the enterprise improves also get better. Keeping the values of the enterprise intact, sustaining quality through continued demonstration of its academic work, while at the same time building in a commitment to continuously improve the organization and meet the needs of users, are all needed to make an effective response.

Internet-enabled learning allows content to be adapted and the updated material made available to every student at the same time. Moreover, unitized elements and the distributed nature of the learning material can mean that the cycle time for repetition and evaluation is much shorter than with conventional ODFL delivery for accredited programmes. Frequent repetition has benefits for quality assurance, giving the opportunity to make improvements more often, thereby optimizing a programme more quickly. Quality assurance in an educational context is guided by the need for balance and compromise between contested elements. These elements are mainly internal, but there are also external frameworks that are in place to provide transparency and comparability, and which serve to respond to the government need for and public interest in institutional performance and evidence of student achievement. An educational enterprise, therefore, needs to commit to the quality-assurance expectations within this environment as well as respond to opportunities and challenges posed by competitors.

VALUE ASSURANCE AND TOTAL QUALITY MANAGEMENT

Much work on quality assurance has its roots in the industrial and commercial discipline of quality (Deming, 1982; Juran, 1962). The dynamic for this quality movement lies in global competition to improve business performance, because there are major costs, associated with quality failure, that can result in a loss of satisfaction and customers. Implementing quality systems presents many management challenges, such as redesigning an organization to create flatter, horizontal structures with teams comprised of highly skilled workers organized around process. There are also significant costs attached to quality appraisal, but in comparison only a relatively small amount of costs involved in prevention. This gives justification to the analysis of prevention, appraisal and failure in the process, which can effect major cost-savings by shifting the emphasis from failure correction to prevention.

Spreading quality assurance throughout an organization, together with a commitment to continuous improvement practice, is a characteristic known as total quality management (TQM). The relevance of the TQM approach in higher education has long been the subject of debate. Advocates perceive it as a straightforward means to provide quality assurance. In many circumstances, however, it is beset with implementation difficulties, and in applying it to higher education it may well be changed out of all recognition (Harvey and Green, 1993: 9–34). Over time there have been many suggestions for implementation at the faculty level and institutional level (Bolton, 1995: 97–100; Eriksen, 1995: 14–29). The prevailing advice is to exercise caution in its application, as in practice the pursuit of total quality brought with it an inappropriate managerialist culture (Holmes and McElwee, 1995: 5–10).

The core problem of the TQM approach is that it brings the terminology of industry to academic staff. It can challenge their professional autonomy by raising the status of students to those of customers and requiring staff to be more accountable for actions. Indeed, debate on the relevance of these processes can be time-consuming and detract from focus on improving quality-assurance systems. QA systems attempt to define services and processes; this entails a precise, accurate and exhaustive analysis of what needs to be done. The QA system then identifies ways of monitoring and evaluating that analysis to build in procedures for seeking to improve practice. For an educational programme, these processes act to provide guidance for a student on the authenticity of the content. Value assurance comes from the effectiveness of monitoring a course, and that it does not suffer a decline in PUV in the face of efforts to improve cost efficiencies. A core competence of an educational enterprise, therefore, is in value assurance.

VALUE ENHANCEMENT

Value enhancement is another core competence. It covers the processes where the existing services are constantly reviewed with the aim of upgrading them. Each dimension of perceived value needs to be monitored and checked for change; the service offer can then be reviewed to match it more closely by continuous development. Such continuous improvement is implicit in the pursuit of a quality strategy. An explicit practice of continuous quality improvement (CQI) exists and forms a powerful and important approach for organizations in other economic sectors. The concept of CQI is conveyed by the Japanese term *kaizen*, which means 'slow never-ending improvement in all aspects of life' (PERA, 1991). It differs from the occidental approach to improvement, principally in being holistic. It also relies on investment in people and not primarily in technology, machines, equipment or systems. The classic western approach to continuous improvement involves spending large sums of money on new systems, applying the latest technology that require specialist input to achieve large-step changes in performance. In contrast, *kaizen* is implemented by a continuous series of small-step improvements on existing systems through the people who work on these systems, a technique applicable to people at all levels, on a team and an individual basis. 'Never-ending improvement' signifies that the method is long-term and continuous.

The approach is similar to conventional problem-solving, apart from the fact that *kaizen* stresses the importance of standardization. The standardization step is crucial as it secures the improvement and maintains its benefit for the organization. A typical structured approach to CQI involves progression through a series of steps (PERA, 1991). These steps, together with accompanying CQI tasks for value enhancement of e-learning, are as follows:

1. Define areas for improvement, such as the significant dimensions of PUV.
2. Analyse and select appropriate problem.
3. Identify causes and distinguish improvement factors.
4. Plan countermeasures and methods for content, support or technology.
5. Implement the plan.
6. Confirm academic and employee perceptions. For each dimension, check for PUV change.
7. Standardize by incorporating improvement in programme and monitoring feedback.

The development of an e-learning programme is an application where CQI has direct relevance because of its process-oriented nature and innovative aspects. It is most effective when it is used in conjunction with innovative-type improvements, such as new programme development. The technique is long-term and produces small incremental improvements that engage teams of people in standardizing the process and, as such, can be applied by an e-learning design and delivery team.

Digital learning differs from conventional face-to-face delivery in many respects, but among the most apparent is the potential for frequent updating and management of the technology. The ease of updating of courseware content allows value enhancement by a CQI path to be followed, with the improvement standardized in the content or delivery model. The technology approach requires a provider to address staff and student support systems to enable them to operate effectively in the new learning environment and to stimulate staff to continuously improve teaching and learning. There are other ways, for example by stimulating involvement and support through team and collaborative working, informing the decision process with facts from evaluation and minimizing controllable quality variations.

CUSTOMIZATION AND CONSUMER QUESTIONS ON QUALITY

Higher education has created ODFL pathways that are equivalent to mass-production methods, to handle more and more people. Conversely, the trend in business is to try to be more responsive to customers to an extent that certain companies aim to customize a product for a particular customer. E-learning offers the opportunity to rebalance this position, since it is possible for each student to proceed, at his or her own pace, with a learning experience that is customized according to personal characteristics. In principle, a course programme with appropriate objects and tests can be compiled as it is needed and tailored for an individual.

Customers in small firms are often clear and forceful in their response to what matters most to them: relevance of learning to their job, preferably gained on the job or at the firm's premises, and not necessarily academic awards. A customized solution can be developed on a non-credit or credit basis, agreed with the firm. In this respect, customer satisfaction with the employee experience implies more than purely academic concerns and judgements over quality.

The range of providers and programmes of e-learning presents a vast range of choice and opportunity for the public. Variety on such a scale presents another set of difficulties for a potential student; how to scrutinize all the information available and then select and decide on a course of action. The student might well ask how to gauge quality in the e-learning setting, what the relevant factors involved are and how to make contact. Potential students need reliable indicators of the quality of e-learning to help navigate the bewildering array of courses and programmes on offer. One approach to help consumer choice is through a number of URL sites developed to offer advice on how to choose an online course, such as learndirect (*www.learndirect.co.uk*),

Degree-net (*www.degree.net*), AboutEducation (*www.about.com/education*) and WorldwideLearn (*www.worldwidelearn.com*).

A guide to help potential students to assess a learning product from the consumer's point of view is given in Table 10.2. The guidelines comprise the desirable features, progressing from the concerns of the customer for relevant outputs and benefits of the programme to the delivery features of the learning service. These guides provide a template against which a potential customer will make a judgement. Competitors will be gauging their capabilities against these criteria. To prosper against global competition, therefore, both the public and privately-funded e-learning enterprises need to establish their credentials in these elements, to find their niche in the new global education marketplace. Guidelines are available at (*www.detya.gov.au/highered/mceetya_cop.htm*) and (*www.futureed.com*).

BUILDING LEARNING RELATIONSHIPS: CRM

Understanding targeted customers is important to success in raising perceived user-value and sustaining competitive advantage. The goal then is to discover the core offer in content, technology and business that clients are happy with and then to develop from this position. The process of creating, maintaining and enhancing strong relationships with customers and other stakeholders is the basis of the business practice of customer-relationship management (CRM). Listening, learning and responding to customers are processes that make an increasingly student-centred enterprise. Data-collection online makes better use of the collection of information to attract and keep customers, to identify at-risk students who might leave and, the most profitable of all, to make them evangelists for the institution.

At the heart of CRM is a technology approach to customer information. Attracting new customers and launching new products are more expensive alternatives than maximizing earnings from existing participants and products. The conditions of the marketplace, the needs of the client and the characteristics of the offer can all change. Effective two-way communications exchange, therefore, needs to be sensitive to these stages and flexible enough to respond to them.

Creating long-term mutually beneficial relationships, in which an enterprise measures success by its customers, is central to CRM. Business principles are at its core, but the issues are relevant for e-learning. In order clearly to understand perceived user-value, it becomes important to keep data on students, to see what they actually do, to identify patterns that emerge and identify any barriers that develop in order to predict long-term behaviour. The number of classes held, the number of referrals or the number of students progressing might measure success.

Table 10.2. Questions to help determine the quality of e-learning courses (developed from Morin, 2000: 21)

E-learning element	Explicit questions
1. Check the accreditation.	Is it recognized by professional accreditation bodies? Is it transferable within programmes and institutions, locally, nationally and internationally?
2. Grade the provider.	Who are the teachers? Is the Website up to date and well designed? What are the success rates for completion?
3. Acquired content skills.	Is the content relevant? Is it transferable? Is it specific for the purpose? Does it require self-directed learning management? What is needed for successful course completion?
4. Return on investment of learner's time, finances and energy.	Is the course accessible as needed, when needed? What are the benefits and utility of the programme? Will the course be effective in the achievement of personal goals? Does it offer what you expect from an online course? Can you register and take assessments online?
5. View a sample course.	Is it possible to view a virtual class? Is the online format what you want? Does your technology meet technical requirements for the course?
6. Learning objectives linked.	Are the specific learning objectives aligned with current business goals?
7. Solid instructional design.	Does the software adhere to modern adult-learning techniques and feature a self-directed, learning-by-doing design?
8. Appropriate application.	Is the programme custom designed for e-learning?
9. Engaging and interactive methodologies.	Is the content presentation attractive? Are different types of interactivity offered? Is there student–tutor and student–student interaction, and in what form?
10. Practical examples.	Are there practical cases and situations in the content?
11. Friendly navigation.	Does the design allow easy navigation?
12. Effective assessment.	Does the system identify how well learners will be able to apply new skills to real-life situations?
13. Tracking capabilities.	Does the supporting system compile information on performance for analysis by learner and organization?
14. Multiple deployment options.	Does the course use a variety of platforms, such as CD-ROM and Internet?

The purpose of CRM is to build a learning relationship, rather than simply to make a transaction. Few SME customers purchase learning per se; instead, they buy a solution to a business problem, and the initial purchase is the opening of a conversation about the business problem that should continue, if the relationship is to grow. This learning relationship is a scenario in which both sides profit from an exchange of information. Learning relationships are common in face-to-face meetings, but they are rare in an e-environment, in which anonymous customers can gather information, make purchases, diagnose problems and undertake learning through Websites.

WHO IS A CUSTOMER?

The learning relationship involves a constant learning curve for both the provider and the customer. Although the supplier works to collect information, each side benefits. Learning relationships enable a provider to track change and spot trends, giving the provider a built-in focus group and a significant competitive advantage over rivals who may attempt to poach customers by offering incentives. In response to CRM issues, some educational institutions are developing their own software (Rodin, 2002: 172). Others are trying to integrate their university systems with a commercial system for credit and non-credit courses. The big difficulty, though, is to implement an integrated Web-based system that works seamlessly between registration, finance and continuing education systems.

Keeping track of a customer is a key part of CRM, but all kinds of customers and influencers on e-learning can be identified. For instance, in a large organization there are several levels of potential relationship: the human resources department has a client relationship and operates from the position of a customer. Similarly, employees can be registered as learners, but the individual may move out of the company and still continue to study. Multiple relationships are equally evident in small firms, where a decision-maker can decide to enrol employees on a programme. The range of possible customers could include any or all of the following: a parent company and subsidiaries, an individual place of business, individual contact within a business, a family or household, an individual purchaser, a telephone number or a 'cookie'.

Defining such customers makes it possible to track them. The kind of clarifying questions that arise for internal processes are: what information do we want? How will we capture this? Do people tutoring classes, or preparing prospectuses, get enough information? Where do we have customer information today? What customer information do we currently have? How do we consolidate, store and distribute information? The management tools that can be used to clarify the customer are: segmentation, profiling, profitability analysis, needs analysis, sales analysis, customer valuation, Web intelligence and call behavioural analysis. The interface tools to link with the customer include direct mail, e-commerce, Website, e-mail, customer service and call centres.

Customer information comes from engaging in two-way conversations with customers that are observed and documented to give a complete real-time understanding of the customer, which is shared across the enterprise. The customer feel of an enterprise-based CRM site in action can be gained from Amazon (*www.amazon.com*). Here, CRM applications respond to a customer enquiry with helpful information, such as 'purchasers of this book also bought the following titles'. Companies invest in CRM normally to reduce costs, but it may also generate improved customer satisfaction. Applying similar techniques to e-learning students can lead to effective information and course samples up to the point of registration and service afterwards. In reality, very few enterprises have perfect information, so the quest is really for the best possible information. The difficult aspects of adopting CRM, though, come from aligning processes with the aims of a provider.

BUILDING RELATIONSHIPS WITH SCM

E-business affects the way that companies sell their products and services, but also changes the ways they address customer needs and manage their supply chains. Unlocking the influence of the supply chain can prove a successful route for e-learning development work with an SME firm, as demonstrated in chapter 2. It can provide good word-of-mouth referral and value assurance to potential customers in SME firms. A supply chain is a series of companies linked together and supplying parts, materials and services to others. A company that provides publications, for example, will need suppliers for a broad range of equipment, such as computers, printers, disks, paper, card and so forth. Each supplier will get its materials from other sources. Each time a customer buys a product, the company has to ensure that there are enough parts in stock to replenish the supply, by ordering materials through the supply chain. Supply-chain management (SCM) is the business practice, rooted in technology, which tries to streamline this process.

SCM relationships can exert a strong influence on learning for decision-makers in a SME. During negotiations with a decision-maker in a firm in the supply chain, a staircase agreement can be proposed: if we bring benefits to your company, will you recommend us to your suppliers so they can benefit as well? Asking for positive referral from one to other SME supply-chain partners is an easier step than trying to make independent sales to each one. Firms appear willing to do this if they perceive real benefit. Agreement is best at the start, though, since it clarifies objectives and gives time, if necessary, to build relevant content and authenticity.

TECHNICAL STANDARDS MOVEMENT FOR E-LEARNING

Standards can refer to quality or technical issues with e-learning. The former meaning describes the learning experience of a student, linked to the expectations placed on a course and qualification. In the lexicon of quality assurance: 'Standards are the level of requirements and conditions that must be met by institutions or programs to be accredited or certified by a quality assurance or accrediting agency. These conditions involve expectations about quality, attainment, effectiveness, financial viability, outcomes and sustainability' (CHEA, 2001: 4). Technical standards, in contrast, are more specific for e-learning designers and exist to ensure that access to content is possible from different e-learning platforms. They are the key to sharing, maintaining and sustaining educational technology applications. Courseware that complies with a standard can become accessible to students through different platforms and devices. It means that a choice of platform will no longer be based on whether an existing library of e-content will operate on a particular system, although, until recently, the portability of material was still a distant promise.

Technical standards are important to having identifiable and marketable products. The concept behind technical standards for learning technology is that teachers, instructors and designers will be able to put together courses by assembling learning objects. There is a growing consensus around such an object-based approach to constructing content for online delivery. Described variously as learning-object, content-object and information-object approaches, the concept is based on 'chunking' content into reusable components and building a flexible hierarchy to create instructional sequences. Content at every level may be indexed to support search and reuse.

These learning objects, elements or tools, range in shape and size and include text-based materials, audio-visual, simulations, slides and tests, and can be inserted where they are needed into a bespoke course. They will, in principle, fit easily into place inside a programme assembled by a teacher. An agreed set of technical standards will help staff, institutions and students who will be able to search and select different course objects for a course. The potential benefits of having a standards-based integrated teaching and learning system include providing a comprehensive library of learning materials in one repository. It can allow mixing and matching off-the-shelf content and customized content. It can minimize costs associated with the implementation of multiple systems, support a wide selection of authoring to give trackable data and provide reports to allow for better measurements of student usage and performance.

There is a complication, in that an application based on a technical standards model might well allow a large training organization, such as the US military, to operate, exchange, manage, track and reuse all of their learning content and data, no matter what the original source or application, and be sure that all of the products and services will interoperate. It might also be useful to large enterprises, where content can be made reusable. There are limitations in the delivery of such content to small firms, however, especially in addressing issues of authenticity and contextual relevance, which are recurring themes in previous chapters. Similarly, self-profiling for a personalized learning programme becomes a more sophisticated task for an individual, in choosing from a burgeoning number of learning objects.

KEY CONCEPTS IN TECHNICAL STANDARDS

There are increasing numbers of valuable ready-to-use learning objects, although it is still hard to assemble them into a useful product. Creating technical standards for course delivery entails understanding metadata, course framework and student tracking. Metadata is the code for course objects that identifies their content. A learning object is the smallest unit of information that can stand alone and still have meaning to a learner. It offers an alternative to defining e-learning as courses, by breaking down a course into its component parts – text, audio, video, graphics or assessment objects that focus on a specific concept. These small units can then be assembled into an object library so that different products can use the same material, improving efficiency and lowering costs. The principle of metadata is to make learning objects easier to find by attaching tags to them with key information about the contents and how it can be used.

For course objects to be linked into a programme there needs to be an overarching course framework. This gives the course delivery system the order and sequence of course elements, the arrangement for the contents or the optimal sequence. Student tracking of a student taking a course is also required; there must be a standard way to record elements, such as assessment scores, and to transfer this data to an LMS that can track the progress of a student.

KEY EFFORTS ON STANDARDS

Over the past decade several initiatives have emerged to create generally accepted standards for electronic learning, to help efforts associated with content interoperability, metadata-tagging and data-tracking. They are looking for a standardization process that permits courseware to be reusable, portable, accessible and durable. The concept was to develop small packets of reusable and shareable course content that could easily be located and retrieved from a repository. This would help people to find course content or have adaptable systems to meet the needs of learners. Prominent contributions have been made by the IEEE, IMS, AICC and ADL standards committees.

The Institution of Electrical and Electronic Engineers (IEEE) Learning Technology Standards Committee (LTSC) is dedicated to establishing standards for learning technology (*www.itsc.ieee.org*). Groups cover wide-ranging topics, including learning-object metadata, student profiles, course sequencing, computer-managed instruction, competency definitions, localization and content packaging. Most groups around the world doing work in creating specifications for areas related to learning use the standard IEEE LTSC P1484. The EU supports a group applying and integrating the IEEE LTSC learning standards through the European PROMETEUS projects (*www.prometeus.org*). This seeks to apply the technical standards through the various special-interest groups and integrate them into the European context and cultures.

Instructional Management System (IMS) is a standards group which aims to develop the facility for the retrieval and interoperability of online-learning resources. It is driven by a consortium of educational, commercial and government organizations (*www.imsproject.org*). IMS has two goals: first, defining the technical standards for interoperability of applications and services in distributed learning; second, to support the incorporation of IMS specifications into products and services worldwide. The Aviation Industry Computer-based training committee (AICC) develops guidelines for the aviation industry in the development, delivery and evaluation of computer-based training and related training technologies (*www.aicc.org/pages/primer/html*).

SCORM AND ADVANCED DISTRIBUTED LEARNING (ADL)

The most influential initiative in bringing the specific groups of professionals together to agree on the process and flow among them is the Advanced Distributed Learning (ADL) initiative (*www.adlnet.org*), which set out to determine the standards that the US Federal Government would use for its educational technology programmes. The ADL strategy aims to exploit networked-based technologies, create platform-neutral reusable courseware and content to lower costs, promote collaboration to satisfy common needs and enhance performance with emerging learning technologies. An ADL academic cooperation laboratory, or ADL co-LAB, was established in 2000 to promote collaboration between academic providers (*www.academiccolab.org/learn*). This is intended to be an open and collegial focal point for evaluating and demonstrating ADL tools and prototypes and sharing data among universities, government organizations and the private sector, in promoting high-quality, reusable content for distributed learning.

ADL promoted cooperation between standard-setting groups to identify technical interface points from which standards for Web-based learning technologies could be developed. This led to the development of ADL's Shareable Courseware Object Reference Model (SCORM) as a means of technical specification (*www.adlnet.org*). This is a software model that defines the interrelationships of course components, data models and protocols. It defines a standardized run-time environment and addresses the ability to mix and match contents from multiple sources. It allows the development of interchangeable content, so that buyers are not trapped by a proprietary learning technology. SCORM took four major areas – metadata, course-structure format, a data model for learner-tracking and an applications program interface – and selected the methods that worked best for the military's education organizations. To back up its standards, SCORM decided to create software programs to test learning objects, learning management systems and course-creation and delivery tools for compatibility.

These SCORM guidelines provide a foundation for how the US Department of Defense will apply learning technologies to design and operate a learning environment. It means that the US Government as a customer can choose multiple vendors, provided they comply with the IEEE LTSC standards and the SCORM specifications, for various projects and be sure that all of the products and services will interoperate. The standards movement and SCORM are rapidly developing and will have an impact on the development of Web-based course materials and on the availability of Web-based course content.

THE PROSPECTUS FOR QUALITY

In delivery to firms, the authenticity of the product is essential to maintaining credibility. Authenticity extends beyond accuracy and institutional quality-assurance methods. It lies in the confidence of the learner in the programme and the relevance of the content. This can arise from the content and the support staff, at least some of whom ought to have experience in small firms, to ensure that the situations and solutions are real and credible. Course cycles are likely to be shorter and more rapid, so that any lapse in standards will soon be reflected in diminished business. Customers from firms may need to be provided with guidance and assurance on how to gauge quality and make comparisons between modes and providers. For an educational enterprise, ensuring that the fundamental values of the educational enterprise are maintained and that the quality of e-learning provision is demonstrable through student achievement will strengthen relationships. Any failure risks a loss of employee enrolments and intervention from competitors, with a likely loss of revenue.

11

Professional development

Initiating and sustaining e-learning depends on professionals, who design, implement, manage and support the various aspects of a system. Attracting and retaining effective staff is, therefore, integral to an educational enterprise's success. There are many different roles, but in small providers, one or two people may fill all the roles. In larger delivery systems there is usually a higher degree of role specialization. In supporting SMEs and corporate employees, there are roles in business consultancy liaison and in the design of authentic content that are relevant for SME or large-scale enterprises. For decision-makers and practitioners, the challenge is less about transferring content to the Web for delivery and much more about personal networking, communicating with people in firms and about the service-provider moving faster, sharing best practice and improving competitiveness. Applying an e-learning strategy, though, brings with it a change in techniques and ways of working that may cause early anxiety in the minds of educators.

CHANGING ROLES

The knowledge-based economy is bringing with it, for many organizations, a cultural transformation in the workplace, a change in the ways employees work and interact within an organization. The problem is that people in employment not only need specialized knowledge in business, science, engineering or technology that is combined with creativity, problem-solving and evaluation, they also need learning delivered differently from a conventional classroom situation. Many people are unable to attend a conventional campus-based course, and seek more flexible solutions. This change in market demand will ultimately affect mainstream courses. Creating a value proposition for an educational service requires staff with a breadth of understanding, both in specialized knowledge and in the applications of learning technologies. In the case of servicing small firms, this breadth includes learning, technology and business.

The professional development of staff is important in every educational service. Pursuing e-learning for delivery to businesses has practical implications for individuals and educational providers alike. Lively and fundamental issues are involved for staff, including a move to greater team-working, performance analysis, student-centred learning, innovation, value enhancement and the applications of technology for learning. The adoption of e-learning, therefore, brings with it a change in both the techniques and ways of working. Developing the right talent to transform traditional delivery into digital learning is crucial.

E-LEARNING AS E-BUSINESS

Providing e-learning as an e-business puts an onus on a decision-maker in an educational enterprise to lead as well as manage. Simply engaging a competent project-manager to implement an e-learning programme for a certain market and then expecting academic staff to join in and follow through is often unrealistic. Operating as an e-business, however, requires a different management style from that of traditional operations. The challenge at its starkest is in managing and leading a flexible and demanding multidisciplinary practitioner team, compared with that of leading a conventional, traditional academic staff team. Whereas academic leadership can be achieved through research and academic development, e-business, in contrast, requires a broader range of management abilities to cope with a different and enlarged range of contingencies. The challenge in moving into e-business comes not just from technology or content, but from the change of attitude needed to get staff to think differently and react quickly to keep up with the pace of change, often set by external events and clients. Developing and fostering a vibrant, dynamic culture can then be the key factor in developing a practical and sustainable e-learning process.

The goal for a decision-maker, then, is to develop an integrated approach that responds best to the strengths of staff and the variety of expertise. An e-learning team should have academic strengths to give a programme authenticity, technical and tutorial support to provide excellent quality of service, as well as e-business development skills to continue to provide a service to business clients. Operating without such an integrated approach can lead to the segmentation of staff into two camps: academic and project staff. As e-learning and e-business take off, this can create rivalries between the two groups over relative values and rewards. The role of the manager, consequently, is in communicating a new enterprise culture to all staff. This may then lead to redefining the job responsibilities of staff to include e-delivery as well as conventional learning. Minimizing the disruptive effects of change on staff is also very important.

The various roles in providing e-learning for SMEs arise from the functions of operating an educational enterprise: content development as well as infrastructure and learner support. These areas may appear clear-cut, but in practice there is some overlap of functions across them. Although e-learners in an

SME can be supported wholly by technology, they may still benefit from information received explicitly from direct people-to-people contact and implicitly from experience, interaction and application. A variety of skills is therefore required, as is a collaborative approach to bring together individuals with different expertise and strengths. In practical terms this leads to academic staff gaining more familiarity with the processes of student support for distance and flexible learning, the capabilities of the technology for learning delivery and the analysis and support of employees in work-based learning (Roffe, 2000: 327–39).

AUTHENTICITY AND BUSINESS LIAISON

The interface between education and the commercial world involves a growing scale of interactions under the umbrella of knowledge-transfer activity. The required skills in working at this interface are typical of those needed in many professions, such as business planning, business development, selling, negotiation, time-management, influencing, conflict-resolution and planning (Zeitlyn and Horne, 2002). It is the execution of these skills, however, in combination with knowledge relevant for the work of the targeted group, that is important. The principle applies to development work with large enterprises and to voluntary organizations as well as to the working community of SMEs.

Knowledge transfer (KT) is a term often applied to a mix of processes that combine to make potential users aware of knowledge or technology opportunities and help to support its eventual utilization. There are a number of underpinning processes, such as relationship management, knowledge management and communications and consultancy skills. Knowledge-transfer activities are carried out by a diverse set of people, operating in different environments. The work of these practitioners is not in itself complex. Complexity comes from the context – the systems, the politics and the sensitivities of working in an environment where there remains a need to effect real change in the culture and operations of host organizations. Difficulties can also arise from working at the boundary between the internal and external interface, that is, in matching perceived needs for an external community with what it is possible to deliver from internal resources.

Specialized work in market development is required in order to enter and compete in selected SME markets successfully. A challenge exists with e-learning, both in addressing the essential knowledge and skill areas for content, and also in integrating it into the context in which business operates. For example, without a practitioner with background experience of applications in a small firm, authenticity will be lessened and sales reduced. There are so many ways in which liaison staff can interact with e-learning communities, especially in the SME and corporate sector, that this interaction affects the ways that liaison staff operate and the tasks they undertake. There is a compelling case, therefore, for their integration into an e-learning delivery team for a specific market.

SKILLS INVESTIGATIONS FOR E-LEARNING

Authenticity, for SMEs, implies providing learning that is directly relevant to the business, as well as involving people who understand what it is like to run an SME. There is a lack of trainers with expertise in SMEs, as well as a lack of understanding of the best practices for learning and development for SME managers (James, 2000: 85–93), and a lack of skills and training for the development of technology-supported learning for SME managers. This can be a problem, because growth in demand for e-learning can quickly translate into a need for more online tutors, which may lead to management-of-change issues over new tutor roles. Another of the problems in scaling up is that tutors can be very involved with students throughout the course. The extent to which a tutor engages in interactions will limit the number of students for each instructor. This can be addressed, to an extent, by creative course design and other techniques, but in the end there is going to be a limit on what can be done.

Several linked investigations have reviewed and attempted to define the skills and competences required for authoring and supporting e-learning. A review of publications relevant to tutoring within an e-learning environment concluded that tutors needed skills in four main areas: pedagogic, social, managerial and technical (Whitlock, 2000). Examples of good practice of tutoring for the corporate sector focused on the ways that tutors add value training, key competences, the constraints on the use of tutorial support, and the roles tutors play in teaching, developing and supporting learners, where the primary method is CBT/IMM (Goodyear and Steeples, 2000: 12).

A companion project examined effective strategies for deploying human resources in the development of e-learning materials for occupational training (Arenicola Designs, 2000: 8–10). A list of key skills and typical profiles was constructed for authors, covering project management, high-level design and detailed-level design, with much overlap reported between the roles of project manager, instructional designer and courseware designer. This study concluded that project management ought to be carried out by people with e-learning authoring experience, since a full appreciation of the complexity of multimedia development could then be taken into account. Skill shortages are most acute in the area of project management and instructional design. Respondents to the research survey indicated worryingly low priorities for performance analysis, evaluation and validation, which indicated variable standards of design, and an emphasis on technology and an underestimation of the importance of analysis and design among a minority of e-learning developers.

TEACHERS AND TRAINERS

The way that we view technology-supported learning depends on how we view learning. Transitions in the learning media affect the interpretative tasks of the teacher, as Peters observed (O. Peters, 1998). For example, the transition from speaking to writing and from listening to reading create both a change of medium and also different ways of thinking, expressing, studying and remembering. Today the task of e-educators is to exploit the new technology of digital-learning environments rather than imitate face-to-face teaching.

The decision to develop ODFL provision has a direct bearing on teaching staff. The emphasis in this book is on e-learning development by a group or section of an educational enterprise. Many e-learning developments are the activities of an enthusiastic solo developer, however, what Bates has dubbed a 'lone ranger' (Bates, 2000). This can be a mixed blessing, as it creates practical interest in the applications of teaching and learning with technology, but the practice can dissuade other staff members that the effort takes too much time, trouble and effort. An educational manager seeking quantity and quality from additional provision – inexpensively – may see an enthusiast moving conventional course-presentations online, and try to persuade others to follow suit and then expect them to conduct e-learning as an e-business. Time, effort and money, of course, are needed. The underlying question is, though, instead of being an activity for enthusiasts or the more technically-minded, or distance-learning practitioners, or specialist vocational trainers, how does e-learning become a core skill for mainstream educationalists? This is taking place, and a variety of approaches are traced in chapter 6. Whatever the route, the application and development of e-learning support systems does bring with it a need for the development of teachers, tutors and trainers, as well as support staff.

The process of e-learning requires a variety of skills from a tutor (Duggleby, 2000). These skills can be categorized into four main areas: pedagogic, social, managerial and technical. Many teachers and trainers lack specific skills in these areas and so they become the concerns of staff development. Changes in educational practice to extend the range and accessibility of educational opportunities through distributed learning mean that e-learning becomes just another delivery mechanism. Viewed in this way, e-learners become just another student group, albeit with special requirements for support.

There are advantages to e-learning for practitioners, since it can allow a shift of time towards supporting activities that cannot currently be supported even with the most advanced technology: stimulating higher-order thinking, seeing new patterns, making new connections, leading communities, guiding, coaching, encouraging and motivating. Senior teaching staff, however, are in a more difficult position. There are pressures to use technology-supported learning, not only from management, but from students who are technology-literate. For many senior staff there is not a great incentive for a major rethink about how they teach. Time will bring change, in the form of younger staff with more readiness to apply technology. There is, however, an immediate and institutional issue for decision-makers to ensure that adequate development and training is provided for staff.

Technology-supported learning offers an advantage in new career dimensions for teachers: they do not have to be Web programmers, but they do need to understand the technology and where it fits into teaching and learning. New roles and responsibilities emerge as part of the project design team, as well as a longer-term requirement for more online tutors. This role includes reviewing student work, providing advice and counselling, initiating discussion among e-learner groups and scheduling collaboration activities. The term 'e-moderator' is assigned by Salmon to this new generation of teachers and trainers who work online (Salmon, 2000).

THE E-LEARNING PROJECT TEAM

A wide variety of tasks and responsibilities need to be fulfilled in the creation and deployment of an e-learning programme. Some of these are common for delivery to all types of student, while others are particular to the support of small firms, such as the group of activities under knowledge transfer that includes performance consulting. Value assurance and enhancement are familiar mainstream activities, but the emphasis on innovation is more prominent. An innovator in e-learning does many of the same things, applies similar techniques and meets comparable difficulties to an entrepreneur involved in conventional enterprise. The knowledge-creating activities that create a competitive advantage include problem-solving skills, experimenting to build for the future, integrating information across internal project and functional boundaries, and importing expertise from outside the enterprise.

In practice, staff resources may present issues over the extent of in-house development, or outsourcing to contractors or partners, and the balance, if any, between the two. Flexibility is needed. The practice of multiskilling is common in small-scale enterprises and yields the benefit of greater flexibility in scheduling. Individuals within a small project team might take on more than one role, for example a content specialist might also be a writer, instructional designer and an online tutor.

The new team tasks for online learning are to inform learners about the content of the programmes and improve their access to it. The learner determines the start when logging on and can access the material day and night. If the learner is not given the availability to control their own learning, they can find another provider, or simply become dormant. For staff migrating from traditional teaching and learning, this means a shift in control of the learning process and a closer association with learner support. There are also new roles for staff as advisers on learning, content and progression, as well as in improving access to information.

The different roles in the project team might be filled by full-time or part-time staff, either permanent employees or contract staff. Moreover, the resource profile for the project development is likely to show that certain roles are needed for only a limited period and that others, such as online tutoring, are required to sustain the delivery operation. Scheduling roles into a work-plan requires project-management skills. There are various roles and responsibilities within an e-learning project team (Harris and Shepherd, 2000: 14) that are identified by Harris and Shepherd as follows, although in small enterprises an individual is expected to fulfil multiple roles. These include the following:

A *marketer* for marketing development, identification of market opportunities, devising marketing communications mix.

A *project manager* for coordinating team work, setting budgets and schedules, monitoring performance and liaising with clients.

Content specialists to provide accurate and up-to-date content for the e-learning course materials.

A *writer* for the preparation of any text or narrative in the programme script.

An *instructional designer* to identify, analyse and define the training need, establish learning objectives, design, document and script.

A *graphic designer* for design elements.

A *programmer* for creating any custom code needed.

An *author* for assembling the course materials, text, audio, images, program codes into their final form.

An *audio-visual* specialist in the production of audio-visual content.

A *Web master* for Web maintenance of the URL learning-site and *postmaster* for e-communications.

A *tester* for course materials to identify difficulties and conformance with the script.

A *production assistant* providing administrative and logistical support.

A *tutor* to provide online support.

COMPETENCES AND SKILLS FOR LEARNING TECHNOLOGIES

Developing e-learning is often a highly-skilled process requiring a range of skills at each stage. To further complicate matters further, the exact skill requirements are constantly changing as advances are made in technology. Individual staff and educational enterprises, therefore, face a challenge in keeping up to date with these changes. The skills and competencies that enable people to apply learning technologies for HRD work are categorized into thirty-one competences (Sanders, 1998). These fall into four main areas:

general competences, management competences, distribution-method competences and presentation-method competences (Table 11.1).

Table 11.1. Competences for learning technologies for SMEs (developed from Sanders, 1998)

General competence	Management competence	Distribution-method competence	Presentation-method competence
Adult learning	Management of learning	Cost analysis/ROI	Cost analysis
Instructional design	Technology selection	Limitations of modes	Limitations
Performance analysis	Management of design	Benefits of modes	Learners' benefits
Implementation	Management of development	Effects on learners	Integration
Leadership	Management of learning	Remote site coordination	
Industry awareness	Technology implementation	Learner support	
Design and development	Support and evaluation	Buy-in advocacy	
Interpersonal relationship	Change management	Business knowledge	
Consulting	Contracting	Performance analysis	
Project management	Communications		
Evaluation	HRD policies and management		

The development of technology-supported learning requires an unusual blend of skills and, in recent years, several attempts at defining the skill standards have been made. These include the competences for IT training (IITT, 1998), an update on the instructional design competences (IBSTPI, 2000), knowledge descriptions for learning technologies (ASTD, 2000) and necessary skills perceived by practitioners in the field in the UK (Arenicola Designs, 2000: 8–9). Each of these gives a range of skills and competences.

THE TUTOR IN E-LEARNING

The tutor in e-learning may perform a wide range of tasks, with several accounts of the forms that tutorial support might take (Duggleby, 2000: Salmon, 2000). The common activities include diagnosing learners' needs, helping learners to get started, explaining content to them, assessing their progress, giving feedback and encouragement, recording progress, trouble-shooting problems and developing the learning environment (Whitlock, 2000: 6). There are also principles of teaching and learning for adults (andragogy), that are intended to have general application in the education of adults and, as such, all may not be appropriate to every e-learning situation (Knowles, 1990: 93–4). They form an integrated concept of the operational role of the andragogical teacher, with the principles and their practical implications for e-learning presented in Table 11.2.

Table 11.2. Conditions for adult learning and teaching and implications for e-learning (developed from Knowles, 1990: 93–4)

Principles of teaching
Implementation by e-learning

Conditions of learning
The learners feel a need to learn
1. Teacher exposes students to new possibilities of self-fulfilment.
   Design has attractive presentations to enthuse the e-learner about new options.
2. The teacher helps each student clarify own aspirations for improved behaviour.
   Tutor assists student in analysing the learning options.
3. The teacher helps each student diagnose the gap between teacher's aspiration and student's present level of performance.
   Tutor aids student to identify current performance and any prerequisites for progress.
4. Teacher helps students identify life problems they experience because of gaps in their personal equipment.
   Tutor aid for student to explore a wide range of resources to learn the same content, in terms of individual student situation.

The learning environment is characterized by physical comfort, mutual trust and respect, mutual helpfulness, freedom of expression and acceptance of differences.
5. Teacher provides physical conditions that are comfortable and conducive to interaction.
   Tutor provides advice on study time and conditions or technical guidance.
6. Teacher accepts each student as a person of worth and respects feelings and ideas.
   Style of content, tags and responses individualized and respectful.
7. Teacher seeks to build relationships of mutual trust and helpfulness among the students by encouraging cooperative activities and refraining from competitiveness.
   Tutor encouragement to build and participate in local peer networks and to share learning resources and information.
8. Teacher exposes his or her own feelings and contributes resources as a co-learner in the spirit of mutual inquiry.
   Tutor may build e-relationships and share resources and the means of overcoming difficulties.

Learners perceive the goals of a learning experience to be their goals.
9. Teacher involves students in a mutual process of formulating learning-objectives in which the needs of the students, the institution, the subject matter and society are taken into account.

Tutor uses the potential of e-delivery for individualization to ensure that the goals fit individual learner.

The learners accept a share of the responsibility for planning and operating a learning experience and have a feeling of commitment toward it.

10. Teacher shares own thinking about the options available in designing learning experiences and the selection of materials and methods, and involves the student in deciding among these options jointly.
   Tutor explores different strategies with e-learning student for learning development, and for extracting and relating ideas.

The learners participate actively in the learning process.

11. Teacher helps the students to organize themselves, for example, by project groups, to share responsibility in the process of mutual inquiry.
   Tutor facilitates groupings of peer-to-peer students by geography (country, county) or standards. Tutor seeks out 'lurkers' to engage them more fully. Prompt feedback is given.

The learning process is related to and makes use of the experience of the learners.

12. Teacher helps students exploit their own experiences as resources for learning through various techniques, such as discussion, role-playing, case method, etc.
   Tutor provides insight into self-directed learning skills: choosing alternatives, helping peers learn, failure resilience, self-reward, openness to new learning styles, asking peers for help, etc.

13. Teacher gears presentation to the levels of experience of his particular students.
   Tutor prepares individual e-learning study-path with progression points and individual benchmarks.

14. Teacher helps students apply new learning to their experience and make their learning more meaningful.
   Tutor helps e-learner with search outside course for relevant examples, related applications and illustrations.

The learners have a sense of progress towards their own goals.

15. Teacher involves students in developing mutually acceptable criteria and methods for measuring progress toward the learning objectives.
   Tutor engages with learner, contracting on criteria, time and progress towards e-learning objectives.

16. Teacher helps students develop and apply procedures for self-evaluation according to these criteria.
   Tutor assists in prompting critical self-evaluation of self-directed learning, noting strengths and weaknesses, and reflection aided by timely feedback on progress and relevant action.

In the corporate training field, the essence of the role of the tutor is to respond to learner need and this might by done by someone without specific activity of tutoring in their job description (Goodyear and Steeples, 2000: 6). Tutors may work in jobs such as customer support or technical help-desks and carry out their roles very effectively, even though they may have a more limited set of instructional skills, compared with people employed in conventional training. Indeed, an examination of the tutorial role in four different learning settings revealed that in each role an important area of competence concerned the pedagogic approach, as much as technological abilities.

A tutor can support independent learners by means of asynchronous computer-conferencing. The role of the tutor might involve organizing discussion groups, setting online tasks and assisting learners who require additional advice or direction. By evaluating the responses of learners to a particular programme, tutors can help improve an online programme by identifying suitable modifications to a programme in order to enhance its effectiveness. A tutor can also support a group of learners applying e-learning in a face-to-face classroom or laboratory setting. Although the learner will be supported by technology, they may also still rely on information received explicitly from direct people-to-people contact and implicitly from experience, interaction and application. This can arise from asynchronous, synchronous or face-to-face delivery, or blended combinations of these approaches. Synchronous learning puts a co-presence demand on a tutor and removes the 24-hours-a-day availability of asynchronous support. The tutor in this role needs to have subject knowledge, and the capability to deal with IT problems and maintain a group of learners on a learning schedule.

The tutor can support learning in a drop-in learning-resource centre and may play a range of roles within such a resource centre, including administration, technical support and librarianship. The pedagogic tasks might involve helping learners to develop a suitable study plan identifying relevant resources, offering guidance on the learning methods included in the courseware or resolving technical application problems, as well as offering or directing the learner to subject expertise. A tutor may also apply e-learning materials in a demonstration mode for interactive group-learning. The tutor in such a setting needs to have the ability to operate the software and provide insightful lines of enquiry to the learning group, balancing the learner goals and the support provided by the learning materials.

Technology-supported learning offers teachers a choice. It can allow a shift of time towards supporting what cannot now be supported, even with the most advanced technology. This may include stimulating higher-order thinking, seeing new patterns, making new connections, leading communities of learners, guiding, coaching, encouraging and motivating. There will also be a need for advocacy by a teacher.

ATTRIBUTES OF E-LEARNING TUTORS

The operation of an e-learning course on a large scale will probably require the migration and conversion of staff used to classroom delivery into an e-learning role. Good pointers for desirable attributes of individuals for this move have been proposed (Mantyla and Gividen, 1999). These attributes include staff with enthusiasm, as this may help to convert others as the programme develops; anyone with prior successful distance-learning experience and who is enthusiastic about doing more, and who may also act as a mentor to aid tutor development; and excellent classroom teachers, since a sound track-record in delivering learning is a basic requirement for e-learning tutors. The orientation of the tutor to a learner-centred support model, or open-mindedness towards alternative student approaches will assist the transition. Flexibility is helpful, in order to acquire new skills, technologies and ways of working. Adaptability is an important attribute, since an e-learning tutor works in a team, but does not control what each person on the team does. Effective use of humour helps remote e-learners enjoy the learning experience and want to come back for more courses, and contributes to good word-of-mouth referral, which itself is invaluable for ongoing student recruitment. Lastly, a willingness to learn about new technologies is a crucial attribute, as effective distance-learning tutors find out how technology works to support the learning experience.

STAFF CONVERSION TO E-LEARNING

The current dynamic behind e-learning is likely to create a demand for more staff for online work than ever before. This can lead to the recruitment of new staff or the migration of existing staff to work in this area. For many providers, this will mean encouraging, motivating and supporting staff members as they adapt to include the support of distributed learning as part of their repertoire of skills, or even make the complete change from classroom teachers to facilitators of e-learning. Once staff who are considering making the change are identified, then help by means of a development programme can help participants gain familiarity with the techniques of online support.

It is not uncommon for staff to be reticent about volunteering for work on e-learning and it is important to address the real or perceived problems as a first step. Such perceptions ought to be addressed openly to ensure that their decisions are based on facts. One way of doing this is through a forum, workshop or departmental meeting, where negative perceptions can be addressed. The forum will need to build in ways to identify and address people's concerns and resistance to e-learning, with a range of effective arguments on good practice. Among the best arguments are successful outcomes from similar organizations, departments or groups. Conversely, a poorly-delivered course will need to have a strong and persuasive counter-argument, because it runs the risk of moderating the dynamic for change.

The move to e-learning generally needs the commitment of a group and the formation of a team approach to project development. For an academic department or centre, problems are likely to arise if only a part of the relevant teaching staff is committed to implementation and not the whole. In such circumstances, contention can arise between those who perceive themselves as working for the corporate good and those bent on individual professional or personal goals. If the internal culture is primarily individualistic, perhaps due to a research-based culture, or the pursuit of individual teaching-career objectives, or for some other reason, then the formation of a committed group may prove more difficult to achieve. Forming a new dedicated task-team may then be more effective and create fewer vexing managerial problems.

Certain differences in the role of an e-learning tutor compared with classroom teaching might be seen as advantages by a teacher. These include greater flexibility in delivery, away from a fixed class timetable. The lack of requirement for a public on-stage presentation may appeal. In teaching and learning terms, there can be a greater opportunity to focus on individual learner difficulties and in-depth learning, rather than on content delivery. The techniques offer a greater ability to plan, direct and influence feedback and chat sessions in asynchronous working. There are also opportunities to support learners from diverse and different remote contexts, which might appeal to staff with an interest in lifelong learning and diversity.

The challenges of e-learning may cause anxiety at first in the minds of existing staff changing to e-learning. It may make academic staff resist, or repudiate, work in the field for a variety of reasons. They may not be adaptable to supporting people in the workforce, or sympathetic to lifelong learners or to individuals who want to develop cultural interests. There are other reasons. An investigation of the impact of online learning in higher and further education concluded that e-learning presents change, because of a major shift in the conventional student–teacher relationship (Ross and Klug, 1999). Starting e-learning also requires a very considerable amount of application on the part of the teacher. This need for staff commitment in support of an online system is a recurring theme that some observers view as the greatest single factor in implementation (Hammond and Terrence, 1998).

Various actual, or perceived, hindrances may face tutors in the transition to an e-learning environment. The tutor might be sceptical that e-learning is as good as the classroom experience, in which case the tutor is encouraged by an offer of researched documentation with a list of successful e-learning Websites for benchmarking best practices and successful outcomes. There can be fear of applying the technology, so that technology support with staff development on the applications of learning technologies is offered. The tutor is performing where peers can see him or her, hence encouragement is given to arrange a mentor for each staff member making the transition, or to organize team teaching with an existing e-learning tutor. It may seem to the tutor that there is a lack of control in the learning engagement: the need here is to convey the shift from solo effort to team effort in the design and delivery of e-learning. A fear of losing jobs may exist, so encouragement can be given and information on the new types of opportunities created by new e-learning environments. Staff-development support can also be offered with new roles and responsibilities, such as facilitating, moderating and learner support. Staff in research-oriented university centres may question whether providing learning for companies, SMEs or lifelong learners is a relevant activity for the institution and for them in particular. Ultimately, this is a strategic decision for the university, with its roots in the institutional culture, though it may not require each member of staff to participate in every activity. These hindrances can be addressed, in general, by suitable encouragement to help the potential e-tutor to succeed in the migration from face-to-face to e-learning delivery.

ORGANIZATIONAL LEARNING DISABILITIES

Professional development is essentially a personal pursuit with the ownership and responsibility for it belonging to the individual professional. It cannot be delegated to someone else, nor can an organization be expected to take it comprehensively forward beyond regulatory training on behalf of an individual. This fact of working life is more easily recognized by a professional operating in a commercial role; someone with daily concern for the marketing of professional services, acquiring and possessing certain competences that a client organization, as a customer, pays for. To develop these competences means offering to provide enhanced key benefits for the employing organization, such as more profits for a firm, or more students, improved quality or greater financial contributions for an educational enterprise.

The academic system itself, however, can do better in developing a professional approach to teaching (Laurillard, 1993). Teachers themselves need to understand better how individuals experience their subject, how it is understood and misunderstood. Currently, they are neither required, nor enabled, to do this, and the mass system of lectures and assessments means that it is unlikely they will ever find out. A greater focus on the effectiveness of teaching is needed, together with an organizational infrastructure that enables teachers to be as professional in their teaching as they endeavour to be in research. There are several reasons why higher education finds it so difficult to change traditions, values and infrastructure, including pressures for financial input to go down and other performance indicators to rise.

There are other learning hindrances that can arise. In balancing relative priorities in an institution, staff development can assume a low priority for an institution with an accompanying relatively low level of resource. Low priority will usually mean that the operation has low institutional status, esteem and staff grading. Appraisal systems in higher education were introduced as an external initiative and a 'top-down' measure. Although implemented in different ways by institutions, these often fail to provide optimum benefits for the organization. For the individual appraisee within a hierarchical appraisal system this can serve to calcify positions and the option of requesting an independent appraiser can appear as a lack of confidence in the managerial hierarchy. A top-down approach for staff development which is introduced as a senior management initiative, without gaining support from teaching and support staff, may also be problematic.

PERSONAL AND PROFESSIONAL DEVELOPMENT

Creating change in individuals is difficult, not least because people tend to resist unintended or disorganized changes. Moreover, managers aim to produce stable processes within their organizations and staff expect consistency, order and predictability. The process of change is also usually uncertain and accompanied by the risk of losing something. Staff develop differently, have different skills, attitudes, abilities and personalities. Hence, a marked change for one person might be quite simple and take only a short time, but for someone else it might take much longer and even then be less pronounced. The skills and processes that best facilitate development are not required in the same variety or intensity by everyone.

In education circles, the term 'staff development' has become a catch-all expression, synonymous with the processes of professional development for teachers, educational managers and support staff. It is often seen as the main means available to an institution for the systematic development of employees in support of its strategy, together with other human resource actions, such as appraisal, personnel policies, selection, advancement and promotion. In general, staff development has just two main aims, that are aligned with the interests of both the individual and the employer: improvement in performance in the current job, and preparation for future opportunities, responsibilities and tasks.

For the individual staff member, an alignment of professional-development interests with that of the department, or the institution or, where appropriate, a relevant industrial, commercial or professional body, offers particular advantages. Where this alignment can be achieved, the integration of purpose can allow the justification of institutional time and resources for the pursuit of professional-development goals. Approached in this way, a higher priority can be gained if this development is converted into tangible benefits for the provider, for instance, in terms of new courses, more students or better standards.

Laudable as this approach might be, however, it sometimes results in such a low priority being given to resources that it is not successful. In such cases, the process of development can be supported with the aid of the IT infrastructure of the institution. Institutions, in general, have relatively good access to broad bandwidth communications channels, which facilitates Internet and Intranet connection, meaning that professional development can continue through professional electronic networking, access to external information and opportunities for online learning.

Performance intervention is a means of enhancing professional skills (Coleman, 1992: 634–48). In summary, this approach comprises: determine needs; determine existing knowledge, skills and attitudes; define gaps; develop appropriate performance interventions; and evaluate results and make adjustments as needed. Although Coleman is writing in the field of human performance technology (HPT), the core elements are common to four practical processes for staff development: self-profiling, professional and personal development planning, the long-term development of an individual's curriculum vitae and systematic staff appraisal within a supportive framework.

SELF-PROFILING

The rapid advances in technology and professional updating make keeping abreast of the continuously evolving skill-requirements increasingly difficult. It is more effective for staff to take care of their own development needs than to wait for a project or line manager to propose solutions. The foundations of professional development are based on identified skill-needs, knowledge or competences, which inform and shape an appropriate development-plan. The various needs of an individual vary over time. They can arise from changed circumstances, such as a new or changed job-role, new technology or management techniques. The needs can also appear through formal performance-appraisal systems, external assessment, a review of performance failures, self-assessment, or following events such as promotion, advancement, review or job application.

Such an analysis can be done by self-assessment using a series of prompt lists covering the principal areas of responsibility, such as teaching and student learning, curriculum development, administration, guidance, updating subject knowledge, projects and other professional activities. When complete, these prompt lists can identify the current activities and responsibilities, the activities with particular strengths, aspects that need developing, and competences that are not being used in present activities (Roffe, 2000: 327–39). For a particular profile area, such as teaching and learning, a series of prompt statements focus attention on relevant actions and draw awareness to skills in the area. The responses are completed in a matrix that provides a convenient guide to record the responses and to identify actions necessary to address weaknesses or disuse in competences (Table 11.3).

Table 11.3. Self-profile prompt responses

1. Current activities.	2. Strengths	3. Weaknesses
Main duties and responsibilities.	Strengths in main areas.	Aspects that need developing.
4. Unused competencies	**5. Action required/Date**	**6. Action taken/Date**
Any unused competences in the area.	Actions necessary to develop competences.	Record here actions relating to strengths and needs.

Completing such a profile helps to identify professional competences and needs. It also forms a personal record of development and professional activities, which can be used in preparing a curriculum vitae or as an agenda for staff appraisal. Moreover, it can assist in career development and planning for self-development.

Innovation

For any organization intent on starting and pursuing innovation, the initial steps are the same: to identify what is currently being done and the present skills within the organization, and to identify what can be done to improve. A conventional skill-list amongst staff engaged on work on teaching and learning, however, would not normally include innovation and the management of innovation. To be effective in the field of innovation, an individual requires special knowledge, skills and attitudes – knowledge of the organization and its environment as well as of the body of case information that leads to effective innovation (Majaro, 1988), and the skills of an effective and creative manager, with the appropriate attitude that will enable an individual to apply creative talent.

As a service organization, an educational institution's capabilities are embodied largely in the collective knowledge of its staff and the organizational procedures that shape the way they interact. Hence, in order to have individuals capable of initiating innovation, effective development is needed. This is not simply a traditional top-down approach, identifying or devising a suitable training-programme, because the work is complex, interrelated to other institutional activities and continuously changing in nature (Rossett, 1999: 63–8). Rather, it involves the transfer and acquisition of skills by a variety of means. The following are relevant statements to stimulate responses for the completion of Table 11.3: are you able to identify sources of innovative opportunity? Audit the organization's effectiveness in the area of creativity? Manage to transform an opportunity into a viable product or market entrant? Analyse, prioritize and select ideas for development? Communicate ideas clearly?

Manage multidisciplinary team contributions? Undertake project management? Identify market niches and devise marketing strategies for the educational service? Design products or services?

Project management

The creation of an e-learning programme is commonly performed through a project-management process. There are five recognized stages in the production of a Web-based training programme: analysis, design, development, implementation and evaluation, although not all these stages need apply in every case. For example, if content is available from another programme, then the design and development may be less important since this will have already been done. Nevertheless, drawing the development process through to a successful e-learning product requires conventional project-management abilities. Typical prompts for completing the self-profile table are: are you able to develop, lead and manage a technology-based team? Coordinate the work of a project team? Set budgets and determine costs? Determine project schedules? Monitor courseware and project performance? Manage contracts? Evaluate performance? Lead value assurance and validation arrangements? Determine and monitor the dimensions of perceived user-value? Do you have communication skills with clients, funding bodies and other third parties?

E-learning development

Capturing and integrating the 'human component' into an online learning solution is critical, yet difficult. One of the largest challenges of online learning is effectiveness, and to be effective on the Internet the learning experience must be engaging and interactive. Content must be presented in a manner that encourages individuals to read, observe, practise and experience learning in a meaningful and innovative manner. Approaches to e-learning range from those that use the Internet primarily as a distribution channel, to technologies that allow live, two-way interactive connections. Many and diverse skills are needed in e-learning design and development so that typical prompts become: are you able to design and develop learning through computer-based learning packages? Understand different learning technologies? Design and develop learning through suitable learning-media selection? Design for short segments of learning? Build in interactivity and vary the activities to ensure an active learning event rather than a passive learning experience? Create effective visual aids? Set up an infrastructure to support learners at remote sites? Establish learner-support systems before, during and after learning delivery? Deliver the learning experience based on the selected technologies?

E-learning support

The rate of change for e-learning developers is much faster than for classroom trainers. The fastest change is in the technology, the delivery platforms, the media available and the software tools. This leads to prompts such as: are you able to create a learning infrastructure? Develop a delivery platform? Produce materials? Design and develop simulations? Apply authoring software? Programme PCs? Design interactive screens? Manage system design? Implement courseware monitoring techniques? Provide detailed-level design skills, such as media selection? Introduce self-study design skills? Apply editorial skills?

Tutoring e-learning

Greater interactivity between tutor and student can also serve to enhance personalization and improve motivation and retention. Immediate feedback is also possible to questions and practice exercises. A great attraction of online learning is the large numbers of students it is possible to reach, provided that they can find the programme. Typical prompts for self-development include: are you able to identify and record needs through interactive tests or question-naires? Ensure easy registration and identify pre-course administration requirements? Set up an infrastructure to support learners at remote sites? Apply software for collecting, maintaining and distributing content? Record and track learning and assessment? Assess knowledge through online assessment? Develop and contribute to a learning-support team? Market the online service? Promote and maintain the Website? Use all equipment and applications? Prepare evaluation tools?

Performance consultancy

Performance consultancy is intended to diagnose the needs of SMEs by a holistic analysis. It can also be described as part of the practice of management consultancy, or knowledge transfer, in determining the business-performance needs that can be addressed through workforce development. It is the execution in SMEs that is important and, in the particular case here, performance improvement in small firms by e-learning. The kind of prompts that help complete the self-profile table include: are you able to subject complex situations to systematic examination and resolve these into key elements? Examine data produced by analysis and identify the main factors to be considered if an opportunity is to be exploited? Study data and diagnoses to overcome problems and make the best of opportunities? Work effectively with other people? Get other people to accept your proposals? Present findings and recommendations logically and lucidly?

Assess markets and marketing services to existing and potential clients? Persuade potential clients to accept your proposals?

Staff with these skills and the capacity to undertake e-learning roles may be available in a provider. If they are not, then external recruitment may be necessary, with these prompts serving as job descriptions or for scoring candidates during interview selection. These prompts can also provide a basis for appraisal reviews. The skills and attributes of staff detailed by professional self-profiling can be tied into the functional HRD policies and competitive strategies in a structured way, by the appraiser and appraisee, working through the dimensions of perceived value. A pro forma, such as the example in Table 11.4, can be used as a means of discussion for deriving action points.

Table 11.4 Staff attributes for contributing to PUV, a sample form for review by appraisal

Dimension of PUV	Self-appraisal	Appraiser	Action points
Authenticity			
Personalization			
Flexibility			
Support			
Accreditation			

INFLUENCING ACTION BY APPRAISAL

Appraisal can bring a wide range of potential benefits for individuals, including better communications, clearer work objectives, a sense of being valued and working with better-informed managers. Educational institutions may also benefit from these aspects: appraisal can help in departmental planning, aligning departmental needs and priorities as well as in the identification and dissemination of good practice.

A principal goal of appraisal is to improve the performance of a member of staff and for the individual to commit to following an agreed course of action. Unless the appraisee recognizes the need for and agrees a change, though, the appraisal is likely to fail. When a new challenge is presented, there is a danger that the opportunity is so novel, risky and uncertain that the opening is misperceived or even regarded as a threat. It is crucial, in gaining the agreement of the individual, to build on mutual trust, in order to explore opportunities along with solutions and gain commitment from the individual to take action. When the opportunities are realized by an individual, it is possible to maintain enthusiasm and drive for the change.

The natural time for an individual to consider professional aims and a change of direction is at the time of appraisal. Most teachers and trainers keep a personal record of training, development and professional activities which can be used in compiling a curriculum vitae or as a platform for discussion within a system of appraisal. The critical step in appraisal is, however, the interpersonal process, in which the appraiser helps the appraisee to redirect his or her performance while maintaining mutual trust.

The process and options for staff development clearly vary from one organization to another. The method most appropriate for a member of staff is dependent on the inclination of the individual, the work of their department or centre, the way the development methods impact on the individual now and in the future, and the available range of opportunities. These factors are important determinants because they again influence the extent to which an individual accepts the staff-development opportunity. The individual member of staff, in conjunction with line-management, has an important decision-making role in terms of his or her development. Whichever route of development is chosen, it is essential to use the opportunity to address attitudes and behaviour at the same time as skills acquisition. Positive attitudes, with curiosity and creativity, are attributes for professional development to flourish.

CENTRALIZATION–DECENTRALIZATION COSTS

There is a high cost to investment in e-learning. This arises from the technology infrastructure, content development and support, but also from the recurrent cost of staff development. Even when staff become adept at using technology for learning applications, they need to continue to update their skills. There is an organizational tradition in universities and colleges of setting up a central support-unit for providing staff development as well as for learning-technology support. It is common for teaching departments and centres to have their own budgets, that can also include spending on staff development and learning technology. Practice varies from institution to institution in the degree of autonomy and decentralization. The greater the decentralization, however, the more the likelihood of multiple centres of activity pursuing different development directions. There is then a clear and present danger of duplication and inefficiency without transparent areas of agreed responsibilities.

Despite this contention, a balanced approach seems best, between central and devolved activities. The degree of decentralization determines the amount of resource available for the specialized support of learning technologies. This means that the extent of detailed specialization of staff that might occur in dedicated e-learning companies becomes feasible only in universities and colleges with sufficiently large aggregated resources. In practice, a Web specialist and an application coordinator are necessary. The alternative is overextension of staff through multiskilling, on low-scale initiatives with little lasting impact.

THE EDUCATIONAL ENTERPRISE AND THE INDIVIDUAL

A shift in the total resources for staff development occurs with the adoption of learning technologies. The procurement and infrastructure support of IT, video- and audioconferencing, Web-meeting space and access to databases all require resources. This movement for learning resources represents a marked shift from the practice of identifying and applying a staff-development budget for training events and conferences, together with accompanying expenditure on travel and subsistence. Greater accessibility of information from sources, such as the government, professional and commercial organizations, firms, other institutions and research databases, serves to expand greatly the internal community of users of this information, as well as its circulation, and contribute to the professional development of staff. This keeps an individual better informed, but it can be challenging to management in situations where a culture of power through information applies. Professional networking was previously restricted to those individuals with the responsibilities, as well as the resources, to travel and meet people. Electronic communication, however, allows networking to a much wider group of staff, with the time, inclination and access to technology. It helps professional development, which is still a personal challenge for an individual.

Aligning interests with an institutional, departmental, competitive or functional strategy, or an appropriate industrial commercial need, is likely to provide direct benefits to the educational enterprise in terms of more students, better courses, better research and development, or a greater financial contribution. Such alignment, although desirable, might not be achievable, leaving the option for an individual to become an independent learner through formal and informal methods. The ways of mitigating this are becoming much more available, especially through online learning. There are professional networks for educationalists in the UK through the Learning and Teaching Support Networks, such as ESCalate (*www.escalate.ac.uk*), as well as a wide range of opportunities accessible through the Web.

Finally, in circumstances where alignment of professional and organizational interests can be achieved, it can be relatively straightforward to justify time and resources for the pursuit of professional-development goals. Career progression, however, does not necessarily follow. The high-quality competences that can arise from effective professional development do not, as a matter of course, lead to career progression. This depends more on how well they are applied, the actual opportunities that present themselves and an individual's motivation.

12

Evaluation

Creating an e-learning programme takes time, effort and resources. With so much energy expended it makes sense to monitor the results to justify the initial investment. Evaluation as a process can help with decisions that enhance the quality and perceived value of e-learning. It is a multifaceted and dynamic activity that can be applied to the whole e-learning system, or just a part of it, such as at a course level, or for the effectiveness of an innovative action. In applications for firms, success is tied to the ability of the programme to meet the learning needs of the organization in which the system operates. For an educational enterprise, success with e-learning is related to broader criteria: for meeting learning needs effectively, an efficient learning system that assures value, enhances intangibles and innovates successfully is crucial. For providers engaged in partnership working, evaluation involves the assessment of factors at both the partnership level and the individual partner level. Overall, evaluation is essential in sustaining the e-learning value proposition by providing relevant and timely information to decision-makers and practitioners.

THE VALUE OF EVALUATION

Evaluation is a process that professionals carry out all the time and in every discipline, comparing the actual and real with the predicted or promised. The reason for doing so is to determine the effectiveness, efficiency or appropriateness of a particular course of action. The intention is to highlight good or bad practice, detect errors and correct mistakes, assess risk, enable optimum investment to be achieved and also to allow individuals and organizations to learn. The outcomes of the evaluation process can tell people what they have done wrong or that they are about to fail. Evaluation can be most effective, though, when it informs future decisions; then, the purpose is to enlighten decision-makers so that they can enhance value, improving what exists or doing better on the next occasion. Evaluation for this purpose is therefore better used to understand events and processes for future action, whereas accountability looks back to properly assign praise, or blame (Geis and Smith, 1992: 130–50).

Testing and evaluating propositions about the best way of teaching something by e-learning can provide a valid basis for broadening and enriching an educational prospectus. The reasons for evaluating e-learning are, therefore, the same as for any form of learning experience. At present e-learning is still an experimental process for many educational enterprises, so that value can be gained from assessing technology-supported solutions. The literature-base on the evaluation of e-learning is also comparatively underdeveloped, compared with the vast number of contributions on assessing education and training. Consequently, such classic approaches as training evaluation are expected by practitioners and clients in firms and are applied widely.

CLASSIC TRAINING EVALUATION

Classic training is based on instructional systems design (ISD), which originated in order to address the problem of inefficient and ineffective instruction directly. As an innovation, training greatly compresses the time needed to acquire skills, over earlier methods, such as apprenticeship. It achieves this condensation through a process involving the careful analysis of job requirements, the determination of skill needs, the specification of objectives, and the design, delivery and evaluation of an instructional programme. Over the past sixty years or so, each of these components has been critically examined. Even so, intriguing questions still remain around the transfer problem – why the transfer of learning in the workplace so low (Baldwin and Ford, 1988: 63–105). This simple, yet profound issue has led to studies on the effectiveness of learning transfer and helped initiate the movement for performance improvement (Broad and Newstrom, 1992).

Apart from the transfer issue, there are, though, certain limitations in applying a classic ISD approach to e-learning. The essence of the application of e-learning is speed; the ISD model in comparison is comprehensive, but slow. By the time a detailed set of behavioural objectives has been specified by training designers, the business problem may have changed. In the process of perfecting a training design, a business opportunity might be missed. Internet delivery has also blurred the distinction between a content user and a content provider, and in the process challenged the role of an instructor. As a result, much corporate e-learning is a collaborative sharing of knowledge, and ISD does not address the task of engaging in these types of conversation. The ISD model is much better at addressing project-management and problem-solving, applied within a rigid framework. It serves as a good aid to teaching and learning instructional design, but expert designers tend to be more fluid and rapid in the processes that they apply. The problem then is not that the ISD model is poor, but rather that its limitations are not always fully acknowledged.

A primary reason for providing education and training for managers and employees is to address a gap between existing knowledge and a necessary level of knowledge. The individual then has to learn new skills to bridge the gap. Evaluation is a core step in the instructional process that can measure the extent to which students have satisfied the course objectives in acquiring skills and bridging the performance gap. It also provides a means of demonstrating to managers in SMEs the business value of a learning programme and hence its authenticity.

There are a small number of classic evaluation models for training that are widely used by practitioners. The most common is the four-level training-evaluation model, which is a hierarchical model with a specific emphasis for each level (Kirkpatrick, 1994). Other structured-level approaches exist, for example an evaluation-level approach based on performance analysis (Brinkerhoff, 1987), and also a model with a fifth level for translating the worth of training into monetary value (Phillips, 1991). These methods all share a common focus at their highest levels on determining the benefit of training through an expression of financial value. It has always been recognised that it is difficult to isolate and measure the results of training. The long-established Kirkpatrick model is still the blueprint for evaluation used by many trainers, even though the return-on-investment assessment at level 4 is seldom achieved. The model comprises four levels, as follows, and can be adopted for e-learning.

Level 1: Reaction of learners

This stage captures the reaction of learners to a training programme and is typical of an end-of-course evaluation. In e-learning terms this can be integrated with a learner satisfaction and comment form at the end of each course. With e-learning, employee evaluation is essential as it gives a direct source of information on the value of a programme. This merits the careful drafting of questions that draw out the learner experience with content, technology, support and authenticity. Areas where value can be enhanced can also be addressed. The advantages are that it is easy to measure trainees' likes and dislikes about a programme and its delivery, but the disadvantage is that trainees do not have to like a programme to learn.

At this level, the reactions of participants are important since it is believed that the more positive the reaction, the more likely it is that transfer will occur to the tasks of a job. This reaction level can be assessed through several measures relevant to the online learning environment, such as chat, e-mail or online questionnaires. The online delivery and return of questionnaires is very appropriate when the course is delivered online, and has the advantages that the responses can be analysed automatically through a linked spreadsheet programme which can then provide timely evaluation information.

Level 2: Learning at the end of the programme

This level assesses how much people learned as a result of participating in the programme. Feedback on the e-learning design can serve to improve the business performance for future student groups. At level 2, opportunities for e-learning evaluation occur in pre-test, post-test and online evaluation. Evaluation during the course through questionnaires and observation, with rapid feedback, provides an opportunity for individual course adaptation in e-learning. There are advantages because this level is easy to measure, but the disadvantages are that the curriculum can be determined on financial basis, not on needs.

It is commonly accepted that the difficulties of evaluation tend to increase with the level. At the learning level, the techniques of assessment are determined by the type of course and the objectives of the programme. In the case of objectives in the cognitive domain, essays, online tests or problem-solving might be applied. In the case of the affective domain, questionnaires and one-to-one chat might be used. The psychomotor domain is not well suited to online measurement, however, unless the objective of the learning programme is the acquisition of keyboard skills.

Level 3: Performance on the job

This stage determines the extent to which people apply the learning in their work and whether the transfer during e-learning was effective. This level measures behavioural changes resulting from learning. Supervisors and managers as well as learners can provide information on performance changes. The techniques applied are observation, managers' checklists and 360-degree feedback. The advantages are its direct application, but the disadvantages are that this level is relatively difficult to measure, requests for data are disruptive and there are too many job-performance variables.

At the application area, information is sought on the transfer and application of new knowledge, skills and attitudes to a job. The conventional processes for measuring the extent of the impact at this level are through observations, questionnaires, automatic responses and self-reporting. Measurement here is most useful when it can be compared with information on the participant's capabilities before the course.

Level 4: Results for the organization

This assesses the business impact of the training on organizational operations, or job environment, usually in the form of return on investment (ROI). The costs of training can be established, although the benefits are subjective and difficult to quantify and express in monetary terms. Benefits will often accrue over a period of time that may fall outside the scope of the evaluation. Level 4 measures training results, for example increased productivity, sales and employee retention. The methods employed include managers' briefings, before and after analysis of HRD data, cost-benefit analysis and the identification of ROI. The advantages are that results at this level are a crucial benefit to the organization.

Business results are regarded widely as a difficult level to evaluate. Difficulties arise because there are many factors that can affect performance and the transfer of learning, apart from the courses supplied. These can include: personal factors, such as motivation, ability and attention; instructional factors, such as course design and trainers' ability; and organizational factors, such as climate, timing, management, learner support, etc. The classical approach around this problem is to form a control group of individuals similar to the learner group, but with the control not undertaking training. Comparisons on the performance of the two groups may then reveal distinctive characteristics. The time and effort involved for results at this level with all types of client are very considerable. For a provider, the resources might be better deployed in evaluating the e-learning service itself, rather than in evaluating company ROI. Indeed, a four-level analysis can cost more than the design and the delivery of a training programme it measures.

Conventional ROI approaches might be of interest to the corporate and small firm client, but very costly for an e-learning provider to perform. A relatively simple approach, however, is to calculate the costs associated with travel and absence from the workplace. More effort can then be put to determining the dimensions of value perceived by the small firm client, information that can be applied to sustain a competitive advantage for the provider.

EVALUATION AND THE EFFECTS OF TECHNOLOGY

Classic educational evaluation studies are fundamentally about the collection of data relevant to questions of learning needs, in order to make timely decisions about educational effectiveness. Evaluation is a core of the curriculum design process and there are many approaches, including ODFL applications and team-based methods (Calder et al., 1995; Thorpe, 1993). Educational course evaluation has a range of purposes, so it is important to determine at the start what the evaluation will do. It can be categorized into three basic groups: standards, methodology and process (Hale and French, 1999: 165–77). 'Standards' refers to judging the levels of achievement that a student has reached. Methodology refers to whether quantitative or qualitative evaluation is sought. Process refers to either formative evaluation, in which data-collection occurs during the process and the information can be used for decision-making during the event, or summative evaluation, where a determination of the effectiveness of an intervention is made after it is completed and is focused on outcomes. Formative evaluation may influence the design and delivery of training or educational course, while summative evaluation measures its effectiveness.

The application of technology to support learning adds certain features that need to be considered in a comprehensive evaluation framework. For instance, the evaluation of learning technologies is bound together with the authoring and dissemination process. There are many models now available that include the impact of technology. Among the most widely cited internationally is a cost -benefit analysis proposed by Bates (Bates, 2000: 136–46). With a widely distributed population, calculations to underpin academic e-learning have been developed in Canadian university consortia since the mid-1990s and inform this model. The model considers the access, costs, teaching and learning, interactivity, organizational issues, novelty and speed, giving rise to the acronym ACTIONS. It assesses the strengths and weaknesses of learning technologies together with the costs. This model addresses the access and flexibility for a particular target group, the optimum instructional approaches and supporting technologies. The ease of use for the kind of interaction is a criterion, as are organizational issues for the delivery mode, the reliability of the technology and how quickly content can be changed.

A holistic approach to evaluation is advocated by Athanasou, which should include the particular mode of learning, social aspects of instruction, relationship with other components of instruction, learning sequence, presentation medium, extent of interactivity and content-matter interest (Athanasou, 1998: 96–103). He proposes a systematic approach, with questions to determine information from six areas: ethics, needs, costs, objectives, effects and the interests of stakeholders.

Another approach is provided by a conceptual framework of the processes for learning-technology integration into a course of study, and gives another grouping of the main processes (Stoner, 1996):

Initiation: preliminary assessment and recognition of problem and possibilities.
Analysis and evaluation: specifying course objectives, data-collection, evaluation of system, identification of possible development directions.
Selection of learning technologies: to generate alternative learning-technology solutions, compare alternatives with objectives.
Design integration: plan and design learning activities, determine assessments, acquire resources, test learning technology.
Implementation: materials production, installation of learning technology, testing technology on course, staff training, student testing.
Monitor: continuous integrative evaluation and adaptation for the course system.

Evaluation of the implementation: informal and formal assessment closes the cycle.

Evaluation can be designed for different purposes or roles. Integrative evaluation, for example, can help users to make the most of a given application by assessing the integrated use of a particular learning technology on certain programmes. Illuminative evaluation can reveal important features that are latent in a particular application. Formative evaluation can help improve the design of e-learning as the application is being developed. Finally, summative evaluation can aid users to choose which parts of e-learning to use and for what.

EVALUATION OF DELIVERY TO BUSINESSES

The four-level training-evaluation model exercises a powerful influence on practitioners of industrial and commercial training, particularly in North America. Problems which arise with the higher levels, particularly level 4, question its relevancy in its conventional form for assessing e-learning. According to Hall and LeCavalier the most promising strategy for the effective evaluation of e-learning is to focus on level 3, job-performance-based measures (Hall and LeCavalier, 2000). This emerged from collecting information from eleven firms with significant e-learning success, where fewer than half the firms collected ROI data on their e-learning systems. The formal assessment of the effectiveness of e-learning, particularly at the job-performance level, proved difficult. Nevertheless, online testing (level 2 evaluation) is common, well accepted and helpful in replacing anecdotal data on training effectiveness with firm results. No general consensus exists, at present, concerning the importance of measurement at every level. From this small survey for large corporations, Hall and LeCavalier concluded there was no general demand from managers for extensive evaluation metrics on e-learning. Since learning-management systems can provide managers with a wide range of previously unavailable data, the traditional measures, such as annual trainee days and course completions, may become less relevant as an activity measure.

Little consensus on metrics and measurement methods exists, but the case for a more comprehensive framework for the evaluation of e-learning is argued by Phillips et al. (Phillips et al., 2000). They consider that most current evaluations at the business level, or return-on-investment (ROI) level, are driven by the funders of e-learning and not by the designers and providers of e-learning. Moreover, in their view e-learning outcomes are as effective as those of conventional face-to-face learning, but traditional classroom instruction gives more favourable responses from participants, that is, from level 1 evaluation. ROI studies also indicate a positive return for firms utilizing e-learning courses, although the broader range of benefits to a company ought to be assessed together with ROI. In gathering evaluation data, the same strategies and processes applied on other types of evaluations can be applied to e-learning programmes.

Influences on learners' perceptions of e-learning materials have been assessed by an evaluation tool, designed to compare judgements by learners, and applied to five different TSL courses from three design centres (Sambrook, 2002: 157–68). The tool is intended for managers and HRD practitioners to help identify influencing factors on the perception of quality. Among the other top factors influencing learners' judgements of quality were user-friendly instructions, clear and accurate presentation, an interesting engagement, the right amount of information and the right balance of text and graphics.

Collecting answers to evaluation questions is necessary, whichever method is used, and a wide variety of methods exist for doing this. The existence of so many different approaches in regular use signifies that no single methodology is best, and the fact that so many exist reflects on the different types of questions it is possible to ask during evaluation (Harvey, 1998). Technology itself provides unique opportunities to monitor training and generate useful statistical data. For example, comparing cumulative time used to complete an online course with time away from work to complete an equivalent classroom course yields instant data on cost savings. Other data that could be collected, completely transparent to the e-learning user, include the number of logins, average time per session, time of day and other user preferences and even navigation patterns.

EVALUATION ON THE INDIVIDUAL LEVEL

The novelty of e-learning applications brings pressure on evaluators to yield information about its effectiveness and efficiency as a learning solution. Feedback from individual students can inform on the satisfaction with the learning process, the amount learned and the integration of the skills. It can consider the numbers of students who have expressed an interest, registered, progressed and completed the programme. This addresses certain practical marketing questions such as: how far has the coverage extended towards the target population? What is the geographical distribution for e-learning enquiries and enrolments: regional, national, international? In addition, certain indicators could be measured or monitored, including the cost of the programme. Key questions might include: how many enquiries have there been? How many course registrations? Where is the e-learner from: local, sub-region, region and country? How many active and dormant e-learners are there? What volume statistics indicate the level of activity? How many gain the qualification? How long does it take to complete for the fastest quartile and the average?

The experience at Lampeter highlights certain characteristics of our e-learning students and came from a comparison of student' progress on the same course delivered online and face-to-face. Not unexpectedly, the easiest level to ascertain is the reaction (level 1) evaluation on the e-learning programme and learning (level 2) when specific content knowledge gained from the e-learning course was assessed. E-learning yielded learning (level 2) responses similar to those of face-to-face learning, but distinctive differences appeared in the characteristics of online learners, compared to students in a face-to-face learning environment, including: the nature of the students, progress, personal preferences and new client groupings.

Different students engage in e-learning

Students who enrol on the e-learning programme are significantly different from those on full-time, mainstream courses. In age terms, many are more mature, aged forty years or over, and these students derive from professional backgrounds, with a substantial prior learning-history derived from their professional subject-base. The written communication skills of e-learners were stronger than for campus-based students through conventional delivery. In comparison with a group who arrived to study the programme full-time through a campus-based delivery, however, their verbal communication skills were not as strong.

Progression rates and participation vary

The ability to progress on the programme at the pace of the student means that some students could complete in two months, although the average is nine months. A characteristic of e-learning is that some students 'lurk', that is, they receive content and log on, but there is no response from them in terms of chat sessions, even though they may submit coursework for assessment as required.

Anonymity preference

Many distance students prefer the anonymity offered by e-learning. Many managers do not wish their fallibility and learning difficulties to be exposed to people who know them, nor to people who may work with them, or for them. The availability of participation through e-learning, therefore, offers them a new route for professional and personal development, with a degree of anonymity that alleviates the potential for appearing foolish and failing.

Proximity preference

Even though individuals enjoy anonymity, they still express an interest in proximity to other tutors and peers. An opportunity for face-to-face meetings in the form of campus events was created and proved popular for those participating in a short complementary study programme.

New unexpected client-groupings emerge

A major benefit comes from the development of new client-bases of students enrolling on courses. An initial group of SMEs in the local and regional market led to entry into the large corporate university markets as well as attracting independent lifelong learners drawn from the international marketplace.

EFFICIENCY

The costs for a provider fall into many categories, including: curriculum design and evaluation, online tutors, technical support, administration, promotional costs and the costs borne by students – salaries, benefits, etc. Other costs, related to the promotion of the programme and IT infrastructure, might be met by the central services of an organization. A contrast with conventional classroom delivery will show typically savings from delivery, but additional expense in design and learner-support infrastructure.

E-learning ought to provide clients with major efficiencies over alternative methods in both time and cost. In terms of time, a learner-management system will yield information on how long it takes a learner to complete the e-learning course, which can then be compared with progress and completion on conventional courses. For the client there are also time savings to be gained from travel to a classroom. Key questions might include: what are the full costs of the e-learning development? What are the comparable costs for conventional learning for a similar cohort? What are the most sensitive financial factors in e-learning delivery? How can the development process be improved? How efficient is the conversion of enquiries into enrolments? How well is the e-learning programme organized?

Formative evaluation, either online or offline, during a programme makes the evaluation activity much more dynamic and the results more timely. There are advantages in using the Internet for supplying and responding to questionnaires, particularly the speed of response and analysis. Many qualitative questionnaires for formative evaluation are available on the Internet, but fewer models for summative evaluation. There is a degree of complexity involved in the design of computer-based evaluation forms. Instructional pages can be simple HTML documents, but interactive questionnaire forms require background programs that are not HTML-based. These programs consist of an execution file that interacts with HTML documents, but does not appear on any screen while executing. Background programs such as these can provide online testing, grading, recording and data storage. A learning-management system provides an effective way to provide data for formative evaluation. The inclusion of online evaluation instruments aids the efficient collection of information and online testing yields information on knowledge acquisition.

THE EFFECTIVENESS OF RESULTS

The design for e-learning can be based on behaviourist, information processing, cognitive, humanistic or constructivist principles, since e-learning does not imply a particular learning process informed by a single learning theory. The learning may involve acquiring information, skills or competencies, and those may be assessed by processes requiring recall, analysis, synthesis, creative behaviours or hypotheses. Different approaches to e-learning, from asynchronous, through computer-mediated tutoring, to synchronous student–student interaction application, mean that it is not a discreetly definable process. These particular approaches can be evaluated, but an evaluation approach can only assess particular applications of e-learning rather than a general and comprehensive application.

There are assumptions made in e-learning design that priorities for good practice in classroom learning transfer across into the e-learning situation. Challenges are emerging to this, for instance, to the belief that learning-style preferences are key to instructional design in e-learning (Lewis and Orton, 2000: 47–51). Lewis and Orton suggest that e-learning is still too new for most learners to identify online learning as a preference. The development of individuals experienced in TSL, however, is likely to draw out more informed comparisons.

Assessing the cost-effectiveness of TSL can be difficult because of factors that may operate singly or together (Hunt and Clarke, 1997). Relevant factors are that: the indirect costs, such as trainees' time, are difficult to measure; costing information is not kept in sufficient detail; and direct costs are often combined with other non-relevant costs and are difficult to isolate. Key questions on effectiveness can include: what is the overall satisfaction of the learners with the programme? What change is there in the knowledge, skills or attitude of participants? What changes are there in on-the-job behaviour? What productivity changes have occurred as a result of the programme?

There are additional effectiveness-measures that apply to a provider. Monitoring of a Website and a learning-management system can provide a quick and accurate indication of the effect of promotion. Promotion by a fresh and attractive Website can attract enquiries and international registrations, as can holding special promotional events planned to coincide with course-development milestones, and arranging a drip-feed of news stories to stimulate interest and maintain the flow of registrations. E-learning programmes provide the greatest benefit by providing the opportunities to learn, where none existed previously. They also enable managers in companies with an Intranet to host an e-learning programme on their corporate Intranet, without large up-front development costs, but priced on an individual enrolment basis.

RETURN ON INVESTMENT

An assessment of the return on the investment (ROI) for a firm can be made by comparing the cost of previous traditional provision with that delivered through e-learning, with the major cost-savings in travel and out-of-office time. For micro-SMEs, though, determining ROI and comparative benefits can be much more difficult, as no provision existed beforehand. The major benefit occurs through no work absences. The cost of a full ROI evaluation of a programme can exceed the actual development and delivery costs. The ability to collect evaluation data online, however, not only markedly reduces costs but also provides real-time data on the progress of a scheme.

E-learning shifts the resource equation away from direct delivery and into content development and maintenance, similar to other forms of ODFL provision. The e-learning support team needs technology support as well as a development capacity. This increases the variety of skills and raises the core costs for delivery, but can be compensated for by the benefits in greater curriculum adaptability and the scalability of the learning course. Additional students can be accommodated to match demand by adding tutorial and administrative support. The literature contrasts technology-based training approaches with conventional approaches and reports a 30 per cent saving of cost (EC, 1994), 32.3 per cent cost-saving (Employment Department, 1991) or between 12 and 90 per cent (Tucker, 1994).

For the return-on-investment (ROI) category, the financial impact of the e-learning programme in terms of business results is assessed against the investment in the programme. In order to determine the ROI, the first step is to aggregate all the direct and financial costs that have been created by the e-learning programme; the second step is to assign a financial value to the business improvements that have been made over a twelve-month period. The third step is to identify the ROI from the formula:

$$ROI = (benefits/costs) \times 100\%$$

Evaluation at the ROI level (4 and 5) can be very time-consuming and have considerable resource implications. Hence, with a large portfolio of courses, some priority selection-criteria will be needed to determine which programmes to evaluate at this level. The criteria often applied in conventional delivery are: the life-cycle of the e-learning programme, since a long-term implementation and duration would demand an ROI evaluation at some point during the programme; and the linkage of the e-learning programme to operational goals and measures, since a direct linkage should be subjected to ROI evaluation.

Certain e-learning project developments are justified on cost savings alone, when the fully loaded cost of the traditional learning is compared to the cost of e-learning. Cost savings result in a positive ROI. This assumes that the output of the learning process remains the same and the earnings, or net monetary benefits from both approaches are consistent, which may not always be the case. The evaluation of an e-learning project should include a mechanism for forecasting the actual expected benefits, converting to monetary values, and then comparing the benefits to the projected cost. The difficulty is to estimate the actual change in business measures linked directly to the e-learning programme.

A comprehensive evaluation system yielding a full range of six types of data (reaction, learning, application, business impact, ROI and intangibles) would be impractical to use for every e-learning project. The workload will be simply too great in larger organizations, where there are many e-learning programmes. Certain types of e-learning programmes may not be appropriate for evaluating at the ROI level. A sensible approach, therefore, is to identify and classify which programmes are appropriate for comprehensive evaluation on the basis of their significance for the provider.

Key questions for determining ROI might be: how big is the target audience for the e-learning programme? How important is the programme to the strategic objectives of the organization? What are the cost savings of the e-learning programme? What are the direct benefits of the programme? What are the outcomes from sensitivity analysis for a range of outcomes, such as break-even point?

An alternative simplified ROI method offers a way to approach ROI in an educational provider (Collis and Moonen, 2001). Collis and Moonen advocate the abandonment of an absolute and exhaustive ROI calculation and in its place suggest a systematic, but more intuitive calculation and the comparison of one situation with another. The approach is based on a simple grading system, 1 (poor) to 5 (very good). The principles are to focus on a specific factor and local context, with only those parameters that are changing in meaningful ways considered. Factors are grouped together as either economic, qualitative or efficiency. The major actors are identified and each actor considers the perceived impact for all three types of factor. A score is assigned to the perception of each actor. The results are then added and the totals used as the basis for discussion on the e-learning provision.

Table 12.1. Abbreviated and simplified ROI e-learning case (adapted from Collis and Moonen, 2001)

Actors	Institution	Department	Tutors	Actual and potential students
Parameter				
Potential for enrolment	4	4	4	
Marketing value	4	5	1	5
Engaging student interest	2	4	4	4
Enhancing student support	4	3	4	
Keeping content up to date	2	2	1	
Resource control	3	3	2	1
System malfunctions	1	1	1	2
Totals	**14**	**23**	**17**	**17**

An illustration of the method is shown in Table 12.1 for a Lampeter course, where the strong score by students for engaging interest arises through the enhanced access to staff afforded by e-learning over conventional face-to-face methods. Other noteworthy features are the limited impact on the marketing value perceived by some tutors and the weight given to continuing the efforts needed in keeping information up to date. The other drawback is that system malfunctions impact negatively across the range of stakeholders.

MEASURING INTANGIBLES

Education is a service that is intangible. It can be difficult to determine investment returns in e-learning, which is even more intangible than normal learning. Measuring intangibles, though, has attracted lots of attention. The value of intangibles to an enterprise in creating a competitive edge is emphasized by Low and Kalafut (Low and Kalafut, 2002). They cite the intangibles that drive performance as: leadership, strategy execution, communications and transparency, brand equity, reputation, networks and alliances, technology and processes, human capital, workplace organization and culture, innovation, intellectual capital and adaptability. The emphasis given to each factor depends to a large extent on the provider. The key steps are for a particular enterprise to determine the critical intangibles for delivery and determine suitable metrics for them. A baseline is created and then benchmarked against competitors. Initiatives are then introduced to enhance performance across these parameters.

Evaluation can therefore be based on a variety of business factors, such as the cost and the perceived value of the service, with the significant dimensions determined through analysis of client perceptions (described in chapter 7). The system capabilities of value assurance, enhancement (considered in chapter 10) and innovation (chapter 8) are important in improving perceived value. Assessing an e-learning delivery system can be achieved by looking at these generic competences and at specific content delivery areas. Additionally, instructional interest focuses on factors such as completion rates, achievement levels, values, autonomy and relationships, based on the performance of individuals and groups.

CRITERIA FOR EVALUATING INNOVATION

Allowing too many initiatives to proceed has the effect of diverting resources and energy from core activities. As a result, the organization risks losing focus. There is also a need to filter out non-viable or unsustainable schemes at an early stage. Effective screening, therefore, can help eliminate unwanted activities and thereby enhance competitive advantage. There are many forms of media and many strategies for their application. Whatever evaluation instruments and processes are chosen, criteria are needed from which to select suitable matters and questions to evaluate. Four approaches have been distinguished by Inglis et al.: applying the objectives of an innovation; comparing the effectiveness with the previous condition or approach; evaluating against the potential of the technology; and evaluating against a theoretical position (Inglis et al., 2002).

The goals or objectives are often applied as the key criteria for an evaluation. This is suitable for relatively stable situations where the goals are predictable and where unanticipated goals, or outcomes, are not seen as relevant. Evaluating a project against its own objectives, however, can be limiting as it gives no indication of unanticipated outcomes that can have practical importance. The approach does not allow for shifts in the objectives or in the costs. To ignore any additional benefits and other effects simply serves to limit the information that might inform future work.

Comparing the learning outcomes of an initiative with one that does not apply the media innovation is an alternative method. The difficulty with this approach is the practical problem of maintaining constants between the two approaches. Normally the learning environment changes in many ways and the application of knowledge media will affect various aspects of the experience. The roles of learners and teachers change, the learning outcomes or the topic boundaries all might change. These all present limitations to the comparative criteria approach.

Another method is to establish criteria for evaluation that are based on experience or from the literature of the benefits and costs that might arise from the application of an innovation in a digital application in learning. This approach may capture a wider range of benefits and costs than originally identified at the start of the project. The expectations might be that an innovation will yield a new educational experience, provide better monitoring of student progress or broaden access to learning.

Evaluation criteria might also be based on a theoretical position. In terms of learning theory, the criteria adopted for evaluating an innovation will depend on the interpretation held by the evaluator. A behaviourist approach might seek a step-by-step approach, with frequent testing leading to reinforcement appropriate to produce the appropriate learning outcome. A constructivist approach might seek for the learner to engage with content and apply their own meaning with an application to their own situation. This theoretical approach may reveal little about the comparative value of an innovation or the accountability of the innovation in relation to the original objectives, and may prove unsuitable for a project commissioner holding a different theoretical position to an evaluator.

SCREENING INNOVATION

Organizations focus resources on innovation in order to discover and implement opportunities for profitable growth, such as through enhanced student recruitment or improved performance, of one form or another. Successful results are more than simply good fortune – they are the fruit of effective innovation pursued systematically, targeted actively and managed effectively. The process typically requires the monitoring of sources of opportunity, increased investments in research and development, a greater tolerance to risk and incentives for innovation, with a greater emphasis on recruiting, retraining and training employees. The process is predicated, though, on an assessment that the benefits of the innovation will outweigh the costs and accompanying risks. These reasons make the process of screening an innovation desirable.

One way of defining the innovation progressively is by means of a typography covering the innovative domain and dimension, which can help resolve specific features of the value proposition of an e-learning service (Table 12.2). The aim of the grid is to clarify the need and dimensions of innovation by a series of qualitative prompts. In this grid the domain and dimension of the innovation are set out in the first two columns. Addressing the element of audience, for example, a novel client-student group might be described who do not currently have access to an e-learning product. The specific needs are refined in the third column from responses to prompt questions, such as: how is the need of the group defined? What is the nature of the gap between what actually happens and what should occur? What specifically is the new idea or technique? What precisely are the new circumstances which the innovation is intended to address?

Each of the five attributes of innovation has relevance to the screening of an educational innovation (Rogers, 1995). The relative advantage of the innovation in terms of the benefits and advantages, compared with the benefits that existing products and services are able to deliver, is specified in the fourth column.

Table 12.2. Typology for screening innovative learning
(James and Roffe, 2000: 12–21)

Innovative domain	Innovative dimension	What is the particular need?	What is the specific relative advantage?
Andragogy/ pedagogy	New learning delivery, techniques.	What specifically is the new means of delivery?	Will it help trainees to remember better?
Audience	Novel client group.	How is the need of the group defined?	Will the product/ service be more accessible?
Content	New knowledge or interpretation.	What gap is the new learning intended to fill?	How, specifically, will the development fill the gap in content?
Organization	New form of work organization.	What improvement is the new form intended to bring?	To what extent will there be an efficiency improvement or more effective service?
Promotion	New means of reaching clients.	What will the new communications channel be?	How will it be promoted in new areas? How much cheaper will it be?
Technology	New hardware or software.	What precisely is the new technique?	Will it enable people to learn more quickly or easily?

Typical questions here are on price: will the product/service be cheaper? Power: will it enable learners to learn more quickly or remember better? Range: will it be applied in a wide range of areas, not already covered? Gap: will the development close the gap in content or clients?

The other attributes, identified in chapter 8, are also relevant: trialability, that can involve taster and trial events in which clients can sample a product for themselves; simplicity, so that it is easy to understand by the client; observability, so that people see it (this historically had the least to commend itself to the education and training area until the advent of multimedia programmes and Website delivery); and compatibility with existing systems, including both psychological and organizational elements. An innovation which fits easily with existing approaches by teachers and learners will be more easily adopted, as will one which fits into an existing schedule or assessment system. All these approaches will meet with less resistance than those requiring the acquisition of new learning, of either techniques or new equipment, by trainers. These attributes may not be equally important for all respondents, but they are common enough that innovation sponsors should keep them in mind.

The level of resources normally restricts the amount of information that can be gathered to make an a priori prognosis of the outcome. With careful analysis and screening, however, an indication of the likely success of an innovation can be determined. This process of classification serves to determine what information is necessary to produce important measurable parameters for the innovation and the appropriate sources of information, for example on market, technology, technique, or organization. Market research is useful for new products, but very difficult for new audiences. Financial analysis forms a crucial element for the viability of the initiative, for it not to exceed the resources available. This part of the assessment process can yield an a-priori view of the innovation that can provide a framework for demonstration to clients, auditors or senior managers.

Categorizing innovation and specifying measurable criteria make the task of evaluation easier. There are other techniques to aid the process. For example, the earlier in the development process that the viability and suitability of the outcomes of the training innovation are determined, then the more cost-effective the evaluation process will be (James and Roffe, 2000: 12–21). Similarly, maintaining focus on the client's requirements and acceptable-performance indicators for the innovation at an early stage will ease the acceptability of feedback later. Sensitive indicators that can be applied during development to show real-time changes will aid formative evaluation. The process of evaluation should assist the innovation to keep focus and avoid distraction.

THE EFFECTIVENESS OF THE INNOVATION

Every learning innovation has costs that are disbursed across the initiative. A categorization into input, process, output and outcome is a good starting point. Inputs define the activities, information, resources and relationships required to undertake the innovation. Determining the inputs is important because it enables the complexity of the tasks, the scale of work, the quality, the managerial direction and any contractual requirements to be gauged. The process determines how the task is done. Appraising the process level can be used to assess the effectiveness and adequacy of procedures, equipment, system and relationships that are applied to conduct the innovation tasks.

The outputs establish what the task produces and an assessment of the outputs enables the volume of work and the relevance and suitability of activities to be evaluated (Brinkerhoff and Gill, 1994). The outcomes for a learning initiative can take many forms. They can, for example, be improved trainee-performance, better transfer of learning, higher-skills assessments, closer compliance to standards or improvement in the satisfaction ratings for customers, trainees and employees. As such, measures on the outcome level can be used to assess the worth of what has been attained in the innovation.

PARTNERSHIP APPROACHES

Collaboration between educational enterprises in order to share relative strengths is a strategy adopted by certain organizations since the very beginning of e-learning. Collaboration is not the opposite of competition (that would be a monopoly), but in principle it brings together partners synergistically to add value to the individual contributions. Combining the strengths of institutions in principle should form the basis for high-quality education, distributed in the most efficient manner with the highest return. The partnership can add value to the individual members through development at lower unit-costs to create the highest-quality education, research and service. It can then compete on quality to select niches and can support programmes with a strong reputation and brand. There are only a few cases of success in the literature, though, perhaps because of barriers due to politics, legal issues, coordination difficulties or a lack of creativity.

Transnational European projects on e-learning are encouraged by the European Commission (*www.europa.eu.int*) to work together and share results. There is simply not enough funding available for every institution to act independently across a broad range of e-learning development in support of workplace learning. This might lead to massive duplication of effort and non-viable provision. The process of evaluation is a contract requirement in EC contracts, but these processes are well-established (Blackley et al., 1997). Key aspects of undertaking such an evaluation are to avoid specifying too many indicators, or ones which are too complex, and to design an evaluation procedure which is achievable and that will produce demonstrable benefits.

Partnerships can arise between regional groupings of universities and colleges who collaborate in order to address mutual needs. They can also include knowledge-economy clusters, in which an educational enterprise is a partner along with private-sector companies and public-sector economic-development authorities. In such a grouping, an educational enterprise can often be the primary source of expertise on evaluation of e-learning. Arrangements vary in the degree of central control, in budgetary planning and reporting, in the design of the right quality offerings and marketing. The core belief in forming such a partnership is that a combination of strengths is available, which indicate that e-learning product can be delivered efficiently. Common issues arise in this process for evaluation, including the extent to which any planned transfer between partners has taken place; the extent to which involvement in the project has led to measured or perceived change for each of its partners, for example, as a result of the transfer of skills or methods; and whether the participation of each partner in practice occurred as anticipated.

The west Wales e-learning partnership, described in chapter 3, is an example of a regional grouping, whose purpose in essence is to develop an e-learning capability in each partner that can support SMEs. Individual content-development groups inside the partnership operate with much autonomy, leading to a diversity of e-learning techniques and approaches. Evaluation of the pedagogic techniques of members used a protocol that focused on the purpose of each pedagogic element to allow its appropriateness to be evaluated (Rogers, 2002). This allowed an assessment of the purposes, which included to impart knowledge, challenge the existing knowledge and experience of the student, allow assessment of how well that knowledge has been internalized, relate knowledge to a realistic scenario that the student can identify, and so on.

Success in partnership working is the same online or off, and is based on three precepts. First, a genuine need must exist that draws the partners together. Next, the collaborators must have access to expertise that can respond to these needs. Finally, the solutions proposed must make financial and economic sense to all members of the partnership. Evaluation of a partnership can involve assessment at the partnership level and at the individual partner level. Actions to build content need clarity at the outset, as regards the roles, responsibilities and outcomes of members, which also helps with workable indicators for formative evaluation. Providers, then, need to be very agile during the early stages of development. Greater resources and expertise are available in a partnership, but this may bring less autonomy and more inertia, so there is a delicate balance to be struck between securing the overall goals of a partnership and the scope for responsiveness to specific client groups.

EVALUATION AND THE VALUE PROPOSITION

Evaluation is a multidimensional and dynamic activity. It can involve specific actions in providing course support to SMEs, where it is closely tied to the ability to meet the learning and performance needs of personnel and where the primary measure is how well this is achieved. There are direct specific delivery aspects, for instance whether the intended level of learning was achieved, whether the course or curriculum can be improved, its content expanded, or its focus sharpened. There are also systematic aspects, which include the effects of a learning innovation, value assurance, dimensions of efficiency and effectiveness of the provision. Valuable information on how to improve the competitive position of a provider can emerge. Executing an improvement in service will then depend on the external and internal relationships of staff, students and all the personnel who support the delivery system.

Endnote

The subject of this book attests to the electronic evolution that faces an educational enterprise today. All over the world decision-makers and practitioners are seeking to integrate technology into education and training in order to transform the way people learn. The issues in understanding how e-learning can best be used are many and varied, but often common and recurring. In the preceding chapters, therefore, I have tried to probe the relationships that affect an educational enterprise, in particular for supplying SMEs, which meet through the media of the technologies for learning and which form the interrelated themes of this book. It is time to draw together the answers to the principal questions.

An enterprise that applies learning technologies to supply clients becomes engaged in e-business in a highly competitive milieu. This is a key premise. Although couched in business-education language, the subsequent issues on achieving a sustainable competitive strategy are familiar to many educational decision-makers. The answers proposed here are that learning, technology and business are convergent disciplines for formulating a sustainable educational service. Client perceptions of intangibles are important, since competing on price alone is a viable strategy for only the very few. For many, however, a sustainable advantage can come from addressing perceived value.

Taking this approach leads to determining the views of the learner in evaluation and in transferring this information into the dynamic development of a programme. A learner perspective becomes another factor in the assumption of quality in formal learning. Authenticity is the term introduced to capture the genuineness of a course, while assuring value becomes a key process for a provider. This logic helps explain the order in which topics are presented: drawing evidence first from a critical group of SMEs, then considering relevant learning, technology and business principles, which are translated into practical ways to improve perceived value through innovation, value assurance and enhancement.

FIRMS AS CUSTOMERS

The reasons for e-learning appear compelling in large firms. Companies approach learning as a support measure around business needs, and digital delivery allows scalability, timeliness, accountability and cost-effectiveness. Certain large firms are well able to design and deliver their own e-learning, while others choose to purchase services, often from several suppliers. The customer's power increases in these cases, because of the increased information and choice consumers have available to them – often, but not exclusively, through the Internet. We know much about the business of supplying the corporate market and how the performance of managers and employees can best be assisted by learning with the aid of technology. Supplying this sector is a very competitive business that draws new as well as established providers. Some will succeed with their systems and sales, others will choose not to enter or withdraw to a less competitive core by providing e-learning as a flexible delivery option to less-challenging student populations.

What then of e-learning in SMEs? There are pointers from the exploration of strategy, technology and learning in chapter 2. Skill and technology gaps exist in SMEs and always will, so that the real challenge for both SME managers and e-learning practitioners is how to lessen these gaps. The attitude of the SME manager is crucial in determining and influencing solutions, including the application of learning technologies. Moving towards workplace learning delivered just-in-time and away from institutionally-driven learning is a very attractive factor for them.

SME managers usually adopt a pragmatic approach to human resource development. Institutions may offer needs analysis, sales, delivery and support for credit-based e-learning, but this presents a new set of interrelated issues for managers, concerning the applications of IT as well as access to the Internet in the SME. Many clearly need help with the technical aspects of their IT applications. The way in for educational enterprises is, then, not in selling e-learning, but in consultancy, performance improvement and advocacy that focuses on the perceived needs in SMEs. Providing e-learning through this route is not a cheap solution for an educational provider.

SMEs also want to save money. They are reluctant to spend resources on training from institutions and perceive e-learning as less expensive, because not releasing staff from the premises for training for extended periods makes it more affordable. Learning materials could in principle be created by SME employees themselves as a result of engagement in business activities, but this option is not as prominent as in large enterprises due to resource constraints. Managers in SMEs will, therefore, need continuing assistance in finding out what is available and how it may be used. More content by e-learning will also need to be oriented for the context of the SME, rather than for a casebook based on larger-firm practices. For the majority of SME employees, their prior experience of education and training is that of face-to-face instruction in a classroom with other participants. When given an option, many employees enjoy attending such sessions, because they are removed from day-to-day pressures and are able to interact with other learners. The social dimension is an important motivation for many learners, so that creating an appropriate social environment can improve the appeal of learning.

E-learning delivery to SMEs is, therefore, not a cheap market to enter and ought to be justified in its own terms, such as in widening access to lifelong learning, contributing to economic development and creating authentic environments for learning. For an educational enterprise to develop provision in this area means that we must confront not only conventional issues of overcoming resistance to change, motivating faculty and encouraging collaboration, but also a range of issues, including business management, competitive strategy and performance improvement. Concentrating on perceived value helps the provider to stay attuned to the needs of clients in small firms, particularly as regards the differences between the notions of cost and value. Delivering e-learning to other market segments may also create economies of scale for the learning support infrastructure.

LEARNING AND TECHNOLOGY

What appears plain is that learning technologies are now an immense driving force for the development of educational processes across a range of markets, influences that mean e-learning is becoming mainstream in the educational service sector. Although much early attention was drawn to the prospects for large virtual universities, agile providers can design and deliver a variety of content to support an eclectic mixture of groups. It is still feasible to become a niche provider in a borderless economy, for reasons presented in chapter 1. Success is not due simply to technology, though, because technology changes. Technical equity is necessary, but the real competition is in authentic content, personalization of learning support, client perception and business effectiveness.

The advent of e-learning technologies offers the potential learner a range of different learning experiences in topic, timing, format and curriculum plan that can match the expectations and requirements of very discriminating adults. But the brute fact of the matter is that we are not there yet. Constant change in technology is certain to continue, but what is less assured is the real impact that such change will make on teaching and learning. The impact of the Internet's ability to enable learning is changing how people learn and what people learn. Learning how to apply the new technology in an optimum way in an instructional setting always lags behind the introduction of the technology itself. The real challenge for practitioners lies then in recognizing and applying technology for justified use in learning.

INNOVATION

A technology-driven approach to innovation does carry risks. Leading technologies are expensive to acquire and such technology changes quickly. There is a chance that students will not be able to support the same technology, or that it might be quickly superseded, or even bypassed. The appropriate role for an educational provider is, therefore, in applying technologies that are in widespread use, rather than persuading people to adopt a certain technology. This represents the early majority of adopters and subsequent groups on the technology-adoption cycle rather than the innovator group.

Innovation has been more strongly associated with the identification of and delivery to new student groups. Innovation as a system competence is different. Even though the management processes of innovation are well understood, much effort is still under way across the world to discover new teaching, learning and support processes for e-delivery. In Europe, for instance, there is a major effort under way by education providers on investigative work that examines teaching and learning processes by digital delivery to all types of audiences, in order to optimize learning transfer with technology (EC, 2002). This is well-intentioned and necessary work, but we know that concepts of how people learn have concerned educators for centuries, and will continue to generate controversy because of the complexities. Like many innovations in their early stages, much of what e-learning has meant to date is mainly re-purposing existing content without re-conceptualizing. Capturing and integrating the human component into an online learning solution is critical, yet difficult. Content ought to be presented in a manner that encourages individuals to read, observe, practise and experience learning in a meaningful and innovative manner. When the same technology is available to everyone, however, it cannot provide a long-term advantage to anyone. This means that innovation as a competence to enhance value ought to be based on a systemic approach to develop, implement and offer, if feasible, a degree of proprietary control, using technology that is in widespread use by the target student-client group.

A PROSPECTUS FOR AN EDUCATIONAL ENTERPRISE

E-learning is the ideal product for the Internet age: weightless, with high perceived-value and a utility that counters most of the disadvantages of conventional distance-education services. For decision-makers in an educational enterprise, the future prospectus will involve achieving a continuing balance in the resources to support e-learning, which is not a cheap delivery option. It means resolving the continuing demands of technologists for capital infrastructure with the requirements of e-learning curriculum review, design and student support. The eventual balance will probably be attained from the desired technology position, the image of the enterprise, the effectiveness of delivery and support for business development. For some organizations at the cutting edge of technology-driven development, high investment in technology will always be necessary. Their customer-base will expect solutions based on latest technologies, because the technology provides their competitive edge. Most providers, however, will need to settle on a level of support that matches the client needs and the technologies that are in widespread use. For them, the underlying principles of competitive strategy are enduring, however, regardless of technology or the pace of change.

Strategy is about the basic values that an enterprise is trying to deliver to clients and about which clients it sets out to serve. The focus has been on people in employment in SMEs. This group cannot return easily to institutions for knowledge updating. For them, in the future, most education will be self-learning, with much of it arising from electronic sources, with outreach or in-house programmes of learning as a supplement. Learning how to access, learn from and update desired network-based knowledge is becoming the crux of factual training, leaving classrooms for interpreting nuances and relationships through institutionally-based learning. The professions are also involved in SMEs. Areas of factual learning that characterize the professions, such as law, engineering, business and medicine, can all be enhanced by electronic programmes; so can areas such as language learning and softer social-skill areas. Educational institutions, therfore, ought to help learners in their capacity to analyse, interrelate and communicate facts that allow individuals to learn formally and informally in their work.

A strategy must have continuity and ought not to be constantly reinvented. Setting out to achieve economies of scale or scope for e-learning raises the questions, which clients does an enterprise set out to serve, and which of their needs does it intend to meet? An educational enterprise can service one or many client groups, such as distance learners for degree programmes, lifelong learners or corporate learners, and much is already known about these groups. Adult learners are extremely heterogeneous, with large variations in age, prior knowledge, cultural and organizational settings and so on. There are very different motivations for study amongst the individuals. As every e-learning project is unique in terms of learning needs, cost constraints and desired results, the best designs may come from a concerted study of the resources and responses where there is the opportunity for rapid experimentation and fewer constraints. Choosing whom to serve and which of their needs to meet means that an enterprise can align its whole value chain behind the proposition that makes it distinctive.

In developing an e-learning prospectus, the system competences of an e-learning provider that span the activities of the value chain can be a major source of competitive advantage. For an educational service-provider, they are an important point of differentiation from the many other Internet-based providers from non-recognized educational bodies. A major organizational challenge, therefore, is to create the right conditions for the various staff involved in e-learning to address these issues in a way that is timely, collective and relevant.

There is no one 'magic' or universal management-tool that can be applied by decision-makers on e-learning to all situations; each has its own strengths and limitations, and must be used in a particular situation in the right way at the correct time. The success factors are the same as for any business: quality, price and services. The tools, processes and systems described here will help, but the practices of sound management, hiring good people and using resources wisely are also required; together, they enhance considerably the ability to compete with e-learning.

Glossary

The field of e-learning has a range of specialist terms and acronyms. This glossary is intended to provide supplementary information about some of the technical terms involved with e-learning and communications processes used earlier.

application service-provider (ASP). This is a special form of Internet service-provider (ISP) that sells access to software.

asynchronous communication. Communication where participants are not connected in real time, so that messages have to be left. Examples are e-mail, bulletin boards and voice-mail.

asynchronous learning (or **asynchronous, collaborative e-learning, ACEL**). A learning event when participants are not online at the same time and cannot communicate without a time-delay.

Asymmetric Digital Subscriber Loop (ADSL). Converts an existing telephone line into a higher bandwidth channel.

audioconferencing. A multi-point telephone conversation involving people in more than two locations.

authoring tools/authoring systems. Authoring tools are software applications for creating course interactive material. Authoring systems help a course designer to assemble all the components of a course, including text, graphics, questions, links and tracking of student performance.

bandwidth. The transmission capacity of a telecommunications link, measured in bits per second. The greater the bandwidth, the greater the volume of information that can be transmitted over the link in a given period of time.

benchmarking. The ongoing systematic process of measuring and comparing the work processes of one organization with those of another, in order to provide reference points for evaluating improvement.

Bluetooth. This is a wireless technology for the personal connectivity market by providing freedom from wired connections, enabling links between mobile computers, mobile phones and portable hand-held devices and connectivity to the Internet. Bluetooth was originally aimed at cable replacement and for a 10–20 metre range. Newer applications through more powerful radio modules can extend to over 100 metres.

bulletin board. An online function dedicated to a narrow range of subjects, used for posting messages, viewing postings or the downloading of information items.

computer-assisted learning (CAL). Learning that is facilitated via a computer.

computer-based training (CBT). Educational material presented on a computer, mainly by a floppy disk or CD-ROM.

computer-mediated communication (CMC). A collective term that refers to all forms of two-way interaction via computers.

computer conference. Computer-facilitated communication among members of a group, where all the group members see all messages.

content. The intellectual property and knowledge to be imparted. It consists of the course outline, text-based knowledge modules for learning and multimedia.

cookies. Small files that a Website places on a visitor's hard disk to identify and track subsequent visits.

courseware. A generic term for any technology-based training (TBT), computer-based training (CBT), multimedia or Internet/Intranet delivering training.

customer-focused e-learning. Web-based learning programmes targeted at current and potential customers.

customer-relationship management (CRM). Methodologies, software and, normally, Internet capabilities that help a company manage customer relationships in an organized way by identifying and categorizing customers.

digital delivery. delivery of course via the World Wide Web, interactive multimedia or any other media where information is carried in a digital form.

Digital Subscriber Line (DSL). A technology for transferring high-bandwidth information over copper telephone lines.

document sharing. Allows multiple users to view and/or edit the same documents in real time.

downloading. A procedure for transferring or retrieving a file from a remote computer and presenting or saving it on a PC.

Dynamic Hypertext Mark-up Language (DHTML). An enhanced version of HTML that allows easier Web-page updating and greater use of multimedia capabilities, such as sound, video and animation.

electronic performance-support system (EPSS). A computer-based system that receives, stores and disseminates organizational information on demand.

e-mail. The application of an electronic network to send and receive messages.

end-to-end solution. A marketing term which implies that a product or service will handle all aspects of e-learning.

enterprise resource planning (ERP). A set of activities, supported by applications software, that helps a company manage core parts of its business, such as product planning, parts purchasing, inventory management, order tracking and customer service.

ethernet. A local area-network system originally developed at Xerox Palo Alto Research Centre and later made standard. Ethernets operate at 10 Mbps over coaxial cable and link computers and servers in a 'daisy-chain' fashion.

extranet. A local area network (LAN) or wide area network (WAN) using TCP/IP, HTML, SMTP and other open Internet-based standards to transport information. An extranet is available only to people inside and particular people external to an organization.

Extensible Mark-up Language (XML). The adaptation of SGML that is expected to replace HTML as the mark-up language for authored text on the Web.

File Transfer Protocol (FTP). A widely-used protocol for transferring files across networks.

full user-mobility. Wireless classification, indicating that a user can access data on the move, such as from a car.

General Packet Radio System (GPRS). A data-transmission technology that provides cost-efficient Internet Protocol (IP) communication between mobile devices and Internet or Intranet service-hosts. GPRS makes connection from a mobile phone quick and fast.

Hand-held Device Mark-up Language (HDML). A programming language, derived from Hypertext Mark-up Language, that allows Internet access from such wireless devices as hand-held personal computers.

hosting (Web hosting). Outsourcing of the technology and commerce parts of a company's Internet-based learning system to an outside organization.

Hypertext Mark-up Language (HTML). The language of the World Wide Web, with the HTML code for a Web-page determining how a page will look, where the images are and which parts of the page consist of hypertext links to other pages.

Hypertext Transfer Protocol (HTTP). A special language used to communicate between machines on the World Wide Web.

hypertext links. The Web addresses embedded in the body of a HTML document.

Integrated Services Digital Network (ISDN). The narrowband version has been standardized over the last thirty years by telecommunication operators seeking to digitize the customer access network.

internal producer. A team or department within an organization engaged in non-training/TBT business, which develops courseware for internal use.

Internet. The Internet is a worldwide network of computer networks interconnected on an open basis using special communication protocols, such as TCP/IP.

Internet-based training (Web-based training or **online training).** The delivery of educational content via a Web-browser over the Internet, an Intranet or an extranet (LAN/WAN). It provides links to learning resources outside the course, for instance, references, e-mail, bulletin boards, etc. It offers the advantages of computer-based training (CBT) while retaining advantages of instructor-led training.

Internet Protocol (IP). The de facto network protocol for the Internet, able to route and transport all the elements of a multimedia service – text, image, video and sound.

Intranet. A local area network (LAN) or wide area network (WAN) using TCP/IP, HTML, SMTP and other Internet-based standards to convey information. An Intranet is owned by an organization, accessible only to people working internally in an organization and protected from external unauthorized access by security measures.

knowledge management system (KMS). Computer software that captures, organizes and stores knowledge in an organization and enables others to use it.

knowledge media. A collective term referring to interactive multimedia and the World Wide Web.

learning platforms. Internal or external sites, often organized around tightly-focused topics, which contain technologies, ranging from chatrooms to groupware, that allow users to submit and retrieve information.

learning portal. A Website that offers learners, enquirers or organizations consolidated access to learning and training resources from multiple sources. Learning portals can be categorized into content portals, internal portals, community and collaboration portals, affiliation portals and embedded technology portals.

learning service-provider (LSP). A specialized type of applications service-provider, offering training-delivery software and learning management on a hosted or rental basis. Four basic categories of LSP exist: (a) full service, hosting a complete solution by a private network; (b) content-specific, licensing content and a level of learning-management services; (c) tool specific LSP, licensing and hosting a system for an organization; (d) a portal host.

microbrowser. A modified Web-browser that allows users to receive data on a handheld wireless device, where getting good data, not graphics, counts most.

Motion Picture Experts Group (MPEG). A family of standards for the digital encoding of moving images. The family extends from MPEG-1 to MPEG-4. MPEG-2, studio-quality television and multiple CD-quality audio channels are currently the most widely used.

multimedia. A programme featuring any combination of text, images (animated, graphics, still, photographic, streaming), sound and colour.

portable wireless data. Classification of networks that access the Internet via laptops or palm-top computers and small wireless modems.

program. A set of instructions for a computer, often called software.

programme. A course of study that may or may not include a computer program.

programming. The process by which a script and supporting assets are converted into self-contained fully operational courseware.

self-paced e-learning (SPEL). Self-paced e-learning is one of the most common learning engagements on the Web, in which the multitude of sites and the hypertext environment containing self-help pages and guides, resources, courses and reference material are searched for a static document or a hyperlink with a relevant answer.

self-directed learning. Activity in which the learner takes the initiative and responsibility for completing the requirements of a course of study.

simulations. Highly interactive applications that allow the learner to role-play or model a business situation or scenario. Simulations allow the learner to practise behaviours and skills in a risk-free and simulated environment.

situated learning. A learning model that contains four mutually influencing factors: (a) characteristics of the learner, (b) learning goals, (c) the nature of the media for learning and (d) available learning skills and strategies.

streaming media. Allows audio, video and other data to be delivered in a continuous flow to the end-user's PC. The technology allows large datafiles to be streamed to end-users on lower bandwidth connections – a key requirement in making synchronous WBT available to users. Competing technologies, led by RealNetworks RealPlayer and Microsoft's Windows Streaming Video, provide the ability to stream synchronous data to multiple users.

synchronous learning (or synchronous, collaborative e-learning, – SCEL). A real-time, instructor-led online learning event, in which all the participants are logged on at the same time and communicate directly with each other. Examples include audio/videoconferencing, Internet telephony, virtual classrooms and two-way live satellite broadcasts of lectures to trainees in a classroom.

technology-based training (TBT). Embraces the delivery of content via the Internet, Intranet/extranet (LAN/WAN), audio/videotape, interactive TV, satellite broadcast and CD-ROM. It includes computer-based training (CBT) and Web-based training (WBT).

teleconferencing. Interactive communication between individuals at two or more sites using telecommunications.

text-based chat. Allows users to share their ideas during a session, or send private messages to the instructor.

Third Generation (3G). Wireless-technology networks that transmit wireless data at up to two megabits per second, making possible the integration of voice, data and video.

Universal Mobile Telecommunications System (UMTS). This is a key member of the global family of third-generation (3G) mobile technologies, and is being applied by operators with 3G licences.

Uniform Resource Locator (URL). Each item on the Internet has a Uniform Resource Locator (URL). A URL comprises specific parts: the type of protocol used to access the resource, the domain name where the file resides, any directories and/or sub-directories and the file name and type. URLs may have some or all these parts. The domain is the computer on which the material is held. Example: http:// (Protocol) (Domain) (Directory) (Sub-Directory)

Videoconferencing. A medium where individuals or groups can meet in real time for video and audio interaction.

voice-over IP (VOIP). This allows voice to operate over the same channels as Internet data, thus enabling one-way or two-way voice interaction among users.

Web-browser. A program that enables viewing of Web-pages, for example Microsoft Explorer.

wireless application protocol (WAP). This is an open, global specification that enables mobile users with wireless devices to access and interact with information and services easily and instantly. Hand-held digital wireless devices, such as mobile phones, pagers, two-way radios, smartphones and communicators, use WAP. WAP is a communications protocol and application environment that can be built on any operating system, including PalmOS, Windows CE and JavaOS. It provides service interoperability, even between different device families.

wireless local area network (LAN). A network that uses radio or infrared rather than cables and lines to connect data devices.

World Wide Web (or the Web). The Web uses HTTP as a protocol to allow a user with a browser to view materials in a wide variety of formats, text, sound, still and video, on computers all around the world.

x-Digital Subscriber Loop (xDSL). (Where x refers to the current technology.) These technologies exploit the existing telecommunications network of copper-pair cable for high-speed data transmission.

References

Adair, J. (1990), *The Challenge of Innovation*, London: Kogan Page.

Aldrich, C. (2000), 'Customer-Focused E-Learning: The Drivers', *Training and Development*, August.

Alexander, W., Higgison, C. and Mogey, N. (1999), *Video in Teaching and Learning: Case Studies*, LDTI and TALiSMAN, Institute for Computer Based Learning, Herriot-Watt University, available at *http://www.ecbl.hw.ac.uk/ltdi/vcstudies*.

Amabile, T. (1996), *Creativity in Context*, Boulder: Westview Press.

Anderson, J., Reder, L. and Simin, H. (1996) 'Situated Learning and Education', *Educational Researcher*, 25, 4.

Angehrn, A. and Nabeth, T. (1997), 'Leveraging Emerging Technologies in Management Education: Research and Experiences', *European Management Journal*, 15, 3.

Ansoff, H. I. and McDonell, E. J. (1987), *Corporate Strategy*, London: Penguin.

Arenicola Designs (2000), *Authoring for CBT*, Guides for Managers, Practitioners and Researchers, DfEE, Sheffield.

Argyris, C. (1982), *Reasoning, Learning and Action*, San Francisco: Jossey-Bass.

—— (1990), *Overcoming Organisational Defences*, New York: Prentice Hall.

—— (1991), 'Teaching Smart People How to Learn', *Harvard Business Review*, May–June.

—— (1993), *Knowledge for Action: A Guide for Overcoming Barriers to Change*, San Francisco: Jossey-Bass.

—— and Schön, D. A. (1978), *Organisational Learning: A Theory of Action Perspective*, Reading: Addison Wesley.

ASTD (2000), *The ASTD Roadmap for E-learning, http://www.astd.org*.

Athanasou, J. A. (1998), 'A Framework for Evaluating the Effectiveness of Technology-assisted Learning', *Industrial and Commercial Training*, 30, 3.

Bacsich, P., Ash, C. and Heginbotham, S. (2001), *The Costs of Networked Learning-Part Two*, A report for the JISC Committee for Awareness, Liaison and Training (JCALT), Sheffield Hallam University, Sheffield.

Baldwin, T. T. and Ford, J. K. (1988), 'Transfer of Training: A Review and Directions for Future Research', *Personnel Psychology*, 41.

Bandura, A. (1986), *Social Foundations of Thought and Action: A Social Cognitive Theory*, Englewood Cliffs: Prentice Hall.

Bang, J. and Dondi, C. (2000), *The Challenge of ICT to University Education: Networking,*

Virtual Mobility and Collaborative Learning, Proceedings of the ODL Networking for Quality Learning, Lisbon.

BAOL and LLTD (2000), *Learning Centres: A Guide Making It Happen, Guides for Managers, Practitioners and Researchers,* Sheffield, DfEE.

Barker, P. (1999), 'Using Intranets to Support Teaching and Learning', *Innovation in Educational Technologies International,* 36, 1.

Barnett, R. (1997), *Towards a Higher Education for a New Century,* Institute of Education, University of London.

Bates, A. (2000), *Managing Technological Change,* San Francisco, CA: Jossey-Bass.

Bates, T. (1995), *Technology, Open Learning and Distance Education,* London: Routledge.

—— (2001), 'The Continuing Evolution of ICT Capacity: The Implications for Education', in Farrell, G. (ed.) *The Changing Faces of Virtual Education,* Commonwealth of Learning, available at *http://www.col.org/virtualed.*

Beamish, N. G. (2000), *E-learning in the Context of the Corporate University,* Report for the Marchmont Project, University of Exeter, available at *http://www.marchmont.ac.uk.*

—— and Armistead, C. C. (2000), *E-Learning in the Context of the Corporate University,* unpublished review, Centre for Organisational Effectiveness, Bournemouth University, Marchmont project, available from *http://www.lifelonglearning.ac.uk.*

Beckhard, R. and Pritchard, W. (1991), *Changing the Essence,* San Francisco, CA: Jossey-Bass.

Beevers, R. (2000), *Good Practice in Marketing Communications,* Sheffield: Ufi.

Bennis, W. and Mische, M. A. (1995), *21st Century Organisation: Reinventing Through Reengineering,* San Diego: Pfeiffer.

Benson, G. (1997), 'A New Look at EPSS', *Training & Development,* January, 51, 1.

Berthon, P., Lane, N., Pitt, L. and Watson, R. T. (1996), 'The World Wide Web as Advertising Medium', *Journal of Advertising Research,* January–February.

—— (1998), 'The World Wide Web as an Industrial Marketing Communication Tool: Models for the Identification and Assessment of Opportunities', *Journal of Marketing Management,* 14.

Birnbaum, R. (2000), *Management Fads in Higher Education: Where They Come From, What They Do, Why They Fail,* San Francisco, CA: Jossey-Bass.

Bjarnason, S., Davies, J., Farrington, D., Fielden, J., Garrett, R., Lund, H., Middlehurst, R., and Schofield, A. (2000a), *The Business of Borderless Education: UK Perspectives,* Vol. 1, report for the CVCP and HEFCE, London.

—— (2000b), *The Business of Borderless Education: UK Perspectives,* Vol. 2: case-studies and annexes, report for the CVCP and HEFCE, London.

Bjarnason, S. and Edwards, K. (2002), *Towards a Global Metacampus,* Proceedings of EDEN Annual Conference, Granada.

Blackley, S., Goddard, M. and Seymour, H. (1997) *Innovative and Transnational Projects,* Leeds: ICOM.

Blair, T. (2002), 'Challenges of the World Summit on Sustainable Development', Mozambique, 1 September 2002, *www.ukun.org.*

Blandin, B. (2000), 'Open and Distance Learning: an Overall Survey at the Beginning of 2000', *Pre-conference Papers: ODL Networking for Quality Learning,* Lisbon.

Block, H. and Dobell, B. (1999), *The e-Bang Theory*, Bank of America, available at *http://www.bofasecurities.com*.

Block, P. (1981), *Flawless Consulting: A Guide to Getting Your Expertise Used*, San Diego, CA: Pfeiffer.

—— (1992), *The Empowered Manager – Positive Political Skills at Work*, San Francisco, CA: Jossey-Bass.

Boden, D. and Molotch, H. L. (1994), 'The Compulsion of Proximity', in Friedland, R. and Boden, D. (eds), *NowHere: Space, Time and Modernity*, London: University of California Press.

Bok, D. (2002), 'Preserving Educational Values', *Continuing Higher Education Review*, 68, Fall.

Bolton, A. (1995), 'A Rose by Any Other Name: TQM in Higher Education', *Quality Assurance in Education*, 3, 2.

Bolton, J. (1971), *Small Firms – Report of the Committee of Inquiry on Small Firms*, Cmnd 4811, London, HMSO.

Booms, B. and Bitner, M. (1981), 'Marketing Strategies and Organisation Structure for Service Firms', in Donelly, J. and George, W. (eds) *Marketing of Services*, New York: American Marketing Association.

Booth, A. L. and Shower, D. J. (1996), *Acquiring Skills: Market Failures, Their Symptoms and Policy Responses*, London: Centre for Economic Policy Research.

Boyd, R. D., Apps, J. W. and Associates (1980), *Redefining the Discipline of Adult Education*, San Francisco, CA: Jossey-Bass.

Brinkerhoff, R. O. (1987), *Achieving Results from Training*, San Francisco: Jossey-Bass.

Brinkerhoff, R. O. and Gill, S. J. (1994), *The Learning Alliance: Systems Thinking in Human Resource Development*, San Francisco, CA: Jossey-Bass.

Britain, S. and Liber, O. (1999), *A Framework for Pedagogical Evaluation of Virtual Learning Environments*, JTAP Report No 41, available at *http://www.jisc.ac.uk*.

Broad, M. L. and Newstrom, J. W. (1992), *Transfer of Training: Action Packed Strategies to Ensure High Payoff from Training Investments*, Reading, MA: Addison Wesley.

Brockett, R. G. and Hiemstra, R. (1991), *Self-direction in Adult Learning*, London: Routledge.

Brookfield, S. D. (1986), *Understanding and Facilitating Adult Learning*, San Francisco, CA: Jossey-Bass.

Brooksbank, D. and Jones-Evans, D. (2002), *Global Entrepreneurship Monitor: 2001 Wales Executive Report*, Cardiff: WDA.

Brown, J. S. (2000), *The Social Life of Information*, Boston, MA: Harvard Business School Press.

—— Collins, A., and Duguid, P. (1988), 'Situated Cognition and the Culture of Learning', *Educational Researcher*, 18, 1.

Brown, S. (2001), 'Campus re-engineering', in Lockwood, F. and Golley, A. (eds), *Innovation in Open & Distance Learning*, London: Kogan Page.

Brown, S. (ed.) (1997), *Open and Distance Learning: Case Studies from Industry and Education*, London: Kogan Page.

Bruner, J. S. (1961), *The Process of Education*, Cambridge: MA, Harvard University Press.

—— (1966), *Towards a Theory of Instruction*, Cambridge: MA: Harvard University Press.

—— (1971), *The Relevance of Education*, New York: Norton.

—— (1985), 'Models of the learner', *Educational Researcher*, 14.

Burns, T. and Stalker, G. M. (1994), *The Management of Innovation*, Tavistock, 1961, 3rd edn, Oxford: Oxford University Press.

Cafarella, R. and Olsen, S. (1993), 'Psychosocial Development of Women', *Adult Education Quarterly*, 43, 3.

Calder, J., McCollum, A., Morgan, A. and Thorpe, M. (1995), *Learning Effectiveness of Open and Flexible Learning in Vocational Education*, Sheffield: Department for Education and Employment.

Campion, M. and Renner, W. (1992), 'The Supposed Demise of Fordism – Implications for Distance Education', *Distance Education*, 13, 1.

Candy, P. C. (1991), *Self Direction for Lifelong Learning*, San Francisco, CA: Jossey-Bass.

Carr, R. (1990), 'Open Learning: An Imprecise Term', *ICDE Bulletin*, Vol. 22.

Carroll, D. (2002), 'Releasing Trapped Thinking in Colleges. Part 2: Managing Innovation and Building Innovation into Ordinary Work', *Quality Assurance in Education*, 10, 1.

Caruana, S. (2002), 'A Study of Skills in HE for Online Learning', *Proceedings of EDEN Annual Conference*, Granada.

Caudron, S. (1999), 'Free Agent Learner', *Training & Development*, 52, 8.

Cedefop (2001), 'E-learning and Training in Europe', Cedefop series 26, Luxembourg, available from *http://www.trainingvillage.gr*.

Cellerier, G. (1987) 'Structures and Functions', in Inhelder, B., de Caprona, D. and Cornu-Wells, A. (eds), *Piaget Today*, London: Lawrence Erlbaum.

Chaffey, D., Mayer, R., Johnston, K. and Ellis-Chadwick, F. (2000), *Internet Marketing*, Harlow: Prentice Hall.

Chambers, J. (2001), 'E-learning Takes Stage as Next Killer APP', available at *http://www.infoworld.com/articles*.

CHEA (2001), *Glossary of Key Terms in Quality Assurance and Accreditation*, available at: *http:www/chea.org/international_glossary01.htm*.

Checkland, P. B. (1981), *Systems Thinking, Systems Practice*, Chichester: John Wiley.

de Chernatony, L. and McDonald, M. (1992), *Creating Powerful Brands*, Oxford: Butterworth-Heinemann.

Christiensen, C. M. (1997), *The Innovator's Dilemma*, Boston, MA: Harvard Business School.

Chute, A., Thomson, M., and Hancock, B. (1998), *The McGraw-Hill Handbook of Distance Learning*, London: McGraw-Hill.

CIPD (1998), *The IPD Guide on Training Technology*, London: Chartered Institute of Personnel Development.

Clark, K. and Wheelwright, S. (1992), *Revolutionising Product Development*, New York: Free Press.

Click2learn.com (2000), *The Asymetrix Guide to Interactive Online Learning*, available at *http://www.asymetrix.com*.

Close, R. C., Humphreys, R. and Ruttenbur, B. W. (2000), *E-learning & Knowledge Technology*, SunTrust Equitable Securities, available at *http://www.suntrust.com*.

Coleman, M. E. (1992), 'Developing Skills and Enhancing Professional Competence', in Stolovitch, H. D. and Keeps, E. J. (eds) *Handbook of Human Performance Technology*, San Francisco, CA: Jossey-Bass.

Collis, B. (1996), *Tele-learning in a Digital World*, London: Thomson Computer Press.

—— (1999), 'Telematics Supported Education for Traditional Universities in Europe', *Performance Improvement Quarterly*, 12, 2.

—— and Moonen, J. (2001), *Flexible Learning in a Digital World*, London: Kogan Page.

Collis, D. (2001), 'When Industries Change: The Future of Higher Education', *Continuing Higher Education Review*, Vol. 65.

Conley, L. (1999), 'Fordstar: 1,000,000 Students Later', Proceedings of ASTD 99 International Conference, Alexandria, Virginia, available at *http://www.astd.org*.

Cooke, P. (2002), *Knowledge Economies*, London: Routledge.

Coomey, M. and Stephenson, J. (2001), 'Online Learning: It is all about Dialogue, Involvement, Support and Control – According to Research', in Stephenson, J. (ed.), *Teaching & Learning Online*, London: Kogan Page.

Cooper, A. (2002), *Barriers, Borders and Brands*, Observatory on Borderless Higher Education, May, available at *www.obhe.ac.uk*.

Cooper, R. G. (1992), 'The NewProd System: The Industry Experience', *Journal of Product Innovation Management*, 9.

—— and Kleinschmidt, E. (1987), 'New Products: What Separates Winners from Losers?', *Journal of Product Innovation Management*, 4.

Cory-Wright, J. and Keith, A. (2000), *Project Management Issues in Courseware Development*, Guides for Managers, Practitioners and Researchers, Sheffield: DfEE.

Cunningham, S., Tapsall, S., Ryan, Y., Stedman, L., Bagdon, K. and Flew, T. (1998), *New Media and Borderless Education: A Review of the Convergence between Global Media Networks and Higher Education Provision*, Canberra: Department of Employment, Education, Training and Youth Affairs, Commonwealth of Australia.

—— (2000), *The Business of Borderless Education*, Canberra: Department of Employment, Education, Training and Youth Affairs, Commonwealth of Australia.

Curran, J., Blackburn, R., Kitching, J. and North, J. (1997), *Establishing Small Firms: Training Practices, Needs, Difficulties and Use of Industry Training Organisations*, London: DfEE.

Daniel, J. (1996), *Mega-universities and Knowledge Media: Technology Strategies for Higher Education*, London, Kogan Page.

Davenport, T. H. and Prusak, L. (1998), *Working Knowledge: How Organizations Manage What They Know*, Boston, MA: Harvard Business School Press.

Davies, R., Alexander, L. and Yelon, S. (1974), *Learning System Design*, New York: McGraw Hill.

Davis, F. D. (1989), 'Perceived Usefulness. Perceived Ease of Use, and User Acceptance on Information Technology', *MCS Quarterly*, 13, 3.

Davydov, V. (1995), 'The Influence of L. S. Vygotsky on Education Theory, Research and Practice', *Educational Researcher*, 24.

Dearing, R. (1997), *Higher Education in the Learning Society*, Report of the National Committee of Inquiry into Higher Education, London: HMSO.

Deighton, J. (1996), 'The Future of Interactive Marketing', *Harvard Business Review*, November–December.

Deming, W. E. (1982), *Out of the Crisis*, Cambridge: Cambridge University Press.

Dewey, J. (1938), *Experience and Education*, New York: Macmillan.

DfEE (1997), *Training Provision and the Development of Small and Medium Sized Enterprises*, London: DfEE.

―― (1999), *Skills for the Information Age – Second Report of the Information Technology, Communications and Electronic Skills Strategy Group*, Skills Task Force, London: HMSO.

―― (2000), *Guides for Managers, Practitioners and Researchers*, Lifelong Learning and Technologies Division, Sheffield: DfEE.

Dixon, N. (1992), 'Organisational Learning: A Review of the Literature with Implications for HRD', *Human Resource Development Quarterly*, 13, 1.

Dondi, C. (2000), *SUSTAIN*, Presentation at the 1st EDEN Research Workshop on Research and Innovation in Open and Distance Learning, Prague.

Doudikis, G. I., Lybereas, P. and Galliers, R. (1996), 'Information Systems Planning in Small Businesses: A Stage of Growth Analysis', *Journal of Systems Software*, 33.

Douglas, S. and Wind, Y. (1987), 'The Myth of Globalisation', *Columbia Journal of World Business*, Winter.

Dove, R. (1999), 'Knowledge Management, Response Ability, and the Agile Enterprise', *Journal of Knowledge Management*, 3, 1.

Draper, S. W. (1998), 'Niche-based Success in CAL', *Computers and Education*, 30, 1/2.

Driver, R., Asoko, H., Leach J., Mortimer, E. and Scott, P. (1994), 'Constructing Scientific Knowledge in the Classroom', *Educational Researcher*, 23.

Drucker, P. F. (1988), *The Coming of the New Organization*, Harvard Business Review, January–February.

―― (1992), *Managing for the Future*, Oxford: Butterworth-Heinemann.

―― (1994), *Innovation and Entrepreneurship*, Oxford: Butterworth-Heinemann.

DTI (2000), *Closing the Digital Divide: Information and Communication Technologies in Deprived Areas*, PAT 15 report, London, available at *http://www.pat15.org.uk*.

Duffy, T. M. and Jonassen, D. H. (1992), *Constructivism and the Technology of Instruction: A Conversation*, Hillsdale, NJ: Lawrence Erlbaum.

Duggleby, J. (2000), *How to be an Online Tutor*, London: Gower.

Dunn, D. and Thomas, C. (1990), 'High Tech Organizes for the Future', *Journal of Personal Selling & Sales Management*, 10, Spring.

―― Hulak, J. and White, D. S. (1999) 'Segmenting High-tech Markets: A Value-added Taxonomy', *Marketing Intelligence & Planning*, 17, 4.

Durman, P. (2003), 'Broadband Shines amid the Telecoms Gloom', *Sunday Times Business*, 16 February.

Eaton, J. S. (2001), *Distance Learning: Academic and Political Challenges for Higher Education Accreditation*, Council for Higher Education Accreditation Monograph Series, Number 1, Washington, DC.

EC (1996), *Green Paper on Innovation*, Bulletin of the European Union, Supplement 5/95, Luxembourg, available at: *http://europa.eu.int/off/green/index-eu.htm*.

—— (1997), *Green Paper on the Convergence of the Telecommunications, Media and Information Technology Sectors*, Brussels, available from *http://www.europa.eu.int/information_society*.

—— (2000), *The European Observatory for SME*, Sixth Report, Executive Summary, available at *www.eim.nl/docum/observat.htm*.

—— (2001), *Making a European Area of Lifelong Learning a Reality*, available at *http://europa.eu.int/comm/education/life*.

—— (2002), *E-learning Programme*, available at: *http://europa.eu.int/comm/education/elearning*.

—— (2003), *Commission Recommendation 6 May 2003 Concerning the Description of SMEs*, available at *http://europa.eu/int*.

ECOTEC (2001a), *ADAPT Services for Small and Medium Sized Enterprises*, thematic work briefing paper, Birmingham, National Support Agency for ADAPT.

—— (2001b), *Engaging SMEs: Innovative Approaches to Improving Support for Small and Medium Sized Enterprises*, Birmingham: ADAPT Support Unit.

Edpath (2002), 'How's your Course Management System Doing?', *Educational Pathways*, 1, 5.

Eglin, R. (2003), 'E-learning: B&Q Staff Do it Themselves', *Sunday Times Appointments*, 9 February.

Eisenstadt, M. (1995), 'Overt Strategy for Global Learning', *Times Higher Educational Supplement*, multimedia section, 7 April.

Employment Department (1991), *A Review of the Cost Benefits of Computer-Based Training*, National Computing Centre, Sheffield.

Engel, C. E. (1991), 'Not Just a Method But a Way of Learning', in Boud, D. and Feletti, G. (eds), *The Challenge of Problem Based Learning*, London: Kogan Page.

ENSR (1997), *The European Observatory for SMEs*, Zoetermeer, Netherlands: EIM.

Epic Group (2000), *Taking Training On Line*, Guides for Managers, Practitioners and Researchers, Sheffield: DfEE.

Eraut, M. (1999), *Learning in the Workplace*, ESRC Learning Society Programme.

European Observatory for SMEs (2000), *Sixth Report*, Executive Summary available at: *www.eim.nl/docum/observat.htm*.

Eriksen, S. D. (1995), 'TQM and the Transformation from the Elite to a Mass System of Higher Education', *Quality Assurance in Education*, 3, 1.

Evans, T. and Nation, D. (1993), *Reforming Open and Distance Education*, London: Kogan Page.

Evans, T. D. (1994), *Understanding Learners in Open and Distance Education*, London: Kogan Page.

Farrell, G. (ed.) (2001), *The Changing Faces of Virtual Education*, Commonwealth of Learning, available at *http://www.col.org/virtualed*.

Faulkner, D. and Bowman, C. (1995), *The Essence of Competitive Strategy*, London: Prentice Hall.

Freire, P. (1972), *Pedagogy of the Oppressed*, London: Penguin.

French, D. (1999), 'Preparing for Internet-based Learning', in French, D., Hale, C., Johnson, C. and Farr, G. (eds.), *Internet Based Learning: An Introduction and Framework for Higher Education and Business*, London: Kogan Page.

Fryer, B. (1997), 'Are You Caught in the Web?', *Inside Technology Training*, September.

Fullan, M. (1993), *Change Forces: Probing the Depths of Educational Reform*, London: The Falmer Press.

Fulmer, R. M. and Gibbs, P. A. (1998), 'Lifelong Learning at the Corporate University', *Career Development International*, 3, 5.

Gage, N. L. (1972), *Teaching Effectiveness and Teacher Education*, Palo Alto, CA: Pacific Books.

Gagné, R. M. (1965), *The Conditions of Learning*, New York: Holt, Rinehart & Winston, p. v.

—— (1985), *The Conditions of Learning*, 4th edn., New York: Holt, Rinehart & Winston.

—— (1987), *Instructional Technology Foundations*, Hillsdale, NJ: Lawrence Erlbaum.

—— Briggs L. J. and Wager, W. W. (1992), *Principles of Instructional Design*, New York: Holt, Rinehart & Winston.

Garavan, T., Morley, M., Gunningle, P. and McGuire, D. (2002), 'Human Resource Development and Workplace Learning: Emerging Theoretical Perspectives and Organisational Practices', *Journal of European Industrial Training*, 2/3/4.

Garrick, J. (1998), *Informal Learning in the Workplace*, London: Routledge.

Garvin, D. A. (1993), 'Building a Learning Organization', *Harvard Business Review*, July/August.

Ghoshal, S. and Bartlett, C. (1998), *The Individualised Corporation*, London: Heinemann.

Gibb, A. (1997), 'Small Firms' Training and Competitiveness', *International Small Business Journal*, 15, 3.

Geis, G. L. and Smith, M. E. (1992), 'The Function of Evaluation', in Stolovitch, H. D. and Keeps, E. J. (eds), *Handbook of Performance Technology*, San Francisco, CA: Jossey Bass.

Gick, M. and Hollyoak, K. J. (1987), 'The Cognitive Basis of Knowledge Transfer', in Cornier, S. M. and Hagman, J. D. (eds), *Transfer of Learning: Contemporary Research and Applications*, San Diego: Academic Press.

Gilbert, T. F. (1978), *Human Competence: Engineering Worthy Performance*, New York: McGraw-Hill.

Godfrey, M. (ed.) (1997), *Skill Development for International Competitiveness*, London: Croom Helm.

Goodyear, P. (1998), 'New Technology in Higher Education: Understanding the Innovation Process', keynote paper for BITE, *Integrating Information and Communications Technology in HE*, Maastricht.

—— and Steeples, C. (2000), *The Role of the Tutor in Corporate CBT/Interactive Multimedia*, Guides for Managers, Practitioners and Researchers, Sheffield: DfEE.

Gray, C. (1993), 'Stages of Growth and Entrepreneurial Career Motivation', in Crittenden, F., Robertson, M. and Watkins, D. (eds) *Small Firms: Recession and Recovery*, ISBA/Paul London: Chapman.

—— (1998), *Enterprise and Culture*, London: Routledge.

—— and Lawless, N. (2000), *Innovations in the Distance Development of SME*

Management Skills, Open University Business School, available from *http://www1.nks.no/eurodl/shoen/Gray.ht.*

Grow, G. O. (1991), 'Teaching Learners to be Self-directed', *Adult Education Quarterly*, 41.

Hale, C. and French, D. (1999), 'Web-related Assessment and Evaluation', in French, D., Hale, C., Johnson C. and Farr, G. (eds.) (1999), *Internet Based Learning*, London, Kogan Page.

Hale, J. (1998), *The Performance Consultant's Fieldbook*, San Francisco, CA: Pfeiffer.

Hall, B. (1997), *The Web-Based Training Cookbook*, Chichester: John Wiley.

Hall, B. and LeCavalier J. (2000), 'The Case for Level 3', *Learning Circuits*, available at: *http://www.learningcircuits.org/.*

Hamel, G. and Heene, A. (eds) (1994), *Competence-Based Competition*, Chichester: John Wiley.

Hamel, G. and Prahalad, C. K. (1989), 'Strategic Intent', *Harvard Business Review*, May–June.

—— (1990), 'The Core Competence of the Corporation', *Harvard Business Review*, 68, 3, May–June.

Hammond, R. and Terence, K. (1998), 'Implementing a Computer Mediated New Learning Environment', *Proceedings of the 1998 EDEN Annual Conference*, CD-ROM.

Harris, D. (1999), 'Creating a Complete Learning Environment', in French, D., Hale, C., Johnson, C. and Farr, G. (eds), *Internet Based Learning*, Virginia: Stylus.

Harris, J. and Shepherd, C. (2000), *Taking Training On Line*, Epic Group, Guides for Managers, Practitioners and Researchers, Sheffield: DfEE.

Harris, P. (2002), 'E-learning: A Consolidation Update', *Training & Development*, April.

Harte, L., Kellog, S., Dreher, R. and Schaffnit, T. (2000), *The Comprehensive Guide to Wireless Technologies*, Fuquay-Varina, NC: APDG Publishing.

Harvey, J. (1998), *Evaluation Cookbook*, Edinburgh: Learning Technology Dissemination Initiative.

Harvey, L. and Green, D. (1993), 'Defining Quality', *Assessment and Evaluation in Higher Education*, 18, 1.

Hay, D., Butt, F. and Kirby, D. (2002), 'Academics as Entrepreneurs in a UK University', in Williams, G. (ed.) *The Enterprising University: Reform, Excellence and Quality*, Buckingham: SRHE and Open University Press.

Hayes, E. (1989), 'Insights from Women's Experiences of Teaching and Learning', in Hayes, E. (ed.) *Effective Teaching Styles: New Directions for Adult and Continuing Education*, San Francisco, CA: Jossey-Bass.

Hill, R. and Stewart, J. (2000), 'Human Resource Development in Small Organisations', *Journal of European Industrial Training*, 24/2/3/4.

Hoey, R. (ed.) (1994), *Designing for Learning: Effectiveness with Efficiency*, London: Kogan Page.

Hoffman, D. L. and Novak, T. P. (1997) 'A New Marketing Paradigm for Electronic Commerce', *The Information Society*, 13, January–March.

Hoffman, K., Paerjo, M. and Bessant, J. (1998), 'Small Firms, R & D, Technology and Innovation in the UK: A Literature Review', *Technovation*, 18.

Holmberg, B. (1989), *Theory and Practice of Distance Education*, London: Routledge.

Holmes, G. and McElwee, G. (1996), 'Total Quality Management in Higher Education: How to Approach Human Resource Management', *The TQM Magazine*, 7, 6.

Honey, P. and Mumford, A. (1982), *The Manual of Learning Styles*, Maidenhead: Peter Honey.

Huber, R. L. (1993), 'Memory is not only Storage', in Flannery, D. D. (ed.), *Applying Cognitive Learning Theory to Adult Learning*, San Francisco, CA: Jossey-Bass.

Hughes, P. (1998), *Appraisal in UK Higher Education*, Sheffield: UCoSDA.

Hunt, M. and Clarke A. (1997), *A Guide to Cost Effectiveness of TBT*, Sheffield: DfEE.

IBSTPI (2001) *International Board of Standards for Training Performance and Instruction*, available at *http://www.ibstpi.org/index.html*.

Idol, L., Jones, B. F. and Mayer, R. E. (1991), 'Classroom Instruction: The Teaching of Thinking', in Idol, L. and Jones, B. F. (eds), *Educational Values and Cognitive Instruction: Implications for Reform*, Hillsdale, NJ: Lawrence Erlbaum.

IITT (Institute of IT Training) (1998), *Technology Based Training*, Accreditation Programme and Codes of Practice for TBT Providers, Standards for TBT Learning Materials, available at *http:www.iilt.org.uk*.

Imel, S. (1991), *Collaborative Learning in Adult Education*, ERIC, available at *www.ericfactility.net*.

Inglis, A. (2001), 'Selecting an Integrated Electronic Learning Environment', in Lockwood, F. and Golley, A. (eds), *Innovation in Open & Distance Learning*, London: Kogan Page.

—— Ling, P. and Joosten, V. (2002), *Delivering Digitally: Managing the Transition to the Knowledge Media*, London: Kogan Page.

James, C. (2000), *A Study and Analysis of Management Training Techniques for the Heads of SMEs, Particularly using the Information and Communication Technologies*, Leeds: report for DG Enterprise.

—— and Roffe, I. M. (2000), 'The Evaluation of Goal and Goal-Free Training Innovation', *Journal of European Industrial Training*, 24, 1.

Johansen, R., Sibbert, D., Benson, S., Martin, A., Mittman, R. and Saffo, R. (1991), *Leading Business Teams: How Teams Can Use Technology and Group Process Tools to Enhance Performance*, Reading, MA: Addison-Wesley.

Johnson, D. and Johnson R. (1983), *Learning Together and Alone*, New Jersey: Prentice Hall.

Jones-Evans, D. (2001), *Creating an Entrepreneurial Wales*, Cardiff: IWA.

Juran, J. M. (1962), *Quality Control Handbook*, Maidenhead: McGraw Hill.

Kao, J. (1996), *JAMMING: The Art and Discipline of Business Creativity*, London: HarperCollins Business.

Kanter, R. M. (1983), *The Change Masters: Innovation and Entrepreneurship in the American Corporation*, New York: Simon & Schuster.

—— (2001), 'The Ten Deadly Mistakes of Wanna-Dots', *Harvard Business Review*, January.

Kay, J. (1993), *Foundations of Corporate Success*, Oxford: Oxford University Press.

Keegan, D. (1993), 'A Typology of Distance Teaching Systems', in Harry, K., John, M. and

Keegan, D. (eds), *Distance Education: International Perspectives*, London: Routledge.

Kerry, B. (2000), *The Power of the Internet for Learning: Moving from Promise to Practice*, Report of the Web-based Education Commission, US Department of Education, available at *http://www.webcommission.org*.

Kerzner, H. (1992) *Project Management – A Systems Approach to Planning, Scheduling and Controlling*, New York: Van Nostrand Reinhold.

Kiley, J., Beamish, N., Armfield, G. and Armistead, C. (2001), *Learning in SMEs: Flexible Learning to Meet Flexible Training Needs*, Bournemouth University, Marchmont project, available from *http://www.lifelonglearning.ac.uk*.

King, B. (2001), 'Making a Virtue of Necessity – A Low-cost, Comprehensive, Online Teaching and Learning Environment', in Lockwood, F. and Golley, A. (eds), *Innovation in Open & Distance Learning*, London: Kogan Page.

Kirkpatrick, D. L. (1994), *Evaluating Training Programs: The Four Levels*, San Francisco, CA: Berrett Koehler.

Knight, J. (2002), *Trade in Higher Education Services: The Implications of GATS*, Observatory on Borderless Higher Education, March, available at *www.obhe.ac.uk*.

Knowles, M. S. (1970), *The Modern Practice of Adult Education: Andragogy Versus Pedagogy*, New York: Association Press.

—— (1973), *The Adult Learner*, Houston, TX: Gulf.

—— (1975), *Self-directed Learning*, New York: Association Press.

—— (1980), *The Modern Practice of Adult Education: From Pedagogy to Andragogy*, Englewood Cliffs: Cambridge.

—— (1990), *The Adult Learner: A Neglected Species*, Houston, TX: Gulf Publishing Co.

Kolb, D. (1976), *The Learning Style Inventory*, Boston: McBer.

—— (1984), *Experiential Learning: Experience as the Source of Learning and Development*, Englewood Cliffs: Prentice Hall.

—— Rubin, I. and McIntyre, J. (1979), *Organizational Psychology, A Book of Readings*, Englewood Cliffs: Prentice Hall.

Kotter, J. P. (1995), 'Leading Change: Why Transformation Efforts Fail', *Harvard Business Review*, March–April.

—— (1996), *Leading Change*, Boston, MA: Harvard Business Press.

Lane, A. D. (ed.) (1994), *Issues in People Management No. 8: People Management in SMEs*, London: IPD.

Lange, T., Ottens, M. and Taylor, A. (2000), 'SMEs and Barriers to Skills Development: A Scottish Perspective', *Journal of European Industrial Training*, 24, 1.

Latchem, C., Williamson, J. and Henderson-Lancett, L. (eds) (1993), *Interactive Multimedia: Practice and Promise*, London: Kogan Page.

Laurillard, D. (1993), *Rethinking University Teaching: A Framework for the Effective Use of Educational Technology*, London: Routledge.

Lentell, H and Murphy, D. (1992), 'Neats and Scruffies: Approaches to Quality Learning in Open Learning and Distance Education', in Tait, A. (ed.), *Quality Assurance in Open and Distance Learning: European and International Perspectives*, Buckingham: The Open University Press.

Leonard-Barton, D. A. (1995), *Wellsprings of Knowledge: Building and Sustaining the Sources of Innovation*, Boston, MA: Harvard Business Press.

—— Bowen, K., Clark, K., Holloway, C. and Wheelwright, S. (1994), 'How to Integrate Work and Deepen Expertise', *Harvard Business Review*, September–October.

Levitt, T. (1983), 'The Globalisation of Markets', *Harvard Business Review*, May–June.

Lewis, N. J. and Orton, P. (2000), 'The Five Attributes of Innovative E-Learning', *Training & Development*, June.

Lewis, R. (1986), 'What is Open Learning?', *Open Learning*, 1, 2.

—— (1987), 'Open Learning in Industry', in Thorpe, M. and Gudgeon, D. (eds), *Open Learning for Adults*, Harlow: Longman.

Lockwood, F. and Gooley, A. (2001), *Innovations in Open & Distance Learning: Successful Development of Online and Web-Based Learning*, London: Kogan Page.

Low, J. and Kalafut, P. C. (2002), *Invisible Advantage: How Intangibles are Driving Business Performance*, Cambridge, MA: Perseus.

McCarthy, J. (1960), *Basic Marketing: A Managerial Approach*, Homewood, IL: Irwin.

McCollum, A. and Calder, J. (1995), *Learning Effectiveness of Open and Flexible Learning in Vocational Education: A Literature Review and Annotated Bibliography*, No. 57, Sheffield: DfEE.

McCormack, C. and Jones, D. (1998), *Building a Web-Based Education System*, Chichester: John Wiley.

McCrea, F., Gay, R. K. and Bacon, R. (2000), *Riding the Big Waves*, Thomas Weisel Partners, available at *http://www.tweisel.com*.

Macpherson, A. (1997), 'The Contribution of External Inputs to the Product Development Efforts of Small Manufacturing Firms', *R&D Management*, 27, 2.

Mager, R. F. (1975), *Preparing Instructional Objectives*, 2nd edn, Belmont: Fearon.

—— and Pipe, O. (1970), *Analysing Performance Problems*, Belmont: Fearon.

Majaro, S. (1988), *The Creative Gap: Managing Ideas for Profit*, London: Longman.

Mantyla K., and Gividen, J. R. (1999), *Distance Learning: A Step by Step Guide for Trainers*, Alexandria, VA: ASTD.

Manville, B. (2002), *Learning Management Systems and the Corporate World*, UCEA Annual Conference, Toronto, April.

Marchmont Observatory (1999), *Understanding SME Learning: The Challenges for UfI*, Exeter University, available from *http://www.lifelonglearning.ac.uk*.

—— (2000), *Marketing Analysis and Marketing Learning*, Exeter University, available from *http://www.lifelonglearning.ac.uk*.

Maslow, A. (1968), *Towards a Psychology of Being*, New York: Van Nostrand.

Mason, R. (1994), *Using Communications Media in Open and Flexible Learning*, London: Kogan Page.

—— (1998a), *Globalising Education: Trends and Applications*, Routledge, London.

—— (1998b), 'Models of Online Courses', *ALN Magazine*, 2, 2, available at *http://www.aln.org/alnweb/magazine/alnpaga.htm*.

Matkin, G. (2001), 'Top Ten Lessons from Dot.coms', in Book, P. A. and Koble, M. A. (eds) 'The Spirit of Enterprise', *Continuing Higher Education Review*, 65.

Megginson D., Joy-Matthews, J. and Banfield, P. (1993), *Human Resource Development*, London: AMED.

Meister, J. (1998), *Corporate Universities: Lessons in Building a World-class Workforce*, New York: McGraw Hill.

Meldrum, M. and de Berranger, P. (1999), 'Can Higher Education Match the Information System Learning Needs of SMEs?', *Journal of European Industrial Training*, 23, 8.

Messick, S. (1984), 'The Nature of Cognitive Styles: Problems and Promises in Educational Practice', *Educational Psychologist*, 19.

Metcalf, H., Walling, A. and Fogarty, M. (1994), *Individual Commitment to Learning Employers' Attitudes*, Policy Studies Institute, Employment Department, Research Series No. 40.

Millar, G. A. (1956), 'The Magical Number Seven, Plus or Minus Two: Some Limits on our Capacity for Processing Information', *Psychological Review*, 63, 81–97.

—— Galanter, E. and Pribram, K. H. (1960), *Plans and the Structure of Behaviour*, New York: Holt, Rinehart and Winston.

Milligan, C. (1999), *Delivering Staff and Professional Development using Virtual Learning Environments*, JISC Report No. 44, JISC Technology Applications Programme, Manchester.

Mintzberg, H. (1994), *The Rise and Fall of Strategic Planning*, New York: Free Press.

Moe, M. and Blodget, H. (2000), *The Knowledge Web, Part 4: Corporate Learning – Feeding Hungry Minds*, available at *http://www.ml.com*.

Moll, L. C. (ed.) (1990), *Vygotsky and Education*, Cambridge: Cambridge University Press.

Moore, G. A. (1991), *Crossing the Chasm*, London: Harper Business.

—— (1995), *Inside the Tornado*, London: Harper Business.

Moore, M. (1973), 'Toward a Theory of Independent Learning and Teaching', *Journal of Higher Education*, 44, 12.

—— (1977), 'A Model of Independent Study', *Epistolodidaktika*, 1.

—— (1993), 'Theory of Transactional Distance', in Keegan, D. (ed.), *Theoretical Principles of Distance Education*, London: Routledge.

—— (1995), 'American Distance Education: A Short Literature Review', in Lockwood, F. (ed.), *Open and Distance Learning Today*, London: Routledge.

Morgan, G. (1991), 'Emerging Waves and Challenges: The Need for New Competences and Mindsets' in Henry, J. (ed.), *Creative Management*, London: Sage Publications.

—— (1993) *Imaginization*, London: Sage Publications.

—— (2001), 'Thirteen must ask Questions about E-learning Products and Services', *The Learning Organisation*, 8, 5.

Morin, D. B. (2000), 'The E List', *Training and Development*, November.

Nayak, R. P. and Ketteringham, J. M. (1987), *Breakthroughs! How Leadership & Drive Created Commercial Innovation that Sweep the World*, London: Mercury Books.

NCIHE (1997), *Higher Education in the Learning Society*, Norwich: HMSO.

Newby, H. (2002), *Towards a Strategy for HE*, Bristol, available from *http://www.hefce.ac.uk*.

Newidiem (2002), *The New Economy of Wales: An analysis of Digital Media, Information Technology and Software Sector Activities*, report for the Wales Information Society.

Newman, F. and Coutourier, L. (2001), *The New Competitive Arena: Market Forces Invade the Academy*, The Futures Project, Brown University, available at *http://www.futuresproject.org*.

Niemi, H. (2002), 'The IQ Form Tool', *Proceedings of EDEN Annual Conference*, Granada.

Nohria, N., Joyce, W. and Robertson, B. (2003), 'What Really Works', *Harvard Business Review*, July.

Nonaka, I. and Tekeuchi, H. (1995), *The Knowledge Creating Company*, Oxford: Oxford University Press.

Ohmae, K. (1987), *The Mind of the Strategist*, London: Penguin.

Oliver, R. (1998), 'Training Teachers for Distance Education Programs using Authentic and Meaningful Contexts', *International Journal of Educational Telecommunications*, 4, 2/3.

Otala, M. (1995), 'The Learning Organization: Theory into Practice', *Industry & Higher Education*, 9.

PERA (1991), *Total Quality Management*, London: Chapman & Hall.

Peters, O. (1993), 'Understanding Distance Education', in Harry, K., John, M. and Keegan, D. (eds), *Distance Education; New Perspective*, London: Routledge.

—— (1998), *Learning and Teaching in Distance Education*, London: Kogan Page.

Peters, T. J. (1997), *The Circle of Innovation*, London: Hodder & Stoughton.

—— (1998), *Thriving on Chaos – Handbook for a Management Revolution*, London: Macmillan.

—— and Waterman R. H. (1982), *In Search of Excellence*, London: Harper & Row.

Peterson, R. W., Marostica, M. A. and Callahan, L. M. (1999), *Helping Investors Climb the e-Learning Curve*, U. S. Bancorp Piper Jaffray, Equity Research Report, available at *http://wwwinternettime.com*.

Petre, M., Carswell, L., Price, B. and Thomas, P. (2000), 'Innovations in Large-scale Supported Distance Teaching: Transformation for the Internet, not just Translation', in Eisenstadt, M. and Vincent, T. (eds), *The Knowledge Web: Learning and Collaborating on the Net*, London: Kogan Page.

Phillips, J., J. (1991), *Handbook of Training Evaluation and Measurement Methods*, London: Kogan Page.

Phillips, J., Phillips, P. P. and Zuniga, L. (2000), 'Evaluating the Effectiveness and the Return on Investment of E-learning', *What Works Online*, 2nd Quarter.

Phipps, R. (1999), *What's the Difference? A Review of Contemporary Research on the Effectiveness of Distance Learning in Higher Education*, available at *http://www.ihep.com*.

—— and Merisotis, J. (2000), *Quality On the Line: Benchmarks for Success in Internet-Based Distance Education*, Washington: The Institute for Higher Education Policy.

Piaget, J. (1970), *Science of Education and the Psychology of the Child*, London: Longmans.

Poplin, M. S. (1988), 'Holistic/Constructivist Principles of the Teaching/Learning Process: Implications for the Field of Disabilities', *Journal of Learning Disabilities*, 21.

Porter, M. E. (1980), *Competitive Strategy – Techniques for Analysing Industries and Competitors*, New York: The Free Press.

—— (1985), *Competitive Advantage: Creating and Sustaining Superior Performance*, New York: Free Press.

—— (1996), 'What is Strategy?', *Harvard Business Review*, November–December.

—— (2001), 'Strategy and the Internet', *Harvard Business Review*, March–April.

QAA (1999), *Guidelines on the Quality Assurance of Distance Learning*, Gloucester: The Quality Assurance Agency for Higher Education.

—— (2000), *Handbook for Academic Review*, Gloucester: The Quality Assurance Agency for Higher Education.

—— (2001), *Quality Assurance in Higher Education*, Gloucester: The Quality Assurance Agency for Higher Education.

Quinn, J. B. (1985), 'Managing Innovation: Controlled Chaos', *Harvard Business Review*, May–June.

—— (1992), *Intelligent Enterprise*, New York: Free Press.

—— (2001), 'Services and Technology Revolutionizing Higher Education', *Educause Review*.

—— Baruch, J. J. and Zien, K. A. (1997), *Innovation Explosion: Using Intellect and Software to Revolutionize Growth Strategies*, New York: Free Press.

Roberts, B. (1988), 'Managing Invention and Innovation', *Research Technology Management*, January–February.

Robinson D. G. and Stern S. (1997), *Corporate Creativity*, San Francisco, CA: Berrett-Koehler.

Robinson, B. (1995), 'Research and Pragmatism in Learner Support', in Lockwood, F. (ed.) (1995), *Open and Distance Learning Today*, London: Routledge.

—— (2001), 'Innovation in Open and Distance Learning: Some Lessons from Experience and Research', in Lockwood, F. and Gooley, A. (eds) (2001), *Innovation in Open and Distance Learning*, London: Kogan Page.

Robinson, D. G. and Robinson, J. C. (1989), *Training for Impact: How to Link Training to Business Needs and Measure the Results*, San Francisco, CA: Jossey-Bass.

—— (1995), *Performance Consulting*, San Francisco, CA: Berrett-Koehler.

Robinson, J. and Taylor, D. (1983), 'Behavioural Objectives in Training for Adult Education', *International Journal of Lifelong Education*, 2, 4.

Robinson, K. (ed.) (1989), *Open and Distance Learning for Nurses*, Harlow: Longman.

Rodin, K. (2002), 'New Designs for Learning', *Continuing Higher Education Review*, 66.

Roffe, I. M. (1997), 'Developing a Dynamic in a Learning Innovation', *Quality Assurance in Education*, 5, 2.

—— (1998), 'Strategic Direction and Development of a Learning Innovation', *Journal of European Industrial Training*, 22, 2.

—— (1999), 'Innovation and Creativity: A Review of the Implications for Training and Development', *Journal of European Industrial Training*, 3, 4/5.

—— (2000), 'Online Learning, Innovation and Knowledge Management', *Industry & Higher Education*, 14, 5.

—— (2002), 'E-learning: Engagement, Enhancement and Execution', *Quality Assurance in Education*, 10, 1.

Roffe, I. M., Morley, A. and Wettern, L. (2000), 'New Product Development', Institute of Consultants, *Directors Briefing*, December, 4.

Rogers, A. (2002), *KEF e-learning Consortium: Evaluation of Pedagogy*, Report for the Knowledge Exploitation Fund consortium, University of Wales, Lampeter.

—— Roffe, I. and Williams, H. (2001), *Technology, Learning and Language Transfer for SMEs*, a report for the EU ADAPT Programme, University of Wales, Lampeter.

Rogers, C. R. (1951), *Client-Centred Therapy*, Boston: Houghton-Mifflin.

—— (1969), *Freedom to Learn*, Columbus, OH: Merrill.

—— (1983), *Freedom to Learn for the 1980s*, Columbus, OH: Merrill.

Rogers, E. M. (1995), *Diffusions of Innovations*, New York: Free Press.

—— and Shoemaker, F. F. (1971), *Communication of Innovation: A Cross-cultural Approach*, New York: Free Press.

Rogoff, B. (1990), *Apprenticeship in Thinking. Cognitive Development in Social Context*, Oxford: Oxford University Press.

Rosenberg, M. C. (2001), *E-learning: Strategies for Delivering Knowledge in the Digital Age*, London: McGraw-Hill.

Rosenberg, M. C., Coscarelli, W. C. and Hutchinson, C. S. (1999), 'The Origins and Evolution of the Field', in Stolovitch, H. D. and Keeps, E. J. (eds), *Handbook of Human Performance Technology*, San Francisco, CA: Jossey-Bass.

Rosenshine, B. and Meister, C. (1995), 'Direct Instruction', in Anderson, L. W. (ed.), *International Encyclopaedia of Teaching and Teacher Education*, 2nd edn, Oxford: Pergamon.

Ross, G. J. and Klug, M. (1999), 'Attitudes of Business College Faculty and Administrators toward Distance Education: a National Survey', *Distance Education*, 20, 2, available at *http://usq.edu.au./dec/decjourn/v20n199*.

Rossett, A. (1999), 'Knowledge Management Meets Analysis', *Training & Development*, May.

Rowntree, D. (1992), *Teaching through Self-Instruction: How to Develop Open Learning Materials*, London: Kogan Page.

Ruble, T. and Stout, D. E. (1993), 'Learning Styles and End-User Training: An Unwarranted Leap of Faith', *MIS Quarterly*, March.

Rumble, G. (1989), 'Open Learning, Distance Education and the Misuse of Language', *Open Learning*, June, 4, 2.

—— (1995), 'Labour Market Theories and Distance Education: Industrialisation and Distance Education', *Open Learning*, 10, 1.

—— (1997), *Costs and Economics of Open and Distance Learning*, London: Kogan Page.

Rummler, G. A. and Brache, A. P. (1995), *Improving Performance: How to Manage the White Space on the Organization Chart*, San Francisco, CA: Jossey-Bass.

Ruttenbur, B. W., Spinkler, G. C. and Lurie, S. (2000), *E-learning: The Engine of the Knowledge Economy*, 15, available at *http://www.morgankeegan.com*.

Sallis, E. (1993), *Total Quality Management in Education*, London: Kogan Page.

Salomon, G. (1993), 'No Distribution without Individuals' Cognition: A Dynamic

Interactional View', in Salomon, G. (ed.), *Distributed Cognitions*, Cambridge: Cambridge University Press.

Salmon, G. (2000), *E-Moderating: The Key to Teaching and Learning Online*, London: Kogan Page.

Sambrook, S. (2002), 'Factors Influencing Learners' Perceptions of the Quality of Computer Based Learning Materials', *Journal of European Industrial Training*, 25, 2.

Sanders, E. (1998), 'What Knowledge and Skills will Enable People to Select, Manage and Use Learning Technologies for HRD Work?', available at *http://www.astd.org/virtual_community/comm_learntec/Ø*.

Sanders, E. S. and Ruggles, J. L. (2000), 'HPI Soup', *Training & Development*, June.

Savery, J. R. and Duffy, T. M. (1996), 'Problem Based Learning: An Instructional Model and Its Constructivist Framework', in Wilson, B. G. (ed.), *Constructivist Learning Environments: Case Studies in Instructional Design*, Englewood Cliffs: Educational Technology Publications.

Scase, R. and Goffee, R. (1987), *The Real World of the Small Business Owner*, London: Croom Helm.

Schank, R. (2002), *Designing World-Class E-Learning*, London: McGraw-Hill.

Schön, D. (1987), *Educating the Reflective Practitioner*, San Francisco, CA: Jossey-Bass.

Schramm, W. (1974), *Big Media, Little Media*, Thousand Oaks, CA: Sage.

Schriver, R. and Giles, S. (1999), 'Real ROI Numbers', *Training & Development*, 52, 8.

Schumpeter, J. ([1942] 1975), *Capitalism, Socialism and Democracy*, New York: Harper, Torch Books.

Scott, P. (ed.) (1998), *The Globalization of Higher Education*, Buckingham: SRHE/Open University Press.

Scriven, B. (1991), 'Distance Education and Open Learning – Implications for Professional Development and Retraining', *Distance Education*, 12, 2.

Selwyn, N., Gorard, G. and Williams, S. (2002), '"We are Guinea Pigs Really": Examining the Realities of ICT-based Adult Learning', *Studies in the Education of Adults*, 34, 1.

Senge, P. M. (1990), *The Fifth Discipline: The Art & Practice of the Learning Organization*, London: Century Books.

Shannon, C. E. (1948), 'A Mathematical Theory of Communications', *Bell System Technical Journal*, Vol. 27, 379–423. Reprinted in Shannon, C. E. and Weaver, W. (1949), *The Mathematical Theory of Communication*, Urbana, IL: University of Illinois Press.

Shannon, D., Guymon, C., Stanesa, J., Rosen, J. and Pay-Crawford, A. (2003), *Measuring the Value of Continuing Education – Application of the Value Creation Index*, UCEA Annual Conference, Chicago.

Shrewsbury, C. (1987), 'What is Feminist Pedagogy?', *Women's Studies Quarterly*, 15.

Shrivastava, P. and Souder, W. (1987), 'The Strategic Management of Technological Innovations: A Review and a Model', *Journal of Management Studies*, 4, 1.

Sizer, J. (1982), 'Assessing Institutional Performance and Progress', in Wagner, L. (ed.), *Agenda for Institutional Change in Higher Education*, Society for Research into Higher Education, Buckingham: Open University Press.

Skinner, B. F. (1968), *The Technology of Teaching*, New York: Appleton-Century-Croft.

Smith, R. M. (1982), *Learning How to Learn*, Cambridge: Englewood Cliffs.

Søby, M. (2002), 'The Learner and the Teacher of the Future', *Proceedings of EDEN Annual Conference*, Granada.

Song, X., Souder, W. and Dryer, B. (1997), 'A Causal Model of the Impact of Skills, Synergy, and Design Sensitivity on New Product Performance', *Journal of Product Innovation Management*, 14, 2.

Speake, T. and Powell, J. (1997), *Skills for the Missing Industry: An Exploratory Study*, London: DfEE.

Stacey, R. (1992), *Managing Chaos*, London: Kogan Page.

Stahl, T. (1999), 'Stimulating Regional Competitiveness: The Learning Region', in Nyham, B., Attwell, G. and Ludger, D. (eds) *Towards the Learning Region*, Thessalonika: CEDEFOP.

Stahl, R. (1994), *The Essential Elements of Cooperative Learning in the Classroom*, ERIC Digest, *www.ericfactility.net*.

Stanworth, J. and Gray, C. (eds) (1991), *Bolton 20 Years On*, London: Paul Chapman.

Steed, C. (2000), *Web-based Training*, Aldershot: Gower.

Stern, E. (1997), 'The Evaluation of the Teaching and Learning Technology Programme of the UK Higher Education Funding Council', *European Journal in Open and Distance Learning, http://kurs.nks.no/eurodl/eurodlen/index.html*.

Stewart, T. A. (1997), *Intellectual Capital: The New Wealth of Organizations*, New York: Doubleday.

Stolovitch, H. D. and Keeps, E. J. (1992), 'What is Human Performance Technology?', in Stolovitch, H. D. and Keeps, E. J. (eds), *Handbook of Human Performance Technology*, San Francisco: Jossey-Bass.

Stoner, G. (1996) 'A Conceptual Framework for the Integration of Learning Technology', in Stoner, G. (ed.), *Implementing Learning Technology*, Learning Technology Dissemination Initiative, Herriot-Watt University, available at *http://www.icbl.hw.ac.uk/ltdi/*.

Storey, D. J. (1994), *Understanding the Small Business Sector*, London: Routledge.

Swartz, E. and Boden, R. (1997), 'A Methodology for Researching the Process of Information Management in Small Firms', *International Journal of Entrepreneurial Behaviour Research*, 3.

Tait, A. (1992), *Key Issues in Open Learning: An Anthology from the Journal of Open Learning 1986–1992*, Harlow: Longman.

—— (1993), 'Systems, Values and Dissent: Quality Assurance for Open and Distance Learning', *Distance Education*, 14, 2.

—— (1997), 'Introduction: International Perspectives on Quality Assurance in Open and Distance Learning: The Importance of Context', in Tait, A. (ed.) (1997), *Quality Assurance in Higher Education: Selected Case Studies*, Vancouver: The Commonwealth of Learning, available at *http://www.cwol.org*.

—— and Mills, R. (1999), *The Convergence of Distance and Conventional Education*, London: Routledge.

Temple, H. (1995), *Cost Effectiveness of Open Learning for Small Firms*, London: DfEE.

Tennant, M. (1997), *Psychology and Adult Learning*, London: Routledge.

—— (1999), 'Is Learning Transferable?' in Boud, D. and Garrick, J. (eds), *Understanding Learning at Work*, London: Routledge.

Thorndike, E. L. (1928), *Adult Learning*, New York: Macmillan.

Thorpe, M. (1993), *Evaluating Open & Distance Learning*, Harlow: Longman.

Thorpe, M. and Grugeon, D. (1987), 'Moving into Open Learning', in Thorpe, M. and Grugeon, D. (eds), *Open Learning for Adults*, Harlow: Longman.

TLTP (2001), *Teaching and Learning Technology Programme*, available at *http://www.tltp.ac.uk/tltp*.

Torrington, D. and Hall, L. (1991), *Personnel Management*, London: Prentice Hall.

Tucker, B. (1994), *Cost Effectiveness of Open and Flexible Learning*, Sheffield: Employment Department.

Tushman, M. L. and O'Reilly, C. (1997), *Winning Through Innovation: A Practical Guide to Leading Organizational Change and Renewal*, Boston: Harvard Business School Press.

UfI (2001), *Corporate Plan 2002: 2005*, Sheffield, available at *http://www.ufi.co.uk*.

Universitas 21 (2000), 'News Corporation in Global Education Partnership Deal with Universitas 21', press release 7 July 2000, available at *www.universitas.edu.au/press_release.html*.

Urdan, T. and Weggen, C. C. (2000), *Corporate eLearning: Exploring a New Frontier*, available from *http://www.wrhambrecht.com*.

Utterback, J. M. (1994), *Mastering the Dynamics of Innovation*, Boston, MA: Harvard Business School Press.

Van de Westeringh, W. (2000), 'ODL and ICT: New Opportunities for the Teaching Profession?', *Proceedings of the ODL Networks for Quality Learning*, Lisbon.

Venkat, K. (2002), 'Delving into the Digital Divide', *IEEE Spectrum*, 39, 2.

Vickerstaff, S. (1992), 'The Training Needs of Small Firms', *Human Resource Management Journal*, 2, 3.

von Hippel, E. (1992), 'Get New Products from Customers', *Harvard Business Review*, March–April.

Vygotsky, L. S. (1978), *Mind in Society: The Development of Higher Psychological processes*, Boston, MA: Harvard University Press.

WAG (2002), *Winning Wales*, Cardiff: Welsh Assembly Government, *http://www.wales.gov.uk*.

Wagner, E. (2000), 'Research into Open and Distance Learning', European ODL Liaison Committee, *Proceedings of the ODL Networks for Quality Learning*, Lisbon.

Watkins, K. E. and Marsick, V. J. (1992), 'Towards a Theory of Informal and Incidental Learning in Organizations', *International Journal of Lifelong Education*, 2, 4.

Weinberger, L. A. (1998), 'Commonly Held Theories of Human Resource Development', *Human Resource Development*, 1, 1.

Whitlock, Q. (2000), *Tutor Support in Online Learning: A Report on a Literature Search*, Guides for Managers, Practitioners and Researchers, Sheffield: DfEE.

Wiersema, F. (1997), *Customer Intimacy*, London: HarperCollins.

Young, J. (2001), 'Does Digital Divide Rhetoric Do More Harm Than Good?', *Chronicle of Higher Education*, 9 November.

Zeitlyn, M. and Horne, J. (2002), *Business Interface Training Review*, London: DTI.

Zuboff, S. (1988), *In the Age of the Smart Machine*, Oxford: Heinemann.

Index